AT WAR WITH GOVERNMENT

At War with Government

HOW CONSERVATIVES WEAPONIZED DISTRUST
FROM GOLDWATER TO TRUMP

Amy Fried and Douglas B. Harris

Columbia University Press
New York

Columbia University Press
Publishers Since 1893
New York   Chichester, West Sussex
cup.columbia.edu

Library of Congress Cataloging-in-Publication Data
Names: Fried, Amy, author. | Harris, Douglas B., author.
Title: At war with government : how conservatives weaponized distrust from
Goldwater to Trump / Amy Fried and Douglas B. Harris.
Description: New York, : Columbia University Press, [2021] | Includes index. |
Identifiers: LCCN 2021000375 (print) | LCCN 2021000376 (ebook) | ISBN
9780231195201 (hardback) | ISBN 9780231195218 (trade paperback) | ISBN
9780231551243 (ebook)
Subjects: LCSH: Political culture—United States. | Conservatives—United
States. | Political alienation—United States. | United States—Politics
and government.
Classification: LCC JA75.7 .F74 2021 (print) | LCC JA75.7 (ebook) | DDC
306.20973—dc23
LC record available at https://lccn.loc.gov/2021000375
LC ebook record available at https://lccn.loc.gov/2021000376

Cover design: Noah Arlow

AF: To my children, Sarah and Caleb
DBH: To my children, Zoe and Maya

CONTENTS

ACKNOWLEDGMENTS

This book is the result of our close collaboration begun over two decades ago, likely over coffee, in Hamilton, New York. During the height of the Republican Revolution in Congress, we began noticing patterns of behavior and rhetoric that seemed designed to undermine public confidence in the political system. If the scholarship up to that point might have expected this from dissident groups, mostly on the left, the outlines of a conservative effort to seize on public discontent and to wage war on government emerged clearly and disturbingly.

Pursuing our individual research agendas (Fried in the development and uses of polling and Harris in congressional leadership and media politics), we continued to take note of the ways in which strategic uses of public distrust in government pervaded Republican politics and the conservative movement. The weaponization of distrust revealed itself as a consistent theme in the archives that we were researching, both in public opinion and in elite strategies behind the scenes.

Revisiting this subject over the years only strengthened our belief that we had identified *the strategy* of contemporary conservatism. Ever problematic since it emerged in the Goldwater era, the GOP's persistent war on government propelled Reaganism, stopped health reform under Bill Clinton, undermined Barack Obama's presidency, and reached crisis proportions in the age of Trump.

Whereas many observers would bemoan the decline of public trust in government as an unfortunate consequence of the age, we saw its strategic benefits and traced them over the years. We believed then and believe now so much in the structures and aims of the U.S. Constitution and the American political system that we were and continue to be alarmed at the implications of this political project.

While we brought different perspectives and expertise to the project, they were matched by a common interest in broader trends in American political development and shared concerns about the health of our democracy.

Truth be told, this is a book that we wished we would never have had to write—but given the consequences of declining trust for the functioning of American politics, we believe that it needed to be written. These decades-long dots needed to be connected as we tried to figure out what has gone so wrong, how the United States became so driven by distrust and its divides, and what could cure the body politic.

A longtime collaboration like this one incurs many intellectual debts. We would like to thank the legion of editors and discussants who commented on components of this project over the years whenever we would take it out for another spin. It all began with John Hibbing and Beth Theiss-Morse, whose edited book *What Is It About Government That Americans Dislike?*, published the first fruits of our collaboration on this subject. Theda Skocpol edited a Scholars Strategy Network brief based on this initial foray. We returned to the subject years later at the prompting of Jeff Stonecash, whose request that we contribute to a special issue of the *Forum* revitalized our interest in this project. Later, both Shamira Gelbman and Dante Scala solicited pieces from us that applied the lens of strategic distrust to Donald Trump in the 2016 and 2020 elections.

We have benefited, too, from discussants who provided not only encouragement but incisive comments that improved our thinking. At the risk of leaving someone out, we would like to thank Kevin Baron, Michael Cobb, Carrie LeVan, Phil Nicolas, John Pitney, Dan Tichenor, and Richard Vallely. Thanks, too, to Oenone Kubie, who organized a conference on credibility and lying at Oxford's Rothermere American Institute in 2018, at which we presented a first attempt to understand Trump's use of distrust. At each conference throughout the years, we tested the approach with new evidence and learned from our fellow panelists and questioners.

We would also like to thank the many archivists who, behind the scenes, preserved the documents and history of presidential and congressional planning, as well as those who patiently and generously aided us in our search for materials. The University of Maine provided support to Amy for various archival visits and for hiring Kelsey Gordon and Eduardo Medrano to assist with the papers of Otis Bowen and Ronald Reagan. Doug acknowledges the Everett McKinley Dirksen Congressional Research Center, the Carl Albert Congressional Research & Studies Center at the University of Oklahoma, and the Loyola University Summer Research Grant program for their support of elements of this project.

Thanks to Christian Winting at Columbia University Press and, especially, Stephen Wesley, who gave us not only several close and thoughtful reads but stalwart encouragement all along for a book he and we believed should go beyond an academic audience.

Both of us are grateful for our extraordinarily easy working relationship, which bridged multiple institutions, career events, and happy and sad family occasions—all of which we talked about as we planned and discussed all aspects of this project.

Each of us has more personal gratitude to express.

Amy thanks her colleagues who have her backed her in so many respects, including a department extraordinary for its combination of fine work, commitment, and collegiality. She learned a lot about communicating with the public from her *Bangor Daily News* op-ed editors, most recently Susan Young. For walks and talks, Amy appreciates Laura Cowan, Karen Horton, and Marie Hayes. Thanks also to Sandy Caron, Luisa Deprez, Richard May, Alan Rosenwasser, Deb Rogers, and the departed Howard Segal. The love from the Siesfelds has mattered so much. Amy dedicates this book to her children, Sarah and Caleb, who have grown into wonderful adults. Her last one was dedicated to Dave, who is still the best husband she can imagine.

Doug would like to thank Ben Ginsberg, who shaped his thinking on public opinion politics many years ago, and Joe Cooper, whose mentorship (and his own work on declining trust in the political system) has continued to inspire. In addition, Doug would like to acknowledge his colleagues in Loyola's political science department, a most congenial community of learned and valued friends. Additionally, several colleagues have heard some version of this argument over the years and offered insight, including Alison Dagnes, Doug Dow, Celia Paris, and Tracy Roof. Most of all, Doug thanks his best friend, Christine, and their daughters—Zoe and Maya—who, despite having had to live with the mood that this sour subject instilled in him, still believe in the promise of America and trust that there will be happier, kinder days ahead.

AT WAR WITH GOVERNMENT

Chapter One

WEAPONIZING DISTRUST

Donald Trump was on another tirade in the summer of 2017. In speeches, at rallies, and in multiple tweets, Trump repeatedly attacked the media, calling the press "fake news" and "the enemy of the people." Reacting, Republican Senator Ben Sasse accused the president of injuring "the beating heart of the American experiment," the First Amendment.

Sasse also contended that Trump intended to undermine trust in government, by "trying to weaponize distrust," an effort that could spill over into how people view government and the common purposes it is established to achieve.[1] "The Declaration of Independence is pretty dang clear about this, that we think government is just our shared tool to secure those rights that we have by nature," said Sasse.

CNN reporter Jake Tapper, struck by Sasse's phrase, "weaponizing distrust," suggested, "It sounds like you're saying this is more than just lashing out. This is a strategy by the president so as to sow seeds of mistrust in anyone who provides any critical coverage."[2]

Trump's strategic use of distrust was not novel for him, and journalists were but one of his many targets. As a candidate, Trump contended his political opponents were corrupt and promised he would target "globalists" and "elites" by "draining the swamp." Claiming there was a "deep state" within government at work against him, President Trump stoked public distrust in law enforcement, the intelligence community, and the military.

Running against the establishment and sowing the seeds of right-wing anti-elite distrust was at the core of Trump's political message—inciting a distrustful, even conspiratorial movement, sparking his rise in the GOP and his election to the presidency, expanding his power as president and motivating his policy efforts. Backing President Trump provided the basis for Republican Party loyalty, and Sasse, despite his occasional barbs and denunciations, was no exception when it came to his votes in support of Trump's nominations and policies.[3]

Moreover, the "weaponization of distrust" was not new. To the contrary, it had been a staple of the Republican strategic playbook for well over half a century.

During the New Deal, amid the turmoil of World War II, and beyond, Democrats promoted an American national identity linked to national endeavors and a burgeoning American state. Pushing back, the New Deal's principal opponents—Republicans and other conservatives—promoted an American political identity emphasizing suspicion, hostility, and antipathy toward the government, particularly the social welfare state. While decrying government, Republicans backed shifting resources to their donors and to some of their voting constituencies. Although Trump used the politics of distrust in his own ways, the principal thrust of the strategy had been time-tested and long practiced in the GOP.

In contrast to the political science literature that views the postwar rise in distrust in American government as an inadvertent by-product of political, social, governmental, and economic factors, this book argues that the politics of distrust is best understood as an intentional strategy employed by political elites who seek to harness preexisting or potential distrust within the public, sharpen it, and mobilize it to their own strategic ends. We trace the development of this strategy over a half century of Republican politics, treating the strategy as the interplay between a distrustful public and the conservative elite who stand to benefit from that distrust. The intentional cultivation and weaponization of distrust represent the fundamental strategy of conservative Republican politics from Barry Goldwater to Donald Trump.

This book chronicles how conservative political elites seized upon the American public's inherent distrust in government, exacerbated it (often with poll- and focus-group-tested rhetorical appeals), and centered a conservative movement around it. What was in it for the elites who seized upon and nurtured distrust in government?

We argue there are four primary benefits of distrust—organizational, electoral, institutional, and policy benefits. At war with government, conservative elites used distrust to build political organizations, to win elections, to channel power toward institutions they controlled and away from ones they did not, and to promote or thwart policy proposals. This war included repeated skirmishes, shifts in tactics, defensive and offensive actions, and efforts to seize new ground—rhetorical, electoral, and institutional—to position conservatives for future successes. Conservative elites sometimes faced internal rebellions, encountering friendly fire from the distrustful public they had spurred on.

During this period, polarization and messaging on race were important aspects of this long war with government, in which the key weapon was the strategic promotion of distrust in government. Those political forces that oppose the use of government to promote unity and inclusion readily employ this strategy of distrust, which taps into existing American skepticism toward government.

THE DECLINE OF TRUST—AND THE CULTIVATION
OF DISTRUST—IN GOVERNMENT

How has the landscape of distrust changed? American trust in government has been in freefall since the mid-twentieth century. In a summary of the literature on governmental trust, University of California Berkeley political scientists Jack Citrin and Laura Stoker noted trust's "steady decline" since 1964, as measured by the American National Election Studies: "It is beyond dispute that Americans' trust in their national government has declined over the past fifty years."[4]

The same is true of evaluations as measured in the General Social Survey, which tracks public confidence in the "people running" the various institutions of national government. These evaluations have shown public confidence declining since the 1970s, though more slowly for the Supreme Court than for other institutions.[5] If the declines were precipitous at the end of the twentieth century, matters have gotten worse in the early twenty-first century. Political scientist Marc Hetherington finds there has been a "near complete collapse of trust in government" since the early 2000s.[6] As is the case with overall trust in government, partisan trust has continued to decline in recent years, with trust among out-party partisans—that is, members of the party that does not control the White House—"much lower than historical norms" generally and having "almost completely evaporated among Republicans during Barack Obama's presidency."[7]

What accounts for this decline? Some contend that economic performance and economic insecurity diminish confidence in government and that rebounding economic conditions do not lead to rebounding confidence. This spells, perhaps, a downward trend in trust, even if the economy performs cyclically.[8] And, of course, there are political factors to blame. The public's frustration with political processes and government dysfunction fuel the freefall.[9] Negativity in the news and increasingly partisan coverage from increasingly partisan outlets abound and feed partisan distrust, particularly as partisans pick and choose news sources that confirm their preexisting ideological biases.[10] This polarization has led to the growing antipathy from "out-party partisans" toward the party in power and its leaders,[11] a fact that is likely to make the political opposition in America more strident, suspicious, and resistant and less likely to compromise, contribute to governance, and supply the regime the legitimacy that was once central to the stability of the American system.[12]

Though there are multiple reinforcing causes for the trends and conditions that have put the public in a distrustful mood, political elites have also cultivated that distrust for their strategic ends. By identifying and analyzing four strategic uses of distrust, we demonstrate that mounting distrust is not simply a consequence, or a by-product, of scandals, a poor economy, government underperformance, political reforms, decreasing social trust, or generational change.[13] Distrust is also a consequence of a conservative war with government—an overt strategy of weaponization whereby political elites seek to mobilize, channel, and direct this powerful potential force.

Building and Un-building Trust

Why do political trust and distrust matter? The politics of governmental trust and distrust is central to the prospects of national unity and the achievement of collective governance and national policy aims. As sociologist William Gamson put it, trust is "the creator of collective power," and "the loss of trust is the loss of system power, the loss of a generalized capacity for authorities to commit resources to attain collective goals."[14] Trust in government is at once an indicator of national unity and a resource cultivated by those seeking to promote it.

Political scientist Benedict Anderson famously called a nation an "imagined community," tied together by a sense of commonality and nationalism. Nations are "*imagined* because the members of even the smallest nation will never know most of their fellow-members, meet them, or even hear of them, yet in the mind of each lives the image of their communion."[15] Shared symbols, holidays, and institutions build collective trust, national identity, and common purpose. Leaders can forge "political peoplehood" to promote and legitimate collective endeavors,[16] explaining to a coalition how their interests align under a common set of identities or beliefs.

Throughout American history, political figures and groups have worked to build trust and a sense of collective purpose to rally support for the state, political projects, or individual leaders. George Washington, for example, cultivated his image and created a unifying symbol that promoted sacrifice for the common good and willingness to leave power voluntarily, providing a model of civil leadership in the early republic.[17] High levels of trust and national unity, including ethos of voluntarism and sacrifice for the common good, were also fostered during World Wars I and II, in part by elites' political projects.[18] By the same token, trust surged after the terrorist attacks of September 11, 2001, as Americans responded to national tragedy and threat. Building new aspects of the state, politicians used constituents' greater trust and underlying fear to support aggressive domestic security, internal intelligence, and foreign policy security agendas.

But pursuing unity, common purpose, and collective action in the United States has always been especially difficult, given the persistent divisions among states, competing economic interests, and the multiplicity of diverse peoples.[19] More fundamentally, American culture is the product of a perpetual struggle among competing, sometimes inherently contradictory "multiple traditions" that produce political crosscurrents and recurring patterns and tensions in America's national identity.[20] If liberty and egalitarianism are American "traditions," other traditions include racism and nativism, which have been mobilized to divide Americans and to undermine collective endeavors.[21]

While some bonds of trust and nationhood can tie people together, others define *American* exclusively, including only some groups as full members of society and illiberally excluding others. Research shows that this has policy consequences. Political scientist Elizabeth Theiss-Morse finds that while people in the United States with the strongest national identifications are most likely to want to help fellow Americans, those individuals also define what it means to be an American most narrowly. This limits their support for social welfare spending, because those needing support are not seen as full members of the nation.[22] Another political scientist, John Transue, reports on research finding that when white Americans focus on national identity rather than racial identity, they are more supportive of spending "to improve educational opportunities for minorities."[23] Thus, inclusive policies seem to require a strong sense of national identity—but national pride is linked to an exclusive sense of "nation" for those who do not want to extend material benefits or status to out-groups and immigrants.

Successful political projects in the United States organize and mobilize political coalitions. Those who would use the state for collective purposes must overcome the currents of distrust that impose persistent obstacles to collective efforts. Such actors seek—out of political interest, ideology, or both—to broaden definitions of Americanism and forge bonds among unlike groups and individuals to discover, articulate, and pursue a common good. But the trust necessary for such endeavors is unlikely to develop or persist without nurturing.

Acknowledging that public trust is a political accomplishment that must be built to achieve collective purposes, we focus on the opponents of such efforts—those political actors who stoke distrust in government and sow divisions to mobilize their political supporters.

Mobilization and the Cultivation of Distrust

The model we suggest of elites seizing upon preexisting distrust in the mass public to mobilize them has substantial support in historical and behavioral political science. Countering the dominant narrative that distrust produces apathy or anomie, political scientist Jack Citrin observed that "mistrust of government and political apathy do not go together."[24] To the contrary, several studies have found that if certain segments of the population are dissatisfied with government performance, they will be comparatively more likely to participate. Similarly, Vivien Hart found that "the highly competent politically who were also distrustful politically were more active than the highly competent and trustful."[25] And William Gamson found that "a combination of a high sense of political efficacy and low political trust is the optimum combination for mobilization—a belief that influence is both possible and necessary."[26]

Such distrustful mobilizations are most powerful when they represent extreme viewpoints and when they are led by elites. Recent studies of right-wing politics have found that "the perceived illegitimacy" of those in power can be a mobilizing agent for the distrustful rather than simply a source of "alienation" from the system.[27] Other studies have found that what leads the distrustful to action rather than to "apathy, withdrawal, or nonpolitical behavior" is the presence of elite leadership that can "articulate grievances."[28]

Distrust has been a useful prod that conservative elites have used to organize and to win intra- and interparty contests since the New Deal, and especially of late. In 2010, for example, Tea Party members and supporters were "highly motivated" and "participate[d] in both nonelectoral and electoral political activity at higher rates" than the rest of the public.[29] Deeply suspicious of Barack Obama and of government itself, Tea Party distrust became an infectious spur to action rather than a demoralizing deterrent. For decades, conservative and Republican political elites sought to stoke distrust not only to turn off portions of the public but also with the intention (and, increasingly, the public opinion technology-fueled ability) to mobilize their targeted constituencies around anger and distrust, while often selectively demobilizing their opponents.

Extremely wealthy individuals with libertarian inclinations are another source of such mobilization. Since the second half of the twentieth century, these individuals made donations and built donor networks to advance conservative causes—influencing primaries; putting pressure on elected officials via lobbying and via funding and organization of citizen groups; and affecting legal education, the legal system, and the discipline of economics toward these anti-statist aims.[30] These projects crafted and spread narratives that the public should distrust and fear the government, telling tales of elite corruption, unfeeling and distant bureaucrats, public assistance to the unworthy, and damage to the liberty and the lives of ordinary Americans.

Advances in public opinion technology that allow political elites to test their arguments through polls and focus groups with greater precision and a new degree of certainty have made this strategy more reliable. As political scientists Lawrence Jacobs and Robert Shapiro describe, in this strategy of "crafting talk," elites "use research on public opinion to pinpoint the most alluring words, symbols, and arguments in an attempt to move public opinion to support their desired arguments."[31] Using these technologies and tactics, elites learn more about how the public might react to their rhetorical efforts so they may better plan and execute mobilization strategies.

In this war with government, political leaders do not have a monopoly on using the weapon of political distrust. While elites use distrust strategically, shaping, directing, and giving added force to public distrust, it is also true that, once unleashed, this distrust can take on a life of its own. And because "distrust breeds conditions for the creation of further distrust," there is no reason to expect that political leaders could predict, much less control, the long-term consequences of broadened public distrust in government.[32] The politics of distrust is an imprecise art. Leaders seize on it but can manage it only loosely and are apt to lose control of it altogether. These elites are thus playing with fire in a political environment already filled with combustible public anger.

Party Polarization and the Politics of Distrust in Government

American politics is increasingly polarized, and like many other aspects of the contemporary polarized era, distrust is asymmetric. While public trust in government has declined across the board, and levels of trust vary depending on people's party identification and on who controls the White House, patterns of distrust are especially pronounced in the GOP. One Pew study found that "Republicans have been much more reactive than Democrats to changes in political power. [They] have expressed much higher levels of trust during Republican than during Democratic presidencies, while Democrats' attitudes have tended to be more consistent."[33] Although Democratic trust also varies with party control, and although Democrats trusted the government far less when out of power during the last two Republican presidencies,[34] Republican trust varies even more and falls extremely low when Democrats are in power. Because of this asymmetry, Democrats are more likely than Republicans to see a president from the other party as legitimate.[35]

Despite these disparities and our focus on conservatives, we do not argue that Democrats and the left never embrace distrust. Public opinion studies found, for example, that the Vietnam War era produced "greater skepticism" and "more resistance" to government, as well as "considerable popular alienation from the symbols of the American political system" on the left.[36] Scholar Vivien Hart claimed that this "outburst" was best seen as "a return to normal . . . true to the mainstream of the American political tradition," though opponents, ironically many of them conservatives, worried that the undermining of authority, the flouting of norms, and the disillusionment with the government was quite a bit more dangerous.[37]

The left's animosities deepened as the Vietnam War continued and state efforts at domestic counterintelligence operations became known. What started as "borderline anti-governmentalism" in the anti-war movement "became full-blown hatred of 'the system.'"[38] Examining distrustful attitudes in the early 1970s, Jack Citrin noted that "respondents with either 'leftist' or 'rightist' candidate preferences are disproportionately likely to feel politically cynical." Later, Garry Wills argued that anti-government values "can be found in a hippie commune or a modern militia camp."[39] Distrust knows no home on the ideological spectrum.

Since the 1960s, however, the motivations and benefits to stoke distrust have been far greater on the right than on the American left. Although partisan polarization has grown, it is asymmetric, with Republican voters and elected officials more extreme and cohesive than their Democratic counterparts. Critically, Republican leaders have been more likely in the contemporary era to promote distrust strategically.[40]

Democrats and Republicans have been different, not just in their ideological dispositions toward government but also organizationally in terms of how they structure their coalitions. Political scientists Matthew Grossman and David Hopkins argue that, whereas Democrats tend to see politics in terms of social groups and evaluate policies in terms of their effects on those groups, Republicans are more apt to see politics through an ideological lens.[41] Democratic perspectives prompt them to see government, particularly the national government, as a partner to provide assistance and opportunity to constituents (leading them to evaluate policies in pragmatic terms), while Republicans see domestic government action as intrusive, overreaching, and a threat to freedom. Indeed, the Republican Party "has built itself up by tearing down government."[42] And when the GOP weaponized distrust, it often incorporated racialized rhetoric.

Race and the Cultivation of Distrust

As distrust was used to mobilize conservatives in an increasingly polarized political system, racialized politics was linked to the politics and strategic uses of distrust in government.[43] A realignment of the American South, first rumbling in the late 1940s and taking hold especially after the mid- to late 1960s, changed both parties' respective stances on the role of the federal government regarding race. The 1964 Civil Rights Act and the 1965 Voting Rights Act led to disaffection among white southern Democrats, whose party had long been plagued by deep divisions over questions of civil rights. At the same time, these new laws opened up a large propor- tion of African American votes for more liberal candidates and causes. For Republicans, who had played important roles in the passage of civil rights policies, the realignment sparked a strategic switch in the elections of the late sixties and early seventies to a "Southern strategy," an effort of onboarding the most conservative region of the country and the one most historically prone to be suspicious of the national government and espe- cially primed at the time to advocate "states' rights." As a practical political matter, anti-government arguments became a way to capture disaffected white votes, in part by using veiled race-coded language to advocate "states' rights" and to disparage a federal government and its policies that were increasingly responsive to African American needs and demands.

Of course, this was all happening at a time when the national govern- ment was especially prominent in politics and policy making. The policy scope of the American state expanded greatly during the New Deal and World War II and again later during the expansions of social programs and environmental regulation in the 1960s and 1970s. With a core of conser- vatives rallying against New Deal liberalism (as well as against what they viewed as Dwight D. Eisenhower's capitulations to it), Republicans vehe- mently resisted Johnson's Great Society, banding together with disaffected southerners in opposition to increasing federal government action.

This was especially pronounced in regard to redistributive policies. Efforts to stigmatize the beneficiaries of a government program decrease support for that program, and low levels of trust have decreased support for policies designed to address racial inequality.[44] With Republican appeals to disaffected southerners starting as early as the 1940s, the party's anti-gov- ernment arguments have become more attractive not only to libertarians and economic conservatives but also to more racist and nativist elements of American society who share those suspicions.

Not just anti-government but also increasingly divisive and exclusive, GOP rhetoric moved from Richard Nixon's Southern strategy to Ronald Reagan–era dog whistles regarding program abuses by "welfare queens," ramping up with George H. W. Bush's embrace of Lee Atwater's race-based appeals to solidify the coalition. Largely avoiding overt racism in most instances, the politics of division on the basis of race became all the more overt and pronounced with GOP opposition to Barack Obama as lingering subcultures of white racial resentments spilled more into the open and were on full display in the anti-immigrant speeches of Donald Trump's campaign and clear targeting of the administration's black critics (as well as NFL players, all the while excusing alt-right and white supremacist protest) in Trump's first years in office. Political scientists Jacob Hacker and Paul Pierson observe that "race is a major ingredient in the GOP's antigovernment cocktail."[45]

For all the damage they might do to the broader body politic, to national unity, and to key constituencies and identity groups, strategies using distrust provided political benefits that American conservatives exploited to build their movement.

Four Benefits of Distrust

Distrust in government is not simply an unfortunate consequence or by-product of social, economic, and political forces but instead is an intentional effort by conservative elites to seize on and encourage a distrustful public for conservative and Republican ends.

The evidence that we marshal to make this case centers on the benefits of distrust that accrue to the GOP and the conservative cause. Cultivating distrust is a broad, comprehensive strategy of political elites that produces tangible benefits in four realms. The promotion of distrust in government provides: *organizational benefits*, helping elites to build, fund, and unify party coalitions, political organizations, and movements; *electoral benefits*, bolstering campaign efforts and wooing distrustful voters in elections; *institutional benefits*, feeding distrust, though selectively, of key institutions of national government, notably those not controlled by the elites stoking distrust; and *policy benefits*, affecting policy outcomes, mostly focused on passing or expanding redistributive policy in the domestic realm.

ORGANIZATIONAL BENEFITS

Organizations are central to political life and necessary to sustaining political ideas, attitudes, and movements over time, because they provide the common motivations and scripts for participants that build commitment and cohesion. Spurring the creation of organizations, coordinating and funding their work to build political and social movements, and managing a broader party coalition are all essential to political success, but are hard-won and must be planned and nurtured.

Party coalitions and social movements do not just happen; they are devised, crafted, and honed by political elites who labor to explain to the various constituent parts of a coalition what they have in common. While one can point to demographic groups' links to political parties, party coalitions are also networks created from the jockeying and inter-relations of these groups and other movements, activists, donors, interest groups, candidates, and party leaders.[46] Throughout this book we consider this organizational imperative of coordinating and unifying the range of political organizations that comprise a party "coalition."

Following the New Deal era, the Republican Party coalition had to shift, expand, and strengthen if Republicans were ever again to control government on their own terms.[47] The modern GOP coalition is frequently thought of as a stool with three legs: social conservatives, economic conservatives, and pro-military defense conservatives.[48] Though not immune to internecine warfare, these groups are potentially unifiable through shared antipathy toward government, especially its uses in the domestic realm. Although many other factors—social conservatism, militarism, anti-communism, and traditionalism—aided in building the Republican coalition, it was anti-government rhetoric and the distrust it easily bred among a dissatisfied public that was the primary impetus for the Republican Party of Goldwater, Reagan, and Trump.

Much of this was accomplished first ideologically and rhetorically around distrust. To "put its theoretical house in order," as William F. Buckley put it, the conservative movement engaged in "one of the more thoroughgoing and self-conscious projects of ideological construction in American history."[49] This construction was built on Hayekian economic libertarianism, overt opposition to New Deal liberalism, and staunch anti-communism—all of which share deep suspicions of the state and see it as a threat to progress and individual liberty.[50]

These elite articulations meshed well with the touchstones of Americans' cultural suspicions of government, especially prominent in the South. Opposition to the civil rights agenda increasingly supported by Democrats opened up the South to the GOP's anti-government appeals and willingness to employ a Southern strategy to bind the coalition. By the 1980s and 1990s, Republicans, increasingly based in the South and generally suspicious of government, "shared an increasingly cohesive antiregulatory and antitax conservatism" that helped to overcome "coalitional challenges" with "an overarching movement consciousness and esprit de corps."[51]

Ever elaborating, the Republican coalition was fed by a more far-flung conservative "movement" that consisted not only of the party per se, but also of an extraordinarily large and well-funded cadre of media outlets, think tanks, advocacy organizations, and coalitions. The modern conservative movement is a hydra, with innumerable traditionalist, religious, small-government, libertarian, legal-philosophical, and watchdog heads. These component pieces include both the mainstream and the extreme. The University of California–Berkeley's Center for Right-Wing Studies (in association with the People for the American Way) lists well over a thousand such groups existing between 1980 and 2004.[52] This many right-wing organizations cannot all overtly collaborate with one another or with the national GOP, but they can potentially be mobilized by common beliefs— the glue that holds a contemporary party together. For all their different missions and policy emphases, anti-government rhetoric and sentiments motivated unity within the conservative movement since the 1960s.

At its core, the conservative movement is the alliance of these constituencies and organizations, the network, funding operation, and ideological touchstones that spur and unite them. The rise of right-wing media—from talk radio to Fox News to Breitbart to OAN and a growing coterie of right-wing social media activists—has facilitated this communication, connecting these elite circles to one another and to mass audiences. Along with top Republican Party leaders and officeholders, these conservative voices lead the movement rhetorically and ideologically, giving voice to the precepts as they endure and adapt to meet the exigencies of the moment.

ELECTORAL BENEFITS

Elites employ the politics of public opinion—including citizen trust and distrust in government—to build support for their campaigns and influence whether and how citizens vote. Following Anthony Downs, political scientists long contended that America's two major political parties tend to move to the ideological center when competing in general elections in the hopes of capturing the "median voter."[53] But the need to fundraise, build campaigns, and win primary elections to secure the nomination provide strong countervailing tendencies that can pull party candidates to the extremes.[54] Tilting the GOP to the right in its nominating processes has been a consistent aim of the modern conservative movement.

In this era, Republican candidates employed social issues, defense and antiterrorism messages, and other issues to accomplish these ends, but anti-government, particularly anti-tax and anti-regulation, rhetoric has been a staple Republican talking point since the 1960s and 1970s to court conservative interests, activists, and votes. While these issues could build campaign momentum and move voters in general elections, they were especially effective in primaries.

As two-party competition within states and within increasingly red and blue districts was on the decline, candidates, who are notoriously "subjectively vulnerable,"[55] began worrying as much or more about challenges from the ideological fringe in primaries than being beaten in the general election. As the GOP moved rightward, anti-tax pledges became near requirements of Republican candidates, and small-government groups like the Club for Growth sponsored many efforts to "primary" establishment Republicans with candidates who were more likely to support even lower taxes and looser regulations. There is no doubt that this propelled unity within Washington; as a Republican congressional staffer said, "We have to wield Club every now and then."[56] Besides unifying the GOP around anti-government rhetoric, these efforts also pushed Republicans further rightward, making onetime staunch conservatives seem unacceptably moderate to Republican activists and primary voters.[57]

Taken as a whole, the electoral context suggested a move away from the center. If this meant that Democrats would feel the pull to the left on issues like abortion, higher minimum wages, climate policy, and health care, Republicans were under increasing pressure to have near or absolutely "spotless records" on gun rights, many social issues, and, of course, taxes. Not discounting the full range of issues that separated the two parties in the polarized era, we show how small-government, anti-tax, antiregulation rhetoric was consistent dogma for an increasingly right-wing GOP.

In the 1970s, political scientist Richard Fenno noted that an increasing number of members of Congress were "running for Congress by running against Congress."[58] On the Republican side in the decades that followed, the strategy was broader, consistent, and increasingly ubiquitous: Republican campaigns were built, money was raised, primaries won, and electoral strategies hatched that repeatedly sought to run to control the government by *running against government.*

INSTITUTIONAL BENEFITS

The growth of distrust from the 1960s to the 2010s occurred in an era marked by divided government, which often made mobilizing distrust a complex effort for partisan elites to selectively celebrate the parts of government the party controlled while discounting and discrediting the institutions of government they did not.

In the 1990s, political scientists Benjamin Ginsberg and Martin Shefter argued that divided government and electoral stalemate produced an inordinate amount of institutional combat. In that combat, what cannot be won at the ballot box is sought by denigrating the powers of the institution controlled by the other party, or even investigating those who occupy key offices.[59] Parties and partisans champion the powers of the institutions they control and talk down the institutions controlled by the other party. The complications of both divided government and close interparty competition for control of each institution has led to a pattern of convenient parsing of which aspects of government are most worthy of distrust.

Post-1960s separation-of-powers politics has been dominated by instrumental views of the appropriate roles of Congress, the president, the courts, and the nonpresidential executive branch. These views shifted, largely determined by perceptions of which institution each party was more likely to control, a condition associated with what political scientist J. Richard Piper called "situational constitutionalism."[60] Whereas post–New Deal liberals celebrated presidential power under Democratic presidents (as had Progressives before them) and often decried congressional conservatism, Republicans backed greater presidential power after the Nixon administration, when issues of war power, impoundment, and eventually presidential secrecy brought institutional powers questions to the foreground. These newfound conservative affinities for presidential power deepened during the Reagan administration[61] but abated during the Clinton presidency and especially under Obama. But during the George W. Bush era and Trump's presidency, conservatives were once again touting strong executive leadership.

However conservatives or liberals might regard the Constitution as "fixed" or "living," their reads of the document proved remarkably flexible when it came to institutional powers and prerogatives.

Tactical aspects of this war with government included vehement rhetoric criticizing the institutions of national government controlled by the other party and somersaulting vacillations in views about institutional powers and prerogatives. Rather than long-held and long-standing commitments for congressional oversight or a "unitary executive" or against "congressional meddling" or "dangerous executive overreach," conservatives' anti-government claims tended to be of-the-moment, instrumental, and strategic efforts to talk down whatever institutions they did not control and to talk up ones they did control.[62]

POLICY BENEFITS

Political elites also have policy goals.[63] Promoting distrust in government and associating that distrust with opposition to specific policy proposals has allowed conservative elites to decrease support for their adversaries and for policies that benefit disfavored groups and to legitimize their own policy aims.

In the United States, responsibility for many domestic policies is divided between levels of government and often involves the tax code and private entities, thus "submerging" the state and hiding policy instruments and their impacts.[64] Health policy, which we discuss throughout this book, includes a dizzying array of government elements: veterans' health facilities, tax expenditures for employers, payments to providers under Medicare and Medicaid, the Indian Health Service, public health efforts, subsidized insurance through the Affordable Care Act, insurance exchanges, and federal and state regulation of private insurers.[65] Thus large numbers of Americans do not recognize some programs as government policy even when they benefit from them.

Policy making in American national government is difficult, particularly given the separation of powers that slows, moderates, and—not infrequently—stops altogether efforts to engage in policy change. These tendencies against quick action, efficient policy making, and centralized bureaucracies are built-in advantages for those who seek to stall the process and preclude national policy making in America. The politics of distrust amplifies these advantages for conservatives by providing political and electoral benefits if their efforts lead to minimal policy responses or inaction, particularly when the proposals promise to expand government's size, budget, or reach. These tendencies have been particularly acute as Americans have forgotten the benefits of government actions that were central to the prosperity and progress of the "mixed economy" of the twentieth century—what Jacob Hacker and Paul Pierson call "American amnesia."[66]

Where they could not win legislative policy battles, the GOP's "new nullification"—including not confirming appointees to implement those policies or cutting funding or key provisions of programs—has confirmed, for certain parts of the public, the ineffectiveness of government. It is, as Hacker and Pierson say, part of a "self-fulfilling critique: Say the government isn't doing its job, make it harder for the government to do its job, repeat."[67]

To the extent that the GOP (and the Whigs before them) were big-government state builders throughout the nineteenth century, twentieth-century Republicans began a trek, slow at first, toward small-government philosophies and arguments. At first, the top leadership of the GOP was somewhat chastened by the New Deal's political strength and generally supportive of government's role in the productive mixed economy of the mid-twentieth century. Eisenhower, for example, made key concessions to New Deal expansions during his presidency.[68] But by the late twentieth and early twenty-first century, lingering anti-government forces would come to the fore again, and GOP orthodoxy would come to think of staple government action as "socialism."[69]

Increasingly since Barry Goldwater's 1964 presidential candidacy, the modern Republican Party is, at least rhetorically, antigovernment. We can see this in many of its chief policy aims, although the GOP is often pro-government when the positive uses of the state serve the interests of their constituents or meet the policy ends in terms of national security, police powers and social regulation of which the modern GOP tends to approve. Viewing taxes and regulations as threats to freedom, conservative Republicans have resisted state expansions, particularly around domestic spending. During the Reagan administration, a group called Americans for Tax Reform began asking officeholders to sign their "Taxpayer Protection Pledge" not to raise income taxes. As more Republican officeholders took the pledge, there was downward pressure, particularly for the deficit conscious, to avoid expanding discretionary spending (particularly because nondiscretionary spending was expanding and putting pressure on public coffers).[70] This, particularly the anti-tax view, has become conservative dogma. Since Newt Gingrich led a revolt against George H. W. Bush's budget agreement that included tax increases, Republicans have been increasingly reluctant to raise *any* taxes and have portrayed higher taxes as a threat to individual freedom.

The GOP has also applied anti-tax arguments against policies aimed at helping the poor and working class. Here again, the politics of distrust, not only of the state but also of different groups, is key to the politics of redistributive policy. How people see state action affecting themselves and others depends in part on what political scientists Anne Schneider and Helen Ingram termed the "social construction of target populations."[71] Whether helped by programs set up to serve them or via subsidies, direct spending or tax expenditures, some groups are portrayed as deserving of government assistance, while others are stigmatized.

Although "Social constructions are manipulated and used by public officials, the media, and the groups themselves,"[72] these can change over time.[73] For instance, not only has stigma against LGBTQ+ people decreased a great deal, but legal discrimination is far less prevalent. But how conservative elites frame social programs in America has persistently been layered with racialized messages.[74] Politicians explicitly or implicitly associating social welfare policies with people of color are taking advantage of preexisting nativism, racial resentments, or outright racism but may also provoke distaste and opposition for playing the race card.

Racial resentments are also reinforced ideologically. Economic components of anti-welfare appeals are based in traditions going back to social Darwinism and promoted by modern libertarians and movement conservatives who see property ownership and acquisition as the preeminent freedoms. They connect, too, to conservative moralists who might view low-income people as less talented or virtuous than other Americans and therefore unworthy of government resources. A potent mix of these arguments and biases can be found in conservative views that welfare creates permanent dependency among its recipients, corrupting both moral character and motivations to work.[75]

Today, almost everyone sees the establishment of Social Security in 1935 as a major step in shielding the elderly from poverty. Why is it so popular while other safety nets are controversial? Despite Social Security's contemporary universalism, political scientist Nicholas Winter found that it is framed racially as white and, consequently, is viewed positively among racially conservative whites, even those who are purportedly antigovernment.[76] By contrast, welfare is stigmatized, associated in the social imagination with black Americans, particularly black women, a view stoked repeatedly by the right-wing trope of "welfare queens."[77]

The rise of the right-wing politics and policies in the last few decades would not have been possible without the politics of distrust. Marc Hetherington, who argued that the failure of liberal policy consensus since the Great Society resulted not from a rightward shift in American opinion but instead from a decline in trust in government, contended that the lack of trust in government explains why even nominal conservatives favor government programs that benefit them but resist redistributive policies that benefit others. It seems too that distrust in government contributes to the gridlock of contemporary politics as the distrustful "out-party partisans" are less likely to make ideological sacrifices to support compromises and create consensus around policies championed by the party in power.[78]

This book's documentation of elites' strategic promotion of distrust is not to be read as a denial that the public is, in fact, authentically distrustful or necessarily wrong to be so. Throughout this book, even as we cite mounting evidence of conservative efforts to cultivate public distrust in government, we neither assume nor claim that citizen distrust in government is unreasonable or unfounded. Astute observers have questioned whether or not distrust is all that problematic, arguing that distrust "is not an illness to be treated but rather a civic virtue to be celebrated."[79] Thinking of distrust as a product of the gap between citizens' informed, normative sense of how the government should perform and their perception of its actual performance, Vivien Hart observed that distrust should not be regarded as "an antidemocratic outburst of emotion" but rather as "democratic and thoughtful" and "potentially constructive."[80]

The mass public does not necessarily owe its trust to the government or the political elites who run it at any particular moment. If anything, it is just as incumbent upon those in power to win public support for their actions as it is for the government generally to secure legitimacy for itself and the current regime. Although the rise of distrust threatens national unity and undermines policy making, it is certainly not always citizens' duty to obey, approve of, and supply legitimacy to the government. Indeed, as with African Americans' greater distrust toward the American state and, in particular, the police, distrust can be earned.

Neither do we argue that elites manufacture public distrust and foist it on an otherwise trusting electorate. Our claim is only that distrust is politically useful, and the argument that we develop throughout the book includes evidence that the efforts to use public distrust were often planned by elites intending to seize upon its great potential. What we are talking about, instead, is an interplay between political elites on the one hand and the mass public on the other. An example of the "politics of public opinion,"[81] distrust in government is full of political potential for those who wield it in an informed and skillful way. Public opinion is a resource that political actors can employ to their own designs and ends.[82] The interaction between the elite and the masses involves a representational push and pull. Sensing existing, latent, or potential opinion, a strategic elite can crystallize that opinion, refine it, and give it voice, all for political utility.

The rise of distrust in government was in part the result of an overt strategy by conservatives to build on public dissatisfaction to build their movement, to win elections, to engage in separation-of-powers conflicts, and to thwart liberal policy advances. At the same time, this war with government has deep roots in key strains of American culture and politics. In the next chapter we will consider the long tradition of suspicion of government and its consequences—for good and for ill.

Chapter Two

TRUST AND DISTRUST IN AMERICAN POLITICAL DEVELOPMENT

Deeply embedded in mass culture, public distrust of government is "a constant in American history," wrote historian Garry Wills. "The fear of government is sometimes sensible, sometimes hysterical, but always pronounced."[1] This is the backdrop against which twentieth- and twenty-first-century conservative politicians and political groups, looking out at a restive public and aware of its distrustful bent, cultivated distrust in government and used it strategically. Persistent and pronounced, distrust matters as political leaders campaign for election, build coalitions, attempt to shift institutions' powers, and try to block or pass, undermine or implement policies.

This chapter's historical narrative, a retelling of American political history with trust and distrust as the central axis, demonstrates the persistent conflicts about whether and how the national government can further the common good and how elites promote inclusive versus exclusive definitions of Americanism that unify or sometimes divide the nation.

THE ROOTS OF DISTRUST IN THE AMERICAN FOUNDING

The American culture of distrust in government predates the republic. In his speech to Parliament on "conciliation" with the American colonies in 1775, Edmund Burke described Americans as "mercurial" and prone to perceive even theoretical government power as an actual threat to liberty.

Compared to Europeans, who "judge of an ill principle in government only by an actual grievance," Americans "anticipate the evil, and judge of the pressure of the grievance by the badness of the principle." Americans, he said, "augur misgovernment at a distance; and snuff the approach of tyranny in every tainted breeze."[2]

Burke had noted the prevalence of the study of law in America—to which he directly attributed this mercurial distrust—and how the colonies objected to new taxes. American colonists thought what the British government did not only abused the social contract but was evidence of a "settled, fixed plan for enslaving the colonies."[3] In the lead-up to the revolution, those arguing against the British government's power over the American colonies cited their rights as Englishmen *and* their natural rights as defined by Lockean liberalism. In the Declaration of Independence, they specified complaints against the Crown's abuses of power and contended it was legitimate to revolt against too-powerful governments that trampled rights and freedoms. Distrust animated the revolution and helped Americans win independence.

Distrust in the power of a distant government led the founders to adopt the Articles of Confederation in 1781, which stayed in operation until replaced by the Constitution. The Articles' drafters stipulated that "each state retains its sovereignty, freedom, and independence."

As the task of writing and ratifying a constitution aimed at expanding the national government's authority commenced, anti-government sentiment persisted. James Madison went to the Constitutional Convention in Philadelphia with hopes of obtaining a much stronger central government than would emerge, but he lost many key battles. The Anti-Federalists, as well as some more moderate Federalists, gave voice to suspicions of government power[4] and succeeded in limiting its power. Gone were Madison's hopes for a national veto of state laws and national (not state) agency in the selection of the Senate and the president by the House of Representatives. And, limited, at least, were the desires he shared with Alexander Hamilton for a stronger central government with "command [of] all the basic tools of national economic development."[5] What emerged from the convention was a hybrid of national and state agency. National government and its powers were limited and contested by the separation of powers and by federalism, with states potent enough to compete with and, at times, to thwart the federal government's aims.

Whereas the Constitution's intent—with all its consolidative, extractive, and coercive powers—"radically challenged the American political tradition of anti-statism," it thus "became the task of its supporters to calm the fears, and answer the objections of the opposition."[6] The Federalist response to this opposition included more extensive divisions in separation of powers and less usurpation of the power of the states than they originally intended.[7]

If Anti-Federalists could not stop the ratification of the Constitution, they could limit the scope of government power, change the nature of federalism, and protect individual rights. Anti-Federalists used state ratifying conventions to propose amendments to the Constitution, many of which were adopted as part of the Bill of Rights.[8] Thus, where Federalists won ratification, the distrustful Anti-Federalists compelled them to develop a divided state, one whose actions would, at first at least, "be light and almost invisible." This Anti-Federalist legacy of a powerful anti-statist tradition would persist for the whole of American history "as the foremost barrier to American state-building."[9]

Ratification debates were not just about the power of the state or the rightness or wrongness of its institutional arrangements. Anti-Federalists also saw a national identity "that would command citizen allegiance" as a cultural threat that could grow out of the new constitutional system.[10] Madison, by contrast, brushed aside those skeptical of a shared endeavor in *Federalist* 14, writing, "Hearken not to the unnatural voice which tells you that the people of America, knit together as they are by so many cords of affection, can no longer live together as members of the same family; can no longer continue the mutual guardians of the mutual happiness; can no longer be fellow citizens of one great respectable, and flourishing empire . . . They formed the design of a great confederacy, which it is incumbent on their successors to improve and perpetuate."[11]

The Federalist victory won the ratification of a stronger national government, but the Anti-Federalist opposition was itself strong and popular. This political reality not only circumscribed federal power but bequeathed a perpetual struggle for power between those forces favoring centralization and those skeptical of common purposes and distrustful of the power capable of achieving them. Describing this struggle in *Federalist* 46, Madison wrote: "[If] the people should in the future become more partial to the federal than to the State governments, the change can only result from such manifest and irresistible proofs of a better administration, as will overcome all their antecedent propensities. And in that case, the people ought not surely to be precluded from giving most of their confidence where they may discover it to be most due."

Federalists wanted not just a stronger national government but also mutual trust and identification with a national polity that could sustain state action and that might grow in power and scope.

DISTRUST AND DISUNITY IN THE NINETEENTH CENTURY

Many of the nineteenth century's major political conflicts centered on struggles for trust. As centralized government capacity grew during the early republic, it was repeatedly met with staunch distrust of centralized power. Building a national economy and the banks, roads, and infrastructure to support it was essential to the Hamiltonian project and later to its Whig and nineteenth-century Republican ideological progeny. And while the Federalists and Hamiltonians sought to construct a national identity that would empower their state-building efforts, the Anti-Federalists revolted. "Within ten years of the Constitution's adoption," wrote historian Max Edling, "the Democratic-Republicans would organize their resistance against the Federalist administration around the same fear" of distant, centralized government.[12] Opposition to the Alien and Sedition Acts, the American system, and the national bank (as but a few nineteenth-century examples) typically followed the same script: opponents argued for individual liberty and self-governance in the states and frequently cast the national government as a threat to liberty and supposed conspiracies of elites at work together to execute those threats.

Anti-government, anti-elite sentiments were so pervasive in the early nineteenth century that they manifested as both potent opposition to government centralizers and also self-restraint *among* those centralizers. Even the political elite could not "escape a culturally ingrained predisposition to view political power and politics as essentially evil."[13]

Nowhere were these issues of centralization and decentralization, of trust and distrust, more pronounced or consequential than in the matter of slavery. The liberal ideals of the Declaration of Independence were a rhetorical and ideological resource for abolitionists, but during the decades that a series of slavery compromises were crafted and tested, these universalistic notions were often watered down and restricted in scope. As historian Dorothy Ross put it, "Even as northern states gradually abolished slavery and white men gained new kinds of freedom, slavery deepened its hold in the South and northern jurists retreated from the human rights claims of natural law for the limits of positive law. The Union was understood north and south to be a compact between free and slave societies, a hybrid slaveholding repub-lic."[14] Abraham Lincoln endorsed this same constitutional compact in his first inaugural address, delivered in March 1861: "I have no purpose, directly or indirectly, to interfere with the institution of slavery in the States where it exists," because it is "the right of each State to order and control its own domestic institutions according to its own judgment exclusively."[15]

If political circumstance compelled President Lincoln to acknowledge the strength of the countervailing forces as Madison had three-quarters of a century earlier, before attaining the office, Lincoln saw such disunity—"a house divided"—as unsustainable. His resolve to unite the states was fueled not only by a moral case against slavery but also because he knew that who-ever resolved that division would decide what the unified new house would look like. "Unless the power of the present political dynasty shall be met and overthrown," he predicted in 1858, "we shall lie down pleasantly dream-ing that the people of Missouri are on the verge of making their State free; and we shall awake to the reality, instead, that the Supreme Court has made Illinois a slave state."[16] At the same time, Lincoln, a Whig before becoming a Republican, supported economic development by the federal government through "internal improvements" and signed legislation establishing land-grant universities.

After the Civil War, efforts to incorporate the war's aftermath into American national identity began immediately. Those who supported a Reconstruction to empower previously enslaved people promoted a ver-sion of patriotism that "expanded traditional conceptions of willingness to die for one's country with more radical notions of social, political and racial equality."[17] But then the federal government politically and constitu-tionally abandoned former slaves and their descendants, allowing southern states to impose white supremacist policies. White southerners reasserted the "states' rights" philosophy that questioned the legitimacy of the federal governmental power that had led to emancipation in the first place, pro-moting a narrative of "northern aggression" during the Civil War and of corrupt and illegitimate occupation during Reconstruction.

During the Gilded Age, from the end of the Civil War until the turn of the century, America witnessed further expansions of the state, funded by politicized tariffs that generated revenue Republicans used to pay for costly government even as they rewarded friendly industries, interests, and political supporters with protectionist tariffs on their foreign competition. The favoritism of Republican tariff schedules was obvious to all, and once again state power became an object of distrust, as did its claims to equal and fair representation. The people wondered: Whose interests would the state promote?

Opposition to corrupt alliances of partisan politicians and allied interests, particularly wealthy business interests, worked up the ire of Democrats, protest movements, and even third parties—including a new party called the Populists. According to political scientist Vivien Hart, "Nowhere in the history of American politics has the expression of this political distrust been more striking than in the Populist movement whose independent party, based in the agricultural regions of the West and South, and vehement demands disturbed the equilibrium of two-party politics between 1890 and 1896."[18] Aiming their fire at political parties and Congress, Populist leaders seized upon economic anxieties and suspicions that eastern alliances had usurped popular representation in government. As one rural Farmers' Alliance chapter in Kansas proclaimed, they were against "a government of politicians, by politicians, and for politicians" and for a "government of the people, by the people, and for the people."[19]

Suspicions of the state arose within some academic circles. A vision gaining prominence in the late nineteenth century (later to resonate among conservatives and libertarians) was social Darwinism. This perspective was exemplified by William Graham Sumner, who, building on the work of Herbert Spencer, argued that wealth properly accrued to those who worked to accumulate capital, and each person's "big duty" was simply "to take care of his or her own self." Sumner praised and mourned the "forgotten man" who was "hard at work" to pay for "all the plunder, the cost of all the economic quackery, and the pay of all the politicians and statesmen . . . threatened by every extension of the paternal theory of government."[20] Social Darwinists saw government as a threat to individualism and thus a threat to societal advancements that unfettered competition among individuals could produce.

In 1898, the USS *Maine* exploded while anchored in Havana harbor, and soon America was involved in the Cuban War of Independence. What would become the Spanish-American War rallied unity and voluntarism for the war effort.[21] In what Secretary of War Russell Alger called "the apotheosis of patriotism," volunteer soldiers—white and black, North and South—contributed to the cause; even President William McKinley's 1896 Democratic opponent William Jennings Bryan accepted "a commission in the Third Nebraska Volunteers" signaling "the approval" of former Populists and proto-Progressives in the West and Midwest.[22]

From a newborn republic to a divided house, nineteenth-century politics struggled with trust and distrust, union and diffused sovereignty. Different histories were constructed and debated, opposing stories rewritten and retold, and these became the cultural backdrops for the trust and distrust of government that could undergird and undermine government action.

By the late nineteenth century and into the early twentieth century, the predominant historical and cultural construction of the Civil War was represented as an honorable divide: good men on both sides. Abolitionist and former slave Frederick Douglass fought this deracialized version of the war that downplayed the cause and role of slavery and absented its moral and ideological meanings. By contrast, prominent leaders like Oliver Wendell Holmes and later Teddy Roosevelt excused the illiberal aims of the Confederacy and stressed the stalwart spirit of all soldiers, Union and Confederate.

At a major commemoration of the fiftieth anniversary of the battle of Gettysburg in 1913, former Union and Confederate soldiers came together. "No longer a war of secession, orator after orator recast the war as a heroic struggle between brothers whose blood had strengthened and purified the nation."[23] White Americans brushed aside the centrality of slavery and white supremacy to the Civil War and embraced a shared national identity with an agree-to-disagree attitude toward regional policies and positions, including minimal or absent black voting rights and other white supremacist structures. During the Gilded Age and Populist and Progressive movements, some rediscovered the value of the state as a means of countering the power of increasingly nationalized corporations as well as corrupt state and local party machines. Americans would also feel the necessity of the state in times of war.

BUILT TRUST AND THE TWENTIETH-CENTURY
DEVELOPMENT OF THE STATE

As he looked back on William McKinley's call to arms for the Spanish-American War, Secretary of War Russell Alger wrote that, whereas America responded to the call, "The governmental machinery was altogether inadequate to immediately meet the emergency."[24] The twentieth century would reveal many more emergencies—global and domestic—that would compel the development of a more elaborate national state.

With Republicans firmly in control of the turn-of-the-century Congress and the presidential electoral map, the question was not so much whether but how to use the state. The neo-Hamiltonian tendency to cast centralized power as a boon to manufacturing and commercial interests was the touchstone of "regular" (as opposed to Progressive) Republicanism by the end of the nineteenth century. By contrast, Progressive opposition took the form not of questioning state power but of recasting the uses of the state that—for all of its echoes of Populists' preferences for "the people" as opposed to the moneyed "interests"—promised, too, a more technologically sophisticated state guided by experts.[25] But this reliance on well-trained "experts" was subject to racially biased views of the American polity. As Rogers Smith observed,

> Even as they apotheosized democracy, most progressives continued to believe that modern science had shown the reality of racial differences, and that most nonwhites and some whites, at home and abroad, needed tutelary rule before they would be prepared for self-governance . . . Progressives generally supported and sometimes initiated the Jim Crow-era disenfranchisement measures that hindered many poor whites as well as blacks. They also called for policies of both immigration restriction and mandatory assimilation to insure the "100 percent Americanism," rather than the "hyphenated Americanism," of newcomers.[26]

If small-government arguments for individual "liberty" were matched to states' rights and localist arguments against national governmental power (from the Civil War to Reconstruction and civil rights, for example), Progressives, in "glimps[ing] a national community,"[27] explored how the national government might come to be a protector of individual liberty as much as a threat.

Nothing of the era demanded state expansions and transformed citizens' perceptions of government more than America entering World War I. Seeking national mobilization, Woodrow Wilson employed George Creel to propagandize for the war and the necessary expenditure of resources it would entail. Amid sometimes "lurching and ambivalent expansions and contractions of state capacities and bureaucratic authorities," whole-sale transformations of American citizenship were underway as a small-state citizenship ethos of obligation and voluntarism gave way to concepts of citizenship that emphasized individualism and appeals to "rights." This constituted a "massive and sometimes contradictory restructuring of the relationship between Americans and state power."[28] Add to this a "record high protective tariff," a new national budgeting system that empowered the executive branch, and redistributive policies from agricultural crop supports to veterans' bonuses, one can see the massive growth in the poten-tial of the twentieth-century state that emanated from World War I.[29]

Domestically, some Democrats had advocated for more national gov-ernment intervention since the Wilson administration, and they had been fueling national sentiment toward trust in government in support of those aims. With Al Smith's 1928 presidential candidacy, and especially after the Great Depression began, an increasing proportion of national Democrats made the case for greater governmental involvement, which they believed they could leverage to fashion a broad, progressive coalition atop their conservative southern base. The push and pull between the conservative and liberal wings of the party would continue for decades, but the more progressive and liberal elements of the Democratic Party had taken root by the 1930s, and they would continue to explore programmatically liberal policies in ensuing years, including support for the poor, social insurance for the aged and infirm, and health care.[30] These potentially positive uses of the national government were more pronounced, both domestically and in foreign policy, throughout the New Deal, World War II, and the Cold War, as Democrats expanded the state, broadened its influence in society and the economy, and intentionally worked to build public confidence in the state as they were expanding it.

Taking office in 1933 and anticipating a broader use of the state, President Franklin D. Roosevelt called for unity as Americans' "sacred obligation." "We now realize as we have never realized before our interdependence on each other," he said, "that we cannot merely take but we must give as well; that if we are to go forward, we must move as a trained and loyal army willing to sacrifice for the good of a common discipline."[31]

While this speech also called for public investment and limiting monop-olists, by the late 1930s the Roosevelt administration stressed fiscal pol-icy as a tool to manage the economy and allow businesses to develop.[32]

The public philosophy of the New Deal was both a policy program and a "rationale for those acts," according to political scientist Samuel H. Beer. "Roosevelt's nationalism was a doctrine of federal centralization, and under his administration, in peace as well as war, the balance of the American federal system swung sharply toward Washington."[33] Conservatives of the time equated liberty with economic freedom from government, but Roosevelt argued that economic freedom was contingent on economic *security*, promoting an expanded view of rights based in government action.

The push and pull of trust and distrust in government were in evidence throughout the New Deal as opposing voices sought to undermine Roosevelt's agenda. Among conservative opponents, moralistic and religious language was combined with claims about economic freedom. As historians Kevin Kruse and Kim Phillips-Fein note, in the 1930s business groups critical of government programs and regulations worked with religious leaders to criticize the New Deal.[34] However, the American public largely held liberal positions on government's role in the economy. Americans strongly backed Social Security from its start, and support only grew. A 1938 poll found Social Security was viewed extremely positively across regions and races, and a follow-up poll in 1944 found that large majorities favored expanding the program to include the self-employed, people working for government, domestic workers, and farmers. Regulations of banks and wages and programs for housing and farm support were also popular.[35] Yet short-lived public support for government ownership of banks, railroads, and electric utilities declined from the mid-1930s through the mid-1940s. At the same time, support for labor and for strategies like sit-down strikes and the closed shop also fell. Anti-labor sentiment was growing stronger in the South.

In the midst of World War II, Franklin Roosevelt's administration internally discussed seeking a large health-care program after the war and "the right to adequate medical care and the opportunity to achieve and enjoy good health" was included as part of Roosevelt's January 1944 delineation of a Second Bill of Rights. In 1945 President Harry S. Truman reiterated those rights and announced he would recommend "a national health program to provide adequate medical care for all Americans and to protect them from financial loss and hardships resulting from illness and accident."[36]

Framing health care as a right, Truman argued it was a national concern and pointed to health problems among military recruits and military members. Anticipating opposition, Truman explained that people would be able to "get medical and hospital services just as they do now—on the basis of their own voluntary decisions and choices" and "doctors and hospitals would continue to deal with disease with the same professional freedom." What would be different was that getting services "would not depend on how much [patients] can afford to pay at the time."[37] Truman argued this approach was "not socialized medicine," but the label helped to derail the proposal, along with the "conservative coalition of Republicans and Southern Democrats that controlled Congress [and] the resistance of the American Medical Association."[38]

Support for the New Deal was especially precarious in the more conservative South. Race and region had always been key fault lines in Roosevelt's coalition, as they had been throughout America's political development. The New Deal coalition was held together in part by structuring policies to secure support from southern segregationist Democrats. This is why Social Security originally *excluded* agricultural and domestic workers, who were disproportionately African American. According to political scientist Ira Katznelson, "Shaped by the South, national policies in the 1930s and 1940s regarding Social Security, labor law, military race relations, and the treatment of veterans . . . reinforced inequality and deepened the racial divide."[39] In Congress, the New Deal coalition was sustained by Democratic Party leaders—like Texan Sam Rayburn and Bostonian John McCormack who, because they had relatively low proportions of African Americans in their districts compared to other southern states and northeastern cities—were well placed to "finesse" volatile civil rights questions that could divide the party.[40]

Despite these policy concessions, the South was increasingly restive with its place in the New Deal coalition. If conservative southerners bought into the New Deal's economic relief as a "temporary" solution to the Great Depression, their support for FDR waned as the depression slackened. At the same time, Roosevelt was trying to take the party leftward, exacerbating conflict with conservative southerners. After his failed attempt to "purge" conservatives (mostly southerners) in 1938's primary elections, unease grew, and southern Democratic committee chairs turned from supporting New Deal policies to investigating the administration, all the while looking for one of their own to replace FDR in 1940.[41] With all of its built-in ambivalence and the mounting coordinated opposition from a conservative coalition of Republicans and southern Democrats, what sustained FDR's coalition into the 1940 was the skill of Roosevelt's congressional allies in avoiding divisive issues, especially civil rights. This perpetuated the party's unsavory reliance on segregationists, and it meant shifting primarily from gaining new liberal policy wins to merely protecting the domestic policy gains made in the first two terms.[42]

World War II united America once again, in part because war and national security threats tend to bind people together and such threats emphasize the value of the state even to skeptical citizens.[43] As part of New Deal politics, the U.S. Department of Agriculture had carried out opinion research among farmers and others to plan how to implement and market policies. The USDA was on the ground doing polling and interviews right after the attack on Pearl Harbor. Other government bureaus were quickly created to build on this work.

During the war, the federal government invested considerable resources into promoting national unity and exhorting citizens to participate in the war effort whether at home or abroad. Like commercial marketing and advertising, the federal government conducted public opinion research on how best to appeal to Americans and to understand what might undermine unity. For instance, research conducted in June 1942 about Americans' susceptibility to ideas promoting "disunity in America" and "inimical to the war effort" focused not only on how people saw the war going and the aims of the war, but also whether people were anti-labor, anti-Semitic, and xenophobic. Analysts warned that "a strong anti-foreign sentiment can have terrible consequences for our war effort," pitting both those born in the United States against people born elsewhere and raising questions about why Americans were fighting to help people in other nations.[44] Public relations efforts from posters to radio programs to films asked people to ration provisions, purchase war bonds, and otherwise contribute to and identify with the nation.

But the unity of wartime could not resolve the tensions fracturing the New Deal coalition. The racial divisions that plagued domestic policy confronted the war effort too. The federal government monitored and tried to dampen racial tensions in the North and South. It was a difficult task to craft messages that avoided patronizing black Americans while not angering supporters of segregation and white supremacy.[45] This balance was often impossible. A pamphlet published in late 1942 by the Office of War Information (OWI) showcasing contributions by African American servicemen met vociferous objections from powerful southern legislators because of its statements about the pace of and future progress toward racial equality. "If President Roosevelt expects to see his Administration succeed itself," said Representative John Rankin, a Democrat from Mississippi, "he had better crack down on these crackpots who are constantly harassing and insulting the white people of the Southern States."[46] In an "off-the-record discussion among half a dozen Congressmen," anger was voiced "over the OWI handling of the Negro situation," which included its publication of "Negroes and the War." This "southern ire" led Congress to slash the agency's budget and restrict its domestic opinion research.[47] At the same time, the black press, black citizens, and civil rights advocates often saw these efforts to promote "Negro morale" as inadequate when African Americans were doing so much to win the war.[48]

Having lifted the country out of the throes of the Great Depression and then guided it through World War II, FDR's political coalition and the domestic and security state that it built were massively popular, these fault lines notwithstanding. Broad swaths of the American public regarded it with great trust and affection.

Such high levels of trust in government in part resulted from policy efforts. Wartime demands of achieving unity led to considerable state investments in building support for the state and gingerly addressing racial discrimination. While disproportionately helping white men, the post–World War II GI Bill assisted millions of citizens and promoted civic engagement and trust in government.[49]

Still, long-standing tendencies toward distrust and disunity were only ameliorated, not resolved. Whereas unions and civil rights groups worked together during the war to promote racial equality,[50] unions ended the period with decreased support, and public opinion did not change much on racial issues. Not even white veterans were "distinguishable on a wide range of racial prejudice measures."[51]

CULTIVATING DISTRUST IN POSTWAR AMERICA

After World War II, the strategic promotion of distrust solidified as a strategy of opposition to the New Deal—its governance and policy aims as well as its political coalition. Seizing not only on America's traditional anti-statism as a weapon to oppose the nationalizing and centralizing tendencies of the New Deal but also on the emergent weaknesses in that coalition that resulted from civil rights struggles, the GOP eventually brought white southern conservatives into its fold and became the party of small government. This was a fundamental departure for the party that was heir to Hamilton, Lincoln, and other state-builders but one that had anti-government antecedents that, by the 1960s, were decades old.

Since the 1920s, Republicans had transformed party orthodoxy from one in which the government was an active promoter of "order" in the economy and society to one in which government was a threat to individual liberty. Overthrowing Burkean conservatism for a neoclassical vision of free markets and Spencerian social Darwinism, Republicans would denounce government meddling and proclaim it, as Reagan would say, "the problem."[52] As political scientist John Gerring put it, "Whereas in the previous century the party had worked to contain the passions of the individual, largely through the actions of an interventionist state, now Republicans reversed this polarity: the individual was to be set free from the machinations of the state."[53] Democrats' successful and popular uses of the state in the 1930s and 1940s left the Republicans with a clear oppositional path built around antipathy to the government. Thus, in fundamental ways, the GOP had switched places with the Democratic Party to become the anti-statist party and, not coincidentally, the party of the South.

The roots of the postwar American promotion of distrust in government grew out a conservative backlash—Republican and southern Democratic—against a powerful national government involving itself in economics, civil rights, and health care. The American state had worked to build a sense of national identity during wartime, which made it difficult for opposing voices to undermine state power and national unity. After the war, however, opposition voices grew louder. From the 1950s to the 1980s, political rhetoric and organized efforts to shift the bases of national identity refocused understandings of Americanism and citizenship from government as a protector and force for the national interest toward government as a threat to economic freedom and liberal (though it would ceased to be called such) civil society.[54] These oppositional forces seized at once on weaknesses in the New Deal coalition and Cold War anxieties about the dangers of oppressive states and their threats to individual liberty.

It is noteworthy that conservatives took the opportunity of the Cold War to immediately raise fears of large states—and the potential infiltration of

American politics by communists—and, ironically, as a reason to build up the American state's domestic surveillance and national security apparatus. Whereas these state expansions were generally approved to fight the communist menace, it would be Medicare and welfare expansions that conservatives would deem socialistic threats to American liberty. It is equally notable that it would be the left that proved to be the more distrustful critic of the expansions of the military, intelligence, and police powers.

Lurking behind these efforts—to undermine the New Deal, to break the Democratic coalition, and to lure away the South—was, of course, race. The New Deal coalition was always electorally fragile on this count. New configurations of racial groups and white backlash against social programs had changed the formula for winning elections. The migration of African Americans to northern industrialized cities during and after World War II was a political opportunity for Democrats. Black Americans had the right to vote in those locales and, depending on what President Truman did, might swing key electoral votes to him. As a November 1947 campaign memo to Truman put it, "Unless there are new and real efforts (as distinguished from mere political gestures which are today thoroughly understood and strongly resented by sophisticated Negro leaders), the Negro bloc, which, certainly in Illinois and probably in New York and Ohio, *does* hold the balance of power, will go Republican."[55]

Such efforts to attract black voters by supporting civil rights policies dismayed white supremacist, segregationist southern Democrats. Rejecting this significant change in Democratic Party politics, Dixiecrats broke away from the Democratic Party in 1948 and ran Strom Thurmond for president. Even as Truman unexpectedly defeated Republican Thomas E. Dewey, Thurmond won thirty-nine electoral votes from four states plus one faithless elector in the South.

Liberal economic views, regionalism, and race made traditional southern Democrats increasingly uncomfortable. Both parties saw the potential for the emergence of a conservative Republican Party faction based around government's limited role in the economy and race politics. In September 1948, Truman campaign strategists noted there was distaste toward "Truman and the National Democratic Party" in the South. They believed these views could lead to "the commencement of new party alignments in the United States and a two-party system in the South" due to "the racial issue" and "a growing sentiment against centralization, communistic trends in the

Democratic Party, and the disregard of southern views to court the fringe or radical elements in doubtful northern states."[56] According to political scientist Eric Schickler, "From the late 1930s onward, conservative political entrepreneurs saw the opportunity afforded by southern dissatisfaction with the direction of the New Deal and believed that an ideological appeal framed around states' rights had the potential to create a coalition of midwestern economic conservatives and southern racial conservatives."[57]

Even during the moderate interregnum of the Eisenhower years, conservative forces were growing stronger within the GOP. If Dwight Eisenhower's "modern Republicanism" evinced more moderation on questions of governmental power, he was neither immune to criticisms when he expanded the role of the national government nor was he without his own personal qualms about the growth of the state.[58] In a letter to vice presidential nominee Richard Nixon, Eisenhower claimed "that continuation of the present administration in Washington will continue us, perhaps beyond redemption, on the path toward Socialism we are now pursuing."[59] Still, he was political realist enough to expand the state in key ways throughout his administration. Even when using the term "socialized medicine" to describe legislation that provided a benefit for elderly people who could not afford health care, Eisenhower ultimately signed the legislation. And even though he created the Department of Health, Education, and Welfare in 1953, Eisenhower stated in 1954 that he opposed "a Federally-operated and controlled system of medical care" and promised to "use every single attribute to defeat any move toward socialized medicine."[60] Eisenhower's preferred policies relied on subsidizing insurance, which he argued would head off the sorts of plans that did not fit that label.[61]

Over the next few decades, Republicans sharpened their anti-government rhetoric as Democrats looked to expand the state and its potential uses during John F. Kennedy's New Frontier campaign and Lyndon Johnson's Great Society initiative.

The conservative assault against health care, for example, continued. When in February 1961 President John F. Kennedy launched a new effort for a health program, he defended against the claim that it was socialistic. Kennedy stated "The program is not socialized medicine . . . It is a program of prepayment for health costs with absolute freedom of choice guaranteed. Every person will choose his own doctor and hospital."[62] The American Medical Association mounted an extensive campaign to prevent any plan from being adopted that included lobbying, campaign donations, and public relations efforts. The word "socialism" was used in posters the AMA sent doctors to put up in their waiting rooms, along with materials cautioning patients waiting there.[63] Then-actor Ronald Reagan participated in the AMA's Operation Coffee Cup campaign to forestall what would become Medicare by recording a speech that was played to gatherings hosted by doctors' wives. Reagan suggested supporters of the proposed health program were trying to fool others, saying, "One of the traditional methods of imposing statism or socialism on a people has been by way of medicine. It's very easy to disguise a medical program as a humanitarian project."

Ramping up the distrustful rhetoric, Reagan claimed that this was but a next step to a loss of liberty itself. An overweening government, Reagan warned, would tell doctors, in what areas they could practice medicine and where they could live. Ultimately, if the legislation was not stopped, Reagan said, "We will awake to find that we have socialism. And if you don't do this and if I don't do it, one of these days you and I are going to spend our sunset years telling our children and our children's children, what it once was like in America when men were free."[64]

Momentum for health care for the elderly and the poor came after Lyndon Johnson's 1964 landslide victory over Barry Goldwater. While Johnson campaigned for creating a health-care program, Goldwater opposed it. Johnson's win brought with it so many seats for Democrats that they held two to one majorities in the House and Senate. No incumbent backing Medicare lost reelection, a fact interpreted as demonstrating that Goldwater's opposition had hurt Republicans.[65] Those electoral conditions enabled Johnson to sign into law in 1965 two Medicare programs for the elderly, a hospital program and coverage for doctors' visits, as well as Medicaid, a program for low-income individuals.

Johnson and other national Democrats also became increasingly pro–civil rights, winning over black voters outside disenfranchised states and passing legislation to enfranchise southern black voters. The passage of the 1964 Civil Rights Act and the 1965 Voting Rights Act not only appealed to these voters but affected the politics surrounding all manner of federalism and policy questions. In addition to making use of the national government to compel the compliance of reluctant, especially southern, states, race was important in achieving and implementing major pillars of U.S. health policy in Medicare and Medicaid. During legislative–executive negotiations, the

Johnson administration was asked whether funding for hospital care would be contingent on desegregating those facilities. In fact, the Civil Rights Act made the maintenance of segregation unviable. As Zelizer notes, "Southern legislators now had more incentive to vote in favor of new federal services for their region, even if those funds threatened white supremacy, because it was now clear that racial desegregation was going to happen anyway."[66] Indeed, the Office of Equal Health Opportunity in the U.S. Public Health Service, created in February 1966, monitored hospitals and enforced compliance with federal regulations requiring integrated hospitals. But these historic achievements in civil rights exacted a political cost on the fragile coalition that FDR had built.

Meanwhile, the Republican Party was actively trying to pick up the disaffected pieces of a fraying New Deal coalition and integrate them into a new GOP. Sparked by Barry Goldwater, America's "first major politician to embrace the name 'conservative,'"[67] the GOP's right wing took aim at both the party's more pro-state, Rockefeller wing, and at the Democrats by arguing that the New Deal had outlived whatever usefulness it had and had become a threat to liberty.[68] Using anti-elite rhetoric, Goldwater supporter Phyllis Schlafly conspiratorially claimed that "a few secret kingmakers" had previously "successfully forced their choice" of a Republican presidential nominee on the party and called for "a choice, not an echo."[69]

Goldwater's candidacy targeted disaffected white southerners, a long-term investment for the GOP that cost them black voters. Goldwater received only 6 percent of the African American vote, down from 32 percent for Nixon in 1960 and 39 percent for Eisenhower in 1956.[70] Notably, despite LBJ's 1964 landslide, Goldwater captured, in addition to his home state of Arizona, just the "Deep South" states of Alabama, Georgia, Louisiana, Mississippi, and South Carolina giving rise to the belief that the GOP might at long last make lasting inroads in the South.

These long-frustrated GOP efforts finally bore fruit with Richard Nixon's victory in 1968, thanks to both anti-government sentiment and new racial calculations. Building on the Goldwater legacy, the Nixon administration and the Republican National Committee (RNC) promoted distrust of nationalizing policies. Offering a departure from Democratic programs and rule, in accepting the 1968 Republican nomination, Richard Nixon said, "For the past five years, we have been deluged by government programs for the unemployed; programs for the cities; programs for the poor.

And we have reaped from these programs an ugly harvest of frustration, violence and failure across the land." The "ugly harvest" was a deviation from American greatness: "America is a great nation," he said, "not because of what government did for people—but because of what people did for themselves over a hundred-ninety years in this country." For Nixon, at least rhetorically, the new aim of government should not be more programs and more spending but instead easing the burdens of taxes and employing tax credits "to enlist in this battle the greatest engine of progress ever developed in the history of man—American private enterprise."[71]

Nixon's victory benefited from the independent, segregationist candidacy of George Wallace, a former Democrat who bolted the party over civil rights, effectively splitting the coalition. Race politics had been emerging as key to Republican strategy since the 1960s Civil and Voting Rights Acts opened an avenue for the GOP to strip the Democratic Party of its southern base. Paving the way for Nixon's 1968 victory and a soon-to-be reconstituted GOP, Wallace won five Deep South states—Alabama, Arkansas, Georgia, Louisiana, and Mississippi.

Nixon's political planning for 1970 and 1972 hinged on winning over Wallace voters and white southerners more generally. Having read Richard Scammon and Ben Wattenberg's 1970 book, *The Real Majority*, Pat Buchanan advised the president of the authors' crucial observation that the majority of America was "unyoung, unpoor, unblack."[72] Seeking to win white working-class votes nationally and to peel off white southerners disaffected with a Democratic Party that had passed civil rights and voting rights acts, Nixon focused on "social issues," which according to Buchanan were "first discovered by Goldwater and Wallace" and included "drugs, demonstrations, pornography, disruptions, 'kidlash,' permissiveness, violence, riots, crime."[73] Getting voters to focus less on the economic benefits of government policies and more on these issues appealed to Nixon's "silent majority."

The appeals to the "real majority" included a "Southern strategy" message to onboard disaffected white southerners to the Republican coalition.[74] Generally, Nixon's anti-government denigration of "programs" and the national government as well as his promise of a "new federalism" that would return power to state and local governments all had appeal to the former Confederate states chafing under new, intrusive national policies. Still, the racial element of the appeal to America's "unyoung, unpoor, and unblack" citizens was clear whether it was encoded in the language of "law and order" politics or articulated more pointedly in Buchanan's advice to Nixon that Republicans make the Democratic Party "the party of bussing, the advocates of 'compulsory integration.' "[75]

Of course, the Southern strategy typically had to be sub rosa (it was only officially admitted to in 2005 when RNC chairman Ken Mehlman apologized to the NAACP) for fear of alienating other voters as Republicans pursued white southerners. Still, the Republican anti-government orthodoxy allowed Nixon to argue that New Deal and Great Society policies were bad for black America. In the only mention of black Americans in a policy context contained in his 1968 nomination acceptance speech, Nixon said, "Black Americans, no more than white Americans, they do not want more government programs which perpetuate dependency."[76] In this formulation, Nixon began a Republican trope that would allow for denigration of policies that helped African Americans while ostensibly supporting their true interests.

If the GOP's increasing anti-state conservatism attracted southerners already prone to be suspicious of the national government, southerners in turn made the GOP all the more conservative. From the 1960s on, race and anti-statist conservative politics and policies linked rhetorically and politically to the concept of states' rights. As political scientist Joseph Lowndes argues, "In the case of modern conservatism, race has been both an open and coded signifier for popular mobilizations against redistribution, regulation, labor protections, and myriad other aspects of neo-liberal opposition to 'big government.' "[77] To conservatives, the untrustworthy state was one that dismantled racial segregation and sought to reduce racial disparities limiting opportunity. Republicans also attracted evangelical Christians unhappy with the emergence of the women's rights and gay rights movements. Nixon used culture war themes in his 1972 campaign, a race he won in a landslide, painting his Democratic Party opponent George McGovern as the candidate of "acid, amnesty, and abortion." While their strategy did not have a single geographic locus, the combination of white racial resentment, evangelicalism, and anti-feminism was especially potent in the South.[78] As more conservatives came into the tent, they ran the Rockefeller wing out of the party in the 1970s and 1980s, fueling not only America's party polarization but also conservative expressions of distrust in government.

After the 1960s, conservative movement activists, some of whom joined in racialized politics while others merely looked the other way, took increasingly hardline stances against government involvement in social programs and the economy, and very wealthy individuals worked to shift the ideological center of the country toward libertarian notions, defining liberty in terms of property rights and as little taxation as possible and arguing that government attempts to help people promoted dependency.[79]

Since at least the New Deal (and even the Progressive era), liberals and progressives had championed the presidency as a potentially dynamic force for action, whereas conservatives admired Congress's slow-paced, deliberative contributions to policy making and its bias toward inaction altogether. It was really only during the Nixon administration that Republicans began to shift on these questions, resisting resurgent congressional power when issues of war powers, budget impoundment, and eventually presidential secrecy during Watergate brought questions of the separation of powers to the foreground.

The shifts were stunningly abrupt for conservative "fixed constitutionalists." As late as 1968, the GOP platform championed a revitalized Congress, hoping it would be "reorganized and modernized to function efficiently as a coequal branch of government." Republicans also worried that the growth of the executive with "an increasingly impersonal national government has tended to submerge the individual" and an "entrenched, burgeoning bureaucracy has increasingly usurped powers, unauthorized by Congress." Quite apart from later concerns about Congress's role in budgeting and its "meddling" in administration, the 1968 GOP platform called for "strengthened Congressional control over federal expenditures" and for "strict Congressional oversight of administrative and regulatory agency compliance" with the law. Echoing long-standing conservative orthodoxy, Republicans believed an emboldened Congress could "preserve personal liberty, improve efficiency, and provide a swifter response to human problems."[80]

Not surprisingly, with Nixon in the White House but Democrats controlling both the House and the Senate, the 1972 GOP platform ceased calls for more congressional power. Mentions of Congress in that platform were almost exclusively focused on criticizing Congress for inaction on Nixon program initiatives or complaining that Democrats had controlled Congress for "forty out of the last forty-four years."[81]

Republicans' political strength ebbed for a time as Nixon faced investigations into the Watergate scandal and then resigned from office in August 1974, making Gerald Ford the new president. Democrats did quite well in the

November 1974 congressional races and passed legislation requiring greater executive branch transparency and restricting the president in budgetary matters and war making. Ford's chief of staff, Dick Cheney, later to represent Wyoming in the House of Representatives and serve as George W. Bush's vice president, was disturbed by the diminution of presidential power.[82]

By 1976, Republican complaints about Congress reached a fever pitch. Republicans charged that Democrats had created a system of government that is "warped and overnationalized" and one in which legislators regularly "cav[ed] in . . . to special interest demands." Seizing on high-profile scandals, they described Congress as "riddled with corruption" and called for the implementation of a list of internal reforms regarding member and staff salaries, financial disclosures of members and an audit of congressional allowances by the General Accounting Office, changes in the legislative process, and reform of the House Ethics Committee.[83]

Uniting traditional GOP forces with longer-standing anti-government sentiments in the South, conservative Republicans strategically cultivated distrust in government to build conservative organizations, to wage campaigns and win elections, to shift power to the governing institutions they controlled while undermining the Democratic Congress, and to affect policy struggles.

THE STRATEGY OF DISTRUST

Beginning with the presidential candidacy of Barry Goldwater, distrust in government became the primary strategy of conservative Republicans as they chipped away at post–New Deal Democratic dominance. The GOP coalition would be built, too, on a vehement promotion of capitalism and business interests, a growing moralism and belief in social order, and support for a robust American military. But the anti-government strand of Republicanism (even as it conflicted in important ways with these other strains of conservative thought) was as strong and prevalent as any of the party's ideological tropes and strategic commitments. If, like any party coalition, the GOP was multifaceted, it is fair to say that its purported ideology and its strategic rhetoric were centered on distrust in government.

The balance of power in the Republican Party was not only conservative and anti-government, but also predominantly white. By the late 1960s, the party's geographic center shifted toward the South, and it embraced a combination of anti-statist ideology and states' rights views of the newly onboarded southern contingent. Party messages promoting distrust were often infused with racialized rhetoric in opposing Democrats and their policy proposals.

The remainder of this book chronicles these conservative, Republican strategic efforts since the 1960s to promote distrust in government to achieve party objectives. But we stress here that our argument is different than simply asserting that conservative Republicans are anti-government, a point which to some might seem overly obvious. To the contrary, we argue that contemporary conservatives' anti-governmentalism is also strategic. The evidence of a strategic motivation can be found in the inconsistent application of these sentiments. Contemporary conservatives are not against employing government in some policy areas, and they apply their anti-government principles inconsistently depending on whether they are in power and which of the institutions of national government they control.

First, given that Republicans were once the big-government party, the conservative embrace of anti-government rhetoric was central to intraparty struggles. Conservatives sought to best the party's moderate faction, itself emboldened during the Eisenhower years. All manner of conservative insurgents from the John Birch Society to the *National Review* tapped into America's "endemic strain" of distrust in government.

The impetus and broader appeal of this strategy of distrust was a conservative reaction to the growth of the state since the New Deal and the subsequent national government interventions during the civil rights era and the Great Society. The *National Review*'s mission statement, penned by William F. Buckley Jr. in 1955, listed the magazine's first "conviction":

> It is the job of centralized government (in peacetime) to protect its citizens' lives, liberty, and property. All other activities of government tend to diminish freedom and hamper progress. The growth of government (the dominant social feature of this century) must be fought relentlessly. In this great social conflict of the era, we are, without reservations, on the libertarian side.[84]

But to "stand athwart history, yelling 'Stop!,' " as Buckley proclaimed the *Review* did, was to run afoul of the popularity of the New Deal, and as some argue, to discount the benefits (and economic growth) that big government had provided.[85]

Second, the contemporary GOP, for all of its anti-government stances and pronouncements, seems still to be "antigovernment in rhetoric if not always in practice."[86] Even when the modern conservative movement was developing and came to dominate the GOP, many of the staunchest conservatives were proponents of state action (and increasingly so) when it came to police powers, the military, aid to economic elites, and rooting out "subversive" elements of society, at least those on the left. If it is true that liberals are more apt to favor government action when it comes to domestic social welfare spending and redistribution, economic interventionism (including economic regulation), and use of government to expand civil rights protections, it is conservatives who favor expanded government in terms of military spending, government police powers and surveillance, and, for social conservatives, a "role" for "government in enforcing moral standards."[87]

Consider how prone conservatives are to state action in these policy areas and, especially, when they themselves control the government. What is more, the modern conservative movement, for all of its anti-government rhetoric seems to be much more open to government spending (and regulation) when such policies support its interests or the interests of those with whom it identifies or of whom it approves. In a 1964 survey, Lloyd Free and Hadley Cantril found that whereas a majority of Americans give voice to an ideological conservatism in the abstract, a larger percentage nevertheless is "operationally liberal," tending to support government action when faced with specifics.[88] Revisiting these questions in a 1997 survey, Albert H. Cantril and Susan Davis Cantril found continued evidence of this American ambivalence toward government among liberals and conservatives alike. They said, "To understand people's thinking about government, one needs to know a lot more than the way they describe their own philosophy."[89]

It is simply wrong to say that contemporary American conservatives—supportive as they are of significant portions of the state and of policies that benefit friendly constituencies—oppose government across the board and that liberals favor it. Despite the distrustful anti-government rhetoric they employ for strategic ends, the full story is more complex, with each side holding some pro-government and some anti-government views.

Conservatives' constitutional prescriptions about appropriate institutional roles in the separation of powers are equally fluid. Whereas traditional conservatives celebrated congressional authority and decried presidential activism, modern conservatives support expansive powers of the presidency when Republicans control the White House but decry presidential power in the hands of Democrats.[90] By the same token, they are apt to complain of activist or obstructionist Congresses and their meddling oversight when Democrats have majority control but deem these same activities appropriate constitutional prerogatives when the GOP controls Congress. This is not to excuse liberals who play the same situational game, but simply to point out that rhetoric about the "meddling oversight" of Democratic Congresses or the abusive, even dangerous, executive orders of Democratic presidents seems less like principled constitutional prescriptions when they are so unevenly applied, and more like a clever strategy to spur a restive public.

Contemporary conservatives are only selectively anti-government. The effort to stoke government distrust is strategic and instrumental. There are benefits to distrust, and this book will explore four of them: organizational, electoral, institutional, and policy benefits. The rhetoric employed by conservatives has not only tapped into Americans' long-held suspicions of government, but it has become so extreme as to make war on the very legitimacy of the government itself. That these concerns are not expressed universally but only selectively and situationally strongly suggests that when conservatives try to stoke distrust in government—and in one's fellow citizens—they are less sentinels guarding liberty than they are politicos ambitiously and strategically (perhaps even cynically) capitalizing on public skepticism to breed anti-government sentiments. We turn next to strategic uses of political distrust in the Reagan era.

Chapter Three

HERE TO HELP?

Movement Conservatism and the State
in the Reagan Era

"The nine most terrifying words in the English language are 'I'm from the government, and I'm here to help,'" alleged Ronald Reagan in 1986 at a press conference in Illinois.[1]

Yet Reagan immediately followed this precept by touting "a drought assistance task force" and "the availability of price-support loans for all the grain in this year's crop." Many of the problems facing farmers, he contended, were caused by the government, and so his goal was to establish "economic independence for agriculture" and to "return farming to real farmers." Yet he readily acknowledged that spending on agriculture had risen rapidly under his watch and that his "administration has committed record amounts of assistance, spending more in this year alone than any previous administration spent during its entire tenure." Per his own conservative ideology, help from the government should give farmers pause, but Reagan reassured them with promises of even more future government assistance: "America's farmers should know that our commitment to helping them is unshakable. And as long as I am in Washington, their concerns are going to be heard and acted upon."

But when faced with questions in the same press conference about the needs of a decidedly different population—the citizens of Chicago, a city with a sharply declining white population—Reagan eschewed direct federal action.[2] Harold Washington, the city's first black mayor, had charged that the president's policies were enormously destructive, creating budget gaps that would lead to tax cuts or slashing the ranks of firefighters and police. When asked about Mayor Washington's claims, Reagan argued instead for block grants to states and cities to reduce, as he claimed, administrative waste. In stark contrast to his stance on funding farmers, the president argued that the best policy for Chicago would be an indirect effort to cut federal taxes, which "would then open areas to where a local government or a state government that had a need for additional revenues could take those revenues."[3]

Somewhat surprising given his historical reputation, Reagan's anti-government stance was not so much a consistent ideology as it was situational, applied unevenly, and dependent on the constituencies that stood to benefit.

For all the small-government rhetoric that is Reagan-era lore, the Reagan revolution had an ambivalent relationship with the state. Reagan wanted to decrease taxes and was for small government in domestic spending and economic regulation, while favoring increasing domestic spending to build support among groups, like farmers, who were important to his coalition. But, departing from conservative predecessors like Barry Goldwater, Reagan conservatism also carved out a role for a more intrusive government in moral and social issues, exhibiting what the political scientist Theodore J. Lowi called a "commitment to highly coercive government controls of many areas of conduct."[4]

Reagan also backed an expanded presidency and considerably more government when it came to building up police powers, the military, and the national security apparatus. Against decades of conservative thought championing a strong Congress, Reaganites reversed course and invented a "unitary executive" theory of administrative politics to accompany an invigorated presidency. The strong presidency they championed would have been anathema to the early twentieth-century conservatives who mistrusted presidential power and centralized executive authority. And those elements of the state that are more coercive and surveilling—the military, law enforcement, and intelligence—were championed by Reaganites. Ironically, a burgeoning domestic state was seen as a lumbering threat to liberty, but the more coercive and physically constraining aspects of the state somehow were not deemed to be similarly threatening by Reagan or his followers.

Given these complications and contradictions, what are we to make of all this anti-government rhetoric? Part of it reflected Reagan's deeply held beliefs, the zeal of a midlife conservative convert. It was also a strategic

effort to seize upon existing distrust among the public that he could cata-
lyze and cultivate to build a lasting Republican coalition. Reagan employed
this tactic to benefit his conservative movement, to win elections, to wage
separation of powers conflicts, and to make policy. In doing so, Reagan-
era conservatism actively undermined post–World War II national unity
and trust in government. As formidable and lasting as Franklin Delano
Roosevelt's coalition was, like most built things, it was precarious, and the
postwar rise and development of conservatism had the intention and effect
of undermining the public trust in the national government that was at the
New Deal's core. Weaponizing distrust in their war with government, the
movement instead promoted a view of American identity in which citizens
are suspicious of government, particularly the federal government.

Reagan's rise to prominence—his conservative takeover of the Republican Party and his landslide election and reelection in 1980 and 1984—
were stunning historical achievements. For a party that had suffered
disgrace with Richard Nixon's 1974 resignation and withered at the polls
in 1974 and 1976 after Gerald Ford pardoned Nixon, the Republican Party
rebounded quickly with a strong showing in 1978 and regained the White
House and achieved Senate control by 1980. Reagan's victory over President
Carter brought Republicans as close to majority control of the House in the
Ninety-Seventh Congress as they had been since the 1950s.[5] Capitalizing
on distrust in government, Reagan reconstructed America, fashioning a
new governing coalition, including a new conservative vision of separation of powers politics, and began efforts—if halting and incomplete—to
dismantle federal government power and programs.

Reagan's ambivalence in these efforts was not so much lack of will as it
was lessons learned (sometimes at great political cost) about the remaining
strength of the public's affinities for what FDR and the Democrats had built
and the recognition of how even the most conservative parts of America,
like the farmers Reagan addressed in 1986, had come to rely on the government for economic benefits and security.

REAGAN'S RISE

Ronald Reagan's rise to political power paralleled the trajectory of the public's view of the New Deal. Reagan himself was once a New Deal Democrat.
His father worked for the Works Progress Administration. Even after

Ronald Reagan's conversion to conservatism he spoke about the importance of the WPA and his father's work. In later years, Reagan would be
cagey about the duration and depth of his support of Franklin Roosevelt,
but he never deviated from admitting to having voted for FDR in 1932 and
sometimes copped to supporting him in all subsequent elections too.

As a Hollywood actor and labor leader, Reagan was part of liberal politics and causes in California into the 1940s. He supported Helen Gahagan
Douglas (dubbed the "Pink Lady" by political foes, including opponent
Richard Nixon, who insinuated that she sympathized with communists) in
her 1950 bid for the Senate. Reagan was even considered a potential surro-
gate spokesperson for the campaign, though notably some Douglas operatives resisted because of Reagan's "leftish reputation" at the time.[6]

Reagan liked the New Deal as much as the next American in the 1940s.
Americans so approved of the New Deal that Dwight Eisenhower's 1952
and 1956 candidacies offered what he called "a modern Republicanism" that
strategically accepted New Deal expansions of government and focused the
public's attention instead on "Korea, Communism, and corruption."[7] Given
the anti-government distrust that would follow in the 1960s, it is easy to
forget that during the mid-twentieth century, America's postwar consensus
exhibited a great deal of trust and confidence in government. In 1958, a Pew
survey found nearly three-fourths of Americans trusted the government
"just about always" or "most of the time."[8]

During the 1950s, Reagan turned right. He joined Democrats for Eisenhower and took a job delivering conservative pro-business speeches for
General Electric. Reagan was hired by GE to host a weekly television show
and to tour the country giving speeches. Under the tutelage of GE vice
president Lemuel Boulware, Reagan, already staunchly anti-communist
and willing to follow a GOP that was becoming more hardline on that score,
adopted more conservative views as he preached the company's "essentially
conservative message" to its employees and to civic groups, aiming to affect
politics by "establishing a better business climate."[9]

On that GE talk circuit from 1954 to 1962, Reagan took the company's
message to "many small and medium-sized towns." Ever the performer,
Reagan was persuaded by audience reactions "to abandon liberalism,"
one GE public relations executive said. One review of the sparse record of
Reagan's speeches observed that "most applause lines, once they found their
way into a Reagan speech, did not vanish. Reagan told the same stories about

communism in Hollywood, government waste and abuse, and encroaching federal control to audiences for years."[10] Reagan referred to his GE years as his "postgraduate course in political science."[11]

This new conservative Reagan ascended abruptly in the 1960s. He supported Nixon in 1960, offering to switch his party affiliation to Republican but postponed the act because Nixon thought him a better spokesman as a pro-Nixon Democrat.[12] Reagan registered as a Republican in 1962, less than two short years before delivering, with a convert's clarity and fervor, his famous "A Time for Choosing" speech in favor of Barry Goldwater at the Republican National Convention and only four years before his first election as governor of California.[13]

Reagan rode the rising tide of government distrust as it crested—on both the left and the right—in the 1960s. The 1950s' patina of placidity was washed away by social change, burgeoning federal government, and an increasingly ominous Cold War. Amid fear and uncertainty, change seemed to cause apprehension across the political spectrum. In their 1962 "Port Huron Statement," the leftist Students for a Democratic Society claimed that Americans had "deeply felt anxieties about their role in the new world" and wondered whether "something *can* be done to change circumstances in the school, the workplaces, the bureaucracies, the government?"[14] Just two years later, Barry Goldwater accepted the Republican nomination for president, championing "private property" as "the one way to make government a durable ally of the whole man, rather than his determined enemy."[15]

Distrust was ubiquitous and mounting in a decade marked not only by overdue realizations of civil rights for African Americans (and the dislocations those changes brought) and broad expansions in government exhibited by the New Frontier and the Great Society but also by an unpopular war, civil unrest, and the assassinations, in order, of Medgar Evers, John F. Kennedy, Malcolm X, Martin Luther King Jr., and Robert Kennedy.

On the right, conservatives, suspicious of taxation and regulation and resistant to federal government expansions into states (including civil rights efforts that would eventually transform the South), captured the GOP after Goldwater's candidacy. Their beliefs were cemented by fervent anti-communism, which offered bogeymen to which the GOP compared Democrats, as well as instantiations of the dangers of big government. This broader conservative appeal found a downright fervent voice in the right-wing John Birch Society, which imagined communist infiltration of American government and spun or echoed wild conspiracy theories, including that the fluoridation of drinking water was a "red conspiracy" that would produce "moronic, atheistic slaves . . . praying to the Communists."[16]

On the left, tumult over the Vietnam War and instances of the FBI and other law enforcement targeting and infiltrating civil rights and antiwar organizations drove distrust of government even as the GOP's New Right fought "Eastern establishment" and Chamber of Commerce Republicans. From Vietnam to Watergate, trust in government dropped precipitously. By the time of the Carter administration, only about a quarter of American citizens said they trusted the federal government. (In the years since, public trust has exceeded 50 percent only one time, and that was for a brief period after 9/11.[17]) Beginning in the 1960s, public distrust in government has been the prevailing condition of the American mind.

Anti-government sentiment prevailed in Ronald Reagan's rhetoric during his two terms as governor. When Reagan announced his candidacy for governor, he blamed the 1965 Watts riots, which erupted after violence by police toward an African American man, on "the philosophy that in any situation the public should turn to the government for the answer."[18] In his inaugural address on January 5, 1967, Reagan said of himself and other elected officeholders, "We are of the people, chosen by them to see that no permanent structure of government ever encroaches on freedom or assumes a power beyond that freely granted by the people." He added, "We stand between the taxpayer and the taxspender."[19] The consistent themes of Reaganism, forged on the GE lecture circuit and highlighted in the 1964 Republican Convention, would be staple messages of his governorship.

Still, foreshadowing his presidency, Governor Reagan's rhetoric and his governing reality diverged frequently, revealing what one longtime observer of California politics called a "startling disconnect between ideological principle and gubernatorial practice," pointing to "the open secret that Reagan "made pragmatic compromises between ideology and political reality" even as he "almost never acknowledged in public having compromised."[20]

Reagan raised taxes in his first year as governor and signed the Therapeutic Abortion Act, liberalizing abortion in California, that same year. He notably expanded government's role in conservation and accepted other concessions in efforts to get things done in a state more moderate than conservative. Notably, Reagan's conservative rhetoric and reputation survived, with only minimal backlash from the right, thanks to a combination of the consistency of his public statements, his "actor's skill," his "famous coating of political Teflon," and California's "persistent preference" of "political fantasy over reality."[21]

This is not to say that Reagan disbelieved what he said about government but rather that he was willing to suspend doctrine in the service of actually governing. And he looked for and found important ways to cut government's growth and make real at least some of his convictions. As governor, he advocated in 1973 a "tax-cutting initiative" known as Proposition 1 that built public sentiment toward the successful Proposition 13 and earned Reagan the nickname "the Father of the Tax Revolt."[22]

After two successful terms as governor, Reagan challenged incumbent Gerald Ford in 1976 for the Republican nomination. Although this failed, his campaign against Ford began the electoral juggernaut, built around anti-government sentiment, that would eventually take him to the White House in 1980. As his aspirations turned toward national politics, cultivating distrust in the New Deal state he had once championed was the heart of Reagan's electoral and governance strategies.

Reagan came at Ford as an outsider from the right, and he targeted otherwise popular government programs that mainstream Republicans had come to accept. Reagan had portrayed John F. Kennedy's proposed health program as socialistic, so his call for the federal government to retreat from its commitment to heath care was not surprising.[23] He argued that the federal government was too powerful and spent too much on Medicaid, a federal–state partnership that provided health coverage to those with low income, and on an array of other programs, and instead argued that funds and control should be held by states. Reagan also implied that recipients did not deserve taxpayer support, even that they were swindlers. Both themes came together in a 1975 speech to the Chicago Executives' Club, in which Reagan argued for cuts to core social welfare programs to reduce federal spending.[24]

Reagan's first forays into this new politics were difficult for a traditionalist like Ford to interpret. Like most traditional Republicans since Eisenhower, Ford believed there were elements of the New Deal that were untouchable for Republicans. Undoubtedly, these beliefs had been reinforced with Goldwater's 1964 trouncing at the polls, when the conservative's pioneering candidacy lost the popular vote by over 12 percent and won but six states (Goldwater's home state of Arizona and, notably, five Deep South states).

Ford's career had been built as a conservative, but he was committed to sound governance and compromise, and he demurred each time Reagan explored opportunities to weaken the most popular government programs. When Reagan called for a $90 billion cut in Washington spending during his Chicago speech, the response from the Ford campaign was "The American people will not go back to a system where you don't take care of people in need."[25] And, when Reagan espoused major changes in 1976 that would make Social Security voluntary and allow for some funds to be invested in the stock market, Ford strongly disagreed with both, saying, "I believe in the firm integrity of the Social Security program."[26] Democratic representative and eventual Speaker of the House Tip O'Neill believed Reagan's position on Social Security was a major error, and years later wrote that he expected it to be so electorally lethal that he hoped the GOP selected Reagan as the nominee.[27]

Traditional insiders perceived these and other policy statements as missteps, but unbeknownst to them, Reagan's appeal was deepening among "movement conservatives." Reagan was building something new around long-standing, but growing, fundamental American misgivings about government. This line of attack could potentially unify a new GOP coalition by fusing libertarianism with traditional conservatism and anti-communism.

This anti-government alchemy had particular appeal in the South, where suspicions of centralized government are perennial but were particularly pronounced in the decade following the Civil Rights and Voting Rights Acts. Building on the post-Wallace "Southern strategy," Reagan used race-coded language to bolster his appeal, particularly against President Gerald Ford, who had voted for both acts. Reagan was on record opposing both. Reagan also opposed affirmative action policies, casting them as discrimination against whites.

Avoiding overt racism in public, Reagan walked right up to the line. He blamed Martin Luther King Jr.'s assassination on the lawlessness born of King's embrace of civil disobedience.[28] He used the term "welfare queen," a race-coded term that connoted fraudulent use of benefits, during his 1976 campaign. He spread the story of a cheating welfare recipient, Linda Taylor, saying she was collecting Medicaid, food stamps, and welfare all while receiving funds on multiple Social Security and veterans' benefit accounts.[29] He contrasted "hardworking people" who pay their bills and put up with high taxes to a "slum dweller," who could get a fancy apartment at vastly reduced rates, the cost of which Reagan misstated.[30] Galvanizing his support among white southern conservatives, Reagan told a Mississippi rally, "If there's a Southern strategy, I'm a part of it."[31]

Strength in the South helped Reagan to slow Ford's campaign when, with the support of Jesse Helms, he scored an unexpected victory in North Carolina. With that win, Reagan put an end to calls for his withdrawal as a candidate and racked up more southern support to add to his dominance out West. In the end, Reagan bested Ford in eight contests out of the eleven held in the states of the former Confederacy.

Reagan was building ardent support among conservative activists across the country. That Reagan's adherents were more committed than Ford's was a repeated refrain among party watchers. Comparing the two, one observer said, "If Ford aroused apathy, Reagan instilled dedication and interest."[32] By the same token, the columnist Jules Witcover wrote that Reagan, "the candidate of the Republican emotions," stoked an ideological fight with Ford at the 1976 convention in the hopes of closing the small delegate gap between the two: "His strategists would try somehow to confront this basically conservative party with some basic test of ideology that would set enough sparks flying to ignite an upset victory."[33] This became the party's platform fight; there and throughout, "the conservative element of the party . . . did effectively dominate the convention."[34]

Ultimately, Ford eked out enough delegates to win the nomination. But Reagan's star was on the rise among the growing conservative wing of the party. In 1976 the parties' platforms diverged on abortion; Reagan took a firmly antiabortion position, and social conservatives were on the ascent in the GOP. The convention was not the only place where Reagan's activists became potent opponents to Ford. Besides the South, Reagan had also done well in "nonprimary states, where the organization and intensity of his supporters were crucial. Throughout the country, Reagan gained support, built organization, and developed contributor lists that would prove crucial four years later."[35] New-breed southerners, Moral Majority social conservatives, and doctrinaire, tax-revolting, small-government activists were shaping a powerful coalition.[36]

With this burgeoning conservative movement, Reagan was the Republican to beat in 1980, despite persistent rumors that Ford might run again. Flanked to his left by the likes of George H. W. Bush, John Anderson, and Howard Baker, Reagan withstood conservative opposition from Bob Dole and John Connally and narrowed the race to a head-to-head against Bush, bested him—conservative over moderate—and then consolidated the GOP coalition by taking Bush as vice president. Reagan united these wings of the party under a lower-tax, less-government philosophy and, with his social conservative credentials rock solid and baked into his candidacy, Reagan's 1980 presidential run focused on the economy, the national debt, national security, and an overarching critique of Jimmy Carter and of government itself.

Reagan's rise can be understood as built atop Goldwater and Nixonian Republicanism with roots going back to the 1920s, but he sharpened its critique of government, crystallizing it under his rhetorical and performative mastery. Throughout his pre-presidential political career, Reagan had made the case for limited government, mirroring contemporary fiscal conservative arguments about how taxes, regulation, and deficits limited freedom. At the same time, Reagan, like Nixon, promoted government power to ensure "law and order" versus student and other anti–Vietnam War protestors and rioters in black, urban neighborhoods, and supported anti-crime measures and a "War on Drugs" that would disproportionately hit people of color.

The coalition being built was formidable. The New Right, writes Rick Perlstein, presented "conservativism as an ideology for working people." It saw "the true exploiters" not big business but "federal bureaucrats grasping for tax dollars, and the media elites who shoved 1960s libertinism down Middle America's throats."[37] Anti-feminist cultural commitments helped bring evangelical Christians to the Republican coalition. In 1980 the Republican platform dropped its support for the Equal Rights Amendment after including it since 1940. Reagan seized upon social issues like abortion and opposition to the Equal Rights Amendment to solidify growing support among evangelical Christians, fusing them to this new GOP coalition with these issues and broader cultural appeals.

Also, like Nixon, Reagan abandoned prior conservatives' affinities for congressional power and fears of a strong presidency in favor of a set of separation of powers prescriptions that would expand presidential power and restrict Congress. According to the 1980 Republican platform, "the twenty-five years of Democratic domination of the Congress have cost us a generation of lost [economic] opportunities" and have produced "our current crisis of overregulation."[38]

In his 1980 Republican National Convention acceptance speech, Reagan spoke of a federal government "overgrown and overweight," one that needed "to go on a diet." It had not only ceased to function but had become a clear threat to Americans' fundamental liberties—"dominating their lives." He believed post–New Deal Americans failed to see government expansion's cost, and he spoke of the "danger" of the state: "Government is never more dangerous than when our desire to have it help us blinds us to its great power to harm us."[39] But to tame it, conservatives believed, required a much stronger presidency. In a 1980 meeting between Gerald Ford's former chief of staff Dick Cheney and James Baker, who was to be President Reagan's first chief of staff, Cheney stressed the need for the executive branch to restore power and authority and regain independence from congressional strictures.[40]

Reagan's coalition, when it remained taut and unified, was tied together by a small-government philosophy, largely in explicit opposition to the New Deal and especially the Great Society. According to political scientist Andrew Busch, "By 1979 the conservative movement was highly developed both intellectually and at the popular level. It had fused three basic thrusts (economic freedom, anticommunism, and social coherence) and two general orientations (libertarian and traditionalist)."[41] Reagan built his political legacy on these principles and coalesced a disparate and somewhat ironic (given the military buildup and the big-government social regulations advocated by the Moral Majority) Republican coalition around small-government precepts. Conservatives believed the small-government philosophy and its pairing with anti-communism were "the glue that held the movement together."[42]

None of this is to say that Reagan spun this out of whole cloth. Public discontent was real. Antipathy to government action was deeply embedded in American culture, and many Americans believed the New Deal philosophy of government had outlived its usefulness and the Great Society had taken it several steps too far. "Reagan was the catalyst, not the creator"[43] of this movement, a leader who built a successful electoral career riding an anti-government wave.

A REPUBLICAN REALIGNMENT?

Concordant with the Republicans' hope to dismantle the New Deal state was the effort to displace its electoral and governing coalition with conservative one—to achieve a "Republican realignment." Developed by political scientists V. O. Key Jr. and Walter Dean Burnham, realignment theory holds that American political history is punctuated by a handful of "critical" elections that produce new electoral patterns in which a significant portion of the electorate adopt new partisan affiliations. This alters the partisan and governing coalitions at the national level, wherein those patterns and coalitions endure for several succeeding elections.[44]

FDR's New Deal coalition realigned American politics in 1932. What happened to that coalition depended both on what national leaders did but also, as political scientist Eric Schickler stresses, on developments in and pressures from organizations, local party leaders, and activists on national leaders.[45]

Reagan's advisors and adherents, some explicitly using the term "realignment," were eager to claim that they had displaced the New Deal with their own realignment that, like prior realignments, would last for decades to come.

There was some reason to believe that they had accomplished just that. The 1980 election was a stunning victory for Reagan and the Republicans and a rebuke to Carter, who had been weakened by economic problems and the Iranian hostage crisis. Besting Carter by nearly 10 percentage points in the popular vote (John Anderson was running as a third-party candidate), Reagan's 50.7 percent popular vote total translated into a massive electoral college victory: he won forty-four states. At the same time, winning twelve new seats, the Republicans took control of the Senate for the first time since the 1950s. Reagan had also made decisive inroads in the longtime Democratic stronghold in the South, a regional shift typical of many realignments.

But the realignment was not total. The Republicans failed to capture majority control of the House of Representatives. Though the GOP gained nearly three dozen seats, it topped out at 192 seats in the Ninety-Seventh Congress, only matching (exactly) the number of seats it held after both of Nixon's 1968 and 1972 victories. And Reagan's electoral victory hinged not so much on large numbers of new Republican voters but instead on what were famously called "Reagan Democrats."

Early analyses of Reagan's 1980 win revealed ambivalence in the electorate. Rather than a conservative mandate, Burnham thought the election was dominated purely by an anti-Carter mood: "A negative, highly general, public rejection of a failed incumbent administration."[46] Thus, as large as his victory was, the Reagan "mandate" had to be manufactured retrospectively. It had to be found in an electoral message "distinguished by ambivalence and searching" with a "strong call for moderate change" and, at best, a conditional willingness to "try something different."[47]

Republicans, though, looked at the realignment glass as half full and proceeded as if the 1980 started a new party era.

It is easy in retrospect to mistake the Reagan coalition as a natural occurrence in which economic liberalism, social conservatism, and foreign policy interventionism converged into an all-around "Republicanism" of the Cold War context. But like so many multifaceted coalitions, if it was to be durable, Reagan's was one that needed to be nurtured, explained, and politically finessed.

Just as the New Deal threw together a mix of liberals and conservatives (from immigrants to Klansmen), the conservative coalition was a Frankenstein's monster of different, sometimes seemingly antithetical groups. Once the party of the northeastern establishment, the post-Goldwater Republican Party was increasingly western, often openly hostile to the "eastern establishment." Individualistic, western conservatives were not only drawn to the GOP's low tax policies, but they were just as incensed by the federal government's management of public lands, producing the 1970s "sagebrush rebellion." Reagan established a broad coalition: rural and urban, libertarian and moralizing, working class and wealthy. Far from being natural, the GOP coalition was constructed and built on what Lowi called a false "concordance" between "capitalism and Christianity"—it was "coalitional not organic," with elements that were "strictly tactical."[48] Having been out of power for most of the post–New Deal era and much better at opposition than governance, the Republican Party's majority coalition had to be built.[49]

And it *would* be built, mainly by doubling down on government distrust and using it as a strategic weapon to galvanize the Right.[50] Antipathy toward government had the potential to connect the elite centers of the conservative movement to rank-and-file voters. Even as political scientist Everett Carll Ladd sought to throw cold water on Reagan's "mandate," he noticed some movement on confidence in government evincing a "growing public ambivalence on many major policy questions, especially on the role of government itself."[51] The public still had to be moved along on this question, though. If Reagan opined that government was "the problem," "people had not stopped looking to government for solutions and assistance," and "the public's antigovernment mood was balanced by its progovernment mood."[52]

If not the first to mobilize distrust, Reagan was a talented manipulator of the rhetoric that helped forge this coalition. Using small-government arguments, social issues, and some racial tropes, he transformed the New Deal coalition by turning its "southerners into Evangelicals," its workers into patriots, and the beneficiaries of government programs into taxpayers.[53]

The onboarding of the South was the key feat of the Republican realignment. Goldwater and Nixon had displayed strength in southern states in 1964 and 1972, but Carter had regained the region for the Democrats in 1976. Just as he had tried to do in 1976, Reagan built on the "Southern strategy" fusing race politics and states' rights to his anti-government message. Notably, he "launched his 1980 campaign for the White House from Philadelphia, Mississippi, best known as the site of the murders of three civil rights workers during the Freedom Summer of 1964."[54]

Besides this and other "Southern strategy" nods, Reagan's small-government philosophy found ideological kinship in the South. Coupled with his "new federalism" promise of returning power to state and local governments, Reagan decried welfare and government assistance to draw in white southerners. As the journalist Thomas Edsall wrote in 1980, "The public image of the Republican Party became again sharply more conservative on racial issues. That year, by a margin of better than 6 to 1, the electorate saw the GOP as unlikely to help minorities."[55]

Reagan also made surprising inroads with young voters in cities, a group known as "young urban professionals" (yuppies), who were too young to have personal recollections of FDR or the assistance the New Deal offered and wealthy enough to see the appeal of the GOP's lower tax-and-spend policies. If Reagan's success with voters under thirty—who were less likely to share the racial or social views of southerners and evangelicals—was among "the most momentous" factors of 1980, it was his economic argument that attracted and could keep them, despite them being "more supportive of abortion rights, women's rights, racial tolerance, and environmentalism and less supportive of the Moral Majority than any other age group."[56]

The anti-government message was the glue that seemed to hold the party coalition together. Reagan had mobilized southerners, Evangelicals, tax revolters, and westerners, but that did not erase the Reagan coalition's persistent fault lines. Uniting southern populists with urban professionals was a coup for Reagan but a precarious mix. Increasing political engagement among evangelical voters and the rise of politically active religious organizations produced increasing demands for changes in social policy and culture war politics. As a result, tensions emerged within the Republican Party.[57] Political scientists Thomas Cavanagh and James Sundquist spotted this inherent weakness in the coalition: "White southerners fear hard times and dislike the GOP's country club image, but they admire Reagan's foreign policy toughness and his social conservatism. Yuppies' preferences are almost precisely reversed: they are attracted by Reagan's free market philosophy and his promises of economic growth and affluence but are relatively progressive on social issues and dovish on foreign policy." Cavanagh and Sundquist believed that efforts "to legislate morality" would undermine "Republican gains among young people."[58]

As useful as they could be, Moral Majority issue stances or the kinds of overtly race-based appeals that could be narrowcast to some parts of the coalition were increasingly off limits. If these and other social issues like immigration threatened either to split the Republican coalition or thwart reaching independents and wayward Democrats, small government, low taxes, and less spending could always hold the coalition together. But Republicans would find that the practical strength of these anti-government sentiments was stronger if such sentiments were regularly espoused but not so regularly applied in such a doctrinaire way as to deny coalition members the government benefits they needed or wanted. If policy views were articulated clearly enough, purportedly as overarching principles, then those within the coalition could be deemed "worthy" and political opponents could be thought "unworthy" of government assistance.

DOWNSIZING GOVERNMENT

The dire consequences of government run amok were the very first themes in Reagan's inaugural address. He blamed stifled enterprise on government's cost and mounting deficits and summed up his grim diagnosis with one of his more famous anti-government proclamations: "In this present crisis, government is not the solution to our problem; government is the problem."[59]

In the first months of his new administration, Reagan quickly moved to cut taxes and federal spending. Key policy achievements, including the Economic Recovery Tax Act (also known as the Kemp-Roth tax cut), the Gramm-Latta budget, and eventually the Omnibus Budget Reconciliation Bill (known as Gramm-Latta II), passed Congress and reduced taxes and government spending so severely that budget scholars dubbed the Omnibus Budget Reconciliation bill "the most sweeping legislation in modern American history."[60]

Owing to the freshness of Reagan's "mandate," his honeymoon as the newly elected president, and the outpouring of public support following a March 30 assassination attempt, Reagan made good on campaign promises "to curb the size and influence of the Federal establishment and to demand recognition of the distinction between the powers granted to the Federal Government and those reserved to the States or to the people."[61] Key federal programs were on the chopping block, and many new executive appointees were confirmed with the suspected (sometimes avowed) purposes of downsizing the departments and agencies they were selected to lead. Subsequent memories of Reagan as a cutter of "big government" rely mostly on the first year, when the war with government was on the offensive and these legislative accomplishments were secured.

Even in these early and historically successful months, Reagan felt the limits of political backlash. When official Washington balked at White House requests for voluntary budget cuts and entrenched interests moved to protect their favored programs, even Reagan's advisors and allies warned against pushing too hard. Fearing a public reaction against "draconian" budget cuts, the White House "felt forced" to promise that a "social safety net" of programs (Social Security, Medicare, veterans' benefits, Head Start, and Supplemental Security Income) would be spared the severest cuts. According to political scientists Joseph White and Aaron Wildavsky, the programs that were spared were "those whose recipients were hardest to stigmatize—the elderly, the elderly sick, veterans, the handicapped—or had most political power."[62] Within the administration, even these exceptions were viewed as "major concessions." As one Reagan administration member put it, "Bear in mind that Reagan and his supporters feel that Social Security should be voluntary and Medicare should not exist."[63]

Notwithstanding these concerns, in a speech laying out his budget priorities to a joint session of Congress one week later, Reagan called for large cuts to Medicaid, saying the program was "not cost-effective." Shifting costs to the states, Reagan proposed "a cap on how much the Federal Government will contribute, but at the same time allow the States much more flexibility in managing and structuring the programs."[64] Reagan's caps meant cost shifting and placed downward budgetary pressure on the program: cutting federal Medicaid funds going to the states in the 1981 fiscal year by $100 million "and by $1 billion in the fiscal year 1982. After that, the Federal contribution would rise at the same rate as inflation. States would have to make up the difference, either by changing eligibility requirements, reducing payment rates or increasing efficiency."[65]

But this push toward devolving federal power provoked pushback. Early negotiations between Reagan administration officials and a group of governors fell apart when the governors rejected the proposed financial and administrative responsibilities.[66] And although his initial budget cut Medicare and Medicaid, Reagan was thwarted in implementing caps to limit Medicaid increases to below the rate of medical inflation.[67] He also failed in his promises to promote competition in the health-care industry.[68] Even as the administration racked up big political wins, dismantling some federal programs proved unfeasible and undoing others came at great political cost.

None of this is to deny that the public mood supported Reagan's anti-governmentalism. By late 1981, pollsters were advising Democrats to "avoid excessive use of the word *program*" because, except in the case of Social Security, "program" had "strongly negative connotations in the electorate." Sensing vulnerability and anticipating conservative strategies, pollsters warned: "The GOP PR folks will try to force us into this type of discussion, particularly 'programs' relating to poor people and minorities."[69]

But the public, if angry in general, was ambivalent about government in terms of specific policies and thus would only follow Reagan so far. Time and again, Reagan would probe the possibilities of reducing the federal government but acquiesce to political realities. Political scientist Hugh Heclo and economist Rudolph Penner described the White House's "strategic management" of Reagan's policy program: "A typical script found the president enunciating some simple principle, followed by reports of the president resisting counterpressures with great stubbornness, then an eventual compromise sufficient for the president's proposal to win passage without the president himself appearing to engage in political bargaining, and finally a White House claim of victory."[70] The kabuki theater implied here suggests that Reagan's well-known anti-government philosophy was a useful negotiating tool that had the added benefit "that the basic political theory behind the Reagan economic policy—that of reviving the economy through retrenchment in government—was itself never open to question and debate."[71]

Reagan's budget plans faced frequent resistance within Congress. Moderate Republicans were less supportive of some of Reagan's budgetary proposals, including the Medicaid cuts and program transformation, than were southern Democrats.[72] When these moderate Republicans joined colleagues to support the Gramm-Latta budget (GOP support on the budget vote was unanimous), Tip O'Neill vowed to hold votes on individual-cut proposals later in the process. Recognizing that, however popular budget cuts might be in the abstract, the specific cuts could be unpopular, O'Neill seemed willing to let congressional Republicans walk the plank if they chose. Of the Gramm-Latta budget vote, he said, "Wait 'til Middle America realizes what's happened with these budget cuts . . . Am I going to get some Republican scalps down the road? You bet I am."[73] This seemed to be O'Neill's broader strategy: to let public opinion either sway House Republicans' votes or to lay claim to their seats in 1982. When asked by reporters if he had tried to "woo" northeastern Republicans as Reagan had with southern Democrats, he said, "They know the consequences . . . I would hate to be any one of those fourteen Northeast Republicans, come election day, lying in the sun with a beer and the Latta-Gramm vote."[74]

The big public opinion hit came after the first Gramm-Latta budget vote passed in Congress. It became clear to voters that, once these cuts were completed, Social Security was next. When proposed Social Security cuts in benefits surfaced within the administration, Reagan's political advisors were horrified, but Reagan approved. Going public with a plan to reduce benefits and begin a congressional debate in mid-May, the administration saw public support collapse and immediately pulled back.[75] By July, with the political debacle in full swing, Reagan backed down, but not without denouncing what he called "the opportunistic political maneuvering" by Democrats in Congress, claiming they were "cynically designed to play on the fears of many Americans."[76] The successful opposition was a potent reminder early in the administration that the public placed a high value on some key government programs and benefits and would follow Reagan's efforts to downsize only so far.

Despite occasional opposition and quite a bit of nervousness, the early policy accomplishments of Reagan's first term made the rhetorical assault on government concrete. Decentralization and shrinking the national domestic policy state were central to Reagan's policy and political agendas. Political scientist Richard Nathan summarized Reagan's first-term domestic efforts as reducing the public sector in favor of private entities; shifting power from the federal government to the states; and "a concept of programs to aid the poor that consists of providing adequate benefits to the 'truly needy,' and removing from welfare able-bodied persons who can make it on their own."[77] The language of "deservingness" took hold, as did the idea that "for their own good, people who can work should be prodded into doing so."[78] These pillars of small government—devolution and support only for the "deserving"—built on antecedent trends in the conservative movement that were frequently racialized and became conservative staples after Reagan.

Some programs and interests would be spared—succumbing to the political potency of opponents or public opinion or because the beneficiaries were on Reagan's team. When his tax cut legislation faced stiff opposition in Congress, Reagan opened up the bill to allow exceptions, breaks, and "giveaways" to save the bill's prospects—a process White and Wildavsky called "Christmas in July."[79] And for all the rhetoric about government spending and deficits, military spending skyrocketed in Reagan's budgets, as did the budget deficit overall. As reporter James Fallows noted, military spending from 1982 through 1985 was greater than "any four years of the Vietnam or the Korean War." In constant dollars, military spending rose from $200 billion at the end of Carter's administration to $300 billion in 1986.[80]

The Reagan record on dismantling Washington government was mixed as well. There was a deregulatory thrust, to be sure. With a February 1981 executive order, he expanded White House control over proposed administrative regulations, including everything from environmental to economic regulations, a move that "the architects of the Reagan order believed" would be a "substantial force" in achieving conservative, political control over federal rulemaking. This process, called administrative clearance, led to a "precipitous decline in the number of proposed rules since Reagan took office."[81]

Thus, Reagan did not oversee the demise of the regulatory state and the bureaucracy but instead advocated stronger presidentialism atop it. Lowi observed that Reagan sought "no legislation from Congress terminating or permanently reducing regulatory powers or jurisdiction," but instead "enlarged the powers of the presidency by putting all regulatory agencies under closer supervision to make them more sensitive to presidential preferences."[82]

Reagan's pragmatic and mixed record extended beyond budget and administrative questions. Building law and order credentials, the War on

Drugs and other enforcement initiatives expanded federal government police powers on Reagan's watch. If the southern Evangelicals wanted more social regulation, then Reagan's coalition would tolerate it, much to the chagrin of Goldwater and other more libertarian Republicans, who applied the small-government doctrine to more than budget and tax cutting. Reagan's anti-government reputation is belied by a record that was only intermittently and inconsistently applied.

By October 1982, Democrats were stressing that, for all the small-government rhetoric and rosy promises, the budget deficit for fiscal year 1982 would be nearly three times what Reagan had predicted. To counter criticism, that summer Reagan backed a proposal for a constitutional amendment for a balanced budget. The amendment was sure to fail, and Democratic talking points dubbed it "a public relations gesture to obscure the fact that he produced the largest deficit in history." House majority leader Jim Wright accused Reagan of "show biz and razzle dazzle" on the amendment, which he said was "as devoid of serious meaning as a Bugs Bunny comedy."[83]

In addition to claiming that Reagan's "small-government" approach was more posture than reality, Democrats had settled on "fairness" as their theme for the midterm elections, in the hope that the public would place firm limits on just how far Reaganism could go in cutting government. Democratic talking points painted a dire picture of the economy—unemployment, struggling small businesses, housing starts, "the future of Social Security," and the death of the family farm—if the country was to "stay the course" as Republicans hoped.[84]

But plausible deniability on the deficit was essential to Reagan's image development, which was carefully cultivated by political advisors who linked domestic policy aims to electoral politics in the hopes of charting a path to reelection in 1984 and completing the realignment they hoped had been sparked in 1980.

Such links were laid out in a private February 1982 meeting at Camp David involving high-level administration officials, strategists, and an array of political staff. According to polling memos prepared by Richard Wirthlin, Reagan's most vehement opponents remained "strong Democrats, Blacks and those with incomes under $10,000," while "Reagan's strongest supporters are the more conservative, upper income and white respondents." He advised Reagan to appeal to the racially divided electorate through policies and symbols. "In the briefing book prepared for that meeting, the domestic strategy emphasized the policies of budget cuts, federalism, and in developing 'symbolic actions for key constituencies—aged, Spanish-surnamed, white ethnics/blue collar, populist/rednecks, (other?)."[85]

To maintain support from Reagan Democrats, the president was advised that he should be mindful of their concerns about social issues and "the administration should continue to take a high profile on the issue of voluntary prayer in the schools" but should stress values over policies.[86] Detecting this strategy, some Christian conservatives like Pat Robertson complained that Reagan was "more talk than action" and "more symbolic than restrictive" on social issues.[87]

Despite this planning, the GOP lost twenty-six seats in the House, though they added two seats to the Senate majority. With this, Reagan's most significant anti-government legislative achievements were over, and the policy aspects of the war with government were put on the defensive.

Reagan's allies in Washington worked to protect their domestic policy gains. They had already been compelled to raise taxes in 1982 (something they would repeat several times in the remainder of the decade).[88] Then the president turned his focus in 1983 to foreign policy, pressing quick fait accompli wars, such as the 1983 invasion of Grenada just days after a terrorist bomb killed 241 service members in Lebanon. Reagan stepped up prosecution of the Cold War, touting the "Star Wars" strategic defense initiative in an effort to challenge the "Evil Empire" Soviet Union while pursuing nuclear arms control.

AN INCOMPLETE REALIGNMENT, A UNITARY EXECUTIVE

Reagan's hopes of completing a Republican realignment loomed large in 1984. With Reagan's poll numbers strong in the fall ahead of the election, his political advisors had been talking privately about the possibility, and on the Wednesday before the election, Reagan speculated about "the beginnings of a new phenomenon," namely a "historic electoral realignment," the following Tuesday. Obviously rehearsed in at least some of the criteria needed for realignment, he said,

> I believe that next Tuesday we'll see a large number of voters joining our Republican ranks for the first time . . . This is no mere political cycle, nor has it anything to do with the personality of the candidates. We're attracting

the support of people who have never voted with us before, not because they're deserting the Democratic Party, but because the Democratic Party has deserted them.[89]

Reagan predicted extraordinary strength with urban voters, particularly the black vote, which one of his consultants predicted could go as much as 15 percent for Reagan.[90] Of course, this was unlikely (Reagan won only 9 percent of the black vote in 1984 compared to 64 percent of the white vote), though Reagan was solidifying his support in the South (which would be the strongest, if still incomplete, evidence of a realignment) and winning a record high percentage of the Catholic vote for a Republican and a whopping 69 percent of evangelicals.[91]

More telling on the question of realignment was that, despite Reagan's 49-state landslide, Republicans failed to take the House of Representatives (their seats increased to 181 seats but they were still 11 short of the mark they set after 1968, 1972, and 1980) and barely retained their Senate majority—they lost two seats there as well.

Congressional Democrats had laid the political groundwork to insulate candidates from Reagan's landslide. In early October, pollster Lou Harris presented the results of a nationwide poll he had conducted to the House Democratic Caucus. If the news was grim for Democratic presidential nominee, Walter Mondale, who had been Carter's vice president, things were more promising down ballot. Contrary to Reagan's contention that the election was about party rather than personality, Harris found high levels of personal support for Reagan but also a strong preference for continued Democratic control of the House as a check on the rightward turn: "By 2–1, the voters *don't* want to see Republicans in control of Congress. They also are saying they don't like nor trust Reagan and the Republicans on most issues." Harris emphasized, "Remember, by 2–1 they *don't* want a Republican Congress. That's your secret weapon."[92]

For Reagan and Republicans there were demonstrable gains in the South, but Harris found that Reagan had "traded the West for the South." In the West, Reagan won his narrowest margin over Mondale (seven points), but in the South he held a twenty-two-point lead. Harris warned that this had "cut the Democratic lead in House races in the South to only 48–43 percent."[93] But the fact that House Democrats still led in Dixie emphasizes just how premature and optimistic were Republican dreams of realignment.

Reagan continued the GOP's newfound advocacy of presidential power and strategically promoted its contempt for Congress as an institution. The 1984 Republican platform called the congressional budget process "bankrupt" and argued that the president should be given the line-item veto. Republicans claimed that "twenty-eight years of a Congress rigidly controlled by the Democrats" made the institution "out of touch with the people."[94]

Somewhat ironically for a president running for reelection, Reagan's 1984 campaign emphasized the same anti-government themes he embraced when challenging incumbents Ford and Carter. Despite his lifelong affinity for FDR and notwithstanding the policy wins of his own first term, Reagan doubled down on his critique of the twentieth-century American state and the path the New Deal had forged.

In this war with government, Reagan framed government as a threat to liberty through excessive taxation and echoed sentiments first offered by Goldwater and Nixon that government assistance promoted dependency. Claims of this type were particularly pronounced when he spoke of cities and racial minorities. Not only did Reagan oppose income support programs for the poor, but he also promoted the idea that many people using these programs were lazy and corrupt and were made so by the government. In his 1984 nomination acceptance speech, Reagan said that before his taking office, "Urban neighborhoods and schools deteriorated. Those whom government intended to help discovered a cycle of dependency that could not be broken. Government became a drug, providing temporary relief, but addiction as well."[95]

Describing the "New Beginning" for America that he pursued in the first administration, Reagan's second inaugural address promised that he would continue down that path. Reagan turned from discussing policies that he charged "increase dependency, break up families, and destroy self-respect" to a discussion of the economic needs of "blacks, Hispanics and all minorities" that go beyond "civil rights."[96] He charged that the New Deal's growth of the state was a betrayal of the Founders' idea that government "was not our master, it is our servant." Said Reagan, "We asked things of government that government was not equipped to give. We yielded authority to the National Government that properly belonged to States or to local governments or to the people themselves."[97] Reagan's criticism of the New Deal was consistent with the long-held Republican belief that one can love one's country but fear one's government. "We are a nation that has a government," he said, "not the other way around."[98]

As this rhetoric persisted into his second term, so too did the need for compromise and the concessions that typified his first term. To avoid lame duck status setting in too soon, a robust second term required shoring up political support.

In one notable example, Reagan proved willing to explore expansions of government—even in the area of health care—to build support with a key constituency. According to the Wirthlin Group, "the Reagan Administration was unpopular with the elderly." A program to provide catastrophic care insurance through Medicare was meant "to soften the image" and with "with an eye to the upcoming 1986 congressional elections . . . to win points with this crucial voting group."[99] An internal poll conducted in December 1985 found that providing "insurance for families that could be destroyed financially by a catastrophic illness" was ranked as more important than strengthening U.S. defenses—a core Reagan focus—even as Reagan himself was seen as mishandling the care issue. Seniors viewed this health coverage issue as important to them personally, with an 8.3 average on a 10-point scale. They rated Reagan's efforts on the issue a mere 5.4.[100]

In his 1986 State of the Union address, Reagan called upon Health and Human Services secretary Otis Bowen to develop a plan for catastrophic care, a remarkable step for the longtime opponent of Medicare and Medicaid. Bowen, a physician and former Indiana governor, was personally motivated because, as he recalled, he "had seen people including my patients spending themselves down to nothing and having nothing left to live on as a result of prolonged illnesses."[101]

Still, the forceful anti-government rhetoric remained, with Reagan proclaiming in his 1986 State of the Union address: "Government growing beyond our consent had become a lumbering giant, slamming shut the gates of opportunity, threatening to crush the very roots of our freedom."[102]

It is perhaps another irony that Reagan-era efforts to shrink government required a strong leader and a strong presidency. Nixon had begun a radical departure from decades of conservative pro-Congress orthodoxy, but the Reagan revolution was at the forefront of expanding executive power, primarily as a means of achieving administratively and politically what could not be won legislatively. Even more fundamentally, if the Reagan revolutionaries could not complete the realignment through electoral might or with public support, they would instead try to accomplish their aims by rethinking the separation of powers, opening up a much broader legal front that would strategically link constitutional arguments to conservative causes for years to come.

Recognizing the need to build legitimacy for presidential government, the Reagan Justice Department, under Edwin Meese, was hard at work creating the notion of the "unitary executive," a bundle of constitutional rationalizations that threatened Congress's traditional role in administrative oversight and control and brought the executive branch even more firmly under the control of the president.[103] The most full-throated statement of this philosophy was an internal Justice Department Office of Legal Policy report on the separation of powers that "laid out a revolutionary vision of the president's powers under the Constitution."[104]

Looking for a "comprehensive way of 'thinking clearly' about separation of powers," the 1986 report, entitled "Separation of Powers: Legislative–Executive Relations," traced the Founders' thoughts regarding the need, in the late eighteenth century, to limit the potential for a predominant legislative branch, including by building up a strong and independent executive.

Denigrating Congress, the report argued that "the institutionalization of the 'welfare state' has transformed members of Congress from individuals representing nationally defined interests into individuals acting as ombudsmen for parochial spending interests" and that Congress had become atomized to the point that stronger centralized leadership was needed: "The prevailing consensus in the 1980s is that, in view of the fractionalization and decentralization of Congress, a relatively strong presidency may be especially necessary now to ensure national leadership."[105]

The Reagan Justice Department asserted a stronger presidency as the solution to congressional gridlock: "Our majoritarian democracy may work better if, when Congress is significantly divided, a President can exercise strong leadership to effect the will of the majority that elected him."[106] The democratic presidency that Reagan performed and that was imagined in this report was more Wilsonian (which celebrated the president's popular leadership) than it was Hamiltonian (which mistrusted it).[107]

With the "unitary executive" view that the president alone would lead agencies (regardless of past practice or the power of the purse residing in Congress), the report also recommended being aggressive with congressional requests for information and testimony, including picking and choosing the members of Congress and internal congressional organizations from which the executive branch would comply with requests (party leaders over committee chairs and committee chairs over other members and staff) and by deeming some congressional requests more appropriate than others (legislative being more important than oversight, and specific oversight being more important, in their eyes, than general separation of powers "checks"). Aggressive in their protections of the executive branch, other recommendations included an executive branch assertion regarding what Congress "should" and should not legislate with respect to its contempt power, what internal rules it should adopt, and what witnesses would show up when Congress called for executive branch testimony. For strict constitutionalists who ostensibly valued the internal integrity and separateness of (as well as an overall balance between) coordinate institutions, each of the items on this wish list seemed specifically to assume that the executive branch could dictate to Congress how to exercise its constitutional obligations.[108]

While the authors framed the strong presidency as a clear emanation from the Constitution and the founding, there were indications it was less a timeless exploration of original intent than it was a strategic effort to shift institutional power to a Republican president. Noting, for example, that "the strong leadership of President Reagan seems clearly to have ended the congressional resurgence of the 1970s," the report took note that "some conservatives now are also finding separation of powers frustrating because it is sometimes an obstacle to the conservative political agenda, thereby serving to preserve the liberal status quo. They are thus inclined to make an exception to their usual respect for separation of powers and advocate a very strong President—primarily for the practical reason that an activist conservative currently sits in the White House."[109] Although the memo counseled taking the "longer-term view," such short-term considerations were embedded in the report. Of course, that is not how prior conservatives had viewed the Framers' intent or how subsequent conservatives would view presidential power under Clinton and Obama.[110]

In the near term, though, there were significant, concrete steps taken to expand presidential power. Reagan made unprecedented, official use of the statements presidents make when signing legislation. With Justice Department guidance, Reagan felt empowered to sign legislation, even if he deemed parts of it unconstitutional. In these cases, should a veto of the overall legislation prove politically "impracticable," he could sign it but use the statement to direct administration lawyers to seek judicial challenges to the offending components of the legislation that he had just signed.[111]

More and more frequently, signing statements would be used to influence subsequent interpretations (by both bureaucracies and courts) of legislative language by putting the president's own interpretation into the official record. As then-Deputy Assistant Attorney General Samuel Alito put it, it was an effort "to ensure that presidential signing statements assume their rightful place in the interpretation of legislation."[112] Institutionalizing this practice in 1986, Attorney General Meese arranged for West Publishing Company to publish these presidential statements "for the first time in the *U.S. Code Congressional and Administrative News*, the standard collection of legislative history" to which judges and bureaucrats might turn for insight on how to interpret law.[113] Collectively, these actions "convert[ed] the signing statement into a systematic mechanism of presidential direct action that frequently overrides the intent of Congress."[114]

For all its legalism and selective reference to the *Federalist Papers*, there was more than a little politics in this document that appeared to have been reverse-engineered primarily for yielding a pretext for strong presidential action. If at least some of the participants believed that they were faithfully interpreting the Constitution, it is notable that they were only now just discovering these justifications for a strong presidency (and on the eve of the Constitution's bicentennial). In a sign that even they were unsure of their premises, the report's writers were wary of provoking "judicial scrutiny," because "the prerogatives of the executive branch may be infringed upon more substantially by the judicial branch than by the legislative branch."[115] The point, it seems, was not so much finding what the Framers had intended as it was asserting one quite contested set of claims over others because it fit the political project at hand.

The growth of presidential power in the Reagan era would play out in foreign policy, too.[116]

To the extent that the Reagan era might be considered to be a return to traditional conservative values and to less government power (as Reagan's supporters wished it to be viewed), the growth of the presidency (and the denigration of Congress) was a departure from this vision. Rather than decrying strong presidential leadership as radical, progressive, or an undermining of the legislative branch, Reaganites saw it as essential. Conservatives now championed sidestepping Congress and seized opportunities to undermine congressional powers in war, policy making, and the separation of powers. So dramatic were these changes that David Stockman, Reagan's first budget director, wrote that Reagan's vision of presidential government required that "the Constitutional prerogatives of the legislative branch would have to be, in effect, suspended" and what was "required" of Congress was "complete surrender" to the Reagan revolution.[117]

ENDGAME

The juggernaut that was Reaganism in the 1980s was weakening by its last two years. Like most "second midterms," the 1986 elections were particularly damaging to Reagan and the Republicans. The Democrats, having picked up seats in the House, elected an ambitious and policy-hungry new Speaker in Jim Wright of Texas and, even more devastating to the GOP, Democrats retook majority control of the Senate, netting eight seats in the 1986 election, returning Senator Robert Byrd to the majority leader's post.

Ever pragmatic, Reagan turned, in part, to a government solution to boost his political standing. In his first cabinet meeting after the election losses, cabinet members were told that a catastrophic care bill was on Reagan's agenda.[118]

In addition to Republican losses, the emergence of the Iran-contra scandal amplified the need for a focus on catastrophic care, if only to change the story. While the earliest news reports related to this scandal emerged just before the 1986 elections, its major elements were revealed later in November 1986. One main component of the Iran-contra affair was the administration's going against explicit instructions of Congress to fund Nicaraguan rebels, the contras, a group fighting against a government with ties to the Soviet Union and Cuba. These monies were in part raised from private sources and against congressional dictates, raising serious constitutional concerns, especially regarding oversight and presidential accountability. In addition, the plan entailed selling arms to the Iranian government to try to secure the release of hostages and using the profits to support the contras. When the story began to be revealed publicly, National Security Council staffer Oliver North destroyed documents and created false chronologies.[119]

Secretary of Health and Human Services Otis Bowen recalled that Reagan "welcomed this publicity about the catastrophic to take people's minds off the Iran-Contra thing."[120] Health and Human Services staffer Joseph Antos observed that White House chief of staff "Donald Regan was trying to find some good news." Antos further observed, "I think the question really was, 'Okay, what do we have on the shelf?' What do we have that is ready to go? Well, this was the 'ready to go' that wasn't foreign policy. And so from something that looked completely dead that rose to astonishing heights." While others were important in promoting catastrophic care within the administration, timing mattered. Per Antos, Iran-contra figure Oliver North was the "one person who is really responsible for the catastrophic coverage act."[121]

As a catastrophic care bill was being negotiated within the administration and between it and Congress, the Iran-contra affair dominated headlines. The decline in Reagan's approval was precipitous and sustained.[122] Investigations began. In late November 1986, Reagan named the Tower Commission, and in early December, he called for a special prosecutor. A House–Senate investigating committee was established in mid-December.

Reagan formally proposed a catastrophic care bill in February 1987. Cabinet members who had held elective office—Bowen and Labor Secretary Bill Brock, a former senator and House member who had also headed the Republican National Committee—argued it had political benefits.[123] Reminding the Domestic Policy Council of "the President's commitment to do something this year," Brock reasoned, "Otherwise the issue will be taken away from us."[124] After touting his conservative credentials as a tax-cutting governor, Bowen said that he "would like to see this administration get the credit," predicting that Congress would "act soon on some form of" it.[125]

Others in the administration judged the bill more ideologically. Influential opponents, including Attorney General Edwin Meese, Economic Adviser Beryl Sprinkel, OMB director James Miller, and Secretary of the Interior Donald Hodel, questioned the legitimacy of expanding the federal government's role, raised budget concerns, and predicted that Congress would vastly increase the scope of any proposal the administration made.[126] True to Reagan's small-government philosophy, these critics called for policy options such as vouchers and giving states greater ability to craft solutions. One memo argued for the "principles of free choice, federalism and encouragement of private enterprise." Miller said, "We should let the market work."[127] Multiple Reagan advisors contended that markets should be trusted and used, not government.[128]

Opponents in the Reagan coalition focused both on the anathematic role of government and politics a catastrophic care act promised. Writing to White House chief of staff Don Regan, Phil Truluck of the Heritage

Foundation pronounced his organization "shocked and disturbed" at the prospect of the Reagan administration supporting "an expansion of the Medicaid system," an approach he called "the reverse of privatization." Truluck contended, "It would be hard to imagine a domestic policy that would elicit more opposition from the Administration's conservative supporters."[129] Predicting backlash, Stuart Butler, also of at Heritage, told a reporter, "I expect implacable conservative opposition."[130] However, conservatives would stick with Reagan, and relatively little political upheaval ensued.[131] This would change, however, early in the Bush administration.

Catastrophic care continued to unfold as Iran-contra raged on. The first public witness to the joint congressional committee on Iran-contra testified in early May 1987. During that summer, some witnesses—particularly Oliver North—drew a great deal of media attention, and committee members largely divided along partisan lines regarding institutional powers.[132] The committee's report was issued in November 1987. All Republicans but three—Senators William Cohen of Maine, Warren Rudman of New Hampshire, and Paul Trible of Virginia—signed onto the minority report, which argued that Reagan and his administration acted within his (now expanding) constitutional orbit. Strongly arguing on behalf of Reagan and strong presidential institutionalism was Representative Dick Cheney of Wyoming, the ranking member of the committee. Later, as George W. Bush's vice president, Cheney (and his chief of staff David Addington, who had staffed the Iran-Contra Committee) would be a proponent of even more sweeping presidential power.

Toward the end of the Reagan administration, conservative frustration peaked with a stalled realignment and the Iran-contra scandal. conservatives were especially tired of decades of Democratic congressional dominance. Newfound conservative ire toward congressional power, muted while Republicans controlled the Senate, was reignited after Democrats recaptured the Senate in the 1986 midterm elections. This created an even more vehement anti-congressionalism in conservative circles. Building on the Reagan Justice Department's mid-1980s "unitary executive" rationales for presidential power, the conservative movement became not only pro-presidency but also decidedly anti-Congress.

Co-opting the language that executive branch critics used to indict the "imperial presidency," a Heritage Foundation–sponsored book warned against an "imperial Congress" threatening the separation of powers and liberty itself. *The Imperial Congress: Crisis in the Separation of Powers* was an edited collection published in 1988 recommending a restoration of separation of powers principles purportedly closer to the Founders' vision.[133]

According to the work's editors, Gordon Jones and John Marini, America faced a constitutional crisis stemming from Congress's "failure to observe traditional limits on its power" and the other branches' "acquiescence" in their disempowerment.[134] Michael Hammond and Peter Weyrich maintained that this institutional breakdown resulted in a House of Representatives that was "a self-perpetuating oligarchy in which the political choices of a majority of Americans have been offset by an elaborate system of electoral jury-rigging, and in which the interests of a few districts predominate in the decision-making process."[135]

Echoing Reagan, Meese, and Cheney, these conservatives were most concerned about what they saw as a beleaguered presidency and aggressive Congress, especially the House. Conservatives charged that Congress—neither representative nor focused on its legislative work—was left to usurp executive power, "micromanaging" a massive administrative state to influence policy without actually legislating.[136] Thomas West wrote that the system, "fosters and thrives upon" corruption.[137] Gordon Crovitz thought congressional investigations of the executive branch in the 1980s criminalized Congress's policy differences with the Reagan administration.[138]

In *The Imperial Congress*, Hammond and Weyrich concluded that all of this purported malfeasance and abuse of power revealed a "banana-republic style electoral politics"[139] in the House of Representatives and compared the House to a Soviet-style system with "the shell, but none of the substance, of democracy."[140] Compared to the Senate, they claimed, the House was "a totalitarian regime."[141] In the view of Jones and Marini, aggressive oversight of the president was "a threat to the separation of powers and ultimately to democratic rule."[142]

If Congress was, as the conservatives had diagnosed it, imperial, out of control, corrupt, and a threat to the separation of powers, democracy, and even liberty, the prescription was clear. In "Comes the Revolution," Gabriel Prosser (a pseudonym) argued the first step toward the constitutional "restoration" was for the president to "deny legitimacy to his congressional opponents and to the systems and structures which they control."[143] In "Overthrowing Oligarchy," Jones wrote, the only potential counterbalance to "legislative tyranny" was for conservatives "to wield the weapon of a reinvigorated executive."[144] West put it even more simply: "The cause of the presidency against Congress *in today's setting* is the cause of free government."[145] As we discuss in chapter 4, Republicans incorporated these anti-Congress criticisms in their 1988 and 1992 party platforms and in planning congressional campaigns in the late 1980s and early 1990s.

The end of the Reagan years paled in comparison to 1981, when the administration had been on the offensive. Weakened by scandal and unavoidable lame duck status, Reagan had not one but two failed Supreme Court nominations—Robert Bork and Douglas Ginsburg—before Anthony Kennedy was confirmed. After a conflict with congressional Democrats over a provision in the Omnibus Trade and Competitiveness Act that would compel employers to notify workers of layoffs, Reagan threatened a veto, only to relent when Democrats moved the plant-closing provision through the legislative process on its own. Reagan allowed the bill to become law without his signature.

These inauspicious losses notwithstanding, many conservatives saw the conclusion of the second term as a beginning rather than an end, continuing at least to believe in the political promise of Reaganism and its small-government rhetoric. In a plan developed by White House staff and the Heritage Foundation, Reaganites acknowledged a loss of momentum in Reagan's last years but with hopes to regain it. The report noted, "With the Congress now controlled by the opposition, legislative victories will be fewer and more difficult. By stressing broad themes we can regain the rhetorical high ground, recapture the support of the American people and eventually increase our success with specific policy initiatives on The Hill."[146]

How could conservatives successfully "regain," "recapture," and "eventually increase" these elements of their agenda? According to the report, it would take reinforcing the rhetorical frames that brought them this far and, with the help of coalition partners, reiterating and rolling out policy ideas, for the "Reagan Revolution has fundamentally altered the framework of the political debate." Writing with confidence, the report contended that such an approach would "set and reinforce a solid foundation for the next ten years' growth of conservative majorities in key constituencies—[via] a strategic plan for a permanent majority party."[147]

While Republicans were not giving up on realignment, there were nevertheless major concessions during the Reagan administration, including in health care, a move at odds with Reagan's decades-old distaste for the nation's core health programs.

THE BUSH CODA

Though a loyal vice president, George H. W. Bush's support was relatively weak among staunch conservatives. Some thought Bush had a questionable record on abortion rights and other social issues, and most did not forget that, in 1980, he had called Reagan's core economic policies "voodoo economics." Wondering if he would stay true to the small-government and social conservative philosophies of the era, movement conservatives did not afford him the same leeway and pragmatic maneuverability.

But it had been Reagan who pressed for the passage of a law that increased Medicare coverage for catastrophic care for the elderly. In the midst of the 1988 presidential campaign, the Medicare Catastrophic Care Act of 1988 (MCCA) was passed by huge margins in the House (328–72) and Senate (86–11).[148] Despite years of railing against a federal government role in health care, one of the legislative acts Reagan was to sign in his last year "was characterized as the largest expansion of Medicare since the program's implementation."[149]

Then-Vice President Bush praised MCCA after it passed, and he supported it during the campaign. Bush, however, also deployed familiar antigovernment tropes, saying, "We should shun the various Democratic health care proposals, which would involve government bureaucrats in people's personal health care decisions."[150] Criticism came from one unexpected place, as Democratic presidential nominee Michael Dukakis asserted that backing the added Medicare premium meant that Bush had already contradicted his promise not to raise taxes as president,[151] an argument that both presaged the coming public and legislative turn against the law and signaled a similar Bush vulnerability in 1992.

The bill would be repealed in Bush's first year. While seniors initially liked the policy, they did not understand its fine details,[152] and neither the federal government nor the AARP, the bill's strongest organizational defender, devoted significant resources to educating beneficiaries about its benefits and costs. The AARP's legislative director described an "unsophisticated" approach to communication, without "focus groups, message testing." The prevailing philosophy, later echoed after the passage of the Affordable Care Act under Barack Obama, was that "people would appreciate [the program] once in place." "It would grow its own constituency."[153] Poor planning made the bill all the more vulnerable.

The anti-government philosophy Reagan had nurtured continued to marshal opposition, too. Anti-tax sentiments were central to the law's eventual repeal. As Brian Biles, a staffer for the House Ways and Means Committee, put it, Reagan had "taught the American people that paying taxes was certainly at least unnecessary, if not un-American."[154] The bill's funding mechanisms were an outgrowth both of Reagan-era deficits and the Gramm-Rudman pay-go provisions that required that all new programs be financed within the same fiscal year. Rather than having the program financed through general revenues or the payroll tax, all beneficiaries were to pay a new Medicare premium, and some would pay an additional premium based on income.[155] The Democratic Congress also piled on benefits in the coverage, increasing its cost. And because of the fiscal rules, in the first year of its operation, premiums would be levied but no benefits would be provided. Low-income seniors were to pay little, while moderate-income and higher-income seniors would pay more. "That tax, little noticed at the time, led to a well-organized protest campaign that ultimately buried members of Congress under an avalanche of angry mail."[156]

This, like so many other political costs of the Reagan era, came home to roost after the Reagan presidency ended and the George H. W. Bush administration began. As president, Bush initially supported catastrophic care but faced early pressure from Republicans to limit or change the law. When, in early April 1989, Representative Bill Archer (R-TX), was to meet with White House chief of staff John Sununu to advocate a delay to the bill's implementation and the formation of a study committee, Robert Porter, the director of the White House Policy Council, advised Sununu to remember Bush's campaign remarks and to say he did not back Archer's bill. But Porter also warned that "dissident groups [were] exploiting discontent with the legislation, in particular the surcharge, to build grass roots strength."[157] A few weeks later, President Bush wrote to Dan Rostenkowski (D-IL), the chair of the House Ways and Means Committee, saying, "It would be imprudent to tinker with Medicaid catastrophic insurance literally in its first months of life. We should not now reopen the legislation."[158] Republican committee members pushed back, criticizing Bush for meeting with Rostenkowski and not consulting with them beforehand and asked to "delay the implementation of the new catastrophic program"[159]

Bush's support faded. By early fall of 1989, the MCCA was in real danger.[160] Wealthier seniors and seniors who thought the income-based premiums would hit them harder voiced their displeasure, most famously in an August 1988 confrontation between Representative Rostenkowski and seniors in his district.[161] "Sen. John McCain (R-AZ) claimed, 'Every member of Congress has been accosted at town meetings.' "[162] Noting that Washington elites had stoked some of this opposition, AARP's Rother said, "Also, there were a lot of, quote, grassroots groups that had received financial backing from the [pharmaceutical] industry."[163]

In September 1989, White House press secretary Marlin Fitzwater acknowledged the pushback against catastrophic care, saying, "the people at home in the August recess obviously made their views very clear about paying for this benefit . . . The elderly complaints are rolling in in tidal waves of immense proportions."[164]

Although Representative Rostenkowski visited President Bush to urge him to oppose the bill's repeal, by December 1989 multiple administration agencies and the director of the Office of Management and Budget recommended he sign repeal legislation.

Unlike health reform fights to come, party polarization played virtually no role in enacting or ending the MCCA. Having passed with strong, bipartisan majorities, it was repealed by even larger ones.[165] OMB director Richard Darman rightly called the repeal "the congressional response to the vocal objections by Medicare beneficiaries to having to pay the entire cost of benefits" and "an unprecedented rollback of a major social welfare program so soon after its creation." Although the Council of Economic Advisors noted it would be "useful" for the administration to develop its own legislation,[166] it was not until February 1992 that Bush introduced a set of health-care policies, but he hardly talked about the package and did not provide a way of paying for them.[167] These policies went nowhere, but health care was to become a central part of Harris Wofford's special election win of a Pennsylvania Senate seat in November 1991 and Bill Clinton's successful challenge to Bush's reelection campaign.

This was just one of many instances where George H. W. Bush was left to pay Reagan's tab. As a candidate and as president, he would have to shore up the GOP's image in Reagan's wake while living up to the promises that had proven too difficult for Reagan to achieve in two terms. Bush's struggle to be the "kinder and gentler" Republican who campaigned as both the "environmental president" and the "education president" can be read as a recognition of the need to shore up the public image of the party that always had difficulty matching Reagan's "Teflon" when it came to cutting programs and with respect to "fairness" and other Democratic issues.

Reagan left it to his successor to finally make good on the elusive promise of deficit reduction that the GOP had espoused throughout the 1980s. As with the prelude, when Dukakis weighed in on the catastrophic care fight, when Bush agreed to "revenue enhancements" to achieve deficit reduction in 1990 budget negotiations with Democrats, it provoked a revolt in the House led by Newt Gingrich: 105 House Republicans abandoned Bush on a budget vote. It also yielded new charges, from Bill Clinton, that Bush had reneged on his "read my lips: no new taxes" campaign pledge.[168]

If peeling back the New Deal and dismantling the Great Society had been the chief aim of conservatives since Goldwater, many conservatives saw not only lost opportunity in the Bush years but even retrenchment. Many also claimed that Bush lost reelection in 1992 because he had abandoned his anti-tax pledge specifically and conservative dogma generally.

But fulfilling the promises of the Reagan era was politically perilous for Bush, who was in the unenviable position of trying to complete the Reagan project, which was always more successful as rhetoric than as policy, but lacked Reagan's communications skills and inherent trust from conservatives.

More daunting than anything, though, was to live in Reagan's shadow. His image and rhetoric became touchstones of Republican and conservative orthodoxy for decades to come. It no doubt took its toll on others as well. So full-throated and doctrinaire were Reagan's rhetorical flourishes that conservatives would come to view Nixon as too liberal, Ford as ineffective, and Bush as wimpy.

A FRUSTRATED MOVEMENT, AN EMBOLDENED PRESIDENCY

Marshaling effective opposition to the New Deal regime, Reagan wielded national Republican political rhetoric that was increasingly anti-government, anti-Washington, and race-coded, and it would shape the GOP for decades to come, including in ways that Reagan himself both would and would not avow.

If Reagan's anti-government rhetoric was clear, his view of governing was complicated. A president who came to office to shrink the federal government, Reagan would expand the government in key areas and would allow— either by design to aid favored constituencies or by concession to political realities—significant slippage in the budget and tax retrenchments of his first years in office. While a harsh critic of income support programs and frequently also of the people who used them, Reagan's small-government view had blind spots for those he deemed hardworking and deserving or for areas in which expanding government might shore up his coalition.

None of this is to say that Reagan secretly favored big government or that his ideological commitments were mere posturing, but instead that Reagan's conservatism, both as California governor and as president, had a more complex, sophisticated, and even pragmatic view of the state than many of his GOP successors would adopt. In some ways, given resistance in Congress and in public opinion, the political system simply would not admit of a wholesale displacement of the New Deal state.

Because Reagan did not achieve all that he wished to in policy terms, his defenders could always deny responsibility for their economic impacts. The recession, the growing deficit, and the growing income gap could just as easily be blamed on the fact that Reagan did not get everything he wanted as they could on his program and performance. Early in the administration, Reagan's defenders could claim that the "president's program had not yet taken effect." Later, they could claim that his theory of government was never actually implemented because congressional Democrats had stopped him or government policies from prior administrations had bespoiled his free market approach.[169] Whereas Harry Truman famously had a sign on his desk as president that read "The Buck Stops Here," the "buck" never stopped with the conservative movement during the Reagan years.

A related consequence was that Reagan's political project—his conservative movement and party coalition—could continue to benefit from public dissatisfaction with the government. Going forward, promises of "tax relief" continued to unify the party in elections and in Congress, with everlasting complaints about "burdensome regulation" and persistent claims that Republicans meant well for the poor even when they denied them resources. Reagan's forces, unified by their opposition to big government, could continue to build an oppositional movement, strategically basing it on government distrust, *even as they were the government*. The movement's bête noire—big government—persisted, and thus Reagan's conservative theory of governance remained untested and the GOP's struggle against government continued.

In Reagan's rhetoric, the government needed to be made "worthy" of the people by making it a "help, not a hindrance" and the growth of government spending was "dangerous" and taxpayers needed "protect[ion]."[170] Taking aim at the Great Society's costly elaborations of the New Deal, Reagan asked pointedly, "What has all this money done? Well, too often it has only made poverty harder to escape."[171] Such statements weaponized resentment of government throughout the rest of Reagan's presidency and became key to his legacy in the GOP.

This stance compelled a deeply conservative following, alarmed by the harm they attributed to government and ready to view Democrats not just as adversaries but as enemies of Reagan's America. Unleashing an ideological movement based on government distrust, post-Reagan conservatives' strategic efforts went to prodigious lengths that not even Reagan would affirm. Reagan himself demonstrated commitments to compromise and governance much more than his progeny would.

In Reagan's time, any challenge to the core of the New Deal was premature. It still had considerable support from the public, including those within the Republican Party. It would take years for Republican efforts to build government distrust to support efforts to "reform Medicare" by cutting billions of dollars out of it or to "privatize Social Security."

Reagan also left a legacy on rhetoric regarding race. As Frances Fox Piven argued, "Ronald Reagan made the image of the 'welfare queen' a staple of American popular culture. This was the politics of spectacle, a spectacle designed to evoke and intensify popular antipathies against Democrats, against blacks, against liberals, against licentious women, and against government, or at least those parts of government that provided support to poor and working people."[172] Such rhetoric was consistent with what Republican strategist Lee Atwater explained as a way of appealing to white southerners without overt racism.[173] The care Reaganites took was to mask the Southern strategy with small-government, anti-Washington, and "new federalism" rhetoric that questioned the appropriateness and value of national government action.

Reagan's claims and insinuations on race issues mattered, because they had staying power for the conservative movement he inspired. Here again, the rhetoric extended well beyond what Reagan would have said, in public at least. Although Reagan used racialized language to decry social welfare policies, his farewell address heralded hardworking immigrants seeking political and economic freedom. In it, Reagan explained that "in his mind" John Winthrop's phrase "a shining city upon a hill" referred to "a tall, proud city . . . teeming with people of all kinds living in harmony and peace; a city with free ports that hummed with commerce and creativity. And if there had to be city walls, the walls had doors and the doors were open to anyone with the will and the heart to get here." The outright xenophobia of Donald Trump and others would emerge later.

The Reaganism on which he had run—the vision of a market unfettered, a "New Beginning" that dismantled the New Deal state—was only partially realized. Frustrated by a Democrat-controlled House and a Senate recaptured by Democrats in 1986, Reagan's domestic ambitions were muted by compromise or halted altogether thereafter, especially after the Ninety-Seventh Congress (1981–82).[174] Even when Reagan initially cut programs that supported the middle class, those efforts were "corrected" by subsequent legislation, and the only budget cuts likely to stick concerned politically "vulnerable" groups—like welfare recipients—who could not fight back.[175]

What did last were the anti-government arguments Reagan had marshalled since 1964 and on which he had built his career and then his presidency. Political scientist Stephen Skowronek viewed Reagan's political and policy impact as "bringing permanent pressure to bear against programs that maintained formidable political and institutional support."[176] Reagan did this, as one of his contemporary observers put it, by "fundamentally chang[ing the] tone and approach" of the conservative movement.[177]

The frustrated realignment and the persistence of divided government in the Reagan years—the failure to take majority control of the House and the loss of the Senate in 1986—meant that Republican supporters of Reagan who wished to stoke anti-government sentiment had to carefully dissect which parts of the government to attack while championing their own power. Politicians view the proper balance between institutions through self-interested lenses,[178] and Reagan-era conservatives focused the promotion of distrust on Congress (and toward an "activist judiciary"). They united complaints about internal congressional practices with broader charges about the inefficiency and intrusiveness of government, while advocating for an expansive view of presidential power.

With Congress seemingly permanently under Democratic control, conservatives lambasted it. Simultaneously they found new hope in the presidency and, led by Meese, began devoting intellectual efforts to building a case for presidential power. With presidential power increasingly a cause célèbre in conservative circles, decades of argument from earlier in the twentieth century championing congressional deliberation, inspired by Willmoore Kendall and other conservative intellectuals, were set aside. The new theory, emerging in the Nixon years and taking hold in Reagan's 1980s, held that "an institutionalized presidency forged for liberal purposes could be redeployed for conservative ends."[179]

For all their anti-government rhetoric, these Reagan-era conservatives were not against governmental power so much as they were against others exercising it. They were quite willing to empower the presidency and the executive branch, all the while stripping from Congress the key mechanisms of oversight the GOP had once recommended. The Bush years continued a conservative embrace of presidential power versus that of Congress. William Barr, then an assistant attorney general at the Office of Legal Counsel, wrote a memo warning of congressional encroachments on the presidency, in which he described the president as "the head of the unitary executive branch."[180] The next year, he claimed that Congress could not always use its budgetary powers to limit presidential actions.[181] Dick Cheney also had more to say about institutional powers in foreign policy, writing in a 1989 essay that the presidency "was designed as a one-person office to ensure it would be ready for action." Opined Cheney, "On the scale of risks, I am more concerned about depriving the president of his ability to act than I am about Congress's alleged inability to respond."[182]

Throwing off concerns about the potential for an unchecked presidency, the new conservatism looked to the White House for leadership in its causes to disrupt congressional dominance of the Washington establishment, tame an overgrown federal bureaucracy, and decentralize federal power.

Reagan's assertiveness, his belief in a "unitary executive," and his commitments to a strong presidency for conservative purposes became new conservative touchstones. Conservatives became presidentialists until, at least, the next Democratic president, at which point they would rediscover the value of a strong Congress as a strategic weapon in their war with government.

Chapter Four

A REVOLUTION AGAINST GOVERNMENT?

The Promotion of Distrust in the Clinton Era

On Wednesday, April 19, 1995, at 9:02 a.m., a fertilizer bomb detonated at the Alfred P. Murrah Federal Building in Oklahoma City. This act of anti-government, right-wing domestic terrorism killed 168 people, among them 19 children.

Four days later, President Bill Clinton traveled to Oklahoma to speak to the mourning city. The Murrah building had housed offices for federal agencies, including the U.S. Department of Housing and Urban Development, the Drug Enforcement Administration, the Bureau of Alcohol, Tobacco, Firearms and Explosives, the Social Security Administration, and a counseling center for Veterans Affairs. Clinton pointed to the deaths of people "who worked to help the elderly and the disabled, who worked to support our farmers and our veterans, who worked to enforce our laws and to protect us. Let us say clearly, they served us well, and we are grateful." These people were not apart from the community, for they were, Clinton said, "Also neighbors and friends" seen "at church or the PTA meetings, at the civic clubs, at the ball park."[1]

But just one day later, Clinton's rhetoric sharpened. He criticized the "loud and angry voices in America today whose sole goal seems to be to try to keep some people as paranoid as possible and the rest of us all torn up and upset with each other." Clinton contended that "Some things that are regularly said over the airwaves" promote "hatred" and "violence," and so answering anti-government acts and speech was essential.[2]

In the coming weeks, Clinton rebuked the rhetoric of talk show host G. Gordon Liddy and the Michigan Militia, an armed right-wing anti-government group. Clinton told them, "If you appropriate our sacred symbols for paranoid purposes and compare yourselves to colonial militias who fought for the democracy you rail against, you are wrong."[3]

In the Clinton years distrust toward government was pervasive,[4] and Clinton's opponents stoked it even when it inspired extreme and dangerous elements. The Republican Party seized on distrust to fuel its potent opposition to the Democratic president and propel itself to power in Congress.

President Clinton was one of two key players in this epic clash. The young president had been first elected as governor of Arkansas at the age of 31, lost reelection in 1980, but was reelected in 1982 and served for the following decade. Rising in national prominence, Clinton chaired the National Governors Association and was a onetime chairman of the Democratic Leadership Council (DLC), a centrist group of Democrats trying to develop new issues to steer the party to the ideological center. He won his first term as president in 1992. Charismatic and skilled in practical politics, Clinton's ascent was, in part, a product of the Reagan era, as the Democrats sought what the DLC called a "third way" between Reagan's small-government conservatism and traditional Democratic liberalism.

The other key player of the era was Newt Gingrich, a member of the House of Representatives from Georgia whose antiestablishment strategies helped him to rise through the ranks of the House, first as a lead dissident railing against Democratic majority control, then as minority whip, and after the 1994 "Republican Revolution" as the first Republican Speaker of the House in forty years.[5] Gingrich was at the center of efforts to force the 1989 resignation of Speaker Jim Wright, a moment historian Julian Zelizer called "precisely the moment our toxic political environment was born."[6] Not only aggressive and partisan, Gingrich was also a skilled strategist who had been head of a group in the House called the Conservative Opportunity Society (COS) that plotted ways to challenge and embarrass the Democratic leadership, including using C-SPAN's national television audience to take these conflicts into America's living rooms. He also led GOPAC, a group that aimed to train Republican candidates and officeholders at the state and local level and to build a "farm team" of future Republican national leaders. Notably, Gingrich trained them in rhetoric, tactics, and arguments to discredit government and the Democrats in efforts to foster a GOP that "talked like Newt."

But Clinton and Gingrich, the principal antagonists of the 1990s, had much in common. Both were of the same generation and each presented himself as a policy wonk. Each man's political career began in a state that had been part of the Confederacy and had suffered fatal white supremacist violence. Like many southern politicians in the post–Civil Rights Act and Voting Rights Act era, both were steeped not only in the politics of race but also in a culture suspicious of national government. If Clinton was practiced in the arts of connection and concession, Gingrich went on the offensive to provoke conflict and stoke distrust.

If not a departure from past efforts to use distrust strategically, the 1990s was a turning point, a time when distrust in government was more consciously and even more artfully embedded in conservative messaging and political strategies.

In their war with government, the GOP used tools more expertly and effectively than in the past: message testing, polling, and focus groups, crafting their communications to widen their coalition and whip up distrust in government to build the Republican "Revolution." Distrust defeated Clinton's health-care reform legislation, and Republicans employed racial tropes to attack prevention policies in Clinton's crime bill. Railing against decades of Democratic control of Congress and Clinton's first moves as president, Republicans seized on public distrust and took control of Congress in 1995.

Distrust in government became particularly salient in Republican strategies in the 1990s for several reasons. First, a recession bred dissatisfaction. And George H. W. Bush's broken "read my lips" tax pledge and congressional scandals exacerbated the public's distrustful mood. With the public eager for the "change" that Bill Clinton and Independent candidate Ross Perot offered in 1992, Republicans, after Bush's defeat, were freed from governing responsibilities and doubled down on anti-government sentiment.

Second, at the end of the Cold War, foreign policy took a backseat. This removed a staple issue that had unified Republicans and at least somewhat had tempered their anti-government rhetoric. As Republican National Committee (RNC) director of strategic planning Don Fierce said in the mid-1990s, "Washington has replaced communism as the glue for conservatives . . . The [new] evil empire is Washington."[7]

While party politics in the 1970s and 1980s stressed resolve in the face of foreign threats, and politics in the 2000s was shaped by the September 11 attacks, a war on terrorism, and wars in Iraq and Afghanistan, Clinton-era politics largely focused on domestic politics.[8]

Third, many Republicans were frustrated with the incompleteness, even the irreconcilability, of the Reagan era. While Reagan had long criticized government, as president he sometimes beat a strategic retreat in the war against it and so did not meet conservative hopes for retrenching social welfare policies. Late Reagan efforts to pass catastrophic care coverage did not help. Bush's acquiescence on tax increases—contrary to his 1988 "Read my lips" pledge—seemed to confirm a mounting suspicion that Reagan's promise to cut taxes while reducing the deficit was chimerical.

A growing conservative movement came together around anti-government themes brewing since Goldwater and Reagan. In 1990, Newt Gingrich led an intraparty revolt against Bush's budget and tax deal. By 1992, Pat Buchanan challenged Bush's nomination from the right, fueled by social conservatives' ire and a right wing that thought Bush had given away too much and did not share their values. After Bush lost the White House, congressional Republicans shifted into full opposition mode.

COMPLETING REAGAN'S STALLED REALIGNMENT?

Frustrated by a thwarted Reagan realignment and Bush's capitulation in the late 1980s and early 1990s, conservatives moved to recapture their party and the government. Building the GOP's congressional majority required, first, attacking Democratic control of Congress and then changing course to celebrate congressional power and undermine the Democratic president. Once they controlled Congress, conservatives dropped their hangups about a meddlesome Congress. Instead, they used their new perch to launch investigations of Clinton, eventually impeaching him.

In the 1980s and early 1990s, cultivating distrust and undermining public confidence in Congress was essential to restoring the constitutional system that conservatives felt had slipped away.

At the center of these efforts was Newt Gingrich, who had written the foreword to *The Imperial Congress*. Behind the scenes, Gingrich instructed GOP leaders to wage "an all-out effort to arouse, mobilize, and lead the American people . . . to break the leftwing machine's illegitimate grip on the House of Representatives."[9] One way to do this was through the national media. According to a Gingrich press staffer, "We were constantly working the *New York Times*' editorial boards on the problems of the liberal welfare state (it's one word in our lexicon)."[10]

All of this was explicitly done in service of completing the Reagan realignment, an aspiration the GOP could not shake. A late-1980s Conservative Opportunity Society planning document explicitly stated that the goal was to "translate the conservative realignment that has occurred at the Presidential level into Republican seats in the U.S. Congress."[11] Republican electoral strategies focused on stoking public anger to undermine the legitimacy of the New Deal, the Great Society, and Democratic control of Congress. In an early 1990s internal document entitled "If House Republicans Are Ever to Become a Majority," Gingrich proposed a "fundamental change" in electioneering with strategies that "nationalized congressional elections around discontent with Congress" and where challengers focus constituent "anger on an illegitimate incumbent."[12] One diagram juxtaposed the GOP against "The Left; Labor Unions; Corrupt Governments; Democrats." Another depicted building a Republican coalition by "informing, arousing, empowering, training, and helping the anti-left."[13] "Arousing" the public and "focusing . . . anger" rested on a strategy of "defining the Democrats as the party of radical left-wing activists, unionized bureaucracies, and corrupt political machines."[14]

The GOP began to use new public opinion techniques in their efforts to stoke distrust. While preparing for the 1992 congressional elections, a Congressional Institute seminar for the House Republican Conference offered data on existing "psychological, demographic, and public opinion trends" and tips on how to "market" messages to a distrustful public. Trainers asserted the premise that "American citizens are disaffected from their government and cynical about their leaders" and planned to "define the crisis of legitimacy that Congress faces" and explain "tools that marketers use."[15] The skillful use of language to shape public opinion was as central to Gingrich's ascent as was the content of his anti-government messages.

With more GOP activists and officeholders thinking and speaking "like Newt," Gingrich's star was on the rise. He formally entered the House Republican leadership when Dick Cheney vacated his whip role to become secretary of defense in March 1989. Besting Ed Madigan, a staid and traditional conservative in the mold of Minority Leader Bob Michel, Gingrich's COS and GOPAC roles helped him demonstrate his more combative strategy's effectiveness.[16]

Gingrich's election to a formal leadership role signaled the acceptance of the "running against Congress" strategy. The staunch anti-Congress/

anti-Washington positions he championed became official party state-ments included in the 1988 and 1992 platforms. While the 1980 and 1984 platforms included only one negative mention of congressional processes, by 1988 and 1992, anti-Congress rhetoric was everywhere. The 1988 plat-form contained twenty-seven criticisms of Congress, which the Republi-cans charged was "no longer the people's branch of government." Instead, they dubbed it the "broken branch" run by "an arrogant oligarchy that has subverted the Constitution."[17]

These abuses by Democrats, the GOP claimed, undermined "account-ability, order, and truth in government." Blaming their opponents for the nation's mounting deficits, Republicans claimed the Democrats had "sabo-taged the Republican program to control the federal budget" with "pork barrel deals," and they charged Democrats with "excessive interference" in foreign policy, no doubt referring in part to the Iran-contra affair.[18]

The 1992 platform contained eleven negative mentions of Congress and a subsection entitled "Cleaning Up the Imperial Congress." The GOP claimed that Democrats' "entrenched power has produced a Congress arrogant, out of touch, hopelessly entangled in a web of PACs, perks, privileges, partisan-ship, paralysis, and pork." Republicans also compared Democratic rule to a con, calling the budget process a "shell game." Echoing *The Imperial Con-gress* and the 1980s Reagan Justice Department, the platform charged that Congress encroached on executive authority, saying " 'Advise and Consent' has been replaced by 'slash and burn,' " and charging Congress with per-mitting "rogue prosecutors to spend tremendous amounts to hound some of the nation's finest public servants."[19]

For a party that had spent much of the twentieth century trying to "restore" Congress, strengthening it as a bulwark against presidential aggrandizement, the turnaround on separation of powers questions that started under Nixon was abrupt and complete.[20] And, just as quickly, Republicans let go of these new anti-Congress positions when contexts changed again, especially after the 1994 elections.

"REAGANISM WITHOUT REAGAN"

The historian Garry Wills once portrayed the Reagan coalition as a "tot-tering edifice" and argued that "Reaganism without Reagan [was] unsus-tainable."[21] Lacking Reagan's political skills and personal popularity, the GOP always struggled to match Reagan's Teflon status in the face of public backlash. Moreover, the dubious math of Reaganomics' pledges of lower taxes, more military spending, and decreased deficits and debt—what George H. W. Bush had called "voodoo economics" in 1980—failed to prove out. And Reagan's core promise to dismantle the New Deal turned out to be too steep a political hill to climb. Unenviable then was George H. W. Bush's effort to "stay the course" set by his predecessor. Bush's task was to govern effectively despite the currency of Reagan-inspired distaste for government within his base.

To challenge Bush in 1992, Democrats selected a reformer in Bill Clinton, a southern governor and Washington outsider with more moderate credentials than 1984 and 1988 nominees Walter Mondale and Michael Dukakis. Bush's approval ratings had soared with the perceived success of the Persian Gulf War, which ended in February 1991, but this faded as public interest turned to domestic matters. Democrats had been on the defensive regarding government action since the early Reagan years, and Clinton was a leader of an attempt to move his party to the center, the DLC, which formed in March 1985, after Reagan's landslide reelection defeated several moderate Democrats.[22] By the early 1990s, many national Democratic leaders— Clinton, Al Gore, Sam Nunn, and Richard Gephardt, for example—had internalized Republican criticisms that they were too enamored of government programs.[23] In a "message grid" exercise examining what Democrats and Republicans elites said about themselves and the other party, the Democratic view of "Republicans on Democrats" focused almost exclusively on government as the party's weakness: "Tax and spend; free-spending; waste and spend; dangerous, irresponsible; pork barrelers; big government."[24] The DLC strategy was not so much to shift the party to "the center" on issues with Republican advantages (taxes, foreign policy, and crime) as to selectively emphasize issues helping Democrats (economics, jobs, and government benefits).[25]

During his 1992 campaign, Clinton pursued a complex racial strategy. Clinton had a history of ties to his state's black community, pursued racial equality, and made his share of symbolic gestures of outreach to African American constituencies. But Clinton also criticized rapper Sister Souljah for her comments on race and flew back to Arkansas to oversee the execution of an intellectually impaired African American man. Each of these moments helped to burnish Clinton's credentials as a "New Democrat," being both willing to call out traditional Democratic constituencies and "tough on crime."

Having "stolen" several Republican issues while advancing a promise to expand national health insurance, Bill Clinton's first presidential election was defined by public distrust in government and restlessness for change. Riding a wave in 1992 reflecting economic dissatisfaction and in favor of "change versus more of the same," Bill Clinton became the first Democratic president since his fellow southerner, Jimmy Carter. Clinton combined wins through the Northeast and West Coast and much of the Midwest with Montana plus five southern states.

But this was far from an unalloyed, progovernment victory. Although Clinton had a decisive electoral college win, he won only 43 percent of the popular vote in a three-way race against President George H. W. Bush and billionaire Ross Perot, whose candidacy, built largely around opposition to debt and the deficit and in favor of smaller government, garnered 19 percent but won no electoral votes. With New Democrat Clinton advocating a "new covenant" of "opportunity, responsibility, community," critical of the Reagan era but eschewing traditional liberalism, all three major presidential candidates employed critiques of "big government."[26] In the wake of an early 1990s recession, Bush reneging on the "read my lips" promise, and high-profile congressional scandals in the House Bank and Post Office, Clinton took office when trust in government was plummeting.[27]

With Clinton's victory, the "Reagan Revolution," if it was to be sustained, had to become a congressional revolution. GOP leaders in Congress and the RNC took on more prominent roles in forging coalitions, linking Beltway Republicans to activists and voters and mediating and coordinating Washington-based allies. When Republican leader Bob Michel announced his retirement, a newly energized congressional leadership under Newt Gingrich and House Republican Conference Chairman Dick Armey strengthened these bonds with the RNC and other coalition partners and planned a successful strategy to win the House of Representatives. The Washington center of this disparate and far-flung conservative movement now resided in the emerging leadership of Newt Gingrich in the House, Bob Dole in the Senate, and Haley Barbour at the Republican National Committee. Conservatives also found informal movement leaders in talk radio personalities like Rush Limbaugh, activists like Paul Weyrich and Grover Norquist, and Christian conservatives like Ralph Reed, who, with Pat Robertson, spearheaded the movement's Christian conservative wing.

To overcome the party's natural fault lines, these leaders harnessed the coalition's ire at Bill Clinton and Democratic-controlled Washington, all the while spurring anti-government sentiment in their hopes of "completing" the Reagan revolution. Anti-government anger was the cornerstone of the coalition, existing in what reporters Dan Balz and Ronald Brownstein called "concentric circles of alienation from government," with the rhetoric at the outer reaches—the NRA, the western property rights movement, "extremist tax protesters, survivalists, and elements of the militia movement"—particularly militant and even dangerous at times.[28] Washington-based elite groups focused on lower taxes (the National Taxpayers Union and Americans for Tax Reform) and constitutional issues (the Federalist Society and US Term Limits). Americans for Tax Reform's Grover Norquist, who held weekly coordinating meetings attended by Republican leaders and officeholders, dubbed this group "a 'Leave Us Alone Coalition.' "[29]

At the RNC, Haley Barbour made it a strategic objective to strengthen the connections between voters, Beltway Republicans, and conservative activists (many who also worked inside the Beltway) that he believed atrophied during the Bush years. Barbour's survey to Republicans found common views about taxes, budgets, and regulations as well as about "line-item vetoes, welfare reform, increased defense spending, congressional reform." The survey also showed uniform views on social issues though Barbour hoped to at least partially correct "the perceived supremacy of social issues over economic and national security issues" in the party.[30]

Employing a conscious strategy to ride the public's "anger" with Washington politics, the "antigovernment coalition" in the GOP would become "the preeminent force in the party" in the Clinton era.[31] The 1992 elections emboldened that force by convincing conservatives that Bush's concessions caused his defeat and allowed the GOP to invigorate its anti-government rhetoric unencumbered by the responsibility of controlling any elected institution of government.

In 1993, pollsters Anthony Fabrizio and John McLaughlin wrote to Bob Michel that Republican voters wanted the GOP to focus on government waste, a balanced budget, the deficit, and individual liberty. Doing so would put "Democrats on the defensive" and restore a "winning electoral coalition."[32] With this messaging recommendation, Republicans set out to mobilize their base and win over Perot voters. Republicans decided on a full-throated opposition focusing on Clinton personally and on the scope of Democrat-controlled government in the two years of unified Democratic rule.

Nothing united the anti-government coalition of professional lobbyists and grassroots movement, moralists and libertarians, intellectuals and populists like Clinton's policy proposals. Conservatives believed his policies on the budget and taxes, health care, abortion, and gun control exemplified a return to big government and 1960s "counterculture" values. During Clinton's first budget fight, Republicans repeatedly claimed it included the "largest tax increase in history." They would double down on their criticisms when Clinton sought to make good on his 1992 campaign pledges to provide "universal health insurance coverage" and get "tough on crime."

ATTACKING GOVERNMENT, ATTACKING CLINTONISM

Republicans strategically wielded distrust in government to defeat health-care reform, hoping to spark a political debacle for Democrats and set the stage for longer-term wins. Conservatives similarly opposed the Violent Crime Control and Law Enforcement Act of 1994, also known as the Clinton Crime Bill, and incorporated racialized language in their attacks. Since the 1960s, Republicans had portrayed themselves as the party of law and order and attacked Democrats as weak on crime. Reflecting the centrist, New Democrat approach that helped Clinton win the presidency in 1992, the crime bill involved complicated racial politics. Although in later decades scholars and activists saw the law's provisions as racially discriminatory and harmful, the bill was supported but criticized by many black local elected officials and members of Congress.[33]

Undermining Clintonism required perpetuating the GOP's war with government, questioning its role and competence regarding health, crime, and all manner of policy concerns.

Clinton's 1992 presidential campaign had focused on the economy ("It's the economy, stupid"), but health care was a top priority. After talking about health care as a right in the 1991 special election for a Senate seat in Pennsylvania, Democrat Harris Wofford overcame a polling deficit of forty points to solidly defeat a much better known Republican. Wofford's campaign managers James Carville and Paul Begala then led the Clinton campaign.

As scholar Paul Starr notes, although it seemed like an "auspicious" time for health-care reform, Democrats were divided. Some preferred a single-payer approach, "while conservative Democrats favored market-oriented reforms without a commitment to universal coverage or spending caps. Between these two groups were more centrist liberals."[34]

An avowed New Democrat, Clinton supported welfare reform and a health plan that targeted cost control and greater coverage through a model called "managed competition" with a global budget.[35] The plan would control costs and expand coverage through highly regulated insurance providers operating in regional alliances. Rather than government paying health providers, coverage was to be expanded by subsidizing premiums for low-income individuals.

Built on candidate Clinton's proposals, details were developed by a White House task force created in January 1993 and headed by First Lady Hillary Clinton and Ira Magaziner. This process, which drew litigation focused on its secrecy, and its policy mechanisms had troublesome political implications. As political scientist Theda Skocpol argued, this approach divided "experts who designed a technically compelling policy" from "operatives who were supposed to sell the finished program to those who would have to live with it."[36]

Meanwhile, the Clinton administration was also considering how to employ crime policy to reposition the Democratic Party. In June 1993, Rahm Emanuel wrote to other top administration staffers that Clinton must avoid being defined by divisive social issues, and crime would serve "as an effective counterweight to gays in the military and abortion," defining Clinton "as strong and moderate."[37]

Clinton's Republican opponents actively cultivated distrust in government, mobilizing it to kill health-care reform and undermine his crime legislation. About a month before President Clinton gave his September 1993 health-care speech to Congress, the House Republican Conference acknowledged the health-care system needed change but framed reform as endangering "the best health care system in the world" with rationing and harming the economy by destroying jobs and raising taxes. Using charged language that portrayed government as risky and frightening, the conference claimed Clinton viewed "America's health care system as a laboratory for a gigantic social experiment—an experiment that has less to do with the public health than with expanding the government's power."[38]

Republicans also warned of the plan's political peril.[39] House Republicans quoted Stuart Butler of the Heritage Foundation, who compared the reform effort to the Vietnam War. The GOP report also compared the repeal of the 1988 catastrophic care legislation to the Bay of Pigs, a "fiasco whose unlearned lessons led to a far greater disaster." While initial polls looked positive for health-care reform, GOP insiders predicted that Congress would "face an inferno of public outrage that will make the catastrophic episode seem, in comparison, like a campfire."[40]

Policy and long-term electoral goals were firmly intertwined for conservatives. Franklin D. Roosevelt and Lyndon B. Johnson had created highly popular public pension and health-care policies that linked Americans to the state and the Democratic party. Republican leaders did not want Clinton to strengthen those ties and saw killing health-care reform as improving their political position in the short and long term. A year before Clinton announced his presidential run, Gingrich confided to two reporters that a Democratic loss on health care would allow Republicans to win a congressional majority. Defeating a Democratic health plan would be "their Stalingrad, their Gettysburg, their Waterloo," enabling Republicans to "defund the government and "destroy the liberal constituency groups."[41]

Conservatives painted Clinton's plan as laden with "bureaucrats" and "big government." Sen. Phil Gramm (R-TX) proclaimed he opposed the plan to protect his own mother: "When my momma gets sick, she is going to end up talking to a bureaucrat and not a doctor."[42] A September 1993 Republican National Committee memo said, "The Clinton plan severely restricts the right of families to choose and instead lets government bureaucrats randomly make the choice for you."[43]

Besides "Washington bureaucrats,"[44] other types of government actors ranged from the relatively innocuous to frightening. Conservatives were fond of saying health care would be delivered with the "efficiency of the Post Office and the compassion of the IRS." One Republican memo called for events in front of post offices to highlight "health care will become as bureaucratic, costly, and inefficient as the U.S. Postal Service."[45] Quite ominously, Congressman Christopher Cox of California claimed the Canadian health-care system could be called "Gestapo medicine." Said he, "The only surprise is that there are not guards armed with AK-47s posed in every doctor's office."[46] Using the same sort of arguments Reagan employed decades earlier, Cox claimed government officials would tell doctors where and how to work.

Soon after Clinton's well-received congressional speech on health care, at which he held up a health security card as a tangible symbol of the benefits

Americans would receive, Bill Kristol openly discussed the political benefits of rejecting any health-care bill. In October 1993, he said, "We don't want to wound the plan. We want to kill it." The next month he asserted, "there's a political opportunity here," as defeating health care "can lay the groundwork for defeating Clintonism across the board" and "lay the agenda for advancing a conservative reform agenda in '95 and '96."[47]

Kristol also fired off a series of memos to congressional leaders. In December 1993 he pointed to Republican benefits in preventing a health-care bill from passing and defined the plan as "a serious political threat to the Republican Party."[48] Kristol called for "an aggressive and uncompromising counterstrategy to delegitimize the proposal." He predicted that if Clinton could achieve health-care reform, "It will relegitimize middle-class dependence for 'security' on government spending and regulation. It will revive the reputation of the party that spends and regulates, the Democrats, as the generous protector of middle-class interests. And it will at the same time strike a punishing blow against Republican claims to defend the middle class by restraining government." But if Clinton's plan were defeated, "it would be "a monumental setback for the president, and an incontestable piece of evidence that Democratic welfare-state liberalism remains firmly in retreat." As compromises were proposed, Kristol stood firm against any policies to establish broader coverage.[49]

But Clinton and health policy were not the only foci of conservatives' antigovernment strategic moves. During 1993, another book like the 1988 *The Imperial Congress*, displayed the decidedly anti-Congress mood of late 1980s–early 1990s conservatism and how its rhetoric about representation, legislating, and oversight was crafted to discredit and delegitimize the institution.

Eric Felten's *The Ruling Class: Inside the Imperial Congress*, was published as Republicans were taking aim at gaining the congressional majority. In the context of decades of Democratic rule, Felten employed populist language against the "ruling class," the "barons in an Imperial Congress." He wrote: "Washington has been poisoned with their machinations and our political system sickened as well."[50]

Although it built on and made explicit reference to *The Imperial Congress*, *The Ruling Class* was different in at least two respects. First, it was less academic and more for public consumption, and second, because Clinton became president the year before its publication, it was less overtly pro-presidency and more anti-Congress. Shifting from conservative 1980s pro-presidency views, Heritage Foundation president Edwin Feulner wrote that reestablishing, "a clear separation of powers may serve more to limit the executive than the legislature."[51]

Conservative critics complained that gerrymandering, congressional perquisites, and constituent casework insulated members of Congress, and hence the Democratic majority, from democratic checks. Felten claimed that a congressional "casework scam" had produced "a rigged and fraudulent system" in which "voters manage to like their own particular Member while holding the institution and the rest of its inmates in contempt."[52]

If Congress's representation of the people through elections was suspect, its legislative activities were on equally shaky ground. Committee and subcommittee hearings, the authors claimed, had degenerated into "showmanship"—a "Barnumocracy" wherein committee members clamored for television coverage and hearings were "used to embarrass administration officials."[53] Elected members focused on publicity rather than policy. All the while, the growth of congressional staff imperiled representation, because "Congressional staff run a shadow government."[54] Increased congressional oversight of the executive branch drove "good people out of public life."[55]

Demonstrating his New Democrat stance, in his 1994 State of the Union address, Clinton linked the domestic security achievable by reducing crime to economic opportunity and to personal responsibility, community empowerment, and achievement. In February 1994, Clinton staffers argued internally that the crime bill would assist the Democratic Party and "cement public perception" of Clinton as "tough on crime." The law increased funding for police on the streets, supported drug courts and boot camps, expanded the federal death penalty, and incorporated three-strikes provisions, drug treatment funding, an assault weapons ban, the Violence Against Women Act, and prevention programs. Noting that Democrats had done poorly when races focused on crime issues, they argued crime legislation would "help House Democrats in particular identify themselves with the issue of crime" and benefit gubernatorial candidates.[56]

Meanwhile, health-care reform was becoming increasingly bogged down. Moderate congressional Republicans sometimes offered compromises, but that became politically difficult. The Chamber of Commerce had advocated for health-care reform, in large part because of the costs involved in providing benefits, but turned against the plan in February 1994 after "politicians lobbied the lobbyists. Representative John Boehner, head of the Conservative

Opportunity Society in the House, told the Chamber's national leaders they had a duty to oppose the administration, and he and other House Republicans contacted local Chambers, urging them to disaffiliate from the national organization."[57] Other business groups announced opposition or support for a moderate alternative to the Clinton plan, the Cooper plan.[58]

Some groups consistently opposed health-care reform and lobbied elected officials, advertised to the public, and activated member organizations. The National Federation of Independent Business, which organized small business owners, consistently opposed the plan. Surreptitiously, the tobacco industry undermined the bill by channeling money to a group supporting single-payer health care "to attack the Clinton plan from the left and specifically attack the cigarette tax as falling disproportionately on the poor."[59] Health insurers organized local business owners to contact members of Congress with whom they had preexisting relationships and to write letters to local newspapers.[60]

The Health Insurance Association of America (HIAA), ran ads with actors playing a middle-aged, middle-income white couple named Harry and Louise. They combined vague invocations about needing "a better way" with anti-government rhetoric. In one ad, Louise said, "This plan forces us to buy our insurance through these new, mandatory government health alliances."

"Run by tens of thousands of new bureaucrats," Harry replied.

"Another billion-dollar bureaucracy," said Louise.

"You know, we just don't need government monopolies to get health coverage to everyone," said Harry.

Another HIAA ad referred to "untested government agencies run by tens of thousands of new bureaucrats."[61] Research is mixed about the ads' effectiveness, but the ads made their way into elite discourse.[62]

Health insurers also appealed to Republican legislators on electoral grounds. Bill McInturff, who did polling for them and the RNC, spoke with Republicans who had long worked on improving the health-care system. He "said, essentially, 'Hey, what do you want? Do you want a Republican majority in the Congress or do you want health care policy?' "[63]

Conservative movement groups organized. In February 1994, Kristol and the Christian Coalition's Ralph Reed announced an outreach plan with radio ads in forty congressional districts in eighteen states, newspaper advertising in Washington, D.C., and thirty other places, and postcards distributed to sixty thousand churches to generate thirty million cards arriving to congressional offices. The messages focused on abortion coverage, wait times for service, decreased quality, higher costs, and tax hikes.[64]

Another organization, the American Conservative Union, encouraged members to reach out to their representatives.[65] Raising the specter of an overly powerful government, the ACU warned that the bill would "abolish our free market approach to health care, and substitute it with a complete federal government takeover. That's called socialized medicine." The mailer confided, "I consider losing our freedoms to government a very frightening proposition, and I think you do also."[66] Whether soft or highly charged, distrust constituted a shared, frequently repeated message among nearly all Republicans and their allies.

While elected Democrats disagreed about policy, all recognized that many Americans had qualms about increasing and financing the federal government's role in health care.[67] On the right was Rep. Jim Cooper of Tennessee, who "was almost as skeptical of government bureaucracy as his Republican neighbors" and presented an alternative health policy.[68] On the left were single-payer advocates like Senator Paul Wellstone of Minnesota. Wellstone promoted single payer to get momentum for policy change[69] but acknowledged to administration officials that "trying to sell the Canadian plan to the public could mean 'being clobbered or accused of wanting to raise people's taxes.' "[70]

Government distrust bled over to Democrats, the health-care task force process, and Bill and Hillary Clinton. One effort starting in spring 1994 tied Whitewater—an Arkansas land deal under investigation, first by special prosecutor Robert Fiske and then by Kenneth Starr—to health care. Representative Lamar Smith of Texas sent a letter to all House Republicans encouraging them to make this link. Rush Limbaugh said, "Whitewater is about heath care," suggesting that people who had been backing health-care reform were taking Clinton's word on it but should question whether Clinton had integrity.[71] Republican Representative Joel Hefley of Colorado said Clinton "promised health care reform, but delivered an unworkable socialist health care scheme. He promised the most ethical White House in history, but has delivered the most scandal-ridden administration in memory."[72]

In working on the crime bill, Clinton's rhetoric and policy approach enabled him to build a coalition with black leaders, who supported the bill's efforts to make neighborhoods safe and to foster healthy local economies.[73] The legislations included some progressive efforts, such as drug courts, funding for community-based programs to prevent crime, the Violence Against Women Act, and an assault weapons ban. Still, black legislators' support was tested after the bill was modified in June 1994 to include more severe punishments, cut prevention funding, and remove the Racial Justice Act (RJA), which enabled people facing the death penalty to provide evidence of racial discrimination based on statistics for where they were sentenced.[74] Walking a tightrope, Clinton was advised that dropping the RJA "may be the only way to get the bill passed in the Senate" but "this course will produce severe damage to our relations with the [Congressional Black Caucus]—which is already incensed about the Crime Bill's 'tough' provisions."[75]

When the White House lobbied Congressional Black Caucus (CBC) members in July 1994, they stressed the president's commitment to new guidelines countering racial discrimination in the death penalty, the bill's potential to become more conservative if it initially failed, the prevention programs and the assault weapons ban, and the support of ten mayors of majority black cities.[76] These mayors wrote to Representative Kweisi Mfume (D-MD), the chair of the CBC, and argued that, while they supported the Racial Justice Act, taking it out should not "bring down the entire bill."[77] Ultimately, Mfume and a majority of the CBC voted for the bill, which passed 235–195 in the House of Representatives and 61–38 in the Senate in late August 1994.

As health-care reform struggled, the passage of the crime bill was a much-needed legislative victory for Democrats heading into the midterms. But while Clinton saw this legislation as a potential political winner, Republicans had been trying to undermine its electoral value. Upon its passage in the Senate, Minority Leader Bob Dole warned that "all the ludicrous, ridiculous items in this bill" would appear in campaign ads.[78]

Conservatives' use of crime, welfare, and urban issues had long evoked racial stereotypes,[79] and arguments against the crime bill were no exception. Republicans emphasized crime and criminals over policies meant to prevent crime and divert young offenders from jail. They characterized the bill as "soft on crime." They often mentioned one prevention program, "midnight basketball," community-based basketball leagues typically played at night. Republicans portrayed it as liberalism run amok, combining the coddling of criminals with welfare, federal overreach, and overspending. Sociologists Darren Wheelock and Douglas Hartmann contended that "the racial images and ideas associated with midnight basketball appear to have fit better with punitive Republican arguments about the nature of crime and criminals and how best to combat them."[80] Anti-government rhetoric was thus linked to racially charged language.

Race did not just figure in the midnight basketball debate when it came to crime, but was also implied in invocations of "welfare," "social workers," and "the war on poverty" and by language pitting "criminals" against "taxpayers" that fit into decades-old patterns of Republicans' race-coded welfare language. Representative Jerry Lewis (R-CA) characterized the crime bill as ineffective and wasteful, saying it was "soft on crime as the logic that billions of dollars for arts and crafts, self-esteem, dance, and midnight basketball programs deters murders, rapists and robbers. Americans want a crime bill that makes criminals extinct, not taxpayers."[81]

Other GOP legislators built on the messages that midnight basketball and programs like it epitomized the failed welfare state and, if provided, should only be funded and implemented by state and local governments. Representative John Duncan (R-TN) said, "Yes, to basketball, but no to turning even more hard-earned money over to Federal bureaucrats."[82] Representative Christopher Cox (R-CA) labeled the program part of "a prolonged failed liberal social experiment that has explained away and justified criminal behavior; indeed, subsidized it with ever more Federal programs. Like the war on poverty, the Great Society war on crime has failed."[83] And Newt Gingrich said, "When people dial 911, they want a policeman. They don't want a social worker."[84]

The derisive language Republicans used for prevention programs mirrored that used by an alliance of conservative groups led by the public relations firm Craig Shirley and Associates.[85] Jeering at the prevention provisions, they presented Clinton and Attorney General Janet Reno with "Crime Busters Action Kits," which, "symbolic of the social welfare provisions" of the bill, contained "a Mighty Morphins Power Rangers coloring book, toy handcuffs, Play-Doh, toy basketballs, paint brushes, and other 'get tough' crime fighting implements."[86] An ad narrated by Charlton Heston for the National Rifle Association said, "Almost a third of it, nearly 9 million dollars, is for social welfare programs. Dance lessons, arts and crafts, midnight basketball and kids programs."[87]

Some crime bill opponents portrayed the young people who would dribble, pass, and throw basketballs as already criminals. Michael Wilbon, a sportswriter for the *Washington Post*, noted that police officers and community leaders found that the program involved young people in healthy activities, prevented crime, and had been named a "point of light" by President George H. W. Bush. Yet Republicans claimed midnight basketball was "symbolic of what's wrong with President Clinton's crime bill."[88]

In promoting prisons, evoking suspicion of government assistance, and employing racialized language, conservatives sought policy and electoral benefits. As a Clinton White House study put it, the treatment of the crime bill reflected the same strategic requisites as health-care reform—"a decision not to give the President any victories, for if they did not, they could potentially gain significantly at the midterm elections."[89]

While the crime bill passed, its approach was tarnished by mockery from the right and disappointment from the left. Through media rhetoric and "thirty-second spots," Republicans lampooned it as weak, even though years later the bill would be widely regarded as overly punitive.

And then, in September 1994, Democrats conceded health-care reform without a vote. Clinton's health-care effort reform had failed.

Democrats later attributed the failure to unfair portraits of the Clinton plan that played into public distrust of government. According to a retrospective prepared by the first lady's office, the bill had been repeatedly mischaracterized.[90] Although the bill did not promote "big government" and was not "overly ambitious" compared to its more progressive alternatives, that is how "it was how it was portrayed to the American people by opponents of reform, as 'bureaucratic social engineering.'" This information spread to the public, so that "at town hall meetings, angry people would state their vociferous opposition to the Clinton plan, waving mailings that claimed the plan would have the government taking over and running all the hospitals in the country."[91] An October 1994 report on polling found that one of the most common responses in focus groups was, "We just didn't know enough and we got scared." According to the report, "Much of what the public thought they knew was in fact wrong, a function both of deliberately spread mis- and disinformation and of natural assumptions by the public, on the basis of their cynicism and mistrust in government."[92] Reform opponents had successfully used the climate of distrust to characterize Clinton's plan as a government takeover. The White House provided insufficient attention and resources to bring together and mobilize a progressive, pro-reform coalition to work with a president they did not fully trust.[93]

Ironically, public disappointment that government could not deliver health-care reform helped reform opponents in the 1994 congressional elections.

Americans had wanted government to improve the health-care system, even as many were afraid that the Clinton plan made government too large. An October White House report presaged that in the 1994 midterms, congressional Democrats would be the focus of public unhappiness with government. Their specific target was not President Clinton, who they saw as earnestly trying but held back by the "old guard" and "entrenched politicians" in Congress. Instead, there was "a belief among participants that longevity and tenure in office leads to corruption and pursuit of self-interest rather than the power to get things done." Distrust of government thwarted health policy, but this failure only created more distrust. As political strategist Stanley Greenberg put it, Republicans' electoral success was "less about big government than it was about the failure of the Democrats to be able to succeed, perform, to make change in something that really mattered to people."[94]

If trust in government was declining even as Clinton took office, according to Deputy Assistant to the President for Health Policy Chris Jennings, it was only after the health bill was defeated that the president recognized "the discomfort and distrust that the public at large had about government in '93 and '94." They "didn't fully understand the impact of twelve years of Republicans in office, basically criticizing everything government does, questioning its ability to respond in a positive way to public needs."[95] Republicans did understand, however, and they were preparing to deploy distrust in their electoral strategies.

THE CONTRACT WITH AMERICA

"To say that the electorate is angry would be like saying that the ocean is wet." So communications consultant Frank Luntz told House GOP leaders just two months before the 1994 elections. "Voters in general, and our swing voters in particular," he said, "have simply ceased to believe that anything good can come out of Washington."[96]

After halting Clinton's health-care legislation and weakening the political benefit of the crime bill, congressional Republicans looked to capitalize on public anger and the historical pattern that the president's party loses seats at midterm. Riding 1994's wave of antipathy, GOP elites and the angry public fed off one another. Republican leaders discovered—according to reporters Dan Balz and Ronald Brownstein—that "it was virtually impossible to overreach in attacking Washington or the federal government" and that they were "continually prodded to greater militance" by their base.[97]

A stalwart of the Reagan Revolution, Gingrich now fancied himself its torchbearer. The principal architect of the next wave of Reaganism, Gingrich thought that building a House Republican majority required a renewed focus on dismantling the national state and programs built since the New Deal and replacing FDR's "liberal welfare state" with a "conservative opportunity society." Each word in Gingrich's phrase contrasts with FDR's creation.

In late September 1994, just weeks before the midterms, nearly all Republican House candidates signed on to a document called the Contract with America. When the Contract with America emerged, it was a document designed for Republican campaigns to "transform the way Congress works" and end "government that is too big, too intrusive, and too easy with the public's money."[98] Taking aim at the entirety of left-wing politics Clinton purportedly represented, it said, "It is impossible to take the Great Society structure of bureaucracy, the redistributionist model of how wealth is acquired, and the counterculture value system that now permeates the way we deal with the poor, and have any hope of fixing them."[99] Put simply, it was a means of accomplishing Gingrich's long-standing hope to "replace the welfare state."[100]

Such anti-government messaging was embedded in the Contract from its earliest stages of development. At its 1993 messaging conference at Princeton, the Republican leadership had made a first pass at the Contract's focus and "vision of a smaller government" with "three main goals—cutting taxes, reducing the deficit, and increasing defense spending."[101] At a similar conference in Salisbury, Maryland, Republicans fleshed out this vision into principles largely related to the GOP's anti-statist views: "individual liberty, economic opportunity, limited government, personal responsibility, [and] security at home and abroad."[102]

At Princeton and Salisbury and beyond, the GOP elite used refined opinion polling and focus group technologies to gauge and seize on public anger.[103] With these tools, the GOP could test which words and arguments most likely resonated with a restive public suspicious of government and the politicians in it. When he helped plan the Contract with America, Luntz counseled Republicans to separate themselves from "the rest of Washington" and argue that they were for "the middle class" and grasped people's "hopes and fears." Candidates should tell voters that "Republicans trust you."[104]

Besides Republicans conveying their trust in the American people, the Contract with America explicitly presumed a lack of public trust when it outlined the need for "major reforms, aimed at restoring the faith and trust of the American people in their government."[105] The Contract was presented as "an instrument" that could "restore the bonds of trust between the people and their elected representatives."[106]

Mobilizing public distrust in Congress and government was at the core of the Contract's aims. Thinking the Contract "primarily a communications document,"[107] GOP planners saw it as an electoral vehicle that seized on public anger to galvanize Republican unity while also attracting Ross Perot supporters. The Contract lambasted Congress and took aim at the federal government, which, Republicans contended, threatened seniors, tied small businesses in "bureaucratic red tape," and put families "under attack."[108] In addition to institutional changes such as term limits, a balanced budget amendment, and cuts to congressional staff, it included punitive crime and welfare bills, tax cuts, and limits on regulations and liability lawsuits. Unifying conservatives, the Contract became an electoral vehicle to undermine trust in government and win Congress.

The strategies and rhetoric of the "leave us alone" coalition had a new megaphone. With Rush Limbaugh ascendant, talk radio galvanized anti-elite conservative voices, even though conservative elites amplified them.[109] Seizing what one Republican press staffer called "a singular moment [when] talk radio was both powerful in politics and overwhelmingly on our side,"[110] House Republican leaders established a program called "Talk Right" that routinely sent GOP talking points on current issues to talk radio programs and established a booking operation for House Republicans.[111] More distrustful but "less indifferent" about politics than radio non-listeners and listeners to liberal or moderate talk radio, Limbaugh listeners were more politically active and had a higher sense of political efficacy. Distrustful and active, they fit the mold of sociologist William Gamson's "optimum combination for political mobilization."[112]

The anti-Clinton, anti-Washington sentiments united a potentially quarrelsome GOP coalition and unified the House Republican Conference around its Contract with America. The singular emphasis in the construction of the Contract was party unity. Although it included some issues obvious to leadership, there was a two-stage process for compiling items. First, the leaders submitted surveys to House Republicans and Republican House candidates to determine consensus issues. Second, the issues that rose to the top were poll tested; those that enjoyed 60 or 70 percent approval were included. Also, item language was honed through extensive public opinion testing,[113] giving the Contract with America both the potential to unify a would-be GOP majority and capture non-Republican support.

Picking up on a decade's worth of conservative complaints about Congress, the Contract promised a series of House reforms to vote on the first day of the Congress. Among other things, these reforms would compel Congress to live under the laws it passed, audit the House books, and cut the congressional budget and staff. On the heels of recent congressional scandals, these congressional reform aspects of the Contract "aimed at restoring the faith and trust of the American people in their government."[114] Internal Republican planning documents confirmed a sense that riding a wave of public dissatisfaction could reap benefits. After conducting focus groups on the Contract, the Tarrance Group found that focus group participants complained that Congress and its members were "no longer accountable for their actions."[115]

The Contract assailed government more generally. Proposals to shrink government—promises of a balanced budget, welfare reform, deregulation, tort reform, term limits, and tax cuts—dominated the Contract while standing alongside proposals to expand government through anti-crime legislation and stronger national defense.[116] The GOP's antiregulatory agenda, on which some believed George H. W. Bush had softened, was also prominent in the Contract and would continue to be part of the conservative cause thereafter.[117] As Dick Armey and John Boehner wrote to colleagues in late December 1994, "The Contract is a comprehensive plan to reform nearly every aspect of government."[118]

But consider, too, what was not in the Contract. Social issues that might appeal to Christian conservatives and to the NRA were muted, because they were deemed divisive and potentially damaging to the Contract's appeal to swing voters. As Tony Blankley put it, social issues would "cloud the clarity of our message" just as a proposed plank to repeal the assault weapons ban was "too controversial" for inclusion.[119] When social conservatives pushed a "family values" agenda item into the Contract, after tense meetings with GOP leaders, it was for a child tax credit, an issue that had the advantage of being both "pro-family" and "anti-tax."[120] But few other social issues made the cut. As reporter Major Garrett summarized it, "no gun control, no abortion, no school prayer."[121]

Government was defined as anti-family. Limiting the size of government, Republicans argued, would "take money out of the pockets of Washington bureaucrats and [put it] back into the pockets of America's families."[122] In suggesting "the values of the family are under attack from all sides—from the media, from the education establishment, from big government," partisanship mattered. Democrats put "government first"; the GOP would "put families first."[123]

Touting the possibility of taking over the House for the first time in forty years, Republican leaders committed each component of the "leave us alone" coalition to support the whole Contract, not just its pet projects. This unified the conservative elite coalition to support the contract and expanded the coalition of public support needed to pass the agenda.[124] As Armey and Boehner told their colleagues, the leadership created a "core coordinating group" of elite coalition allies, "those fully committed to the Contract as a whole" who "have 'grass roots armies' to mobilize."[125]

If it takes grand strategy to produce or complete a realignment and to sustain a broad party coalition, elections are won or lost by the ability to activate and mobilize constituencies. As the midterms approached, capitalizing on anti-government sentiment stirred the Republican base, helping those employing the strategy to garner electoral success. Nigel Ashford described the "diverse range of constituencies"—the "community of the disaffected"—that Republicans mobilized through the Contract: "the Christian Right, the Perotistas, small business, anti-tax groups, the term limits movement, property rights groups and the gun lobby."[126]

The list also included a large bloc of swing voters who had voted for Ross Perot in 1992. Securing the Perot voter was one aim of the Contract organizers, and to do so they adopted tenets of the Perot agenda, particularly balanced budgets and term limits.[127] Describing these Perot voters, as "hostile" as they were, as "one of the keys" to winning, Gingrich was aware of the difficulties of using public anger to mobilize without turning them off altogether, saying Republicans knew Perot voters "were mad at Congress, but knew they were also generally mad at politicians and were likely to be turned off by a negative campaign."[128]

Recounting a focus group of Perot voters, Luntz (who had worked for Perot's 1992 campaign) observed, "None had anything nice to say about Bill Clinton, Congress, or either of the political parties. In fact, they were literally the most negative, hostile voters I have ever assembled for a focus group."[129] Reaching out to them by cultivating their ire might also open the door to persuading them on other issues. Think of a balanced budget as an "attention-getting device," Dick Armey proposed. "If you're anxious about the deficit, then let me use your anxiety to cut the size of the government."[130]

It was the careful construction of the Contract—with its focus on smaller government and governmental reform and its aversion to social issues—that helped the GOP unite conservatives and swing Perot voters around a common enemy: the federal government.[131] The Contract's framing, including its claim that Republicans wished voters to throw them out if they did not live up to their promises, was designed to "capitalize . . . on the voters' disgust with 'politics as usual' in Washington."[132] Contract allies like the Christian Coalition and the NRA mobilized voters, as did "the angry diatribes of talk radio hosts."[133] These efforts reshaped the electorate; conservatives went from 30 percent of voters in 1992 to 38 percent in 1994, and "religious conservatives" from 24 percent to 33 percent.[134]

The anger voters felt in 1994, stoked by the Contract and GOP strategy, produced a tidal wave. The Democrats lost fifty-four House seats and eight Senate seats—and with them, they lost majority control of both chambers, the House for the first time since 1954.

Clinton's policy failures, a labor movement discouraged by Clinton's passage of the North American Free Trade Agreement, and Clinton's personal scandals contributed to Americans' sense that government did not work. The inability to pass health-care reform was a linchpin, along with an ambivalent Clinton coalition that did not entirely trust the New Democrat vision, distrust of Clinton, and unresolved anger on the right and among Perot voters. It did not help that there was more than a little mistrust of the Democratic Congress, particularly after it had controlled the House for four decades.

For all their celebration of the communications and electoral value of the Contract, Republicans understood that its underlying rationale was more than just anti-Clinton, it was anti-government. Framing the conflict as Gingrich outlined in his plan to take over the majority years before, Republicans claimed that the choice "was actually about some fairly big ideas—Which direction do you want to go in?—and those who argued for counterculture values, bigger government, redistributionist economics, and bureaucracies deciding how you should spend your money, were on the losing end in virtually every part of the country."[135]

The "clear undeniable message" that voters delivered, according to GOP leaders, was based around how Democrats and Republicans "envisioned the role of government in their lives."[136] As one Republican staffer put it, "The important thing is to define to the American people what the election results mean—and this election was about the issue of big government."[137] Not only did it disproportionately mobilize conservative groups, angered by the first years of the Clinton presidency, it also appealed to Perot supporters. Citing GOP gains with working-class and reformist Perot voters, Luntz said, "That means the Contract worked."[138]

THE REPUBLICAN REVOLUTION

Republicans now controlled both chambers of Congress and the first hundred days of the 104th Congress saw some of the most extraordinary productivity and unity Republicans ever demonstrated. As Gingrich ally Vin Weber put it, the Contract with America was "a device for managing the first six months."[139]

United they were. House Republicans brought every Contract item up for a vote, passed most of its provisions, and several items became law. Intraparty unity vote scores in Congress reached heights that had not been seen in years. One Gingrich staffer claimed it was "the only way to govern . . . we couldn't have been as cohesive as we were without [the Contract]."[140]

Having held votes on all of the Contract's provisions in the first hundred days as advertised, House Republicans could run for reelection having lived up to their promises. The National Republican Campaign Committee (NRCC) bragged that the "Contract with America looked beyond the Washington-based solutions that have worsened the problems they were meant to solve."[141]

Emboldened, Republican members were eager to press their advantage. Some of the 1994 Republican class began to report having been "very disappointed" that Reagan's budget-cutting performance did not meet his anti-government rhetoric.[142] Soon they wanted "to go 'beyond Reagan,' to bring his priorities of less government, a strong America and traditional morality into new spheres."[143] In his 1995 book *To Renew America*, Gingrich used florid moral terms, blaming the liberal welfare state for grave damage.[144] Welfare deprived youth "of their God-given rights to life, liberty, and the pursuit of happiness" by trapping them in a "welfare bureaucracy."

Personalizing anti-government outrage, Gingrich asked critics "to imagine that their children were the ones dying on the evening news."[145]

With an eye toward the federal budget and another rhetorical nod toward the neglected social conservative wing, the NRCC prepared House Republicans for an April recess, arming them with the argument that balancing the budget was a "moral responsibility" to be achieved "for our children's sake."[146] Among the talking points were broadsides against welfare and centralized federal bureaucracy.[147] Connecting anti-statism with social issues, Republicans claimed that by "reducing government's influence," the Contract "alters the relationship between American families and government."[148]

Still, for all their anti-Washington talk, the GOP leadership was hard at work making Washington their own. Gingrich was working the elite press, espousing conservative causes with nationally televised daily press conferences and more media appearances than any Speaker of the House in history.[149] Majority Whip Tom DeLay organized and led Project Relief, an antiregulatory "coalition of more than three hundred business and other lobby groups as well as individuals that wanted regulations rolled back." DeLay also devised his "K Street Strategy," which required D.C. lobbyists to hire Republicans to deal with House leadership.[150] Meanwhile conference chairman John Boehner headed up the "Thursday Group" of business groups and conservative organizations to persuade members by pressuring them from outside Congress.[151] Their war with government was anything but anti-elite.

After they won control of the very institutions they had maligned, conservatives shifted course on separation of powers rhetoric.[152] Against the admonitions of the 1980s Meese Justice Department report—to "take the longer-term view of separation of powers" and "Republican control of Congress would be no reason to relax our interpretation of the Constitution's requirements on separation of powers,"[153] conservatives flipped once again, becoming pro-Congress on separation of powers.

A foot soldier in the Reagan Revolution and now a top commander, Newt Gingrich marched in both directions for the conservative cause. As a founder of the COS, head of GOPAC, and the lead opponent of decades of Democratic rule of Congress, Gingrich developed and publicized broadsides against congressional power. In his 1988 foreword to *The Imperial Congress*, Gingrich, a former history professor, referenced the *Federalist*

Papers and argued that the Founders "tried to insure against the rise of an imperial Congress."[154] In 1988 Gingrich charged that, counter to the Framers' vision, Congress had become unrepresentative, arrogant, and corrupt and "at stake is the liberty of the American public."[155]

But once he was Speaker, Gingrich saw the separation of powers and the *Federalist Papers* differently. In early 1995, he told a group of congressional scholars at the Library of Congress that "as we leave the Cold War era, you're going to see a reassertion of Congressional initiative" pursuant to "the natural pattern" that "in peacetime" the *Federalist Papers* holds a "bias toward the legislative branch." Elaborating, he said, "The very dispersion of the power in the legislative branch will protect freedom and, therefore, over time, we have greater freedom because of the legislative branch than we would by putting our faith in an elected temporary kingship."[156] Seemingly referring to James Madison's observation that "in republican government, the legislative authority necessarily predominates," Gingrich and other Republicans had read this starkly differently in the 1980s and early 1990s, when Democrats controlled Congress.

Once in power and apparently no longer worried about an imperial Congress, Republicans went to work to employ the powers they previously decried. Rather than correct Congress's "imperial" tendencies, Republicans expanded those tendencies and sought to govern from Congress. The Democratic president was left, for some time at least, to proclaim the mere "relevance" of his office, in part because Clinton was "willing to work with the Republicans."[157]

The Gingrich-led Republican Congress of the 1990s became a tour-de-force of congressional power versus the Clinton White House. Political scientist William F. Connelly Jr. wrote that Gingrich was "a legislative supremacist" who "clearly acted as if the center of political gravity should reside in Congress" and that during Gingrich's speakership the GOP Congress "came to dominate the agenda-setting function in American politics."[158] Connelly called Gingrich's expansion of Congress's role after his long-standing critiques of the institution under the Democrats "ironic" and compared Gingrich to " 'Czar' Cannon," arguably the most powerful Speaker of the House in American history because Gingrich sought to recreate "congressional government."[159]

Congressional Republicans began to make robust use of oversight mechanisms, despite erstwhile statements of Constitution-based "principles" to the contrary. Republicans had complained in their 1992 platform that, under Democrats, congressional "committee hearings are no longer for fact-finding; they are political sideshows."[160] Once party control reversed, Republicans used oversight to sway public opinion.

In fact, away from public gaze, the House GOP had planned to make the most of committee hearings if it won the majority. In 1993, the House Republican Conference began a project for "Enhanced Oversight of the Clinton Administration," which would train members and staff on "all aspects of effective oversight" of the administration. This included "filing FOIA requests, working with the press, using investigative tools, building coalitions, and understanding ethics rules and legal tools on our side," in an effort to "systematically scrutinize" executive branch personnel and activities.[161]

An internal GOP leadership document from the summer of 1994 discussed using hearings to "expose and punish" the consequences of Democratic rule, including exposing the "bad people and their bad policies." Emphasizing that the focus would be on "yes, bad people, not just people with whom we disagree," Republicans planned "month after shocking month" of putting Democrats "on trial" in what they called "our Nuremberg."[162]

Once in the majority, Republicans abandoned their purported concerns about the "showmanship" and "Barnumocracy" with which they had charged Democrats. In 1995, the Conference offered "training sessions" for members and staff dubbed the "Oversight Institute: Guarding the Public Trust."[163] In this war with government, what mattered to Republicans was the institutional ground they held to wage battles with political opponents.

Almost as dramatic were GOP efforts to continue to legislate their revolution. An important political consequence of the Contract's design— selecting the issues that most unified Republicans and were most popular elsewhere—was that the party had front-loaded those issues, placing them as far away from the next election as possible. Leftover issues were not only more divisive and less broadly supported, but also entailed the more difficult policy challenge of meeting commitments while balancing the budget, a feat that had eluded Ronald Reagan and for which George H. W. Bush had paid a price at Gingrich's hands in 1990.[164]

As Republicans tried to pivot from the Contract's script to more wide-ranging efforts at "remaking the federal government and balancing the budget by 2002," the stakes were laid bare. Republican leadership staff offered message coaching for town hall meetings in congressional districts, a way to "frame our debate as a campaign to change a Washington government that is leaving a legacy of fiscal and moral bankruptcy for our children."[165] Balancing the budget was difficult enough in the George H. W. Bush approach, with tax increases. With Republican tax cuts requiring reductions from significant budget areas, it would be even harder.

By late 1995, Republicans took a politically dangerous pass at "reforming" Medicare and by year's end were locked in budget negotiations with Clinton. These eventually stalled and government shut down. Public opinion turned against Republicans, blaming the shutdown on their overreach. Much like Reagan, with his politically disastrous attempt to reform Social Security in 1981, Gingrich and House Republicans found there were limits to cutting government, no matter how well poll tested.[166] Although "reforming" Medicare to the tune of $270 billion in cuts was needed for balancing the budget while cutting taxes, Republicans paid a steep political price for the attempt. Still, Gingrich led the fight in the House to bring the deficit to zero in seven years. Both efforts hurt Republicans in the 1996 elections.[167]

As the elections approached, Republicans continued their anti-government rhetoric, though with a softer tone, cowed by their shutdown failure and voter concerns over Medicare. Preparing Republicans with "Words that Work," Frank Luntz counseled, "We need to restore COMMON SENSE to government . . . After all, who knows better about what each community needs, a local leader or a Washington Bureaucrat?"[168] Considerably less "revolutionary" in tone than in 1994, this more measured approach to reform was nevertheless based squarely on distrust of distant government in Washington. The House Republicans' strategic plan for 1996 defined the election as "a choice between America and Washington; a compassionate America vs. a well-meaning but failed effort to create a compassionate bureaucracy."[169]

The GOP's anti-government rhetoric, toned down since 1994, aimed to win by mobilizing the base and appealing to swing voters, some of whom had cooled on the "revolution," and many more of whom were likely to turn out in the presidential year. For the base, Rush Limbaugh demonized Clinton and the Democrats in Washington, an exercise in "identity building and enemy creation" designed to rouse passions through the use of "moral outrage" to "spur political engagement."[170]

But Republican pollsters advised that the revolution's excessiveness and tone was losing its appeal. Independents and Perot voters were frustrated.

As pollster Glen Bolger reported, "Swing voters do not believe that reform is happening, and they do not believe in the Revolution."[171]

This put Clinton in a favorable position for reelection.

If Clinton initially governed more liberally than his New Democrat rhetoric promised, he famously pronounced in January 1996 that "the era of big government is over." While softening that proclamation with the proviso that America "cannot go back to the time when our citizens were left to fend for themselves," Clinton's return to the New Democrat philosophy had at least faint echoes of Reagan's limited government "reconstruction" of America. Said Clinton, "We know big government does not have all the answers. We know, and we have worked to give the American people a smaller, less bureaucratic government in Washington."[172]

Clinton returned to his New Democrat script in time for the reelection campaign, and, after vetoing two welfare reform bills, Clinton signed one in August 1996, dismaying progressives and undermining the safety net. But as Clinton pollster Mark Penn saw it, "Clinton won the election because on every issue that the Republicans hoped to dominate—balancing the budget, welfare, crime, immigration, and taxes—Clinton staked out a centrist position early on."[173] Clinton's focus on symbolic issues concerning the family and American culture helped him to maintain distance over Dole, while Republicans were put on the defensive over Medicare and their perceived overreach.[174]

Even as it opened the door to Clinton's reelection in 1996, the Republican Revolution's historic 104th Congress was an apex of legislative power in American separation of powers politics. Congressional power and conflict with the executive branch were not only high by historical standards but were notable, given past conservative concerns over the "imperial" Congress, particularly concerns once aired by the Speaker himself.

BEYOND THE REVOLUTION

Although Republican congressional majorities were spared in 1996, Clinton's reelection was a sign that America was not ready for the revolution Republicans had promised. While some Republicans tried to blame Bob Dole's "issue-less and colourless campaign,"[175] RNC chairman Haley Barbour used the results of a postelection national survey to argue to congressional leaders that Clinton's victory resulted from Clinton diminishing "the Republican advantage on issues like balancing the budget, fighting crime and drugs, reducing government waste and protecting families from the encroachment of moral decay."[176]

Behind the scenes, even Gingrich and Representative Dick Armey seemed convinced they should soften their anti-government messages, becoming more "reformist" than "revolutionary." Gingrich and Armey returned to orthodoxy—lower taxes, less regulation, and a smaller government—and searched for government reform and anti-government stances to unify the coalition.

At the top of the list was taxes. Not only was raising taxes apostasy for congressional Republicans, but Grover Norquist's Americans for Tax Reform was building a grassroots anti-tax movement in the states and compelling an increasing number of elected Republicans to take the ATR pledge that they would not support tax hikes.[177] For years to come, taxes— much more than any matter of spending or budget balance—would be the consistent issue that unified the GOP. It certainly seemed promising for the House GOP, who were hoping to reignite a distrustful public in 1997. Writing to Armey just before April 15, Frank Luntz noted that "tempers flare" around tax day and that GOP messaging could seize that moment when "the call for government reform is clarion . . . and public enemy number one is the tax code."[178] Months later, Luntz advised Republicans that tax reform "is part of a larger story of a greater vision you need to tell."[179]

Believing that, even after Clinton's reelection, Republicans could achieve a lasting party realignment, GOPAC went back to work (as it had for over a decade at this point) on training candidates to speak with the press and the public. Delivering their message of "less taxes and more freedom" could help Republicans win big, reaching "a 62 percent governing majority similar to Roosevelt's New Deal Democrats," they thought. Gaining that congressional majority and the presidency and keeping it over time were to be built electorally around distrust and could lead to policy change.[180]

But upending the policy course of the New Deal and Great Society with a persistent conservative governing majority eluded Republicans. However angry they were, Americans would only follow the GOP so far. Another politically damaging impasse occurred in 1997 when Republicans held up relief to flood victims over provisions precluding government shutdowns and disallowing sampling techniques for the U.S. Census.[181] After the Christmas 1995 government shutdown and Medicare reform efforts, this became the third showdown with Clinton that Republicans misjudged. They had once again underestimated how necessary most Americans—their distrust notwithstanding—viewed the federal government to be.

Perhaps the best hope the GOP had was to count on a historic pattern: the party of the sitting president tends to lose seats in the second midterm election. Gingrich pinned his hopes to the 1998 elections a little more than a year out. He sought a "twenty-seat pick-up" by working to "pick our legislative fights so we win them (and define 'win')" while uniting the conference. No doubt this involved claiming credit for how the contract had "changed Washington" and the size, scope, cost, and accountability of government since 1994.[182]

But the Republican House leadership was not united. Armey began to distinguish himself from Gingrich. Armey planned to deliver a series of speeches on "freedom and responsibility," a set of views that became an orienting force for FreedomWorks, which later developed as a major Koch brothers–funded Tea Party organization during Barack Obama's presidency.[183]

Building a small-government and "reformist" message, Armey planned, for example, to promote reforms of the FDA with the message that Republicans "are bringing long-overdue relief to millions of Americans who have been kept from life-saving drugs and technologies by callous, mindless bureaucratic obstacles at FDA."[184] Armey championed flatter (and outright flat) tax proposals appealing to the anti-tax wing. He also devised what he called a "property rights agenda," contrasting property owners' rights with environmentalists and "UN bureaucrats." Armey's target audience was the "Western and Conservative press," and he aimed to "whip up conservative talk shows as each bill approaches House floor."[185]

With Armey on point, the Republican leadership launched a "long term government accountability project" in 1997 and expanded it in 1998 into a "public campaign targeting waste, fraud and error." The idea was to "convince the public that our goal is a smaller, smarter, common sense government that can be restrained with limited taxes."[186] Coordinating oversight by committee chairs, Armey hoped to build a record for elections in 1998. Staff would produce materials to coordinate House Republican messages on accountability and less government.[187] Behind the scenes, Armey's staff was clear that the purpose, even after the elections, was public relations ("Use this memo—not as a policy wonk memo—but strictly as a communications opportunity"). This was an attempt to stoke public ire at the federal government even as Republicans continued to hold the House majority, suggesting that "the archenemy, the man with the black hat, the sinister man twirling his long mustache, should be Washington bureaucrats—not Washington Congressmen—and definitely not the Republican Party."[188]

Meanwhile, Gingrich was polishing up his grand vision for the next wave of Republicanism. That agenda came to be known as "Goals for a Generation."[189] Months before unveiling it, Republicans poll tested four items, asking respondents what impression they would have of a Republican congressional candidate who proposed "expanding efforts to save children from failing schools, drugs, and crime, allowing people to control and invest their own Social Security Retirement, and capping the maximum total tax burden at 25 percent of your income?" The results were very encouraging; even registered Democrats indicated majority support. Gingrich handwrote to staff: "This is *very* strong support and means maniacal repetition will yield positive results."[190]

Before the release of the Starr Report on Clinton's relationship with Monica Lewinsky and his statements about it (which, with the push for impeachment, would dominate GOP messaging), articulating the "Goals for a Generation" was the GOP plan for the 1998 midterms. With faint echoes of the messages that had driven the Contract, the Republicans' "communications playbook" stressed government supporting "faith, family, personal freedom, and responsibility."[191]

With Clinton in the White House, in 1998 conservatives were far less concerned than they had been in the Reagan years about how wide-ranging special counsel investigations and congressional encroachments hampered the proper functioning of executive power. Gone, too, for the time being, was the GOP's commitment to restraining Congress and empowering the presidency.

Ultimately, Republicans would unify around both the small government goals and the investigation and impeachment of Bill Clinton for Clinton misleading legal authorities about a sexual affair. But they would pay a price. Republicans lost five House seats in the 1998 midterms, and in response to an emerging challenge within the Republican Conference, Gingrich resigned from Congress and the speakership.

The Clinton years marked a leap in the conservative promotion and use of distrust of government. While anger and frustration typified the early

1990s electorate that produced the Republicans' 1994 victory, Republicans waged a war with government to stoke that sentiment.

Without any levers of government in the first two years of Bill Clinton's presidency, Republicans built coalitions and used public opinion technologies to develop messages to unify a broad coalition of conservatives and independents. Newt Gingrich and other Republican leaders were highly focused and strategic and, for a time, successful. While Republicans increasingly had to be pro-life or to give lip service to federal budget deficits to survive electorally, they had to be anti-tax and opposed to "big government" even more. Leaders and insiders employed this messaging to mobilize the base, unify the "leave us alone" coalition, attract Perot voters, and give the GOP a message reinforcing their criticisms of Bill Clinton.

During the Clinton years the benefits of the strategic use of distrust in government reached their peak in the 1994 elections, as important a moment in modern conservatism as any since Reagan's election in 1980. On the eve of November 1994, when it looked increasingly likely that their efforts to build the first Republican House majority since the 1950s would bear fruit, behind the scenes the House Republican leadership thought in broad historical terms, anticipating the retrenchment of the New Deal government that they had pursued for decades. In a memo to his boss, Dick Armey's chief of staff Kerry Knott predicted the election would "herald the biggest political shift since the 1930s." Because the election was "fought over the size and scope of the federal government," winning both houses of Congress would mean "the American people will have overwhelmingly chosen our side." Knott concluded, "A hundred years from now, historians may look back and see this election as the real beginning of the Republican counterrevolution."[192]

Emboldened, GOP leaders pressed the case against government with sometimes disastrous political consequences. Within a year of winning their congressional majorities, the GOP was blamed for the Christmas federal shutdown and for seeking to "reform" Medicare. Bill Clinton used these weak points to reemerge as the defender of popular government programs. In this era, Republicans were never able to recreate the angry moment of 1994 when trying to drum up public outrage over taxes and regulation. The split decision of the 1996 elections, which produced the reelection of both Clinton and Republican congressional majorities, followed a New Democrat return to welfare reform and eventually led to bipartisan collaboration between Clinton and Republicans that balanced the budget and even created a surplus by decade's end.

The Republican war with government had yielded some political successes. Political scientists Hacker and Pierson argue that, by the late twentieth century, anti-government Randians had taken over the GOP with the aim of undermining government altogether. "Trust but verify," they say, became "distrust and defeat."[193]

But in the end, realignment eluded the Republicans. If there was "persistent hostility toward government," internal polling revealed again that public support for individual programs and issue areas was consistently higher than was support for the government in general.[194] After Republicans killed Clinton's health-care reform in 1994, Clinton worked to expand health care for low-income children and add other safeguards. Toward the end of the millennium, the GOP struggled to toe the line where their weaponized anti-government rhetoric mobilized their base without threatening to drive off middle-of-the-road voters.

Chapter Five

"WE'RE ALL MAD HERE"

The Tea Party and the Obama Era

In 2012, on a stop in the swing state of Virginia during his reelection campaign, Barack Obama spoke about government support for entrepreneurship. After calling for funding infrastructure, job training, and education and explaining why he rejected the Republican emphasis on cutting taxes and slashing regulations, Obama told his audience that no one's success came from his or her efforts alone. He explained, "If you were successful, somebody along the line gave you some help. There was a great teacher somewhere in your life. Somebody helped to create this unbelievable American system that we have that allowed you to thrive. Somebody invested in roads and bridges. If you've got a business—you didn't build that. Somebody else made that happen . . . The point is, is that when we succeed, we succeed because of our individual initiative—but also because we do things together."[1]

Republicans immediately pounced on one phrase: "You didn't build that." Presidential candidate Mitt Romney called Obama's remarks "insulting to every entrepreneur, every innovator in America." He continued: "I tell you this. I'm convinced that he wants Americans to be ashamed of success."[2] Later that summer, Obama's statement was featured in attacks at the Republican National Convention, where "We Built It" became a daily theme.[3] Vice-presidential candidate Paul Ryan talked about how small businesspeople established and ran their operations and said, "After all that work, and in a bad economy, it sure doesn't help to hear from their president that government gets the credit. What they deserve to hear is the truth: Yes, you did build that."[4]

As reporter Aaron Blake observed, the government programs Obama espoused were "broadly popular," yet "Republicans have gotten great mileage out of labeling Democrats as big-government liberals and tax-raisers over the past few decades."[5] Throughout the Obama era, Republicans' campaign messaging—in 2010, 2012, and 2014—fit the same pattern: undermining Obama's policies and strategically promoting distrust in government.

The circumstances that gave rise to Obama's presidency and his handling of health-care and economic matters demonstrate the power—but also the limits—of strategically promoting distrust. Obama came to the presidency in 2009 during a severe economic recession, succeeding George W. Bush, a two-term Republican president who left office with low approval ratings—32 percent in his last Gallup poll, after a low of 25 percent before the 2008 election. Support for Bush surged after the September 11, 2001, terrorist attacks, fell, then enjoyed an uptick after the 2003 launch of the Iraq War. After winning reelection in 2004, his standing was undermined the very next year by his effort to partially privatize Social Security and his administration's inept response to Hurricane Katrina.

Bush's perceived callousness and administrative incompetence hurt his approval rating, which goes to show that Americans support a robust government role at some times and in some matters. Democrats gained seats in the House of Representatives and the Senate in the 2006 midterms, and this trend carried into the 2008 presidential election. Amid the 2008 economic meltdown, Senator John McCain and Alaska governor Sarah Palin ran on the GOP ticket, but they could not overcome the tide of unhappiness from the Bush years.

Obama mobilized new voters around a direction rooted in a shared sense of American values, economic opportunity, and quests for equality and change. Offering "hope" and a new direction where government was called upon to address a severe financial crisis and to bail out ailing industries, Obama's early years refocused public attention on the pros and cons of government action.

Soon after the start of Obama's presidency, media personalities, ordinary Americans, and conservative groups organized under a loose rubric called the Tea Party, coalescing the backlash against Obama. The movement opposed policies such as government bailouts and health reform and disparaged immigrants and young, diverse Americans. President Obama himself was often a target, with racist images and tropes frequently seen at Tea Party events. Participants also promoted conspiratorial views and marginal takes of the Constitution. Yet it became a significant political force that influenced the path of the Republican Party and American politics.

The Tea Party took the well-worn conservative strategy of distrust in government to new heights. It is also a prime example of elites using public distrust of government to mobilize public opinion.

Scholars debate whether the Tea Party was a grassroots movement, an organic mobilization of everyday citizens, or an astroturf movement, which is one that is organized and directed by elites and only appears to be grassroots. But this debate misses the point of how elites use distrust as a political weapon.[6] Except in very narrow policy or issue campaigns, elites do not manufacture discontent (or any mass sentiment) out of whole cloth. Instead, they seize on real and socially grounded trends of distrust and dissatisfaction, stoke them and give them a voice, and then mobilize, harness, and crystallize them into a political force. As powerful as they are, such efforts are also fraught. In mobilizing public opinion, elites do not exercise Svengali-like powers over the mass public. To the contrary, the politics of public opinion—and the politics of distrust specifically—is an imprecise art. Leaders seize on existing sentiments and attitudes for strategic purposes but can only direct them loosely. And they are apt to lose control of popular passions altogether.

The Tea Party and Republican opposition to Obama were not simply cultural movements that swelled up from the grassroots. Nor were they merely an elite-driven astroturf affair masquerading as a democratic wave. The oppositional movement, which continued the conservative war with government, was an interplay between mass-based resistance and resentment on the one hand and conservative elite opposition and promotion of public anger on the other. These two distrustful forces—one broad, mass-based, enduring, democratic, and difficult to predict or control and the other elite-driven, strategic, institutionally located, and armed with opinion polls—sometimes clashed with each other as each tried to harness the Tea Party toward its own ends.

Twenty-first-century conservatives continued the post-Goldwater strategy that had worked so well before: stoke distrust in government to build organizations, mobilize for elections, feed selective distrust of institutions, and influence policy debates. After spending most of nearly three decades developing pro-presidency views of the Constitution and employing them when George W. Bush was president, conservatives once again turned against the idea of a strong executive when Obama was elected president. And when the Tea Party rose in opposition to Obama, the GOP establishment worked to build and later to manage it and its untethered congressional cohort. Tea Party members argued constantly against Obama's policies by claiming that he wanted a government that was too powerful. Here again, distrust of government was a potent resource for those who sought to gain and keep power.[7] But this strategy has its dangers, as elite efforts to promote distrust can quickly get out of hand—the distrustful public is apt to turn its ire on its erstwhile leaders and allies.

With both elite and grassroots conservatives propelling each other, Tea Party energy impeded what Obama could accomplish. Obama's grappling with this war with government followed the ambivalent place of government during the administration of George W. Bush.

THE "NEED FOR GOVERNMENT" UNDER BUSH

When George W. Bush ran for president in 2000, he promised to be a "compassionate conservative." The term was coined by the academic and journalist Marvin Olasky, and its philosophy was that civil society and religious organizations, rather than government, should provide social services and poor support.[8] To the extent that "compassionate conservatism" was associated with policies, it also fit the mold of prior concessionary campaign messages, like Dwight Eisenhower's "modern Republicanism" or Bill Clinton's "New Democrat" philosophy, both of which aimed to tack their party to the center and win moderate voters.

Decades of anti-statist rhetoric and policies, dating at least to the draconian cuts of the first Reagan budget, had taken their toll on the Republican Party image, which some saw as uncaring and callous. Bush's campaign message therefore resembled his father's 1988 promise to lead a "kinder, gentler" Republican Party and Newt Gingrich and GOPAC's subsequent strategy to portray "a caring, humanitarian reform Republican Party" that could build a majority.[9]

George W. Bush's first term was marked by this same ambivalence about the role of government. More conservative than his father, Bush's proposal for a large tax cut and a space-based missile defense system seemed reminiscent of Reagan-era conservatism. But having campaigned on "compassion," Bush also advanced a domestic agenda that included "faith-based initiatives" and his No Child Left Behind reform, which incorporated a notable expansion in federal education spending. By 2003, he even instituted a massive expansion in Medicare that included the addition of a prescription drug benefit for Medicare recipients. If, true to his conservative word, Bush pressed for smaller government through lower taxes and less regulation, his appeal to the center meant concessions to government programs that might secure him reelection in 2004.

But it was the terrorist attacks on September 11, 2001, that proved the necessity of government. Soon after the terrorist attacks aimed at New York City, Washington, D.C., and the Pentagon, there came a series of high-profile anthrax attacks against government and media figures. Bush's administration began massive mobilizations: a war in Afghanistan; the Patriot Act's expansions of government surveillance and investigatory, border, and police powers; and the consolidation of government protections of domestic security under the newly created Department of Homeland Security. The ramp-up to the Iraq War and the invasion in early 2003 evinced a mass mobilization of state power. Most such uses of government were consistent with the modern GOP's willingness to accept state activism when it came to security and police powers, and the post-9/11 world was a potent reminder that, for all their protests, conservatives would rely on the state, trust it in crisis, and expand it when in power.

Empowered by his 2004 reelection, which afforded him his first popular vote victory, Bush claimed to have earned "political capital" that he intended to "spend." But his second term was characterized by key missteps. Particularly costly for Bush was a domestic initiative to allow citizens to divert their Social Security savings into individual investment accounts, taking control over the savings from government. Democrats in Congress dubbed this a privatization attempt, and eventually a majority of Americans who—despite their antipathy toward many government programs—largely trusted Social Security as it was and began to suspect the proposal.

In response, the White House mounted a concerted media effort to undermine trust in the solvency of Social Security. This effort built on longer-standing conservative doubts in Social Security's long-term stability. In the late 1990s, for example, conservatives seized on poll data that dubiously asserted that young people believed more in UFOs than that Social Security would still exist when they retired.[10] Despite these efforts to weaken public trust in Social Security, the Bush plan ultimately failed politically. Just as Reagan had run afoul of public opinion on Social Security during his first term, Bush also felt the limits of public distrust in government when Social Security (or, for that fact, Medicare) was involved.

The stubborn need for government became obvious during the cavalcade of crises that plagued Bush's second term. Public support held steady for post-9/11 antiterrorism initiatives, including the war in Afghanistan, though the public's appetite for the Iraq War waned.

When the landfall of Hurricane Katrina broke the levees around New Orleans in August 2005, it demonstrated that the federal government was needed during and in the aftermath of natural disasters. The damage of landfall and subsequent flooding produced a humanitarian crisis: nearly two thousand dead and $81 billion in property damage. The immediate death and suffering and the chaos and looting that followed caught federal officials flat-footed. In response, they criticized state and local officials. Public frustration with the failure of government response reached new heights, buffeted by the expectation that professional, competent government had an inescapable responsibility and irreplaceable role in addressing a crisis on this scale.

Even as conservatives struggled to reconcile their conservative ideology with the need for government, Republicans unleashed a new cycle of situational constitutionalism in their war with government—one that privileged the presidency. During the Reagan years, the Republican Party surrendered its pro-Congress ambivalence about presidential power to become a pro-executive, anti-congressional party, championing President Reagan's expansions of executive power and decrying the politics of the Democratic-controlled Congress. Then, during the Clinton years, arguments that the Democratic Congress and President Clinton were corrupt helped the Gingrich wing of the Republican Party take control of the House and the Senate. The Republican Congress then proposed a subsequent pro-Congress view of the separation of powers that fueled the investigations that ultimately led to Clinton's impeachment.

During the first six years of the George W. Bush administration, Republicans controlled at least one house of Congress, and often both chambers. Reversing course once again, Republicans became pro-executive power, and

Bush "aggressively used executive orders and directives to achieve ambitious and controversial policy goals in both foreign and domestic affairs without congressional action."[11] Republicans discovered anew the merits of a strong presidency, particularly during wartime, so the Democrats' victories in the 2006 election and return to majority status in the House and Senate must have felt familiar to Republicans who cut their teeth in the Reagan era.

Republicans complained about excessive oversight and meddling, and the Bush administration, particularly Vice President Dick Cheney, was back on the march to reestablish executive branch power and presidential autonomy. In March 2000, before becoming selected as Bush's vice presidential nominee, Cheney recalled the Iran-contra minority report, calling it "a reflection" of his experiences in the Ford administration when they were "doing battle with the Congress on so many different things, including Vietnam," with "arms embargoes and sanctions and so many other areas where Congress was really, I thought, encroaching on executive authority."[12] Early in the administration, Cheney pressed his case, refusing to turn over to Congress documents about the membership and activities of the Energy Task Force. As Cheney biographer Barton Gellman explains, when the case was heard in federal court in February 2020, "The vice-president's legal arguments included a stunner. Because each branch of government had unique spheres of authority, and the executive powers vested solely in the president, Congress had no enforceable right to demand *any* information from the executive branch that was not already available to the public." Even more, these congressional–presidential disputes, argued Cheney, were not matters for the judiciary to resolve. Instead, Congress had only brute tools at its disposal—cutting budgets, sending the sergeant at arms to arrest executive branch officials, or impeachment.[13] The GOP's pro-presidentialism was continuing to grow. That march would be suspended again after Barack Obama became president, only to resume in full force during the Trump years.

The Bush administration faltered politically. Public approval steadily declined after mid-2005, and the Republicans lost majority control of Congress in 2006. Conservative Republicans looked for opportunities to distinguish themselves from the administration that they had so closely supported. Bush faced blowback from two elements of his coalition—libertarian, small-government advocates and anti-immigration forces. Despite strong prior support for Bush's aggressive governance in the military and domestic surveillance, small-government advocates returned to form when Bush expanded the domestic state, particularly with Medicare reform and its prescription drug benefit. Bush expressed positive views toward immigrants and had strong ties with Hispanics when he was governor of Texas. Bush's chief strategist Karl Rove hoped to bring Hispanic voters into the Republican coalition, but emerging opposition from Republicans thwarted this plan and stalled comprehensive immigration reform legislation.[14]

Then, in 2008, with the financial collapse, the wheels fell off the cart. Banks, unhindered by regulators, had engaged in risky practices involving the trade of complex financial instruments such as bundles of subprime mortgages. As overextended homeowners began to default, these investments lost their value. Lehman Brothers and other bank and investment entities ran into serious difficulty, leading the stock market and housing prices to crash and foreclosures, unemployment, and personal and business bankruptcies to skyrocket. To stop the bleeding and to stabilize the economy, the Bush administration turned again to a government solution: bailing out the financial markets and affected industries and individuals. On top of billions of dollars on No Child Left Behind, hundreds of billions on prescription drugs, not to mention the vast amounts spent on foreign policy and defense, the Bush administration signed off on a $700 billion Troubled Asset Relief Program (TARP) bill in August 2008—the final blow to his small-government promises. Securing trust for the actions of the administration and the rebuilt financial system was its own problem for the Bush and Obama administrations, particularly in a persistently anti-statist culture in which the public did not trust in government.[15] But even conservatives conceded that government action was necessary to rescue the economy from the brink.

For all of the antipathy toward and suspicion of government that conservatives had espoused for decades, the Bush administration produced massive spending in the domestic realm as one crisis after the next demanded it. Politically hobbled, Republican nominee John McCain, speaking from a campaign stop in Orlando, Florida, said that "the fundamentals of the economy are strong." But the financial collapse had damaged the GOP and, seemingly for a time, the conservative cause and its anti-statist ideology.

With parents from Kansas and Kenya, Barack Obama was brought up by his mother and her parents and became a community organizer, a law professor, and a state legislator and U.S. Senator. Obama ran his presidential primary and general election campaigns around the themes of "hope and change" as he had to navigate false claims about his religion and birthplace meant to portray him as not fully American. Obama would win the 2008 presidential election with an electoral vote margin of 365–173 as Democrats gained seats in the House and the Senate. Although he had an ambitious policy agenda, his administration also needed to deal with the economic crisis, for he came into office as hundreds of thousands of jobs were lost each month.

OBAMA, DISTRUST, AND THE RISE OF THE TEA PARTY

In his 2009 inaugural address, President Barack Obama brushed aside ideological purity. "The question we ask today is not whether our government is too big or too small," he said, "but whether it works—whether it helps families find jobs at a decent wage, care they can afford, a retirement that is dignified."[16] This contrasted with President Bill Clinton's famous 1996 State of the Union remark about the end of the era of big government.

But, like Clinton, soon after taking office, Obama saw his project tested—2009 brought an intensely renewed anti-government sentiment, and establishment GOP opposition to Obama started immediately. Going far beyond the "permanent campaign" of jousting, issue framing, and appeals to public opinion, key national Republicans worked to fundamentally undermine Obama's presidency. At a 2009 steakhouse dinner convened on Inauguration Day by political strategist Frank Luntz, a group of Republicans decided they would oppose everything Obama proposed. Former Speaker of the House Newt Gingrich was there, as was the journalist Fred Barnes and about fifteen Republican legislators, including Representatives Paul Ryan and Eric Cantor and Senators Jim DeMint and Jon Kyl. Ryan told attendees that "everyone's got to stick together," and a strategy was born: "Show united and unyielding opposition to the president's economic policies."[17]

Ryan and other attendees knew that unified opposition could belie the "hope" at the center of Obama's campaign. First, GOP unity would make it impossible for Obama to keep his promises to go beyond political divides (and possibly prompt distrust about his character) and make it all the more difficult for Obama to deliver on his policy proposals, especially health care. Against a united GOP, centrist Democrats faced the unhappy prospects of pure party-line votes tying them to leaders who were unpopular in their constituencies or of separating themselves from and undermining the majority's endeavors. Even if legislation passed, it could seem less legitimate without bipartisanship, as the difficult decisions centrist Democrats might face to support Obama would imperil their seats. The dinner attendees hoped this strategy would win them back control of the House in 2010 and the presidency in 2012.

Whatever its design, the conservative elite plan to stall Obama's program might have faltered without a deep reservoir of public discontent and distrust. After 2008, economic distress, a mistrust of a Washington that was perceived to care more for Wall Street than Main Street, and a slow recovery fed two social movements: a scattered Occupy Wall Street movement on the left and a resentful Tea Party movement on the right.[18] If leftist populists objected to the unaccountable economic elites, conservative critics saw a threat to America's free market and traditional values in government efforts to address the crisis. Some conservatives tried to actively distinguish themselves by arguing that even the Bush administration had demonstrated too great an affinity for government, not only in the Medicare prescription drug benefit but especially in the hundreds of billions of dollars in TARP spending in late 2008, which Representative Jeb Hensarling called "the road to socialism."[19]

By early 2009, without the cross-pressures of party loyalty to the president, the GOP was in full opposition mode. Conservative media figures told their audiences to forego the honeymoon in favor of early and vehement opposition. Before the inauguration, Rush Limbaugh took issue with Republicans who he claimed, despite their political differences, hoped Obama would succeed. He told his audience, "I hope Obama fails."[20]

Obama attempted to gain bipartisan support by including substantial tax cuts in his stimulus bill, the American Recovery and Reinvestment Act. He also negotiated with three Senate Republicans, Susan Collins, Olympia Snowe and Arlen Specter. In the end, those Republicans were the only legislators from their party who voted for the bill. However, the lower spending they insisted upon, which Obama later said had "no economic logic" behind it, decreased the bill's stimulative effect. This likely harmed congressional Democrats in the 2010 midterm elections.[21]

Two days after Obama signed the recovery act, CNBC broadcaster Rick Santelli objected passionately on air to an announced Obama mortgage bailout plan, a moment that catalyzed the Tea Party movement. Political scientists Theda Skocpol and Vanessa Williamson found that Washington-based FreedomWorks (led by Dick Armey) and the Koch-funded Americans for Prosperity (AFP), used the moment to build ties to the Tea Partiers at the mass level:

> With the opening provided by the Santelli rant, FreedomWorks built activist connections. It helped to orchestrate the angry town hall protests against health reform in August 2009, co-sponsored Tea Party rallies, and gained new leverage in 2010 with GOPers elected with its endorsement or the support of other Tea Party-identified groups . . . AFP ballooned its contact lists from about 270,000 in 2008 to 1.5 million in 2011, while also expanding its network of coordinators to reach 32 states . . . AFP is also building extensive state networks.[22]

Both FreedomWorks and AFP, parts of the Koch network,[23] were among the key players at the elite level working to connect Washington-based conservatives to a distrustful public at large.

Tea Party protesters, often donning revolutionary-era costumes and displaying the "Don't Tread on Me" Gadsden flag, connected their opposition to Obama and Washington to long-standing historical American distrust in distant and powerful government. As we discussed in chapter 2, anti-government rhetoric was key to the American Revolution and the founding of the republic. Anti-Federalists, early Democrats, and populists resisted strong centralized government and were leery of the influence that might be wielded by economic elites, particularly those from New England. Suspicion of government "meddling" in the economy has a long lineage in American thought. In its earliest iterations it was Democratic, and it became especially Republican only after Progressive attempts to regulate the economic realm when, in the 1920s, Republicans began their active resistance to government intervention in the economy. Many Tea Party adherents claimed that their name also stood for "taxed enough already."

Building on decades-long GOP resistance to taxes, Tea Party aims meshed well with what Beltway Republicans had come to call "constitutional conservatism," a small-government view of the founding era that declared its interest in restoring the Constitution from its degraded state. As law professor Christopher Schmidt wrote, the Tea Party espoused a conservative version of popular constitutionalism that believed citizens had "a responsibility to read their Constitution, to stake out claims about its meaning, and to demand that public officials act in accordance with these claims."[24] Many took their constitutional lessons from Cold War figure W. Cleon Skousen, who denied that the founding had its philosophical roots in the Enlightenment and instead claimed that its primary influence was the Bible.[25]

Fueled by opposition to government, Wall Street, economic elites, and sometimes scientific experts (especially on climate change), the Tea Party movement also had clear antecedents in Republican right-wing populism. Along with distrust in government and Obama, these forces fueled the rhetorical furor Tea Partiers leveled at the "crony capitalism" of corporate bailout policies, government contracts to solar panel maker Solyndra, and accusations that Obama's IRS had targeted right-wing groups. Echoing Newt Gingrich's characterizations of Democrats in the 1990s, Tea Party rhetoric portrayed President Obama, Speaker of the House Nancy Pelosi, and Senate majority leader Harry Reid as manipulators of the state, fueling a political machine that rewarded Democratic allies and punished Republican opponents.

The Tea Party was ostensibly a coalition of Americans worried about the size and scope of government, but it often included racism and nativism. White racial resentment was associated with the election of America's first African American president, and race became a component of the opposition's animus and strategy. As studies found, white racial resentment and nativism were more pronounced in the Tea Party than among other conservatives, Republicans, or the overall population.[26] Political scientist Christopher Parker situated Obama's election in reactionary discourse of societal decay and America's history of exclusion. According to Parker, the Tea Party believed "America to be in decline—a decline associated with the rising status of marginalized groups such as women, people of color, immigrants, and homosexuals. Similar to the Know Nothings of the 1850s, the Ku Klux Klan of the 1920s, and the John Birch Society, the Tea Party is a reaction to social change; now, the change is represented by Obama's election."[27] These racist and nativist sentiments are perennial touchstones with legacies as long as America's commitment to democracy, and together they fueled the Tea Party movement.[28]

The Tea Party was a cocktail of ideologies—government distrust, racial resentments and nativism, and even an authoritarian taste for state-imposed "moral order." This led Tea Party members to complex, sometimes inconsistent policy stances. On social policy, Tea Party Republicans were more apt to prefer a role for the state in social regulation, a notable inconsistency for a small-government movement focused on "individual liberty," seen in a vehement streak of social conservatism that, compared to other Republicans, was much more to the extreme on abortion and gay rights, "overwhelmingly oppos[ing] affirmative action," and more right-leaning on immigration.[29]

Tea Party members carved out exceptions to their anti-government views, especially wherever they stood to benefit. They were likely, for example, to support Social Security and Medicare, which were particularly relevant to them, because Tea Party demographics skewed older than the rest of the population. As political scientists Bryan Gervais and Irwin Morris explained, "Tea Party supporters tend to focus not on the programs but on the recipients. They oppose benefits—of any type—for recipients they deem unworthy or underserving. This is not the same as opposing the program itself because of an ideological aversion to large government or expensive federal programs."[30] Looking at Tea Party activists, Theda Skocpol and Vanessa Williamson observed that for all of their ideological pronouncements, they "evaluate regulations and spending very differently, depending on who or what is regulated, and depending on the kinds of people who benefit."[31] Far from being consistently or exclusively anti-government, Tea Party attitudes were sometimes inconsistent and often extreme.

Political elites recognized the mobilizing potential of anger and began to stoke it. Some right-wing critics portrayed Obama's policy agenda as evidence that he intended to destroy America out of a mindset against colonialism or as part of a large Muslim plot or simply because he hated Americanness itself. Two notable examples connect this politics to the past and future of the GOP. Newt Gingrich said that one must "understand Kenyan, anti-colonial behavior" to "piece together" Obama's actions.[32] Obama's most vociferous opponents, including Donald Trump and others in the "birther movement," questioned his birthplace, religion, and commitment to America's success.

More cautious GOP leaders, including the deep-pocket far-right groups connected to the national Tea Party, were more wary of backing their followers' most extreme stances. In some respects, this was because, despite large areas of agreement, elite and mass views in the conservative movement did not always overlap.[33] They differed on policy emphasis, tactics, and tone.

Given the many sources of anger fueling the movement, Tea Party leaders strategically kept some of it under wraps while playing up more politically palatable issues, like broad anti-government sentiment. In a study of "quality control" in Tea Party messaging, sociologist Francis Prior noted that there was "a deliberate technique of management and instruction" from the top down.[34] Organizers policed messaging to focus on economic issues and anti-government sentiment as opposed to "social issues" (including "immigration, poverty or homelessness"); " 'tinfoil hat theories,' " and limited anti-Obama signs or rants "to prevent framings that either were racist, could be construed as racist, or were otherwise inflammatory."[35]

The challenge of maintaining this "master frame" of anti-government views in local activism was a microcosm of a much larger strategic problem facing the national Tea Party movement. How does an ideological movement achieve message coherence and political influence when its organizations are far-flung, and its followers are not centrally organized?

One way was through considerable financial and organizational support centralized in Washington. According to several studies, the Tea Party was "united" by shared ideological commitments, cable news messages, cyber connections, and a shared partisan identity.[36] Most accounts of the Tea Party's founding and its early maintenance include the roles of CNBC, Fox News, Glenn Beck, Dick Armey, the Koch brothers, and Washington organizations like Americans for Prosperity and FreedomWorks.[37] Conservative billionaire donors and other would-be leaders of the Tea Party movement devoted considerable money and attention to sanding down its rough edges, enforcing message discipline, and channeling anger toward government. In short, conservative elites were indispensable to organizing and focusing the public anger toward Obama and muting its less politically palatable aspects.

Second, shared ideology is a cheaper way to build and maintain the unity of a movement. Because the Tea Party was disparate, decentralized, and loosely affiliated,[38] it was difficult to identify its members. Local Tea Party organizers had relatively meager means of coordinating action, and not even the Koch brothers could supply the financial and organizational resources that would build the organizational structure necessary to tame such a multifaceted group or maintain the grassroots aura from which the Tea Party benefited. A simple story simply told, with broad cultural and historical resonance, could unite them.

Anti-statism bridged these divides, as distrust in government strategically brought together this loose-knit movement of organizations and local chapters. Everywhere, Tea Party supporters and elected officials took up mainline conservative Republican criticisms of domestic policy and regulation. The close alliance of this purportedly grassroots movement with the modern Republican Party is not surprising. Elite media and conservative-leaning groups supported this movement, and for all its purported anti-Washington and insurgent motivations, the Tea Party was incorporated into the national Republican Party. The anti-government leanings of the Tea Party were right at home in a party that had long used the same arguments when it favored them. By 2013, Pew Research found that only 3 percent of Republicans and Republican leaners who agreed with the Tea Party trusted the federal government all or most of the time.[39]

This anti-government philosophy not only stood to unite the Tea Party, but it could also link the movement to long-standing and powerful strains in American political history and culture. Anti-government sentiment fit easily into American culture, and in this way it enjoyed broad appeal even outside the Tea Party. By muting racism, nativism, "tin-foil hat" theories, and strident anti-Obamaism, the focus instead fell upon taxes, spending, deficits, and the size of government. Just as they had done when constructing the Contract with America, leaders viewed social policy arguments as impolitic distractions and opted instead for the low-hanging fruit: public anger toward government. This was culturally resonant and politically appealing, and it preserved the movement's reputation and broadened its political reach.

Given how disparate in organization these groups were, the soft politics of ideology and identity became the glue of their cohesion. Anti-government perspectives were at hand. They had held together conservative coalitions for decades, long-standing tools in election campaigns and during policy fights. Racism, nativism, and social conservatism were also key motivating forces for the Tea Party, but without anti-government rhetoric, the Tea Party would have lacked its central pillar of internal agreement and the fig leaf that masked its illiberal beliefs.

The Tea Party was neither purely grassroots nor completely astroturf. As was the case when Ronald Reagan forged the modern conservative movement and the Republican Revolution took an oppositional stance in the Clinton years, again the solution was found in a message the elites could communicate to a restive public: do not trust the government.

From FreedomWorks and Fox News to the local activities of the grass-roots across the country, the Tea Party was built on such anger, and its more aggressive proponents tried to bend the national Republican Party to amplify the anti-government strain of conservative ideology and Republican policy. Simultaneously, conservative elites seized upon anti-government sentiment among the public, distilled it, guided it, and ultimately wielded it for their own purposes. The GOP organized its opposition to Obama and brought together its elite members and the Tea Party under a single roof during Obama's first term.

But political elites who seek to mobilize public anger run the risk of losing control of it.[40] Even with wealthy benefactors and national organizations, wrangling the Tea Party rank and file was difficult.

Harnessing anger also risks accidentally turning that anger on oneself. Establishment Republicans appealed to Tea Party activists and used their support in campaigns and in governing, but they could not control the Tea Party. Many Tea Party members knew "little or nothing about Freedom-Works or the other national free-market organizations promoting the Tea Party brand."[41] When activists did know about Washington-based groups, they did not necessarily trust them. Political scientist Rachel Blum found in interviews with activists that "some people's distrust of elites ran so deep that they discriminated between real Tea Party groups like their own and the large national Tea Party organizations, which they saw as mouthpieces of the Republican Party."[42] According to Blum, activists developed into an "insurgent faction" that wanted to hold Republicans accountable to conservative principles and saw elections as a main way to do so.

With increasing frequency, candidates affiliated with the Club for Growth and the Tea Party began to challenge establishment Republican incumbents in the primaries. In 2010, Tea Party candidate Mike Lee ousted incumbent Senator Bob Bennett in the Utah Republican caucus. In later years Republican Senator Dick Lugar and Representative Eric Cantor were deemed unacceptable by Tea Party activists, in part because of their ties to Washington or to K Street, and they were ousted in Tea Party–driven primary elections. The volatile populist fervor was potentially dangerous to other elements of the coalition. For example, whereas business conservatives prefer the cheaper labor markets that come with liberal immigration policies, the social conservative and nativist wings of the GOP were concerned about "porous" borders and the economic and social impacts of immigration. Efforts by national Republicans to pass immigration reform provoked restive anti-immigrant forces.

If the Tea Party's potentially dangerous anti-government passions and prejudices were deeply embedded in the mass public and American culture, they were useful to the conservative cause in Washington. The Republican establishment stoked these sentiments to activate publics that they hoped could accomplish two goals: rebuild a Republican congressional majority midway through Obama's presidency and defeat the Affordable Care Act.

DISTRUST AND THE POLITICS OF THE AFFORDABLE CARE ACT

At the signing ceremony for the Affordable Care Act in March 2010, President Obama declared that the law "will set in motion reforms that generations of Americans have fought for and marched for and hungered to see." Indeed, the passage of the Affordable Care Act was a major domestic accomplishment of President Obama and the realization of a long-term liberal policy objective dating back at least to Harry Truman. In the past, Republicans used widespread anti-government sentiment to defeat Bill Clinton's health reform plan in 1994, and many Democrats worried the same would happen to Obama's health reform plan.

Conditions had changed, and Obama could succeed where Clinton had failed. For one, the reform process within Congress had changed. Shortly after the 2008 election, Senate Finance Committee chair Max Baucus (D-MT) issued a white paper based on discussions and negotiations with health-care stakeholders (including hospitals, pharmaceutical companies, and insurance companies) that had begun after Democrats swept into power after the 2006 congressional elections. Obama held a White House forum on health care in March 2009 that included a bipartisan group of legislators, labor leaders, insurance executives, and policy experts. Unlike Clinton, Obama let Congress lead on developing the policy and legislation.

While electing large congressional Democratic majorities in 2008 increased the likelihood of passage, health reform proponents assiduously avoided upending existing health coverage arrangements, and Democratic leaders persisted even after the January 2010 election of Republican senator Scott Brown seemed to preface significant political fallout.[43] Moreover, as the Tea Party mobilized starting in 2009 to prevent the law's passage, proponents also organized, mounting an intensive door-to-door grassroots campaign in favor of it.[44]

Although attempts to stop the Affordable Care Act were not successful, distrust was again key to the Republican playbook. As health policy scholar Jonathan Oberlander noted, Obama's efforts faced "the perennial problem of building popular support for reform in a country where many citizens had little faith in government and where most insured Americans were satisfied with their own health care coverage."[45] Moreover, trust in government has fallen a great deal since Medicare and Medicaid were passed a half century ago and even since the 1993–1994 Clinton effort. A whopping 69 percent agreed they "trusted the federal government to do what is right most of the time" when Medicare passed in 1965, but only 23 percent agreed in 1993 and 19 percent in early 2010.[46]

Unsurprisingly, Republicans returned to the strategic use of anti-government messages to stall health-care reform. As in several prior GOP efforts, Republican strategist Frank Luntz supplied language, telling reform opponents they "simply MUST be vocally and passionately on the side of reform," but that anti-government messages should play a large role.[47] Luntz recommended that the proposal's opponents, after asserting they wanted reform, should say they wanted to prevent a "government takeover" of health care by "Washington bureaucrats" "while ratcheting up the rhetoric against insurance companies."

While the argument was anti-government, it was also decidedly not pro-free market. In a memo based on his public opinion research reported in *Politico* in May 2009, Luntz noted, "Nobody is asking for 'private healthcare' or 'free market health care.' There is no demand for 'more competition.'" Given low public support for the insurance industry, Republicans were told not to frame this fight as government versus the market but rather to focus on quality of care and individual choice. Luntz advised Republicans to say they "are firmly committed to providing genuine access to affordable, quality healthcare for every American" and "oppose any politician-run system that denies you the treatments you need, when you need them."

The framing boiled down to government and politicians on the one hand and individuals and families on the other. Instead of adopting a "Washington takeover of health care," Luntz advised, the nation should "say yes to personalized, patient-centered care." Republicans should bring up harms that would "jeopardize our quality of care and access to good doctors by putting politicians in charge of your healthcare." Noting that Americans care about being denied care, "It is essential," Luntz wrote, "that 'deny' and 'denial' enter the conservative lexicon immediately because it is at the core of what scares Americans the most about a government takeover of healthcare. Then add to it the source of that denial and you have the perfect antigovernment, anti-Washington and anti-Democratic message." Putting "politicians in charge of your health care" was scarier than invoking a role for "bureaucrats"; "Washington" was worse than "government"; and "Washington takeover" more frightening than "Washington control." After all, Luntz said, "Takeovers are like coups. They lead to dictators and a loss of freedom."

Republicans in Congress invoked the specter of government control. Tying the ACA to rationing, Representative Ted Poe (R-TX) said, "In a government-run system, the government decides who gets treatment in medicine and who doesn't. That means the government decides who lives, who dies . . . When government bureaucrat gatekeepers have control over who lives and who dies in America, freedom is the first casualty."[48] Representative Steve Scalise (R-LA) held that a "new health care czar" would have "the ability and the power to interfere between the relationship of a patient and their doctor."[49] Representative Sam Johnson (R-TX) asserted, "Congress needs to wake up and realize that Americans know more about their health care needs than the government bureaucrats. They know exactly what a Washington takeover of health care means, and they're shouting from the rooftops: No, no, no."[50]

Luntz was not the only one from the Clinton opposition who reemerged in 2009. Conservative Betsy McCaughey—who claimed in 1993 that Clinton's reform would make it so that patients would not be able to keep their doctors—cast Obamacare in an even more dire light. McCaughey said that the Obama plan would lead to mandatory end-of-life counseling, which eventually would morph into the notorious (and false) claim that it would establish government "death panels."[51]

Prominent Republican politicians leapt at this claim and replayed it to an already anxious public. Former Alaska governor and 2008 Republican vice presidential nominee Sarah Palin's invocation of "death panels" embodied, too, Luntz's instruction that "what Americans fear most is that Washington politicians will dictate what kind of care they receive." Asking, "Who will suffer the most when they ration care?," Palin answered,

"The sick, the elderly, and the disabled, of course. The America I know and love is not one in which my parents or my baby with Down Syndrome will have to stand in front of Obama's 'death panel' so his bureaucrats can decide, based on a subjective judgment of 'level of productivity in society,' whether they are worthy of health care."[52] Representative Virginia Foxx (R-VA) said old people would be "put to death by their government."[53] Senator Chuck Grassley (R-IA) said Americans "should not have a government-run plan to decide when to pull the plug on grandma."[54] Even GOP House leader John Boehner (R-OH) suggested that paying for end-of-life counseling "may start us down a treacherous path toward government-encouraged euthanasia."[55]

These emphases redeployed long-standing frames about government to apply to health reform. As one analysis observed, "It's no surprise, then, that health reform opponents [were] most likely to cite 'the government [has] too big a role in the health care system' as the reason for their opposition."[56] Another found that for "mass- and elite-level opponents of the ACA, the legislation's cost and the increased governmental role it authorized were central reasons behind their opposition," and these shared concerns did not shift appreciably through the reform effort.[57] Without frames emphasizing economic fairness and equality, supporters had no potent alternate rhetorical approach.[58]

Still, there was no claim more dramatic than the death panels claim that bureaucrats would execute the sick and infirm. Feeding the worst dystopic vision of government, the notion that health reform would lead to the government euthanizing citizens was really aimed at producing more heat than light. Ultimately, the viral nature of this false claim—repeated at health-care town hall events and in the media—produced and reflected fear and anger toward government. These extreme claims take hold, multiply, and deepen opinion about policy. They are also "especially insidious precisely because" they are imagined and mythical.[59] Just like the misinformation spread during the Clinton reform effort, the myth of death panels was persistent and stubborn.[60]

While attempts to use distrust in government to stop the Affordable Care Act failed, they had policy consequences. The provision to pay doctors for end-of-life counseling (the source of the death panels myth) was struck from the bill. Later regulations regarding such advising were also axed.[61] As one scholar put it, "The lie has nimbly been used to mobilize opposition, not just against the ACA's provision for advance care planning but also against other parts of the act," including "the Independent Payment Advisory Board (IPAD) and evidence-based treatment recommendations."[62] Under pressure from the right, Senate Republicans involved in negotiations in the Finance Committee ultimately withheld their support after they slowed the bill's progress and made the bill less progressive.[63] After it was implemented, partisanship affected who enrolled in ACA plans: similarly situated Republicans enrolled less than Democrats—unless enrolling was framed as using private, nongovernmental coverage.[64]

Distrust also bred the fear that the ACA would undermine existing government health benefits. ACA opponents targeted seniors with ads that claimed Medicare was threatened, even though the law increased coverage by closing the prescription drug donut hole and covering preventive care without any copay. Older voters saw "social protections" they received as "individual entitlements for workers, or those attached to workers, not truly as social insurance." But while "the individually earned entitlement proved an effective way to package social protection for individualistic, antigovernment Americans . . . [it] also greatly complicates health-care reform. Public opinion polls showed repeatedly that seniors were more opposed to the Obama health-care reform effort than were younger citizens."[65] These long-standing cultural perspectives, dovetailing with Tea Party rhetoric about the relative "deservingness" of some Americans, were linked to specific negative claims about the ACA.

The policy fight over the ACA sharpened the political fight the Tea Party was waging against Obama. If Tea Party adherents often had libertarian leanings and wanted minimal government, many people who associated themselves with the Tea Party were comfortable with some benefit programs, like Social Security or Medicare, all the while regarding the proposal for the ACA as dangerous and illegitimate.[66] Seniors and veterans, they thought, constituted the deserving, while young people and racial minorities were the undeserving. Tea Party supporters saw government helping a group that they believed had not worked for the policy benefits and therefore received them illegitimately. Although scholars disagree about how much racial attitudes affected views toward the Affordable Care Act, race has long been a factor in the design of and attitudes toward social programs, likely affecting the breadth of their political support.[67]

Clearly angry and opposed to the ACA, Tea Party groups organized people to attend town halls during the summer of 2009. During these often rowdy events, ACA opponents used anti-government themes and dramatized their concerns about "death panels." One event hosted by Representative John Dingell (D-MI) started with Mike Sola pushing his wheelchair-bound son, who has cerebral palsy, to the front. Sola proclaimed that, under the ACA, there would be "no care whatsoever" for his son and told Dingell, "You've ordered a death sentence to this young man."[68] Another ACA opponent told a reform supporter nearby, "You may be dead in five years! They may euthanize you." A sixty-eight-year-old man named John Rhen told a reporter, "They're going to take over everything. It's socialism," and, "I don't want some bureaucrat making health decisions for me and my family."[69] Later in the event, a woman with disabilities named Marcia Boehm, who was uninsured because of preexisting conditions, spoke about how the ACA would benefit her, when "a very large man got down on his knees so he could be face to face with Marcia Boehm and said, 'They are using you. You're stupid. They're going to euthanize you.' "[70]

Incidents like this took place all over the country.[71] An unsuccessful Republican candidate for the Iowa House carried a sign saying "Obama Lies, Grandma Dies," at the town hall meeting of Representative Dave Loebsack.[72] In Virginia over the summer of 2009, Lydia Martin, a canvasser for a progressive group called the Virginia Organizing Project reported a change in mood decidedly against the ACA: "At the doors, people would say, 'I heard they were going to kill old people.' "[73] As summarized by Caitlin Duffy, this rhetoric combined hyperbole, vilification, and a narrative of victimhood that obscured policy specifics. Polarizing the debate by portraying President Obama as someone who would kill others by withholding treatment used distrust of government, reinforced it, and took it to new extremes.[74]

Though ultimately none of this proved enough to defeat the Patient Protection and Affordable Care Act (ACA) as it had Clinton's health-care reform, the hyperbole of a dangerous government takeover that would bring death panels and government-determined "euthanasia" did crystallize anger and fear in the mass public. During the summer and into September 2009, the Senate Finance Committee held bipartisan meetings to try to develop a bill with some Republican buy-in. However, as the uproar from the right grew louder and Republican members became intransigent, Senator Max Baucus ended these efforts. In November 2009, the House of

Representatives passed health reform—with a public option—by 220–215. The Senate passed a different version in December 2009 by a larger margin, 60–39. When Scott Brown, an avowed opponent of the ACA, won the special election for senator in Massachusetts on January 19, 2010, there were still two different versions of the bill, and its eventual success was still very much in question. To enact the ACA, the House passed the Senate version of the bill on March 19 in a 219–212 vote, with not a single vote from Republicans and 34 Democrats opposed. Obama signed it into law two days later before a large, enthusiastic crowd in the White House.

But by then, the cultivation of opposition to the ACA had merged into the broader conservative resistance. At a Tea Party march in 2009, protesters were animated "not only by their opposition to 'Obamacare,' but by anger over perceptions of excessive government spending and taxation, government interference with personal freedoms, such as gun ownership, and a belief that Obama is leading the country toward socialism."[75] Straight out of the same GOP playbook that propelled Reaganism and the Contract with America, these arguments against robust federal domestic policy helped the GOP strengthen disparate organizations, unify its coalition, and motivate voters in the 2010 midterm elections.

THE 2010 MIDTERMS

Democrats fared very poorly in the first congressional election after the Affordable Care Act passed in 2010. In what Obama called a "shellacking," Democrats lost sixty-three House seats and with them their majority. They lost seats in the Senate, too, but retained majority control. Even those who thought Obama had enjoyed considerable policy success in his first two years recognized that, politically, something was wrong. On the eve of the 2010 election, Thomas E. Mann noted that Obama's "efforts to explain clearly and understandably to citizens what he was doing and why—to 'craft a narrative'—have been far from perfect."[76]

Much of the oppositional rage that motivated the 2010 GOP resurgence centered on Obama himself. It began during the 2008 primaries, when McCain–Palin (and before that Hillary Clinton) painted Obama as "a radical leftist" far outside the mainstream of American politics. With the rise of the Tea Party, opposition against Obama accelerated in his first years in office, particularly in the wake of the opposition's framing of Obamacare.[77]

Some were disoriented by the election of the first African American president, and many more horrified that he was a purported radical who "palled around with terrorists," as Palin had put it. This Tea Party anger "reached a boil" in the 2010 midterms, "disproportionately" turning out these angry voters.[78]

The anti-Obama attack was not simply about policy or just about race. It was also framed as a reaction to his use of presidential powers. Conservatives once again became "situational constitutionalists," resisting a strong Democratic presidency contra to the pro-presidentialism they honed during the Reagan and Bush administrations. With Obama in the White House, presidential power was once again purportedly a problem.

Conservative critics charged Obama with a dangerous imperialism. In *The Blueprint: Obama's Plan to Subvert the Constitution and Build an Imperial Presidency*, Ken Blackwell and Ken Klukowski expressed concern about White House "czars," who they referred to as a "shadow government."[79] The Obama White House pointed out that Republican critics had not objected to the "czars" who had led similar endeavors in the George W. Bush administration (or the Reagan and George H. W. Bush administrations before that).[80]

These separation of powers complaints articulated the stated Tea Party fear that Obama was a threat to the Constitution itself. As one Virginia woman told reporter Mara Liasson, "The Democrats are eviscerating our Constitution."[81] Covering Tea Party events, Liasson saw copies of the Constitution passed around and heard many constitutional complaints, like defending gun rights and decrying the size and power of the federal government. Conservative pundit Glenn Beck urged activists to carry, read, and study the Constitution and promulgated conspiratorial claims that progressives had hidden the true origins and sources of the Constitution.

The Tea Party was angry at what they perceived was the loss of the Constitution's original meaning, and they worried that America's decline was irrevocable if Obama succeeded. With every step the administration took, the Tea Party trusted it less and less. The group became a bulwark for the classic GOP strategy of polarized opposition. It also became an intraparty means of enforcing discipline around that strategy. Any Washington Republican who entertained compromise with the White House or publicly acknowledged the administration's success (or who simply said something nice about Obama personally) risked backlash from constituents at town halls or retribution at the ballot box in the primaries.

Rhetoric became more uncivil, and this new tone became the new normal as the GOP worked toward "retaking the House and, subsequently, appeasing and appealing to a bitter base."[82]

The electoral strategy of Republicans gearing up for the 2010 midterms was built on the "anger and energy manifested by the Tea Party movement."[83] Just as Newt Gingrich did in the lead up to the 1994 midterm elections, minority leader John Boehner used strategic advantages to stoke discontent and distrust early in the 2010 campaign cycle. After returning from Representative Kevin McCarthy's California district for a Tea Party event in the spring of 2009, "Boehner reputedly described the angry energy of the Tea Party protestors to the Republican Conference" and encouraged members to connect with activists to win the House.[84]

That same year, three Republican House members—Paul Ryan, minority whip Eric Cantor, and Kevin McCarthy—coauthored *Young Guns: A New Generation of Conservative Leaders*. The book was a naked bid to stake out their own future party leadership and presented them as a break with both the governing Democrats and establishment Republicans who had sparked public anger by not sufficiently restraining government growth.[85] Even while criticizing GOP spending of the past, Cantor wrote, "We've seen Democrats who claim to want only government that 'works' never pass up an opportunity to make government bigger and more intrusive."[86]

The Young Gun appeal to dissatisfaction with Washington Republicans and anger toward Democrats resonated with the Tea Partiers. In the book, McCarthy argued that part of the GOP's task was "re-earning trust." He stressed the importance of "Tea Party protests and the health-care town hall meetings," which, he claimed, had made it "apparent that something on the ground had changed" when House Democrats replaced America's promised hope "with a heavier emphasis on government control, mandates, and taxes than Americans wanted."[87] According to Thomas Mann and Norman Ornstein, the "Young Guns" fanned "the seething populist anger that many activist conservatives felt."[88]

Still, for all its claims to youth and new directions, the Young Guns' rhetoric would seem familiar to anyone charting the GOP since the New Deal. Not much seemed new to the playbook. In his characterization of Democrats, Ryan, a libertarian who gave interns copies of Ayn Rand's *Atlas Shrugged*, wrote, "We're seeing how they want to transform this country into a cradle-to-grave European social welfare state and change the idea of

American forever."[89] Gesturing as he would at various times in his career toward budget and deficit cutting, Ryan criticized those who touted "an expanded entitlement state that would make America more like Europe," suggesting that "America is on a dangerous downward path" and that conservatives had only "a handful of years to save our children and grandchildren from a life of economic decline and insecurity."[90]

Claims about the Obama administration only sharpened the long-standing critique against the state, heightening its power among the GOP faithful and matching the dire story of American decline that Obama's reactionary detractors told. Ryan echoed Gingrich and Palin's framing of Obama as an anti-colonialist and a political radical. He accused Obama—whose "upbringing" and "history didn't suggest he was centrist"—of using "the rhetoric of freedom and choice and opportunity to sell an inherently statist agenda." For Kevin McCarthy, the Democratic agenda was a design to set America on an irreversible path: "They think if they make government so large and the debt so big it will be impossible to reverse it."[91]

The tactics matched the rhetoric. On April 15, 2010, Tea Party organizations organized "tax day protests" and unveiled a new "Contract from America." The contract originated from Ryan Hecker, a Houston-based Tea Party activist who called them a list of ideas to help "the Tea Party brand and narrative that we are actually a group of very smart people with ideas" and attract the attention of officeholders.[92] The Contract from America was signed "The American People."

The 2010 document resembled its 1994 predecessor in important respects. Just as Gingrich had strategically avoided divisive social issues to attract Perot voters and independents, the Contract from America was dedicated to "individual liberty, limited government, and economic freedom." Studies of Tea Party attitudes demonstrated that adherents were more extreme on social issues, but the Contract from America avoided any such references—it mentioned neither abortion nor guns, for example—opting instead to promote small government, anti-regulation, lower taxes and less spending, and themes of individual liberty that would balance the budget, audit the government, and limit even the word count of the tax code. It proposed specific policies too: abolishing cap-and-trade policies, passing an "all-of-the-above" energy policy, and vowing to "defund, repeal, and replace" Obamacare.[93]

Taking a page out of the 1990s Republican playbook, the establishment GOP leadership debuted its "Pledge to America" in September 2010.

Whether or not it was an explicit response to the Tea Party wing's Contract from America, the pledge signaled an openness to Tea Party concerns. Leaders promised a more "listening" Washington that would reduce the size of government, "restore trust" in Congress, encourage economic prosperity, repeal and replace Obamacare, provide for stronger defense, and restore "checks and balances."[94]

The Tea Party movement in 2010—as a brand, a faction within a party, and a force fueled by anger—infused affiliated campaigns with funds, supported them with endorsements (even against Republican incumbent officeholders), and turned out Tea Party voters in primaries and the general elections. A hybrid of grassroots and astroturf politics, the Tea Party served as an important component of the Republican Party's base in 2010, propelling its mobilization and turnout and influencing its primaries. With its "pro-fiscal conservatism" linked with its status as a clearly "anti-Obama movement," the Tea Party became an engine of support for the GOP.[95]

In the Senate races, a political action group called Tea Party Express trained volunteers, shaped campaign messages, and promoted candidates like Joe Miller in Alaska and Marco Rubio in Florida. Often these candidates were going up against the party establishment: Miller challenged incumbent Lisa Murkowski, and Rubio battled Governor Charlie Crist. Here and elsewhere, the Tea Party imperiled Republican electoral prospects, and it pushed GOP candidates to the right.[96] And, of course, the deep pockets behind the Tea Party lent support to preferred candidates in primaries. Along with the Club for Growth (which also had long-established small-government leanings and a disposition to challenge "Republican-in-name-only" incumbents in the primaries), the Tea Party spread money around, including important last-minute money for advertising for Miller in Alaska and for Christine O'Donnell's primary challenges to Mike Castle in Delaware.[97]

Between the Tea Party and the Club for Growth, starting in 2010, "primary challenges were no longer isolated occurrences." From 2010 to 2014, serious primary challenges within the Republican Party (those in which challengers capture at least a quarter of the vote) were on the rise, with double-digit increases in the number of such competitive primaries in the 2010, 2012, and 2014 election cycles over those from 2000 to 2008. Indeed, the 2012 election cycle had more than double the number of such "competitive primary challenges" as occurred in 2008.[98] The GOP's center of gravity was shifting rightward.

The Tea Party could deliver votes in the general election too. Tea Party members voted at much higher rates than non–Tea Party members in the midterms.[99] The two tenets of the GOP's electoral campaigns in 2010 became a general distrust of government and a personal animus toward Obama. Congressional elections expert Gary Jacobson has shown that, ultimately, the 2010 election was a response to the policy activity of the first two Obama years and the slow economic recovery. The midterms became a referendum on Obama, both personally and regarding his legislative program. Based on multiple measures, Jacobson claimed that 2010 was "the most nationalized midterm election in at least six decades." More voters "said their vote for Congress would be a vote either for or against the president" than in any midterm for which such data were available.[100]

The effects were felt more in House districts than in Senate races. Tea Party–backed candidates lost Senate races that were potentially winnable in the anti-government tsunami of 2010. Although Rand Paul won in Kentucky and Mike Lee and Marco Rubio in Utah and Florida, respectively, the Tea Party candidates lost in Nevada, Alaska, Delaware, and Colorado. A mix of problematic candidacies, campaign missteps, and extreme intransigence allowed Democrats to barely hold onto their Senate majority.[101] To GOP strategists, these disappointments were an early signal of the riskiness inherent in Tea Party politics: it did not often appeal to swing voters, and victory was often out of reach in purple districts and states.

But none of these qualifiers should take away from the larger lesson that Republicans could learn from 2010. Although the president's party typically loses seats in midterm elections, the devastation that Obama-era Democrats suffered in 2010 was astounding. Even if the continued economic struggles contributed to this dissatisfaction, much of the public anger that helped the GOP win was planned, led, and stoked. As Congressional Quarterly put it, the GOP victory came from "a potent coalescence of forces: a stagnant economy, the sudden emergence of a movement of ideologically driven conservative activists, a broad sense that the federal government was overreaching under the Democrats, and a shift in the demographics of those who came out to vote."[102]

Not only was anti-government anger key to turning out the base, but with echoes of 1994 responses to Bill Clinton, it was key to the GOP's appeal to independents disaffected with both parties and with the system as a whole. Again, as was the case in 1994, this appeal worked by focusing on small government and economic issues largely to the neglect of social issues that might scare voters off. The GOP already had an excited partisan coalition (who turned out to be "the most enthusiastic participants of all"), but this strategy allowed them to add a crucial bloc—"conservative independents, many of whom adopted the Tea Party's view of [Obama] as an extreme liberal."[103] These same independents were "perpetually angry about the perceived failures of the government in Washington and were deeply distrustful of both parties," and they mobilized because of their "rage against the mainstream political machine, no matter which party was in control."[104]

THE TEA PARTY AGAINST THE ESTABLISHMENT

The public anger at government that fueled the Tea Party's rise sharpened during the Obamacare fight and produced historic victories in the 2010 midterm elections. These primary challenges and subsequent victories accelerated changes—more seats but also a rightward drift—in the Republican Party. This was especially true for the House, where Republican gains produced a majority, and returned American politics to a government divided against itself. The 2010 elections produced what political scientist Alan Abramowitz called "the most conservative and ideologically polarized House since the end of World War II."[105]

Riding a wave of anger, the GOP was emboldened in its "Stop Obama" strategy. Senate leader Mitch McConnell claimed that defeating Obama was the "single most important thing," and House minority leader John Boehner pledged on the eve of the 2010 elections that a Republican majority would "do everything—and I mean everything we can do—to kill it [Obama's policy agenda], stop it, slow it down, whatever we can." If McConnell and Boehner had been strong opponents of Obama from the outset, they doubled down when the Tea Party fervor grew stronger. Colorado Senate nominee Ken Buck's stark views of Washington politics represented broader Tea Party attitudes: "When it comes to spending, I'm not compromising. I don't care who, what, when or where, I'm not compromising."[106]

Tea Party messaging was more strident in tone, and its messengers were often less polished and politic. But the philosophy behind them fit well with a modern GOP that had been built on distrust. The Tea Party's anti-statism was more distilled, concentrated, and vehement, and Tea Party–affiliated members were more organized and unified when they entered the House and Senate. If some observers attributed their differences to a purported "citizen legislator" or amateur's zeal, the Tea Party difference was somewhat ideological and especially antiestablishment, even though its candidates were no less likely than other Republican challengers to have held prior elective office.[107] Anti-government and more confrontational, the Tea Party was less a grass-roots or populist movement than a clearer-eyed opposition—more aggressive but just as careerist as the rest of the GOP. In all, the 2010 midterms produced "a Republican majority in the House dominated by right-wing insurgents determined to radically reduce the size and role of government."[108]

Tea Party leaders outside and inside the House pressured the House to live up to the movement's ideological commitments. Back in power in the legislative branch, conservative critics doubled down on their criticisms of Obama's "abuse" of executive power, carrying the argument as though it were long-standing conservative separation of powers dogma. True to provisions from the Contract from America, former representative Dick Armey, then the head of FreedomWorks, exhorted Republicans elected in the midterm wave to "look to the Constitution to govern your policy."[109]

In the new Congress, the Tea Party Caucus, begun by Representative Michele Bachmann in July 2010, started a series of seminars on the Constitution. The body began reading the document on the floor of the House, and the House adopted a provision (dating to the Tea Party's Contract from America) to cite the section of the Constitution enabling congressional action.[110] Here, too, the Tea Party distinguished itself from establishment Republicans in that it was increasingly resistant to compromise.

Tea Party legislators found their fealty and discipline outside Washington. They followed a multifaceted media strategy—talk radio, Fox News, and social media—decrying compromise and railing against GOP leaders who would grant any concessions to congressional Democrats or the White House.

This came to a head when it came time for Congress to set a budget. In those days, there were literally dozens of attempts to repeal or defund Obamacare. Republicans also advocated cuts to the budget and taxes.[111] This more extreme GOP began to break norms that prior conservatives had observed. Party leaders demanded cuts in other programs to pay even for disaster relief funds, fanned rather than countered right-wing conspiracy theories that imagined Obama would impose martial law, and routinely "dismissed nonpartisan analyses and conclusions about the nature of problems and impact of policies."[112] Data, science, and facts were to be disposed in favor of ideological prejudices.

An anti-governmentalism so zealous that it would deny government reports and scientific studies was also prone to discount the potentially disastrous effects of U.S. default on the American and world economies. As legislative fights emerged over budgets and whether Congress would vote to raise the debt ceiling in 2011 and again in 2013, top Republican leaders negotiated hard with the Obama administration. But for the Tea Party, it was never enough. In an informal 2011 poll of the Tea Party–dominated freshman class conducted by whip Kevin McCarthy, only four members of the class said they would raise the debt ceiling under any circumstances.[113] Even if the recalcitrant backbench was a useful bargaining chip for Boehner and McCarthy, more extreme members and their Tea Party constituents believed this was more than just a talking point.

Here and elsewhere, the Tea Party hold on the GOP challenged not only the economic health of the nation but the entire political system, even down to basic governance. In turn, this eroded public trust in government. Watching from the outside, more traditional Republicans decried the strategy, saying it revealed an "astounding lack of responsible leadership" and was evidence that an "apocalyptic cult" had taken over the GOP.[114]

Still, any havoc the Tea Party could wreak on the political system only fed the movement, because it made its diagnoses of untrustworthy government all the more true. According to political scientists Bryan Gervais and Irwin Morris, if the Tea Party's anti-compromise, anti-negotiation cry was based on an appeal to the purity of principle and on emotions such as anger, fear, and anxiety, it also made governing quite difficult, as "less compromise generates more government dysfunction, which only strengthens the antigovernment message of the Tea Party."[115] Democratic politicians, by contrast, want government programs they support to work, and they fear that breakdowns in governance ultimately harm their electoral prospects.

The Tea Party remained a thorn in the side of the establishment GOP. Going forward, Republican leaders would have to grapple with revolts from Tea Party primary voters who, not coincidentally, overlapped "substantially with those Americans angriest at government."[116] The movement cracked open significant and enduring rifts within the GOP, which were laid bare in Congress as Tea Party and Freedom Caucus Republicans challenged John Boehner and as Senators Ted Cruz and Rand Paul led fights against

Republican leader Mitch McConnell.[117] Within the House, missteps and a damaged brand hurt the Tea Party Caucus, but its sentiments (and many of the initial adherents) remained. Its many members reorganized first into the Liberty Caucus and later into the Freedom Caucus.

Even when the Tea Party lost its popularity and went underground in later years, its energy continued in 2012 as the GOP geared up to unseat Obama. The impact on the GOP electorate was lasting. Extreme as ever, "a majority of Tea Party Republicans said that [Obama] was probably or definitely born in another country, and almost as many said that he was a Muslim."[118] Fueled, too, by antipathy to liberal immigration policies and nativist sentiments, "Tea Party sympathizers form the Republican coalition's largest, most loyal, and most active component."[119]

The anger and distrust pulled the GOP to the right in 2012, even as it went back to the drawing board on constitutional prescriptions. Worry over Obama's power and how he might use it moved from Tea Party corners and conservative publications to the 2012 national Republican Party platform. In one of its planks, the GOP decried Obama's "antipathy toward the Constitution," which they said was exhibited by:

appointing "czars" to evade the confirmation process, making unlawful "recess" appointments when the Senate is not in recess, using executive orders to bypass the separation of powers and its checks and balances, encouraging illegal actions by regulatory agencies from the NLRB to the EPA, openly and notoriously displaying contempt for Congress, the Judiciary, and the Constitutional prerogatives of the individual States, refusing to defend the nation's laws in federal courts or enforce them on the streets, ignoring the legal requirement for legislative enactment of an annual budget, gutting welfare reform by unilaterally removing its statutory work requirement, buying senatorial votes with special favors, and evading the legal requirement for congressional consultation regarding troop commitments overseas.[120]

The Republican punditocracy pressed these claims, often using dire and dramatic language. In *Power Grab: Obama's Dangerous Plan for a One-Party Nation*, for example, Dick Morris and Eileen McGann fretted about Obama's open "disdain for the Constitution."[121]

Soon the GOP rediscovered its affinity for congressional power. Regarding judicial appointments, 1990s Republicans, still stinging from their failure to confirm Robert Bork to the Supreme Court, complained in their platform that "'advise and consent' has been replaced by 'slash and burn.'"[122] With the Senate in Republican hands in 2012, the GOP's party platform debuted a new interpretation of the legislature's role in the advise and consent process: "[It] is both a presidential responsibility, in selecting judicial candidates, and a senatorial responsibility, in confirming them."[123]

Similar convenient tactical shifts occurred in foreign policy. In 2008, the Republican platform had warned that "the waging of war—and the achieving of peace—should never be micromanaged . . . on the floor of the Senate and House of Representatives" and that "our next president must preserve all options." But by 2012, their platform reverted to a balanced view of separated power: "The United States of America is strongest when the President and Congress work closely together—in war and in peace—to advance our common interests and ideals."

However revealing these fluctuations on originalism might be, they are a smaller story than the sharp right turn the GOP took under the Tea Party's spell. A significant number of conservatives—Michelle Bachmann, Newt Gingrich, Rick Perry, Herman Cain, Rick Santorum, and Ron Paul—possessed some measure of conservative, antiestablishment appeal to Tea Party elements. They saw their openings in 2012 and joined the primary race for the Republican nomination. Mitt Romney, Jon Huntsman, and Tim Pawlenty pursued the more establishment lane of the race, but even they had to compete in a rightward direction. Comparing rhetorical emphases of Republican presidential candidates between 2008 and 2012, one study found that "the Republican Party has been radicalized in a direction consistent with the libertarian, small-government ideology" of the Tea Party.[124]

Even though Romney eventually won the nomination, along the way he had to "repudiate his political past as a moderate," "disown" his own health-care policy from Massachusetts, and self-identify as a "severe conservative."[125] He chose Paul Ryan as his running mate to excite the base. Despite his lackluster conservative credentials and his own "government-run" health-care plan, Romney had *more* support from Tea Party members than from other Republicans.[126] Obama won reelection as the first president since Reagan to win majorities of the popular vote twice. Reminiscent of 2010, this rightward shift likely cost the GOP seats down ballot too, including prominent Senate seats in Indiana and Missouri; still, the Tea Party influence was marked and enduring.[127]

In March 2013, the Republican's released a so-called autopsy that considered Obama's election and the loss of the popular vote in five of the six
previous presidential elections. Commissioned by Republican National
Committee chairman Reince Priebus, the report counseled the party to
pay attention to demographic shifts and modify certain positions and
the tone with which they were discussed. Participants in focus groups
of former Republicans in Iowa and Ohio said that the party was "scary,"
"narrow minded," and "out of touch" and that Republicans had become
the party of "stuffy old men," a finding consistent with "other post-
election surveys."[128] To change the party's brand, the report recommended
that candidates focus more on opportunity and growth and reach out to
Hispanics with special attention to comprehensive immigration reform
and to younger voters by becoming more "welcoming and inclusive" on
social issues. The report also struck a populist tone with its call for Republicans to "blow the whistle at corporate malfeasance and attack corporate
welfare." Social conservatives and Tea Party figures pushed back firmly,
arguing that establishment Republicans went against and demobilized the
GOP base.[129]

These intraparty struggles marked GOP politics throughout the remainder of the Obama administration. Frustrated, the Tea Party remained
inflexible to compromise with Democrats but also increasingly angry with
top GOP leaders who did not sufficiently share their sensibility. Immigration became a flashpoint. Although the Senate backed a comprehensive
reform bill in June 2013, and Republican leaders in the House supported
immigration reform, there was considerable grassroots pressure *against*
any path to citizenship for immigrants who had entered the country illegally. As reporter Tim Alberta described it, House Republicans' "office
phones shrieked with angry constituent calls." At a rally at the U.S. Capitol
on June 19, 2013, that coincided with the Tea Party Patriots "Audit the IRS"
rally, Republican speakers stoked the distrustful crowd by arguing that they
were defending the rule of law and the Constitution itself from the Democrats: "Right after [a] former Fox News host whipped the crowd of Tea
Partiers into a frenzy, [Rep. Steve] King bounded onto the stage. 'I can feel
it!' he cried. I can feel we're going to defend the rule of law! We're going to
defend the Constitution! We're going to defend our way of life!' " After this,
the Senate passed comprehensive reform with a strong, bipartisan majority
of 68–32, including fourteen Republicans, but Speaker Boehner refused to

bring the bill to the House floor, knowing that the majority of the House Republican Conference opposed it.[130]

The Tea Party began to target establishment GOP figures and primary against them. An early victim was a former Young Gun, the majority leader Eric Cantor (R-VA). Even though he had begun as a Tea Party booster, using the fervor to recruit and campaign, that support went unrequited back home. Cantor had a Tea Party–backed independent challenger in 2010 and had declined to join the Tea Party Caucus in the House. Increasingly caught between his duties to the Republican Conference and a conservative movement in Virginia more in step with the Tea Party, Cantor was upset in a June 2014 primary by a Tea Party favorite, economics professor Dave Brat.[131]

The Tea Party struggled with a brand the party base found exciting, but was increasingly viewed by outsiders as too far to the right and potentially dangerous to the GOP's efforts to win over independent voters or compete in blue and purple districts and states. House members grew wary of the tarnished brand, and by the 114th Congress, the House Freedom Caucus had taken up this oppositional role, though similarly emphasizing intra-caucus unity (sometimes even through an internal caucus "binding" mechanism) and confrontation with their own leadership, with Democrats, and especially with the Obama White House.[132] Like the largely defunct Tea Party Caucus, the Freedom Caucus was conservative, focused on "limited government" and efforts to enhance its position within the House Republican Conference.[133]

Even though the name changed, Tea Party anger and sentiments endured and remained persistently dangerous to the GOP establishment. Several times, the Tea Party consumed the careers of its erstwhile champions—not just Cantor but later Boehner and eventually the two other Young Guns.

By 2015, Boehner announced his plans to step down, facing "a potential floor vote to oust him as Speaker, pushed by Republican Tea Partyers."[134] Poised to face off (even to the point of a potential "no confidence" vote) with conservative dissidents in his conference over a planned compromise with the Obama administration on spending, Boehner suffered when Freedom Caucus forces revolted, and their mounting threats factored into Boehner's decision to end his career only six years after Kevin McCarthy took him to the Tea Party rally that kicked off his 2010 majority-building efforts.[135] The columnist Todd Purdum later wrote, "Boehner and the rest of the GOP establishment assumed they could ride the Tea Party tide to power, and then co-opt that wing of the party, but that proved badly wrong."[136]

With Boehner out, McCarthy, as leader, seemed poised to rise to the speakership. On the leadership ladder, he quickly garnered votes and took the lead, but then hit a series of roadblocks before abruptly withdrawing. One such roadblock was the Freedom Caucus, which announced its support not for McCarthy but for Florida's Daniel Webster. Another was a letter penned by Representative Walter Jones, who cryptically called for any speakership candidate to drop out if they had committed "misdeeds":

> With all the voter distrust of Washington felt around the country, I'm asking that any candidate for Speaker of the House, majority leader, and majority whip withdraw himself from the leadership election if there are any misdeeds he has committed since joining Congress that will embarrass himself, the Republican Conference, and the House of Representatives if they become public.[137]

Rumors swirled that this letter might have prompted McCarthy to back out, though he denied it and, indeed the lack of the Freedom Caucus votes itself made it difficult to see not so much how McCarthy could win the conference vote for Speaker but whether he would keep enough conservatives in line to garner the 218 he needed to win the speakership on the House floor.[138]

McCarthy's withdrawal from the race opened a window for fellow Young Gun Paul Ryan, then Ways and Means Committee chairman and a former 2012 vice presidential candidate. Still, the fault lines were on display even during that run, as the Freedom Caucus weighed its commitment to Webster's insurgent candidacy, and ultimately there were but a few defections against Ryan on the House floor.[139]

Ryan became Speaker, but like Boehner, his speakership was fraught with conflict with the Tea Party/Freedom Caucus right wing of the conference. The outlines of these impending problems seemed obvious even before the 2016 election. During Trump's rise, the *New York Times*'s Jennifer Steinhauer wrote that "the Tea Party's ultimate creation, Donald J. Trump, may be coming for the last young gun unscathed."[140]

In 2009, the political conditions were ripe for the politics of distrust.

At a time of grave economic difficulty, during which the first African American president tried to enact an ambitious domestic agenda, distrust was strategically useful for conservatives in and outside Congress. When comparing the relative political success of FDR's New Deal programs to those of Obama, Anthony Badger noted that the postwar generation had a much stronger belief in government but "by the 1990s fewer than one in four Americans had that same faith in the federal government. Now the figure is even lower. Obama, like any Democratic president, has to live with that profound culture of antistatist suspicion."[141] In their war with government, conservatives marshaled economic anxiety as well as cultural and identity politics to weaken the Obama administration and its political coalition.

In certain ways the Tea Party Obama faced was different from earlier participants in the conservative war with government. There was a conspiratorial strain to the Tea Party. As political scientist Gary Jacobson put it, "Not a few Tea Partiers came to see [Obama] not merely as an objectionable liberal Democrat, but a tyrant (of the Nazi, fascist, communist, socialist, monarchist, or racist variety, depending on the critic) intent on subjecting Americans to, variously, socialism, communism, fascism, concentration camps; or control by the United Nations, Interpol, international bankers, the Council on Foreign Relations, or the Trilateral Commission."[142] And the Tea Party movement not only went after Obama, but also attacked the GOP establishment and, contrary to the business wing of the Republican Party, overtly promoted anti-immigrant sentiment.

But what was really all that novel? Given what came before, the Tea Party's efforts to undermine trust in government, the executive branch, and the Obama presidency were unsurprising. Stoked by anti-Obama rhetoric (and working hard to disguise the more extreme thought among much of its membership), the Tea Party's anti-government efforts were something of a perfection of the Gingrich revolution's efforts to tear down the government in order to retake it.

As the GOP had already been moving toward right-wing populism, its vehement response to Obama propelled it along that trajectory. Republican Party developments—first Goldwater's western prairie libertarianism and later the incorporation of southern whites who fled the Democratic Party after the civil rights movement—severely diminished moderate (and certainly liberal) Republicanism.[143] This left the anti-statist elements as a potent, sometimes dominating force inside the GOP. That southern and rural turn made the GOP more likely to respond harshly toward the nation's first black president and to embrace nativism. Those right-wing populists who held "that all Americans were not equally deserving" and thought their political enemies were not sufficiently "American" echoed Wendell Wilkie's demand to FDR and the New Dealers: "Give our country back to us."[144]

Moreover, the establishment GOP strategy was strikingly similar to that of previous eras, and the atmosphere in which Obama served was still suspicious of government.

Obama faced an intractable Republican Congress dating back to the day of his inauguration. Unflinching opposition made strategic sense for the GOP. While both parties have become more polarized, Republicans have driven polarization and promoted distrust to a much greater degree than Democrats.[145] A conservative philosophy built on expectations of government ineffectiveness and failure feeds on itself when conservative efforts grind government to a halt. When the Democrats controlled the White House and Congress, Republicans wielded institutionalist arguments against congressional power and refused to cooperate with Democrats in committees. When the government subsequently failed to pass meaningful legislation, Republicans employed those failures to win elections.

Policy opposition to Obama was anti-statist, race based, and suspicious. Consider health care. In arguing against Obamacare, conservatives turned to a familiar weapon in their arsenal, distrust in government. After the Supreme Court ruled on the ACA's constitutionality, Medicaid expansion became optional for states. These decisions made within states were racialized; states that supported expansion the least had larger black populations and low support among whites.[146] This link between race and enlarging social programs was part and parcel of a long pattern in the American politics of health care and social welfare.

Despite this opposition, Obama was the first president since Ronald Reagan to win reelection with two consecutive popular vote majorities. During his time in office, he passed major health reform, put in place a large stimulus package, and promoted regulations to slow climate change, control financial institutions, and save the American automobile industry. He left office quite popular and without personal scandal. As the first African American president, he will be remembered for the stunning political feat of his own electoral victories.

In many ways, Obama's persona, the fact that he symbolized racial progress, and his political status (not to mention his considerable skills) were threats to the GOP. Reversing course from the Reagan and Bush years, the Tea Party's distrust of Obama translated into broader articulations of concern about the power of the presidency and executive branch. Given their anti-Obama roots and odd mix of anti-government sentiment and strong authoritarianism, it was predictable that they would reverse course again to favor a strong presidency as soon as a Republican took the White House.[147]

While neither the GOP establishment nor the Tea Party could stop health-care reform or Obama's reelection, its extreme anti-government rhetoric had consequences for civility, public trust, and governance. In this way, it laid the groundwork for who would come next.

Chapter Six

"PUNCH GOVERNMENT IN THE FACE"

Anger in the Trump Era

In February 2018, an indictment by Special Counsel Robert S. Mueller III charged a Russia-based group called the Internet Research Agency with elaborate attempts to "to interfere with U.S. political and electoral processes, including the 2016 U.S. presidential election."[1] According to the indictment, the conspirators' "stated goal" was to "spread distrust towards the candidates and the political system in general."[2] While the Russian military intelligence directorate hacked the emails of Democrats and the Clinton campaign, the IRA "used social media accounts and interest groups to sow discord in the U.S. political system through 'information warfare.'"[3] The Russian plot depended on America's long-standing culture of anti-statism to exacerbate divisions in American society.[4]

As part of their plan to sow chaos, the Russians backed the candidacy of New York real estate mogul and reality television star Donald J. Trump, who had never before run for political office. According to a bipartisan Senate Intelligence Report issued in August 2020, hacks of Democrats' emails and their summer and fall 2016 releases had a clear motivation: "Moscow's intent was to harm the Clinton Campaign, tarnish an expected Clinton presidential administration, help the Trump Campaign after Trump became the presumptive Republican nominee, and undermine the U.S. democratic process."[5]

In July 2015, Russian interference began to affect the 2016 primaries, initially focusing on weakening Trump's competitors—Marco Rubio, Jeb Bush, and Ted Cruz. Once Trump had secured the Republican nomination, conspirator "specialists" were instructed to "use any opportunity to criticize Hillary and the rest (except Sanders and Trump—we support them.)"[6] According to communications scholar Kathleen Hall Jamieson, these messages influenced some voters, in part because they complemented Trump's own rhetoric and tactics.[7]

Before becoming a presidential candidate, Trump floated racist birther claims, boosting conspiracy theories many Washington, D.C.-based Tea Party organizers had sought to keep under wraps.[8] Then Trump built an insurgent candidacy that melded xenophobia with anger, suspicion, and distrust toward elites and government. In the 2016 campaign, Trump took to Twitter and held rallies lambasting Obama (who Trump claimed "created ISIS") and Hillary Clinton (whom he dubbed "Crooked Hillary"), after levying similar insults at a battery of GOP rivals. Trump launched a full-on assault on national institutions and establishment political actors. He labeled the national media "fake news" and Washington, D.C. a "swamp" that needed to be "drained."

In some ways this aggressive and oppositional stance fit with—and was a logical consequence of—the grand strategy that the GOP had nurtured for decades and accelerated during the Tea Party era in the Obama years. Trump's litany of grievances appealed to the GOP base, which had been primed for many years to be suspicious of the national government, to think of Democrats as the "enemy," and to distrust the media.

But Trumpism was not only an intensification but also a shift in the conservative and Republican strategy to undermine trust in government through both language and action. Trump's extreme rhetoric, when he was a candidate and as president, had five elements.

First, Trump adopted more extreme anti-government rhetoric than any Republican leader before him. He promoted marginal views and conspiracy theories and denounced compromise. Like many Tea Party activists, Trump's disdain extended to the GOP establishment, and he used scorched-earth tactics in internecine battles.

Second, Trump used language that was more directly and explicitly anti-immigrant and overtly race based than any major party presidential candidate after World War II. The rhetoric of the GOP had long implied that welfare programs robbed hard workers to give to the undeserving, often lacing such claims with racialized tropes to characterize the "undeserving." But Trump unabashedly expanded that territory beyond its previous boundaries, making norm-breaking claims that in earlier years would have been seen as uncivil and racist. A 2016 campaign press release stated that Trump was "calling for a total and complete shutdown of Muslims entering the United States until our country's representatives can figure out what is going on."[9] In 2017, when a protest of white supremacists marching in the "Unite the Right" rally in Charlottesville, Virginia, ended in the death of counterprotester Heather Heyer, Trump said there was "hatred, bigotry, and violence—on many sides" with "very fine people on both sides."[10]

Third, Trump combined populist language associated with the left—like critiques of corporate power in politics—and combined it with right-wing populism. He stoked suspicions of relationships between special interests and establishment officeholders. But his tax and regulatory agenda would prove this rhetoric hollow.

Fourth, he flagrantly questioned the legitimacy of election outcomes. Throughout the Republican nominating process, Trump complained about his opponents' tactics, suggesting that elections were "rigged" against him and even that the Iowa caucus should be rerun after he lost to Ted Cruz. In the 2016 general election, he laid the groundwork to question a potential Clinton victory, and in 2018 he questioned the integrity of the midterm elections as the Democrats were poised to make large gains.[11] Trump even charged that voter fraud had cost him the popular vote in the presidential election, something no other American president has done.

Fifth, and most troublingly to many "never Trump" conservatives, he expanded the war with government to include parts of the American state that had previously escaped these strategies. Trump targeted the CIA, intelligence communities, and especially the FBI during its investigation of Russian interference in the 2016 election. He would go on to cast aspersions against the special counsel's investigations. For instance, when the FBI raided the office of Trump lawyer Michael Cohen on April 9, 2018, Trump immediately criticized the action and the Mueller investigation: "So, I just heard that they broke in to the office of one of my personal attorneys, a good man, and it's a disgraceful situation. It's a total witch hunt."[12] The Mueller team, Trump said, was "conflicted" and "the most biased group of people," and he reiterated a frequent complaint that Attorney General

Jeff Sessions's decision to recuse himself from the Russian investigation was "a terrible mistake." Trump called the raid a "disgrace" and an "an attack on our country in a true sense."[13]

Trump employed distrust to shift power toward himself. Seizing on distrust of Washington, he executed a hostile takeover of the GOP. He saw that part of the party's base was dissatisfied with past compromises, the failure to make inroads on the conservative agenda, and comprehensive immigration reform, and he gathered these voters to him. Establishment Republicans ultimately made peace with him because Trump served their agenda by appointing Federalist Society–approved judges, cutting taxes, and limiting regulations on business and because they feared blowback from the Trump base. While Trump's uses of distrust in government were more tumultuous and somewhat different from theirs, he built upon them.

Actions by the Trump administration to shape, defund, and depopulate government agencies were driven by two motives: an interest in building a state personally loyal to and protective of Trump and his agenda but also, in the words of Trump strategist Steve Bannon, to "deconstruct the administrative state."[14] In the words of public administration scholar Donald Moynihan, the "United States went from Reagan's 'government is not the solution to our problem; government is the problem' to a more conspiratorial-minded evocation of public officials as not just dysfunctional but determined to undermine the President."[15]

Trump's situational constitutionalism marked the continuation of a partisan pattern, while additionally severely undermining institutional norms. As legal scholars Joseph Fishkin and David Pozen argue, Republicans have engaged in "asymmetric constitutional hardball," promoting strained views of the Constitution for partisan purposes and "attempting to shift settled understandings of the Constitution in an unusually aggressive or self-entrenching manner."[16] With broad references to "an Article II" power to operate often without cooperation or consultation with Congress, President Trump (and unitary executive adherents including Attorney General William Barr), these Republicans took the unitary executive theory and an expansive view of executive power to new heights.

This Trumpian institutionalism undermined the norms and practices of transparency, accountability, and governmental operations carried out by nonpartisan experts, administrators, and scientists.

Messages promoting distrust in government aligned with the administration's practices of cronyism and personal connections over expertise and competence, as critics sounded alarms about benefits flowing to Trump's family and the all too cozy connections between some powerful economic interests and the Trump administration.

This chapter focuses on Trump's candidacy and the first two years of his presidency and shows the four benefits of distrust at work amid the new and more expansive uses of strategic distrust Trump inaugurated. Trumpism employed distrust strategically to win in 2016, shift the center of gravity of the Republican Party and American conservatism, and promote a nearly unconstrained view of executive power. Trump used distrust to promote anti-trade and anti-immigrant policies; anti-labor and pro-corporate efforts; and cuts in taxes and domestic policies while increasing military spending. Ultimately, Trump also motivated counter-mobilization, with active engagement by resistance groups beginning with the 2017 Women's Marches and an electoral backlash in the 2018 midterm elections.

TRUMP'S HOSTILE TAKEOVER

Donald Trump had toyed off and on with possible presidential runs since the late 1980s. During the Obama years, he reemerged as a political force when he began championing birtherism, the conspiracy theory that Obama was born in Kenya rather than Hawaii. The birther myth was politically powerful, because it had the twin political effects of "othering" Obama to make him seem less American and undermining the legitimacy of his administration by throwing into question, for those who believed the claim, his constitutional eligibility to be president. On Fox News with Bill O'Reilly in 2011, Trump wondered about Obama's birth certificate, and in a tweet in 2012, he wrote, "An 'extremely credible source' has called my office and told me that @BarackObama's birth certificate is a fraud."[17]

Polling indicated there was a market for birtherism. A Fox News poll in April 2011 asked respondents whether those who publicized the claim were "nutty conspiracy theorists" or whether "there is cause to wonder." Forty percent of the respondents and 63 percent of the Republican respondents agreed: "There is cause to wonder."[18] A study by political scientist Philip Klinkner found that beliefs in birther claims were highly related to partisanship and views on race and were revived by Trump's statements in the spring of 2011, leading to a mini-boom of a potential 2012 Trump candidacy.[19] Trump also seized on immigration, contrasting himself with business-oriented Republicans and aligning with those who saw a path to citizenship as "amnesty." As former Trump campaign associate Sam Nunberg observed, "Every time Trump tweeted against amnesty in 2013, 2014, he would get hundreds and hundreds of retweets."[20]

When Trump launched his 2016 campaign at Trump Tower in June 2015, he emphasized three elements critical to his campaign: racial resentments, a burgeoning economic populism, and anti-government sentiment. He was an attractive primary candidate because, as political scientist Rachel Blum explained, "Here was a figure whose brazen disregard for political correctness or decorum, derision of the political establishment, and jingoistic rhetoric toward nonwhites and nonnationals fit precisely with the language activists had been using for some time."[21] Trump's approach was in line with Tea Party activists who were wary of Republican Party leadership, not attracted to the small-government libertarianism of Washington-based Tea Party organizations, and prone to reactionary politics.

Trump warned of liberal immigration policies, saying:

When Mexico sends its people, they're not sending their best. They're not sending you. They're not sending you. They're sending people that have lots of problems, and they're bringing those problems with us [sic]. They're bringing drugs. They're bringing crime. They're rapists. And some, I assume, are good people.[22]

Trump claimed that "politicians are all talk, no action" and "controlled fully by the lobbyists, by the donors, and by the special interests." He captured the key anti-Washington theme of his populist and white nationalist campaign when he said, "They will never make America great again."[23] This slogan did not just look forward, it evoked a time of past greatness, when whites were a larger and more powerful force. Trump also appealed to the extremes of the far right with approving comments about violence toward protestors, something his primary opponents criticized while they were still active candidates.[24]

Trump joined a crowded field of seventeen Republican primary contenders. He stood apart, and not only because many of his opponents had barely distinguishable policy views from each other. Trump's angry, antiestablishment views and messages wielded race, xenophobia, and Islamophobia. Primary opponent Jeb Bush denounced the birther charge. Ted Cruz and Marco Rubio, each of whom had finessed a position on Obama's birthplace in the past, were subject to the birther spillover effect during the nomination fight, which challenged their own status as "natural born citizens."[25]

Trump's birtherism tapped into racialized resentments and worked for Trump with some voters. This is not to deny that economic anxiety—after the 2008 financial collapse and the slower-than-expected recovery—was real. A movement had emerged, on the left, critical of the increasing proportion of wealth going to the richest people in the United States and of the political power of "the 1 percent." Similar sentiments emerged on the right and fueled right-wing populist anger at elites, especially Washington elites and their bailout politics. Throughout his campaign, Trump underscored that he understood corrupt politicians and the inordinate power of the wealthy, because he had given large donations to politicians when he wanted something for himself in return. Trump promised to counter this by "draining the swamp" and protecting and expanding programs that helped everyday Americans.

Trump's rise from birther to viable candidate hinged on public anger. His political organization—which was small, opaque, and personalized compared to most modern presidential campaigns—was built as antiestablishment and benefited from significant media coverage, as the novelty of his "celebrity" candidacy had appeal among the American media. Skilled at garnering media attention, Trump's audacious and confrontational statements against opponents, the establishment, and the media enlivened his core supporters, who were also suspicious of Washington and elites more generally. As political scientist Marc Hetherington observed, Trump's "outsider" candidacy (much more than the outsider governors of prior ages) was fueled by rampant distrust in government that discounted establishment leaders, whether inside or outside Washington.[26] House Freedom Caucus member Trent Franks said, Trump "came along when the country needed someone to punch government in the face."[27]

Trump distinguished himself in the primary field with his hostile tone and his proudly "politically incorrect" and antiestablishment attacks, including on GOP rivals.[28] Trump branded former Florida governor Jeb Bush "low energy" and claimed Bush was trying to downplay his family connections, particularly given his brother's—former president George W. Bush—unpopularity. The day after a December 2015 debate, Trump tweeted, "Jeb Bush had a tough night at the debate. Now he'll probably take some of his special interest money, he is their puppet, and buy ads."[29] Jeb's campaign spending became Trump's preferred target for ridicule. On December 24, he tweeted "Poor @JebBush spent $50 million on his campaign, I spent almost nothing. He's bottom (and gone), I'm top (by a lot). That's what U.S. needs!" Through successive tweets, Trump traced Bush's exorbitant campaign spending and his popular stall and decline. By late January, Jeb's campaign had spent $89 million. This came to a head on February 8, when Trump tweeted, "Everybody is laughing at Jeb Bush-spent $100 million and is at bottom of pack. A pathetic figure!"[30]

February also began the Republican Party's presidential nominating contests. The first was the Iowa caucus on February 1. After the onetime Tea Party favorite, Texas senator Ted Cruz, won the caucus with nearly 28 percent of the vote, he skyrocketed to the top of Trump's target list. Trump accused Cruz of stealing the election by spreading false rumors that Ben Carson was dropping out of the presidential race and by claiming Trump supported Obamacare.

Trump's furor at Cruz's Iowa victory was an early sign that Trump would undermine the legitimacy of elections when they did not go his way. In a series of tweets on February 3 that included ten anti-Cruz tweets in seven hours, Trump lambasted him for having "lied" his way to victory in Iowa, even accusing Cruz of fraud: "Ted Cruz didn't win Iowa, he stole it. That is why all of the polls were so wrong and why he got far more votes than anticipated. Bad!"[31] Trump called for the "Cruz results [to be] nullified" and for the state of Iowa to either "disqualify" Cruz or to have a do-over "new election."[32] Trump would later brand Cruz as "Lyin' Ted" and claim that Cruz's father had been involved in the assassination of President John F. Kennedy.

Trump lost to Ted Cruz in Iowa and only narrowly edged out Marco Rubio for second place, but in the next contest, the New Hampshire primary, he would bounce back to a decisive victory. In New Hampshire, he won 35.3 percent in a multicandidate race. John Kasich finished a distant second above Cruz and Rubio, and with this Trump began to solidify the right, stoking anger against the GOP establishment. One study of the 2016 New Hampshire primary found that it was distrust in government, rather than ideology, that affected a choice of Trump over his GOP rivals. Where "the probability of voting for Trump among moderates and conservatives is unremarkable," political scientists Joshua Dyck, Shanna Person-Merkowitz, and Michael Coates found, "a distruster [in government] is more than 20 percentage points more likely to support Trump than any other Republican candidate."[33] Trump elbowed his way ahead of the primary pack by stoking more anger and distrust than they could or would.

By March, Trump had turned his attention to another rival. If Bush was the well-funded, legacy insider, and Cruz was a lying rival battling Trump for the support of the right, Trump cast the younger and more telegenic Marco Rubio as the typical Washington politician who was more style than substance. Dubbing the Florida Senator "Little Marco," "lightweight," and "choker," and, for a brief time, "RobotRubio," Trump claimed Rubio was "just another all talk, no action, politician."[34]

The criticisms intensified as Rubio became, if only briefly, the most prominent anti-Trump candidate, especially around the time of the Florida Republican primary on March 15. After Rubio ran an anti-Trump ad referencing the claims of fraud against Trump University, Trump returned the charge, tweeting that Rubio was a "fraud lightweight." Concerned over Rubio's seeming momentum, Trump complained three days before the election that Florida forces were seeking to "rig the vote" in Rubio's favor: "Word is-early voting in FL is very dishonest. Little Marco, his State Chairman, & their minions are working overtime-trying to rig the vote."[35]

But Trump won nearly 47 percent of the Florida primary vote, beating out the distant second-place Rubio by nearly twenty points. From there, Trump eclipsed the field for the remainder of the primary season. Rival GOP factions began to calcify around candidates based on the calculation of who was best equipped to "stop Trump." His rivals took turns as the "anti-Trump" candidate, but Trump withstood each challenge and went into the Republican nominating convention with the delegates necessary to secure the nomination.

I ALONE: THE TRUMP CONVENTION

The 2016 Republican National Convention in July was the last chance for establishment Republicans to stop Trump. At the same time, it was Trump's opportunity to shore up his candidacy by embedding it within the broader

GOP coalition. His first step was to choose his running mate. He found one in Indiana governor Mike Pence, an evangelical Christian. From there, he began to articulate more traditional Republican positions: he became antiabortion, he highlighted the constitutional importance of the judiciary, and he reiterated the anti-government, anti-Obama views that connected Trumpist anger to the already distrustful GOP. Regardless of the mutual hostility between Trump and some establishment Republicans, Trump's heated, antiestablishment narrative brought disaffected conservative groups together.

The GOP was angry after eight years of Obama. Some of this ire was aimed at Obama's use of presidential power. In yet another turnaround—and again, despite conservatives' long-avowed view that the Constitution is "fixed" in meaning—the GOP proved adept at adapting its constitutionalist views on the separation of powers to suit its situational needs.[36] The Republican Party discovered "a unitary executive" philosophy in the Reagan years and resurrected it for subsequent Republican presidents. In 2016 the abrupt shift came again—this time against presidential power in opposing Obama but ready to switch back when Trump assumed office.

In 2016, the Republican national platform painted a dire portrait of unaccountable governance and an Obama presidency run amok. According to it, the "most urgent task" was "to restore the American people's faith in their government by electing a president who will enforce duly enacted laws, honor constitutional limits on executive authority, and return credibility to the Oval Office."[37] Seemingly promising a return to limited government and presidential restraint compared to Obama, the platform championed "a Republican president who will end abuses of power by departments and agencies, like the IRS and the EPA, and by the White House itself," adding that "a president who will respect the Constitution's separation of powers" was essential to "safeguarding our liberties."

The platform also incorporated a critique of modern government. Of Obamacare, Republicans charged, "It imposed a Euro-style bureaucracy to manage its unworkable, budget-busting, conflicting provisions." This reliance on the administrative state, Republicans argued, led to "cronyism," whereby the government "distorts the free market and erodes public trust in our political system." Republicans blamed the "federal regulatory burden," which they called "the quiet tyranny," for continued economic stagnation since the 2008 financial meltdown, contending that agencies threatened "the ability of the American people to govern themselves." They termed the Consumer Financial Protection Bureau "a rogue agency" led by a director possessing "dictatorial powers unique in the American republic"[38] and argued the centralization of power in Washington was a threat to the Constitution's federal system—at stake was not just federalism but liberty itself.[39]

The GOP said it placed its trust in the American people and the states, countering them to overweening bureaucrats and the federal government. According to the platform, trusting "the people" should lead to "removing the power from unelected, unaccountable government" and relieving the burden and expense of punishing government regulations." It suggested a sense of loss—of power or identity—bearing the desire to "take back their country."[40]

This right-wing populist definition of "the people" employed an exclusive view of Americanness. Republicans presented government as increasingly benefiting only the undeserving: "The more it intrudes into every aspect of American life the more it alienates the citizens who work, pay taxes, and wonder what has happened to the country they love." This language of deservingness has long had a racial component in Republican political rhetoric, at least as far back as Ronald Reagan's "welfare queen."

Republicans' situational constitutionalism swung again toward executive power at the convention and shifted further after Trump took office.

For all the platform's promise of the return to separation of powers and presidential restraint in response to the purported dangers of Obama's presidency and centralized administrative power, Trump offered his own strong, often unilateral leadership as the solution to the country's woes. Trump led chants of "Lock her up" ("her" being Hillary Clinton), and his surrogates broke democratic norms and embraced an authoritarian tendency that presents political opponents as criminals.

At the convention, Ted Cruz, second in the delegate count, refused to endorse the nominee.[41] Never-Trumpers made a last-ditch attempt to deny Trump the nomination, but this failed when Trump was "backed by Republican National Committee officials in a sign of new coordination between the insurgent candidate and the institutional party establishment."[42]

Then, in his GOP nomination acceptance speech, Trump "offered no praise for Republican icons, he remembered no Golden Age of Republican rule, he offered no praise to his erstwhile rivals or their supporters, and he offered no praise or defense of the Republican Congress."[43]

Making the case that "I alone can fix it," Trump was at once touting his outsized view of his own skills while ignoring—and sometimes outright denigrating—the GOP establishment and the current state of America. Appealing to voter disaffection and anger, Trump's "dystopic vision" of "America as a land of rampant homicides, illegal immigrants, poverty, debt, decaying infrastructure, and international humiliation"—all of which were exaggerations or outright falsehoods—"felt true to his listeners," who were more apt to take his word than to believe official sources, elite fact-checkers, or the mainstream media.[44]

Some GOP elites were wary. They proceeded tentatively, hoping that constitutional checks and balances might mitigate Trump's influence should he win the presidency. In one notable case, just before the convention, Speaker Paul Ryan remarked, "There are policies he's pursuing that I don't agree with. And in the legislative branch—a separate but equal branch of government—we will litigate those things in the future."[45]

This cautious reluctance was true of Trump's defeated rivals too, even as they eventually endorsed or otherwise supported Trump. As the pundit Ezra Klein, citing prior anti-Trump statements and subsequent endorsements by several of his rivals, summed the turnaround: "Ted Cruz told Americans to vote for the pathological liar. Rick Perry urged people to elect the cancer on conservatism. Rand Paul backed the delusional narcissist. Marco Rubio campaigned to hand the nuclear codes of the United States to an erratic individual."[46]

In the end, the GOP establishment was not so much reconciled with Trump as resigned to him. For all the initial antipathy of the "Republican establishment" to Trump, one by one his primary foes and even many Never Trumpers caved to his strength with Republican base voters. They turned their antipathy instead toward Hillary Clinton.[47]

SERIOUSLY OFF-TRACK

When a primary candidate wins a party nomination, there is almost inevitably a softening of positions meant to appeal to moderates. Trump now turned attention to courting the restive public for the general election, and while he continued to use xenophobic and racially charged language, he incorporated some moderate signaling. His strategy until November largely focused on voter frustration with Washington, the media, and the government and the electorate's pessimism about the future.

A week after the Republican National Convention, Democrats held a convention of their own in Philadelphia. The Democrats nominated former senator, secretary of state, and first lady Hillary Clinton. But the party was far from unified. Frustrations lingered among supporters of Bernie Sanders, the progressive independent senator from Vermont who had challenged her for the nomination. Sanders was a self-professed democratic socialist, and his supporters were already distrustful of political and economic elites. Once he lost the nomination, they became convinced that Democratic insiders had put their thumbs on the scale. This upset was fueled by WikiLeaks' release of hacked emails from the Democratic National Committee during the Democratic convention that many Sanders supporters viewed as showing a bias toward Clinton and against Sanders. As the Mueller indictments of July 2018 revealed, these email leaks were timed for the convention to maximize conflict.[48] Representative Debbie Wasserman Schultz, the chair of the Democratic National Committee, resigned in response to the leaked emails. Sanders backers protested inside and outside the convention hall.

Tearing down Hillary Clinton and capitalizing on the Democratic infighting was critical to Trump's strategy. One line of attack involved Clinton's use of a private email server as secretary of state; as part of the process evaluating whether this posed a security risk, Clinton's lawyers withheld from review emails involving personal matters. During the Democratic National Convention, Trump, referring to those, made a direct appeal to camera, saying: "Russia, if you're listening. I hope you're able to find the 30,000 [Clinton] emails that are missing."[49] Although Trump would later say he was joking, the Mueller investigation found that "within approximately five hours of Trump's statement, [Russian Intelligence] officers targeted for the first time Clinton's personal office."[50] Moreover, "by the late summer of 2016, the Trump Campaign was planning a press strategy, a communications campaign, and messaging based on the possible release of Clinton emails by WikiLeaks."[51]

Pursuant to their pro-Trump objectives, Russian Internet Research Agency affiliates established Twitter and Facebook accounts—"March for Trump," "Clinton FRAUDation," and "Trumpsters United"—and promoted hashtags like "#Trump2016," "#TrumpTrain," "#MAGA," and "#Hillary4Prison."[52] They were also active on YouTube, Tumblr, and Instagram. Some Russian social media specialists "mimicked real U.S. organizations" including "@TEN_GOP, purported to be connected to the Tennessee Republican Party" and created "fictitious U.S. organizations and grassroots groups and used these accounts to pose as anti-immigration groups, Tea Party activists, Black Lives Matter protestors, and other U.S. social and political activists."[53] In all, Special Counsel Robert Mueller's investigation found that these "social media operations" had "the goal of sowing discord in the U.S. political system" and possessed the means of reaching "large U.S. audiences."[54]

As Russians actively spread distrust in the summer of 2016, Trump forces found their efforts quite agreeable. The Internet Research Agency actively organized rallies (including in New York, Florida, and Pennsylvania) and "represent[ing] themselves as U.S. persons . . . communicate[d] with members of the Trump campaign to seek assistance and coordination" of their planned rallies.[55] Given how consistent the IRA's messages were with Trump campaign efforts to sow discord and promote distrust, Trump campaign principals and surrogates "promoted—typically by linking, retweeting, or similar methods of reposting—pro-Trump or anti-Clinton content published by the IRA through IRA-controlled social media accounts." Among those who retweeted such content were the campaign's digital director Brad Parscale; its last campaign manager, Kellyanne Conway; and candidate Trump's sons, Eric Trump and Donald Trump Jr. The candidate himself responded to one such posting on Twitter.[56] And Trump repeatedly mentioned WikiLeaks at campaign rallies. "I love WikiLeaks," he told followers in Pennsylvania. Matters worsened for Clinton when, in October and November 2016, WikiLeaks released hacked documents that included Clinton speeches and correspondence related to the Clinton Foundation.[57]

Perhaps most of these instances were just parallel efforts aimed at the same purpose, but subsequent investigations found that Paul Manafort, onetime chairman of the Trump campaign, provided important inside information to foreign actors. Manafort had shared Trump campaign "internal polling data and other updates" with Konstantin Kilimnik, a Ukrainian whom the Mueller investigation said had ties to Russian intelligence. Manafort also shared his "strategy for winning Democratic votes in Midwestern states."[58] After leaving the campaign, Manafort sent a "strategy memorandum" to Jared Kushner "proposing that the Campaign make the case against Clinton 'as the failed and corrupt champion of the establish-ment,' " a case, Manafort claimed, was more credibly made thanks to the WikiLeaks releases of Clinton's and Democrats' internal documents.[59]

All the while, the Trump campaign organization was chaotic, with multi-ple staff changes, including three campaign managers, Corey Lewandowski, Paul Manafort, and Kellyanne Conway. But in one focused endeavor, the campaign worked with Cambridge Analytica to use private Facebook infor-mation to target communications—including fake stories—to carefully selected voters. Trump benefited from other organizations' efforts too, like the support of the Fraternal Order of Police, the well-financed National Rifle Association, white evangelicals, and grassroots groups in swing states. Many of these supporters were on hand from the Tea Party. As political sci-entists Michael Zoorob and Theda Skocpol observed, "Such organized and interconnected Americans, most already voting for Republicans, were often thrilled to hear Donald Trump's message of racially tinged anger, fear and resentment." Embedded in organizational networks, these voters heard and passed on such messages. The result was that "Trump garnered very strong vote margins from such constituencies, even beyond usual GOP margins."[60]

Trump's policy platform was scattershot; it included orthodox Republi-canism on taxes and regulations but also what had been heresy in the GOP regarding trade protections and Russia. Trump's strategic view also encom-passed the details of specific policy stances, including on health care. While disavowing the Affordable Care Act, Trump nevertheless made vague if grandiose promises about covering everyone, often adding that this made him unlike other Republicans.[61] In October 2016, Trump promised, "You're going to have such great healthcare at a tiny fraction of the cost, and it is going to be so easy."[62] But he could never explain how he would achieve this, and according to an analysis of the Commonwealth Fund, the plan released by Trump's campaign would have swelled the "number of uninsured indi-viduals by 16 million to 25 million relative to the ACA" and reduced coverage the most among "low-income individuals and those in poor health" while increasing costs for people getting coverage through the individual market and causing the federal deficit to go up.[63] Trump's approach to health policy matched other Republicans, who claimed they could make the system bet-ter than Obama but only tried to undermine and repeal the ACA.

Despite attacks exploiting her weaknesses, Hillary Clinton led through-out fall 2016 as national polling and political oddsmakers thought her the prohibitive favorite. With echoes of his Iowa caucus complaints against Ted Cruz and charges that Florida officials might "rig" that primary for Marco Rubio, Trump laid groundwork to delegitimize Clinton's victory if she won. At an August campaign rally in Ohio, Trump told his audience, "I'm afraid the election's going to be rigged. I have to be honest."[64]

When Fox's Chris Wallace asked Trump during the third presidential debate in late October whether he would accept the outcome of the election were he to lose, Trump responded, "I will look at it at the time."

Wallace responded by citing "a tradition in this country" of "the peaceful transition of power and no matter how hard fought a campaign . . . at the end of the campaign, that the loser concedes to the winner."

"What I'm saying is that I will tell you at the time," Trump said. "I'll keep you in suspense, okay?"

Incredulous, Clinton responded with the litany of Trump's efforts to promote distrust in institutions as well as in legal and democratic processes:

> You know, every time Donald thinks things aren't going in his direction, he claims whatever it is, is rigged against him. The FBI conducted a yearlong investigation into my e-mails. They concluded there was no case. He said the FBI was rigged. He lost the Iowa caucus, he lost the Wisconsin primary, he said the Republican primary was rigged against him. Then, Trump University gets sued for fraud and racketeering. He claims the court system and the federal judge is rigged against him. There was even a time when he didn't get an Emmy for his TV program three years in a row and he started tweeting that the Emmys were rigged against him.[65]

In response, Trump reiterated his complaints against the FBI and the Department of Justice after doubling down, too, on the Emmys—"Should have gotten it," he said.[66]

But the race tightened. Negative coverage of Clinton was having its effect. Press coverage stressed scandals over policy to a remarkable degree, particularly emphasizing Clinton's use of a private server for routing some government emails. This coverage reached a fever pitch after FBI director James Comey announced on October 28—days ahead of the election—that he was reopening the bureau's investigation. As communications scholars Duncan Watts and David Rothschild found, "The New York Times *ran as many cover stories about Hillary Clinton's emails as they did about all policy issues combined in the 69 days leading up to the election* (and that does not include the three additional articles on October 18, and November 6 and 7, or the two articles on the emails taken from John Podesta)." Moreover, scandal coverage was unbalanced. Across cross news outlets, "The various Clinton-related email scandals accounted for more sentences than all of Trump's scandals combined."[67]

A significant portion of the electorate remained undecided rather late into the campaign season. Communications scholars found that "there were more undecided voters in 2016 than in previous elections," even late into the fall, and the one "characterization that yoked them together" was that "they were angry, passionate, and divided."[68] The negativity of elite rhetoric was filtering down to the mass public. Describing focus groups they conducted during the election, Dan Schill and Rita Kirk noted how undecided voters were "adopt[ing] the style and tenor of the campaign rhetoric" and that voters "were palpably angry." On this count, these scholars said, 2016 was different from previous years: "Participants often appeared tense, conversations frequently became heated, and it was not uncommon for discussants to raise their voices, interrupt, and talk over each other."[69] Angry, distrustful, and less predictable than past electorates, 2016 "voters had weaker party loyalty, less trust in government, lacked confidence in the election, and clearly wanted change."[70]

Moreover, there was significant dissatisfaction with both candidates and doubts about their trustworthiness. Surveys taken in the final months of the campaign demonstrated that the electorate had "relatively low trust for both Hillary Clinton and Donald Trump."[71]

Trump and Clinton supporters differed when it came to trust. Surveys conducted by the Edelman Trust Barometer in late 2016 showed that Trump supporters were significantly less trustful of media (21 percent trust preelection and 15 percent postelection, compared to Clinton supporters 57 percent pre- and 51 percent postelection) and government (25 percent and 26 percent among Trump supporters and 57 percent and 46 percent among Clinton voters pre- and post-election).[72] Large portions of the electorate believed that the political system was failing.[73]

Edelman also discovered "a growing gap between elites, who largely trusted their country's institutions, and non-elites, who mostly didn't."[74] Democrats had lost considerable ground between the Obama election and 2016 and now had to contend with the rise of non-elite "populists"—voters who were liberal on economic issues and conservative on "identity issues." Political scientist Lee Drutman found that an overwhelming number of those who voted for both Obama and Trump were populists, and that Clinton won just 59 percent of populists who had voted for Obama. About a quarter of the rest went for Trump and 14 percent voted third party.[75] And these populists who had voted for Obama in 2012 but Trump in 2016 were more negative toward Muslims and immigrants and more likely to see "people like me" in decline. Together, the populist voters who had once voted for Obama but did not vote for Hillary in 2016 were more likely than the rest to see politics as "a rigged game."[76]

Trump's campaign played into these populist fears and resentments. In August 2016, Steve Bannon, executive chairman of *Breitbart* and a friend of the billionaire Robert Mercer, became the head of Trump's campaign. Bannon had "a sweeping, apocalyptic view of history," and his "response to the rise of modernity was to set populist, right wing nationalism against it." Bannon called Trump a "blunt instrument for us"—and by "us" he meant ethnonationalist populists who desire to restore and protect "western tradition."[77] This version of traditionalism was white supremacist, male dominated, anti-globalist, and Christian, though often critical of modern Christianity and Catholicism.

Bannon's ethnonationalist vision extended Trump's rhetoric. Near the end of the race, the campaign aired an ad warning of calculating elites at odds with the American people that drew from an October 2016 Trump speech.[78] The Anti-Defamation League criticized it for "evoking classic anti-Semitic themes that have historically been used against Jews and still reverberate today."[79] The ad repeatedly referred to corruption by the "political establishment" working hand in hand with "global special interests" and the "global power structure," of which Hillary Clinton and several prominent, wealthy Jews were a part. Trump promised he would replace this system "with a new one, controlled by you, the American people."

Some in the Trump coalition could be motivated by anger toward economic elites, but anti-government messaging and policies could bring them all together. Pollster Emily Ekins identified five subgroups—staunch conservatives, free marketeers, American preservationists, anti-elites, and the disengaged—all conservative, but with different policy emphases and dispositions. The disengaged felt "detached from institutions and elites" (including the GOP) and both the anti-elites and the American preservationists shared a view that "the economic and political systems are rigged," while both free marketeers and staunch conservatives were more comfortable with elite, especially economic elite, institutions but suspicious of Washington, government, taxes, and regulation.[80]

This made Hillary Clinton a useful foil for Trump. Personal antipathy toward her as a candidate focused the powerfully anti-Washington views of the would-be Trump coalition. Two groups changed their views on Clinton a great deal between 2012 and 2016. Anti-elites, who saw the system as rigged in favor of elites but were economically progressive, went from 47 percent seeing Clinton favorably in 2012 to just 9 percent in 2016. Of this group, only 26 percent had very favorable views of Trump, and the group divided on whether their vote was for Trump or against Clinton. American preservationists, too, became far more negative toward Clinton, going from 42 percent seeing Clinton favorably in 2012 to but 5 percent in 2016. In addition to being vehemently anti-Clinton, American preservationists also saw their race as part of their identity and were highly nativist and anti-immigrant.[81]

Because the Trump coalition was disparate and far-flung, it required significant maintenance. The more extreme elements were committed to Trump personally, and some of them displayed disturbing nativism, Islamophobia, and racism. As political scientist Philip Klinkner found, the top predictor of support for Trump in 2016 was a respondent's belief that Obama was a Muslim.[82] Race appeals have been a GOP staple since Nixon's Southern strategy, but they have only grown in power since. Data from the American National Election Studies demonstrated that between "the Reagan era and the Obama presidency, there was a marked increase in racial resentment of white voters."[83] Even between the Tea Party and Trump, racialized messaging became more explicit.[84] One study found "racialized perceptions of economic deservingness" to be "strongly related to support for Donald Trump." Even economic anxiety was racialized. Support for Trump was less related to worries about one's own employment than "concerns about whites losing jobs to minorities."[85]

But bringing the more traditional, less Trumpian Republican elements into the fold required stoking anti-Clinton, antiestablishment, and anti-government sentiments that could unite these groups. Trump wooed these traditional forces with aggressive anti-Clinton rhetoric, portraying her as dishonest and corrupt—the WikiLeaks release of Democratic National

Committee documents and the later-retracted revelation that the FBI was reopening its inquiry into Clinton's emails helped this. He also stoked fears of a more liberal Supreme Court and thus brought traditional small-government, conservative supporters back into the tent.

However stark the warning signs of public discontent and late Trump momentum may have been, Hillary Clinton, Democratic operatives, and election prognosticators more generally were stunned by Trump's victory. Picking up surprise wins in Pennsylvania, Michigan, and Wisconsin, Trump won a 306–227 electoral college victory while still losing the popular vote by 2.8 million votes to Clinton.[86]

Much of Trump's electoral college victory he owed to voters' negative assessments of Clinton and general anger toward Washington. Exit polls showed Trump narrowly (49–45) won voters who were "dissatisfied" with "how the federal government was working," while he lost by very wide margins those who were "satisfied" (75–20) and those who were "enthusiastic" (78–20). But Trump kept the popular electoral margin close enough to win by trouncing Clinton (77–18) among those who said they were "angry" about how the federal government was working. The journalist Uri Friedman put it like this, "Trump rose to power in part by tapping into distrust of government and the media in the United States."[87]

Uncomfortable with losing the popular vote to Clinton, Trump sought to discredit the legitimacy of the election results—something the winner does not usually do. Later that November, the president-elect charged, "Serious voter fraud in Virginia, New Hampshire and California—so why isn't the media reporting on this? Serious bias—big problem!"[88]

Immediately following the election, Trump reiterated his campaign claim that any changeover from the Affordable Care Act would be "easy" and seamless. He told reporter Lesley Stahl, "We're going to do it simultaneously. It'll be just fine. We're not going to have, like, a two-day period and we're not going to have a two-year period where there's nothing. It will be repealed and replaced. And we'll know. And it'll be great health care for much less money. So it'll be better health care, much better, for less money."[89]

During the 2016 campaign, some Republicans opposed Trump for a time. Paul Ryan said that Trump's comments about a federal judge of Mexican heritage constituted the "textbook definition of racism" and, after the release of the *Access Hollywood* tape (on which Trump was heard admitting to groping women), Senator Jeff Flake tweeted that Trump must "withdraw from the race."[90] But while the GOP establishment had used distrust in government for their own purposes, after Trump won in 2016, they learned a hard lesson: those who stoke distrust among the public run the risk of losing control of the distrustful.

In January 2017, National Intelligence director James Clapper informed President-elect Trump that "Vladimir Putin personally ordered an influence campaign to try to help [him] win."[91] Eager to reframe the story, Trump pressed Clapper and other intelligence heads to assist in drafting a press release stating that Russian influence had no effect on the election's outcome. Clapper and the rest refused, and Trump took to Twitter to allege that intelligence agencies had leaked a negative story about him (which he called "fake news"). He asked, "Are we living in Nazi Germany?"[92]

Once in office, Trump demanded loyalty from the party, and he wielded the restive Republican base as a weapon. During Trump's first year, the Republican Congress gave the president wins on nearly every floor vote that the president supported. In 2017, Trump won 100 percent of such votes in the House and 98.3 percent in the Senate (115 out of 117 votes, losing twice on health care). Senate majority leader Mitch McConnell delivered on appointment confirmations, too, handing Trump a perfect 94 to 0 record on confirmation votes.[93]

Sometimes past policy commitments were sidelined in favor of backing Trump. Most congressional Republicans gave in, at first only declining to comment on his controversial statements and ultimately exhibiting situational constitutionalism on steroids, backing an exceedingly powerful president who busted separation of powers norms and denigrated congressional oversight in ways never seen in American history.

THE CHAOS PRESIDENCY

Trump assumed the presidency on January 20, 2017. He showed no sign of letting go of his distrustful, oppositional stance. In his inaugural address, he promised a new "America First" nationalism and contended that America had too long suffered decline and neglect—what he termed "American carnage." Stressing the populist anti-Washington themes that were part and parcel of his campaign, Trump said:

Today we are not merely transferring power from one administration to another, or from one party to another—but we are transferring power from Washington, D.C., and giving it back to you, the American people.

For too long, a small group in our nation's Capital has reaped the rewards
of government while the people have borne the cost.
Washington flourished—but the people did not share in its wealth.
Politicians prospered—but the jobs left, and factories closed.
The establishment protected itself, but not the citizens of our country.

Their victories have not been your victories; their triumphs have not been
your triumphs; and while they celebrated in our nation's Capital, there was
little to celebrate for struggling families across our land.[94]

Simmering beneath these words were decades of anti-Washington sentiment on the right.

But Trump quickly faced counter-mobilization. The day after his inauguration, protestors all over the country staged Women's Marches, in what
has been estimated to be the largest demonstration in the history of the
United States. Altogether about 4.2 million people participated in around
six hundred locations.[95] Many of the marchers became involved in new
groups formed to resist Trump and his agenda, they began citizen lobbying
and mounted protests and events, and many ran for office.

Protests seemed to haunt Trump's steps. After he enacted his promised
"Muslim ban" through an executive order on January 27 that banned citizens
from seven majority Muslim countries from traveling to the United States
for the next ninety days, protests sprang up at airports across America.
Legal groups filed lawsuits, and lawyers camped out at airports to counsel
anyone ensnared in the policy. At New York's John F. Kennedy Airport, a
taxi drivers' union snarled traffic by holding a strike.[96]

Trump continued to stoke distrust toward the intelligence community
and the press. When the *New York Times* reported in February 2017 that
"American law enforcement and intelligence agencies intercepted" communications between Trump's campaign "and other Trump associates with
senior Russian intelligence officials in the year before the election,"[97] Trump
issued two tweets complaining "Information is being illegally given to the
failing @nytimes & @washingtonpost by the intelligence community (NSA
and FBI?). Just like Russia." and "The real scandal here is that classified information is illegally given out by 'intelligence' like candy. Very un-American."[98]

Early in his presidency, Trump shrank the role that scientists and experts
had in advising and providing data and analysis to the executive branch.
The growth of the American policy state has depended on increasing its

administrative capacity to gather and assess relevant information. However, as political scientist Philip Rocco found, Trump's "anti-analytic" administration took "steps to discredit experts and analyses that cast doubt on its agenda, subvert rules requiring the use of objective analysis, and construct new institutions to promote 'alternative facts.' "[99] Trump was not the only Republican to sideline scientific advisory boards and the like—President Reagan cut units engaged in policy evaluation and Speaker of the House Gingrich terminated the congressional Office of Technology Assessment—but Trump's actions were particularly sweeping. Trump's rhetoric about some science, such as climate science, which he at times characterized as "a hoax," was dismissive and conspiratorial and accompanied policies helping the oil, gas, and coal industries.[100]

Trump took steps to prove his unfounded charges of voter fraud via a new body of his creation. In May 2017 he established the Presidential Advisory Commission on Election Integrity, ostensibly to shore up vulnerabilities in the nation's elections with regard to voter fraud. Disbanded in early 2018, the group (also known as the Voter Fraud Task Force) had, as political scientist Charles Stewart put it, "a narrower mission: vigorously pursue the claim that there were millions of double-voters and noncitizen voters in the 2016 election."[101] One commission member, Maine secretary of state Matthew Dunlap, sued, claiming that dissenting members were excluded from deliberations and full participation and the purpose of the commission "was not to pursue the truth but rather to provide an official imprimatur of legitimacy on President Trump's assertions that millions of illegal votes were cast during the 2016 election and to pave the way for policy changes designed to undermine the right to vote."[102]

If Trump's efforts to undermine the election outcome were odd for a victor, many of his policy efforts were considerably more normal for a Republican president elected by those who do not trust the federal government. He spent his first years in office delivering on a GOP wish list of tax cuts, deregulation, and the nomination of conservative federal judges who were committed to limiting federal involvement in governance and policy—though seemingly committed to expanding presidential power.

Besides sidelining scientists and pursuing tax cuts and deregulation, Trump's key to "deconstructing the administrative state" was undoing the policy legacy of Barack Obama's presidency, especially Obamacare. Under President Trump, Republican efforts to repeal the ACA demonstrated both conservatives' anti-government bent but also their political limits. A stark partisan divide separated Democrats and Republicans in whether they approved of the ACA but also how much they enrolled in a plan through a federal or state exchange.[103] Resistance to the ACA was unique, for, as political scientist James Morone points out, while Republicans opposed previous health reform efforts, GOP presidents had never tried to completely repeal major health programs. Morone attributes this new, deep resistance to the rise of white nationalism that, with its emphases on race and immigration, undermines "the social capital that fosters social welfare policies."[104] The disconnect between how the conservative base viewed Obamacare and how many Americans viewed its benefits put the "repeal and replace" GOP in a tough spot. Whatever issues remained with the ACA, as Jacob Hacker and Paul Pierson note, the various House and Senate repeal-and-replace bills (and the Trump tax bill) were deeply, even historically unpopular.[105]

Contrary to Trump's campaign promises, Republican bills significantly cut coverage. Proposed bills reduced public funding, mostly through cuts in Medicaid, another program Trump said he would not harm.[106] While the Affordable Care Act prevented insurance companies from discriminating against people with preexisting conditions, Republican bills gave states greater potential leeway to decide whether these limits continued, affecting how much coverage would cost, what treatments would be covered, and whether coverage would even be available.[107] Trump and congressional Republicans adopted an anti-analytic stance, rejecting or simply ignoring what the Congressional Budget Office reported; this strategy was inadequate for such a high-profile issue.

Medicaid might have seemed a relatively easy political target, as a good deal of its funding supported medical care for the working poor, but health policy scholars Colleen Grogan and Sunggeun (Ethan) Park found that most Americans did not attach any stigma to receiving Medicaid, even though they often view other welfare policies critically.[108] Ultimately, Republican efforts to let states deregulate private sector–based health insurance was itself of concern to many Americans, who distrusted the health insurance industry at least as much as they distrusted the federal government. In fact, most Americans want government to regulate insurance companies by requiring them to cover people with preexisting conditions.[109]

The structure of Republican proposals—and who they could and would hurt—motivated many Americans to protect the ACA. To retain the law in the summer of 2017 and stop Republican efforts to repeal it, citizens and anti-Trump resistance groups like the Indivisibles mobilized to push swing legislators. One swing vote, Senator Susan Collins of Maine, was targeted for months. "On health care, Collins did not start where she ended and she shifted after considerable grassroots action . . . Although actions varied through the twists and turns of the legislative process, week after week people visited, wrote and called."[110] Research by Lara Putnam and Theda Skocpol shows that these organizational efforts heavily involved white, college-educated, middle-aged women—a group that supports higher social spending on priorities like health care and education.[111]

Perhaps the most sympathy-inducing group was the parents of children with disabilities and other major medical problems. Under the Affordable Care Act, these children could get coverage despite having preexisting conditions, and many received Medicaid funding, both of which were under threat.[112] Some of these parents could not afford their children's care. For instance, in July 2017, Louisiana parents set off "in a bus full of wheelchairs and ventilators to Washington" to speak out against GOP health-care proposals. They were concerned about a "provision in a Senate draft proposal that would allow insurance companies to impose lifetime caps on benefits, which could make seriously ill patients essentially uninsurable in the private market. [Parents] Lorio and Michot also oppose a projected 35 percent reduction over two decades in federal funding for Medicaid, which they fear would force states to eliminate the programs that help parents of disabled children care for their kids at home. 'They will be cutting off his life support,' Michot, 33, says of Gabriel. 'Without Medicaid, he would either be dead or institutionalized.' "[113] They called for government restrictions on private health insurance businesses and stable government funding of coverage.

After various legislative twists and turns, the GOP's partial repeal of Obamacare came to a vote in the Senate on July 27, 2017. The Democrats needed three Republican defectors to quash it. Many expected moderate swing-state Republicans Lisa Murkowski from Alaska and Susan Collins from Maine to vote no. It came down to Senator John McCain of Arizona, who stood with his arm raised for a few moments before turning a quick thumbs down, delivering an embarrassment not only to Trump but also to Senate majority leader Mitch McConnell who had lobbied hard to pass the Trump bill. With this last-minute nay vote, the repeal effort was over. Despite persistent opposition to Obamacare from the GOP base, it was no match for the wider public opposition to the Trump–GOP health-care agenda. Outside Republican circles, John McCain was broadly lauded, and Susan Collins was met at the airport in Maine and applauded when she stepped off the plane.[114]

Trump tried to stoke social and political ire as a means to maintain his political base, but he found the limits of this strategy with the ACA. After repeal failed, the broad outlines of Obamacare were retained, and Medicaid, which had been expanded under the Affordable Care Act, "survived perhaps its gravest existential threat in fifty-two years."[115] Even in a time of great polarization, partisanship, and GOP control, displacing Obamacare proved difficult. As health policy scholar Jonathan Oberlander put it, "Republicans learned a familiar lesson in health care politics: disturbing the status quo and threatening arrangements for already-insured Americans invite political disaster."[116]

But Trump shrunk the ACA through other means. It was undermined by his 2017 tax bill, which was supported by every Senate Republican and opposed by every House and Senate Democrat. What the administration could not accomplish legislatively, Trump instead pursued through unilateral executive action and lawsuits. Through some executive orders, Trump gave states more access to waivers and exemptions, while through others he restricted individual access to Medicaid and allowed plans that offered less comprehensive insurance coverage to compete in ACA exchanges.[117] All the while, the administration would continue to challenge the ACA in court, first seeking to invalidate some aspects of the law and, by 2019, arguing in federal court that the entire act "was unconstitutional and should be struck down."[118]

At the time of the 2020 presidential election, Obamacare had been neither repealed nor replaced. The GOP effort to do so legislatively remains another object lesson in the staying power of government even in the face of distrust-inducing efforts to shrink it.

The GOP had long seen tax cuts as crucial to shrinking the administrative state, and perhaps Trump's biggest legislative accomplishment was his tax bill passed at the end of 2017. In the final week of conference deliberations as the House and Senate neared approval of the "Tax Cut and Jobs Act of 2017," Trump celebrated delivering on a campaign promise, employing the anti-tax, anti-government rhetoric that typified the modern GOP. Complaining that the "current tax code is burdensome, complex, and profoundly unfair," Trump argued that his bill was removing restraints on citizens and the economy:

> Our tax cuts will break down, and they'll break it down fast—all forms of government, and all forms of government barriers—and breathe new life into the American economy. They will unleash the American worker; they will tear down the restraints on discovery, innovation, and creation; and they will restore the hopes and dreams of the American family.[119]

Connecting tax cuts to his "Make America Great Again" theme, Trump touted his anti-regulatory efforts, too—"We didn't become great through massive taxation and Washington regulation."[120] Trump's tax bill also undermined the ACA, because it included the elimination of the individual mandate and undermined health-care administration and delivery.

The day after Trump's remarks on tax cuts, the White House staged a photo-op where the president literally cut "red tape" that connected stacks of paper meant to represent the growth in federal regulations from 1960 to 2017. He had issued an executive order in January 2017 mandating that for every new proposed regulation, two existing ones must be eliminated. Then, in December 2017, Trump boasted that his administration had, in fact, cut twenty-two old measures for every new regulation.[121]

If tax cuts, deregulation, and opposing liberal health-care policies were staple GOP small-government fare and held true to Trump's anti-government stance, the Trump policy record was more complicated on the question of government's actual role. Trump was quite willing to expand his own power (and that of the presidency) and to implement policies that provided government benefits to favored Republican constituencies. Still, as we have shown throughout this book, such inconsistencies are not new to a GOP quite willing to broaden government's reach only when it controls the levers of power.

THE SPECIAL COUNSEL, KAVANAUGH, THE CARAVAN, AND THE COMING BLUE WAVE

After thwarting Republicans' attempt to repeal the ACA, Democratic voters held out hope that Robert Mueller's special counsel investigation and other inquiries might definitively reveal wrongdoing by Trump ahead of the 2018 midterm elections, which they hoped would return Congress to Democratic majority control. Historically, the president's party tends to lose seats in the midterms. One year before the elections, longtime Republican pollster Glen Bolger advised Republicans that they should "prepare for the worst" and that "it is best to assume recent political history in midterms will repeat itself" rather than hope for an aberration like in 2002, when Republicans gained seats in George W. Bush's first term.[122] Trump's strategy to avoid this typical pattern was to promote distrust in government, provoke resentment, and scare Americans about refugees.

During the spring and summer, as the 2018 election loomed large, the Mueller probe announced indictments of Russians and Trump associates alike—indictments that would lead to high-profile convictions. The GOP had long been ostensibly the small-government party but (somewhat paradoxically) also the law and order party, favoring strict criminal sentencing and a large police state. Critiquing the FBI had always been off limits to the Republicans, until, swatting interchangeably between the intelligence community and the Mueller investigation, Trump opened up a new front in the decades-long GOP war to build distrust in government, extending it to the intelligence and law enforcement communities. In repeated tweets, Trump decried the "Fake & Corrupt Russia Investigation." He repeatedly tweeted about Mueller throughout 2018 and almost exclusively in negative terms.[123] The bulk of the tweets expressed concern that bias—both partisan bias (he described Mueller's team as "thirteen angry Democrats") and personal bias (alleging that Mueller himself was "conflicted" against Trump)—animated the investigation.

But the Twitter campaign was simply the visible one. All the while, groundwork was being laid to defend Trump and normalize his powerful and nearly unconstrained presidency. William Barr, nominated by Trump to be attorney general in December 2018, had long ago spoken in favor of executive power. Honed in the Reagan era, the "unitary executive" theory, as articulated by Barr, placed the presidency at the very borders of checks and balances.[124]

This view would now be exploited to defend Trump. Barr promoted his extreme presidentialist views in the press and cited them in a June 2018 memo to two top officials at the Department of Justice, undermining the Mueller investigation and asserting "illimitable" presidential powers with regard to law enforcement. After stating he was "in the dark about many facts" of the Mueller investigation, Barr asserted that "Mueller should not be permitted to demand that the President submit to interrogation about alleged obstruction."[125] Barr expounded a constitutional theory that allowed the president vast discretion, even "on a matter in which he has a personal stake." He wrote:

> The Constitution itself places no limit on the President's authority to act on matters which concern him or his own conduct. On the contrary, the Constitution's grant of law enforcement power to the President is plenary. Constitutionally, it is wrong to conceive of the President as simply the highest officer within the Executive branch hierarchy. He alone is the Executive branch. As such, he is the sole repository of Executive powers conferred by the Constitution. Thus, the full measure of law enforcement authority is placed in the President's hands, and no limit is placed on the kinds of cases subject to his control and supervision.

According to Barr, the president was not an individual who inhabited an office and remained subject to the rule of law; instead, the president was equivalent to the executive branch itself and personally held all of that institution's powers over law enforcement.

The constitutionalist tone in Barr's 2018 memo was remarkably different from the view of presidential power the 2016 Republican Party platform applied to Obama. Republicans had swung the pendulum on constitutionalism before in their conception of presidential power, seemingly ready to dust off such broad interpretations only when Republicans inhabit the White House.[126]

If the theory of presidential power was sporadically applied, the more momentous change during this time was Trump's shift in the focus of distrust in government. Previously, GOP rhetoric included extreme complaints that the government was potentially tyrannical—a threat to liberty itself—when that power was aimed at expanding welfare and the domestic policy state, but the military, intelligence, and law enforcement apparatuses of government—directly coercive and potentially more threatening to freedom—had eluded Republican criticisms.

In late June 2018, Supreme Court justice Anthony Kennedy announced his retirement, and now Trump had the opportunity to fill a Supreme Court vacancy ahead of the midterms. This was Trump's second. Neil Gorsuch was seated in January 2017; this filled the opening from the February 2016 death of Antonin Scalia, which Senate majority leader Mitch McConnell had left open, refusing to consider President Obama's nomination of Merrick Garland. Trump nominated U.S. Circuit judge Brett Kavanaugh.

Discord between Trump and the intelligence community reached a new low in Helsinki on July 16. Trump singled out former director of National Intelligence James Clapper and former CIA director John Brennan. Asked if he believed "every U.S. intelligence agency" or Vladimir Putin about Russian election interference in 2016 and whether he would warn Putin not to interfere in future elections, Trump deflected to the FBI and the Democrats: "You have groups that are wondering why the FBI never took the server. Why haven't they taken the server? Why was the FBI told to leave the office of the Democratic National Committee?"[127] He questioned Clapper's conclusion while defending the credibility of Russian denials, saying, "With that being said, all I can do is ask the question: My people came to me—Dan Coats came to me and some others—they said they think it's Russia. I have President Putin; he just said it's not Russia."[128] Even as he expressed "great confidence" in U.S. intelligence, Trump, standing beside Putin, publicly countered their conclusions. "President Putin was extremely strong and powerful in his denial today," he said.[129]

Like Ronald Reagan or George W. Bush, Trump had an anti-government message that was not consistently applied. Some aspects of government would grow and become more intrusive, even though Trump's avowed aim was "deconstruction." For example, Trump's economic nationalism was built on a decidedly unconservative use of government power: the imposition of high tariffs. Not only did this shuffle off decades of conservative ideology that promoted free trade and free markets, but it also put the Trump administration in the position of policing business exemptions to such policies (what the USA Today editorial board called "Big Government at its worst—arbitrary and capricious, if not outright political, as it picks winners and losers in business"[130]).

Equally ironic for a small-government GOP was the administration's multibillion dollar bailout of farmers suffering from the fallout of Trump's trade war with China.[131] Processed as direct cash payments to farmers (and with the bulk of the payments going to wealthy farm businesses and partnerships rather than to family farms) from the U.S. Department of Agriculture, these payments totaled over $28 billion and were made without congressional debate or involvement. For a GOP that had been built around small-government arguments that celebrated rugged individualism and the free market, these 2019 agriculture bailouts give lie to the idea that Trump and the Republicans are against big government. Instead, they value big government for preferred constituencies while denying its legitimacy and appropriateness for others.[132]

Here and elsewhere, the Trump administration was willing to open government coffers at extraordinary levels. The national debt and budget deficit mounted during the Trump years even before the coronavirus pandemic.[133] Later, the administration indicated its willingness to use eminent domain to seize property to build its Mexican border wall, even though the GOP had long held individual property rights were sacrosanct and had erupted in anger at the 2005 Supreme Court *Kelo v. City of New London* case on eminent domain. A clear departure from past GOP positions, the use of eminent domain to build the border wall was more consistent with Trump's own aggressive business practices than with conservative orthodoxy.[134]

In August 2018, the administration revoked John Brennan's security clearance and threatened the same for former director of National Intelligence Clapper, former FBI director James Comey, former CIA director General Michael Hayden, former deputy FBI director Andrew McCabe, former acting attorney general Sally Yates, and former deputy FBI assistant director of the FBI's Counterintelligence Division Peter Strzok.[135] In response, dozens of former intelligence officials penned an open letter in objection, writing, "The country will be weakened if there is a political litmus test applied before seasoned experts are allowed to share their views."[136] To Trump, the whole investigation was a "hoax" and a "rigged witch hunt" that would "make Joseph McCarthy look like a baby!"[137]

As summer's attention turned to the midterms, Democrats had the advantage. Recruitment, fundraising, retirements and open seats, and generic ballot polling all seemed to point in the direction of a "blue wave" that would unseat Republicans and reclaim both houses of Congress for the Democrats. The question, especially regarding the House of Representatives, seemed not so much whether Democrats would win seats but how many they would win.

Trump reverted to his 2016 strategy: undermining trust in elections ahead of a projected loss.[138] In July, he wondered aloud whether the Russians would weigh in on the side of Democrats in the midterm elections: "I'm very concerned that Russia will be fighting very hard to have an impact on the upcoming Election. Based on the fact that no President has been tougher on Russia than me, they will be pushing very hard for the Democrats. They definitely don't want Trump!"[139]

Kavanaugh was sent to the Senate Judiciary Committee for confirmation on September 4. The first four days of hearings were eventful but predictable: senators questioned Kavanaugh about whether he was open to criminally investigating or indicting a sitting president, and the hearings were frequently interrupted by abortion rights protestors worried that his nomination could tilt the court conservative enough to overturn *Roe v. Wade*. Then, on September 12, reports circulated that the committee's ranking Democrat, Dianne Feinstein, had received an allegation against Kavanaugh.

A few days later, the *Washington Post* ran the story. Christine Blasey Ford, a professor of psychology at Palo Alto University in California, alleged that Kavanaugh had sexually assaulted her at a party in 1982, when she was fifteen and he was seventeen. Over the next few weeks, two more women came forward to accuse Kavanaugh of sexual misconduct, and by the end of the month the committee reconvened to hear testimony from Ford. The FBI was called in to investigate and delivered its findings on October 4. The next day, the Senate voted 51 to 49 to advance Kavanaugh's nomination for a formal confirmation vote. On October 6, the vote took place, and Kavanaugh was narrowly confirmed to the Supreme Court 50–48.

With Brett Kavanaugh's confirmation, Trump not only delivered by putting another very conservative justice on the Supreme Court but also stoked conservative outrage at the bitter Senate fight. In her powerful and emotional testimony, Ford initially elicited sympathy from Trump. But later, at a rally in Mississippi on the eve of the full Senate vote that confirmed Kavanaugh, he mocked that same testimony. The GOP successfully turned the confirmation fight (and the fight for a conservative judiciary generally) into key voter issues within its base. Republicans won the confirmation fight but still effectively seized on conservative outrage at the allegations and how the Senate Democrats and the media handled them. At a rally in Missoula, Montana, he told attendees, "This will be an election of Kavanaugh, the caravan, law and order and common sense."[140] Still, the Kavanaugh confirmation also provoked counter-mobilization among its opponents.

In October, Trump paid a good deal of attention to the "caravan," a group of Honduran and Guatemalan migrants making their way to the United States to seek asylum. The group quickly became the focus of right-wing groups, Fox News, and the White House, a bogeyman to raise the immigration issue and excite the GOP base. A review of polling from competitive House districts showed that "border protection, safeguarding immigration officers and standing up to illegal immigration resonated with voters," and this convinced Trump to focus on the caravan, in part because it would frame immigration in terms of national security. The caravan had the added benefit of being an issue polling showed would likely be more energizing to Republicans than to Democrats.[141]

As Fox News repeatedly focused on the caravan, Trump and other Republicans also saw the situation as politically valuable, particularly in their hopes to retain majority control of the Senate. With the president referring to it openly as a "blessing in disguise" that could highlight the need for stronger immigration policies and his border wall, Republican political strategists thought it a "political windfall."[142] Turning up the heat on the issue, Trump claimed the caravan was potentially violent and that it included "people from the Middle East," and he vowed to send troops to the border to stop the "assault on our country."[143]

Critics charged that the president was elevating the issue to an impending crisis for mere political reasons. In late October, he tweeted, "Every time you see a Caravan, or people illegally coming, or attempting to come, into our Country illegally, think of and blame the Democrats for not giving us the votes to change our pathetic Immigration Laws! Remember the Midterms! So unfair to those who come in legally."[144] When his opponents and the press charged that his statements about the caravan were exaggerated and often simply false, one administration official told a reporter, "It doesn't matter if it's 100 percent accurate . . . This is the play."[145]

For some voters, it seemed to work. "Trump's grass-roots base is united and on fire," said Steve Bannon.[146] Extreme parts of the base were downright combustible. That distrust, anger, and fear the GOP so persistently stoked erupted in sometimes violent ways toward the end of October. Pipe bombs were mailed to CNN and prominent Democratic leaders (Barack Obama, Hillary Clinton, Joe Biden, Kamala Harris, Corey Booker, Eric Holder, and Maxine Waters), financers of left-wing causes (George Soros and Tom Steyer), and other Trump critics (John Brennan, James Clapper, and even actor Robert DeNiro).[147] Cesar Sayoc, who was convicted and sentenced to twenty years for producing the devices, proved to be a "fervent supporter of President Trump" and had espoused racist beliefs, including the "birther" claim that Obama was not a citizen.[148]

Later that week, a right-wing gunman who had posted anti-Semitic and anti-immigrant messages on social media shot up the Tree of Life Synagogue in Pittsburgh, killing eleven. In his manifesto, the Pittsburgh shooter cited his belief that Jews were promoting the caravan of "invaders," a word he echoed from the right-wing press.[149]

Violence is not the inevitable outcome of the strategy of distrust, but neither is it unpredictable. As we have argued throughout this book, those who wield the strategy are apt to lose control of it. A distrustful mass public contains the angry, the uncivil and suspicious, and sometimes also the downright unstable and dangerous.

Although some conservatives would continue to argue that the caravan was dangerous, a threat to national security, and even a national emergency, Trump and Fox News barely mentioned it once the votes were in and the midterm election was over.[150]

In his biennial analysis of congressional elections, political scientist Gary Jacobson argued that the divisive anger Trump inspired was key to his first years in office and the "referendum" on which voters would make their midterm decisions. According to Jacobson, the "trafficking in white identity politics, xenophobia, racism, and misogyny that characterized Trump's [2016] campaign has continued unabated, even escalating as he campaigned for Republican candidates in 2018."[151] Just as influential were Trump's attacks on the legitimacy of "any institution that declines to do Trump's bidding—the judiciary, the Federal Bureau of Investigation, the Department of Justice, the intelligence services, at times the congressional Republican Party, and always the news media."[152]

These elements—division, distrust, and outright anger—were central to Trumpism since its beginnings, but he escalated them as bulwarks against rising opposition as the midterms approached.

As was the case in 2016, there was plenty of anger to be mined in 2018. A Reuters/Ipsos poll conducted in late summer "asked respondents to rate their emotional responses—including their level of anger, bitterness, worry, fear, hope, relief and satisfaction" on Trump, the media, and policy issues and found that Republican voters were especially angered at a few Democrats' interest in impeaching Trump (notably well before they succeeded in doing so the following year), "undocumented immigrants," and "reporting from mainstream media" more than other issues, though the ACA and the "Senate handling of Brett Kavanaugh confirmation" were close behind.[153]

Trumpism was built on anger and anger continued to characterize the Trump era. According to political scientist Nicholas Valentino, voters were "angrier in 2016 and 2018 than they were in past election cycles."[154] If anger and distrust motivated Republican voters in 2018, they proved no match for Democrats who were even angrier—angry at "child separation at the border," "Russian election interference," and Trump himself. Democrats and Republicans both increased in turnout, but Democrats more so, producing the highest midterm voting participation in a century.[155] Though they lost ground in Senate contests, the Democrats' blue wave netted them forty House seats and returned them to majority control for the first time since 2010. These wins meant House Democrats could pursue more oversight of Trump than congressional Republicans had been willing or able to do.

A little over a year after the 2018 midterms, the House of Representatives voted for charges of abuse of power and obstruction of Congress, and Donald Trump became the third president in American history to be impeached. The Republican-controlled Senate would go on to block witnesses from being called, and only one Republican, Senator Mitt Romney, voted to remove Trump from office for abuse of power.

Many Republican senators argued that Trump's attempt to use a foreign government to investigate a political rival were allowable uses of executive power. For example, Senator Marsha Blackburn of Tennessee argued the impeachment charges concerned "a policy disagreement over the President's foreign relations strategy."[156] In yet another example of situational constitutionalism, Republicans who had criticized President Obama for pushing presidential powers too far embraced Attorney General Bill Barr's vision of executive power, allowing presidents to broaden their powers in emergencies and even threaten to withhold government resources to dig up dirt on a rival to benefit the president's own reelection campaign. A foreign government was involved in 2016 in trying to help Trump and hurt Clinton and, in the lead-up to the 2020 election, Trump was trying to use a foreign government to hurt his potential, eventual rival, Joe Biden.

By the time of impeachment, commitment to Trump personally and Trumpism had increasingly become the center of the Republican Party, eclipsing the other long-held ideologies that had marked conservativism for decades. When the coronavirus pandemic broke out in early 2020, Trump was slow to even acknowledge the threat. By then, anyone who identified problems, inadequacies, or abuses in the administration—whether that person was a war hero, a law enforcement professional, a journalist, a governor (even a Republican governor), or a scientist—was not to be trusted.

An alchemy of conspiracy theories, racial resentments, institutional and establishment distrust, and anti-government sentiment defined Trump's rise and his presidency. Distrust was central to Trump's electoral strategy. In a new turn, Trump's use of the strategy of distrust targeted not only the domestic state but also intelligence, police powers, and the administration of justice in ways that even a modern GOP built on distrust had not done. The distrust crafted by earlier conservative, Republican leaders became a blunt, erratically wielded weapon for Trumpism and Trump's war with government.

Chapter Seven

MAKING PEACE WITH GOVERNMENT

As Republicans gathered for their 1964 national convention at the cavernous Cow Palace near San Francisco, the far right of the party was determined to wrest control away from moderates. Delegates voted down a plank repudiating extremist groups, including the conspiratorial John Birch Society (which had claimed President Dwight D. Eisenhower, a Republican and former U.S. general, was "a secret agent of the International Communist Conspiracy"[1]), the Ku Klux Klan, and the Communist Party. When moderate Republican and Goldwater primary opponent New York governor Nelson Rockefeller advocated for the plank, highlighting "the Birch Society's unacceptable methods, including hate literature, goon tactics, and bombings"; this "brought a storm of boos, chants, jeers, hisses, and catcalls that made it impossible for him to be heard."[2] Speaking later, Republican presidential nominee Barry Goldwater ominously warned of impending government "tyranny" and presented his candidacy as an alternative to "those who seek to live your lives for you, to take your liberties in return for relieving you of yours, those who elevate the state and downgrade the citizen."[3]

Since the founding, Americans have always had some skepticism toward government. But there have also been periods of high faith in the good that government can do. According to the Pew Research Center,[4] in the late 1950s and early 1960s, over 70 percent of Americans said they could trust the government in Washington to do what is right "just about always" or "most of the time," with 77 percent trusting government just a few weeks before the November 1964 elections in which Democrat Lyndon B. Johnson resoundingly beat Goldwater with over 60 percent of the popular vote and nearly 500 electoral votes.

While trust in government waned and waxed since then, in March 2019 the same poll found just 17 percent of Americans trusting government. The record-low trust Americans have in government these last few decades is something without historical precedent.

Americans did not lose this trust on their own. Conservative elites have cultivated, weaponized, and employed distrust for decades. As they have been at war with government, they used political distrust to build and maintain organizations and coalitions, reshape institutions, win elections, and affect policy outcomes. Since the early 1980s, partisanship and asymmetric polarization has grown, and this polarization has yielded right-wing opposition protests like the Tea Party, intensified elite networks like the one facilitated by the Koch brothers, and relied on a new right-wing media ecosystem—talk radio, cable TV, and extremist internet sites—to amplify and rehearse angry partisan messages. The conservative agenda has shifted from emphasizing free markets and trickle-down economics to explicit racial and anti-immigrant appeals. Conservatives went from merely proclaiming, as Ronald Reagan did, that government was "the problem" to much more dire and conspiratorial views that government was the enemy itself. Then, when Donald Trump was elected, he began to rail against "the deep state."

The roots of this conservative Republican strategy run deep. The GOP that Goldwater, Nixon, and Reagan inspired fought forever, as historian William Leuchtenberg might have characterized it, "in the shadow of FDR."[5] While Roosevelt contended that "necessitous men are not free men,"[6] post–New Deal and post–Great Society conservatives painted a range of policies—progressive taxation, civil rights laws, regulations on business, social programs—as limits on individual freedom and bureaucratic overreach. Ignoring politically convenient blind spots that allowed for massive government benefits to GOP constituencies and regardless of considerable concessions to political realities in how some conservatives actually governed, anti-government rhetoric holds the conservative coalition together and has done so increasingly for more than a half-century.

Reaganism was skeptical of the twentieth-century state and its social welfare policies. Building on Barry Goldwater's conservatism and Richard

Nixon's "Southern strategy," Reagan's electoral coalition tapped into anti-government suspicions as old as America itself. Countering the New Deal coalition with a newly mobilized evangelical Christian movement and race-coded appeals, Reagan built his small-state coalition to include white southerners and ethnic whites, effectively taking more conservative elements out of the Democratic Party and creating more ideologically cohesive political parties on the left and the right.

But Reagan's small-government philosophy proved situational in application. While he deregulated industry and cut the administrative state in places, he expanded it elsewhere: the military, social regulation, police powers, and subsidies for certain Republican constituencies like farmers. Budget deficits grew, and he learned to steer clear from cutting the most popular programs. When under political stress late in his presidency after the Iran-contra scandal, Reagan began to favor a new health policy: catastrophic coverage for the elderly. The Reagan years were characterized by many signals for stronger state governments but also an institutionalist push for greater "unitary" executive power within the federal government that built on Nixon's efforts. Although some conservative activists thought Reagan could have gone further right, they did little to challenge him. Instead, they saved their political fire for his successor, George H. W. Bush, who, when faced with reconciling conflicting Reagan-era promises, ran afoul of conservatives by agreeing to increase taxes to reduce the deficit.

Next, Bill Clinton found himself up against an increasingly organized, strategic effort to use distrust in government. Central to this was distrust in "government-run health care," which mortally wounded his health reform effort, and racialized messages that opposed the Clinton Crime Bill. Brazenly situational, Newt Gingrich and other leaders of the Republican Revolution promoted distrust toward Congress and opposed congressional power when Republicans were in the minority, but when Republicans won a congressional majority in 1994, the GOP shifted its support back to an active Congress that could keep the Democratic president in check. The shift came again when George W. Bush became president, and Republicans again embraced executive power and a strong presidency as territories from which they could pursue other goals.

Barack Obama succeeded Bush in the wake of a major economic downturn following the 2008 financial crisis. He pledged to use the federal government as a positive force in the recovery to follow. Although entering with much more electoral support than Clinton, Obama also faced a huge pushback from the right. Partisan identities became increasingly polarized and asymmetric. The Republicans adopted more extreme positions than Democrats and became increasingly willing to undermine the entire political system. The Tea Party, a movement with grassroots support and backed by wealthy interests, used hyperbolic, race-laden rhetoric against the Affordable Care Act and Obama's use of presidential powers. The establishment Republican leaders rode precariously atop this volatile wave of public dissatisfaction, but ultimately found the Tea Party's energy difficult to wrangle.

Given the increasing demographic diversity of the electorate and Mitt Romney's 2012 loss in the presidential race, some Republican leaders and strategists conducted an "autopsy" of the party. They attempted to steer the GOP away from its social conservatism and xenophobia if the party were to survive. But despite these warnings, some Republicans became vehemently anti-immigrant, stoking racist sentiments and blaming immigrants for the loss of manufacturing jobs and a litany of other social ills. From this wave, a new faction, much more preoccupied with racial issues and economic nativism than traditional conservatives, arose, calling itself the "alt-right." It was in this context Donald Trump won the party nomination and ultimately the presidency in 2016.

In the 2016 campaign, Trump sometimes called for expanding domestic social spending, while his governing policy agenda involved attempting to decrease such spending, boosting military spending, cutting taxes, and installing right-wing judges. President Trump also attacked the national security apparatus and political critics in harsh terms, portraying them as unpatriotic and un-American. Situational constitutionalism on steroids emerged, as the GOP, which claimed it feared Obama's use of presidential power, backed near complete executive power. To be a Republican was to back and to be loyal to Trump; to oppose him made one a recipient of attacks aimed at pacification. And to be loyal to Trump meant supporting a presidency of seemingly illimitable power, a supreme irony given the GOP's modern roots and rhetoric were steeped in distrust.

These GOP uses of distrust in government have been durable, culturally supported, and politically lucrative, and so they may seem impossible to reverse. While shifting over time, the distrust weapon has proven potent for a long war with government that has included making electoral appeals, building and maintaining organizations, gaming institutional power, and waging policy battles. Yet there are some possible ways to at least counter distrust and rebuild public confidence in the political system of the United States and in a more activist policy agenda.

WHAT NOW?

Trust in government will probably never return to the levels of the post–World War II consensus that continued through the early 1960s—and perhaps it shouldn't. After all, citizens should question and challenge politicians and make the system work for more Americans. But American democracy is undermined when elites erode political legitimacy for their own benefit.

Given the concerted time, money, and effort that has gone into cultivating distrust, recovering trust is no simple task. Some related dynamics—increased, asymmetric partisanship and the uses of racialized messages by purveyors of distrust in government—would be difficult to overcome.

The partisan cultivation of distrust has taken its toll. Political elites increasingly deploy us-versus-them rhetoric,[7] and research shows that partisans increasingly see their political opposites more negatively.[8] Issue positions and responses to news stories are increasingly linked to partisan identities defined along national divides.[9] Polarized citizens selectively expose themselves to information from news sources that most likely feed their partisan sentiments.

Democrats and Republicans are both polarized, but polarization has not had equal effects on them. It has become asymmetric, as has the willingness to see the broader political system as worth preserving. Although both parties risk backlash from their bases for any compromise, Democrats tend to see compromise as more necessary than Republicans do. Liberals and conservatives both follow media sources that reinforce their views, but conservatives are more likely to gravitate toward ideological echo chambers, and thus the systemwide effects of such echoes are greater on the right than on the left.[10]

Research into patron networks indicates, too, that conservatives disproportionately benefit from asymmetric efforts by political mega-donors to guide and shape politics and policy. Coordination efforts exist on the left, too, but are less prominent. On the right, mega-donors seeking lower taxes and less regulation pony up for influence to achieve those aims. Their efforts are also more sustained. These conservative organizations acted strategically over a long political time horizon and worked to demobilize organizations that lean left, such as public sector unions.[11] Before the rise of anti-Trump resistance groups and for decades, conservatives not only outspent but out-organized their counterparts on the left.

Fundamental questions of government legitimacy and constitutional meaning are at stake. This is true of support for government generally as well as support for each of the institutions of government. Conservatives more likely to trust a president who shares their views than are liberals, and conservatives are less likely than liberals to see the president of the opposing party as legitimate.[12] This asymmetry can also be seen in the greater use of constitutional hardball among Republicans in legislative–executive conflicts, wherein conservatives treat constitutional prescriptions for the separation of powers instrumentally rather than timeless or representing "fixed meanings." The flexibility with which conservatives approach such institutional prescriptions is in evidence in the states, too. In judicial settings, conservatives' separation of powers viewpoints are deployed selectively to promote offices Republicans control and then suspended when Democrats achieve power.[13] As with any war, the conservatives' war with government consists of skirmishes, extended efforts and longer occupations aimed at strategically stripping control or holding territory.

Undoing partisan polarization is a task for another time—the problems are multifaceted, mutually reinforcing, and exist at least in some form at every level of American national government. As political scientists Matt Grossmann and David A. Hopkins write, "Little evidence substantiates the hope that polarization can be easily reformed away."[14]

Neither can we offer much in the way of successful strategies to undo structural racism or erase the disappointing and devastatingly persistent success of racist appeals in politics.

Race has long been a central aspect of American politics, going back far before the period we chronicle.[15] As was the case with the Democratic Party of Thomas Jefferson and Andrew Jackson through Woodrow Wilson and George Wallace, the modern GOP has a persistent race problem. Perceiving a national Democratic turn away from such politics, Nixon deployed his Southern strategy to seize on white racial resentment. Building on the logic of that strategy, Ronald Reagan used racist tropes in welfare policy rhetoric, and the GOP used racialized rhetoric to attack the Clinton Crime Bill, welfare, and many other policies. Race especially affected how Barack Obama's initiatives (and Obama himself) were portrayed and viewed, going beyond birtherism and including attitudes toward the Affordable Care Act, other policies, and even depictions of the president and his family. The anti-immigrant politics of the Trump era, an element of white racial backlash[16] associated with the Tea Party and the rise of the alt-right, is but one more step down a dangerous path for an American polity as marked by persistent racism as it is by persistent efforts to counter it.

Notably, these trends—polarization and racial appeals—do not operate on parallel tracks. They are intertwined historical trends. As political scientist Alan Abramowitz details in *The Great Alignment*, the parties have been realigning along racial lines for decades. Citing the 1994 midterm elections as a turning point, he argues that Newt Gingrich sought to attract white voters who were "racial and economic conservatives."[17] Even though many African Americans hold some relatively conservative views, black voters shifted too. Now most are "steadfast Democrats" whose partisan identities are reinforced by the black community and its institutions.[18]

White racial backlash to the demographic shifts in America shaped other conservative political attitudes as well. For instance, racial resentment affects economic perceptions and views about which racial groups are most likely to benefit from policies—and that influences a voter's willingness to support those policies.[19] Racial attitudes are also affected by more subtle factors of everyday life. An experiment by political scientist Ryan Enos placed Spanish-speaking people on commuter train platforms in Boston. It found that whites who encountered these Spanish speakers in their routine environments held more anti-immigrant attitudes than those in the control group who did not.[20]

Social science research suggests that countering racial resentment is difficult at best, but there is a greater commitment to racial equality among younger Americans. Unless and until political leadership can breed a stronger sense of shared fortunes among diverse Americans, the growing demographic diversity in America—as just and beneficial as it is—will be used as a political tool to divide.

Still, despite all these entrenched suspicions and resentments, we argue that, just as distrust was cultivated over time, so too can trust be built. But these efforts must build political support as they go—not just for particular policies but for the political system as a whole. Today we need, as Franklin Roosevelt called for in countering the Great Depression, "bold, persistent experimentation" to build trust in government and inclusive visions of American politics, governance, and policy.

BUILDING TRUST IN GOVERNMENT

Inspiring trust in government has been done before, both during and after the New Deal and World War II as we detailed in chapter 2. Today, rebuilding trust in government requires multiple actions and steps structured around the sites conservatives have used in strategically promoting distrust in government—organizations, elections, institutions, and policy.

Table 7.1 summarizes the organizational, electoral, institutional, and policy foci for those who want to make peace with government.

TABLE 7.1
Promoting distrust and trust in government

	The strategic promotion of distrust in government	The strategic promotion of trust in government
Organizational	Employ distrust in government to unite different elements of the conservative coalition. Respond to the potential that distrust toward party establishment from far-right activists challenges organizational strength, stability, and leadership.	Build and strengthen a coalition that argues for government's role in increasing prosperity and opportunity for all. Recruit, train, and support candidates (with particular attention to women and working-class candidates) who will pursue those goals. Revitalize state and local party organizations.
Electoral	Use distrust in government (except for the military) as a key message. Incorporate racialized messages. Employ means of dissuading voter participation. Undermine legitimacy of opposition's victories.	Promote active government policies in campaigns. Use approaches that are effective for listening to and turning out voters across class and racial lines. Promote inclusive electoral rules and policy designs that promote political empowerment.

Institutional	Articulate situational, strategic shifts in promoting distrust toward institutions depending on who is in control.	Through civic education, develop beliefs in the constitutional system that are applied even when inconvenient.
		Promote oversight of exercise of government power; protect robust checks and balances.
		Reform institutions to reduce minority rule and make them more representative.
		Shift elite incentives.
		Update anti-corruption laws.
Policy	Work against programs offering health and other forms of security.	Promote positive views of government via policies people support.
	Work for lower taxes (especially in upper-income brackets) and deregulation of businesses.	Develop policy designs that make government more obvious.
		Reduce administrative burdens.
	Seek to prevent the passage of these policies or undermine them by promoting distrust.	Develop appreciation for expertise and professionalism in governance.
		Highlight successful governance and administration.

Organizations and Trust

Republican leaders used distrust in government as the glue to hold together the Republican coalition. Building a counter-coalition in the face of decades of strategic effort requires making the case for effective government action, supporting candidates who will pursue those goals, and revitalizing state and local party organizations.

Whoever will build this public trust must articulate a public philosophy that asserts a role for government and a good reason to support it. This necessarily involves repeatedly reminding Americans of the value of government to their everyday lives, to their mutual defense and status in the world, and to their economic well-being. At different times since the New Deal policies of the 1930s, the state built up the American economy and shared prosperity. After World War II, the federal government made major infrastructure investments and established many agencies focused on scientific and medical research. Reminding citizens about this history helps Americans overcome their "amnesia" about the role government has played in building American economic power.[21]

Part of recovering the collective memory of good government is also reminding voters that there is no party of small government; that Republican coalitions make use of government benefits; that economic redistribution in America includes red states largely taking more from federal coffers than they put in; and that, even as conservatives decry government, key parts of the GOP coalition benefit from corporate welfare, military spending, and agriculture subsidies.

But pointing out inconsistencies and hypocrisies only goes so far. To build trust, groups and their leaders must not argue that all government activities are legitimate or that all political elites are uniformly trustworthy. Such claims would be neither sensible nor credible. The core contention must be that government can be a force for good and can serve the public's needs and promote policies that promote opportunity, freedom, and fairness.

A self-conscious effort to build a coalition in support of government efforts should emphasize the many instances when government has saved the day. Government has created greater freedom and equality in America by promoting opportunity, opposing and mitigating discrimination, and countering private power that limits workers' rights and injures the environment. Federal laws and programs support higher education; provide health coverage to the elderly, veterans, and millions more Americans; protect the right to organize; support people with disabilities; and mitigate food insecurity. Part of this effort should include reminding the public of those many instances in which businesses, economic elites, and other private powerful actors have threatened the people, their freedom, and their self-actualization.

Another way to build public confidence and to promote this strategic focus is to change who runs for office. Groups assisting women candidates, such as EMILY's List and Emerge America, shape who holds power. Although women candidates and elected officials span political parties, they are increasingly Democratic and often focus on expanding access to education and health care. A pro-government coalition would be well served by increasing their numbers as well as the number of working-class and union candidates and elected officials. Political scientist Nicholas Carnes suggests applying and extending the lessons learned by labor unions in recruiting and training workers to run for office. In his book *The Cash Ceiling*, he writes that labor's "programs to identify, recruit and train working-class people have more potential than any other reform effort" to promote candidates who are not professionals.[22] The National Democratic Training Committee provides free in-person training for working-class candidates; the project operates in both urban and rural areas.[23] Making it more possible for these sorts of candidates to win matters. As Carnes showed in another book, *White-Collar Government*, elected officials from the working class are distinctive in consistently supporting higher taxes on the wealthy, health care, and workers' rights.

We must also consider what political parties do below the national level, because the hard work of bringing in new activists and building coalitions that incorporate varied interests and demographic groups happens first locally, whether in cities, suburbs, or rural areas. Revitalizing parties is important; as political scientist Eitan Hersh notes, "Party organizations—not just individuals with partisan attitudes—are essential to building political power."[24] As Hersh discusses in *Politics Is for Power*, while individuals discussing and sparring about politics, often via social media, constitutes "political hobbyism," political organizations and organizing are more effective in making change and require the difficult work of getting beyond a political bubble and taking time to work in concert with people to persuade and mobilize others.

At the start of the Trump administration there was a swell of organizing on the left, and anti-Trump resistance groups rose up around the country to support candidates and public policies.[25] This loose coalition dedicated itself to winning races in the 2018 midterm elections and ultimately to passing policies. But these local groups vary a fair amount in their links to party organizations and other coalition partners. Not only do grassroots activists often treasure their autonomy, but some party leaders are not necessarily hospitable to them.

For Democrats, making arguments for government is important to internal coalition maintenance and to growing the party. And much can be done to modify what state and local parties do. A brief by the Scholars Strategy Network recommends that state parties support local parties and that local parties shift from election activities to year-round engagement, becoming a welcome presence to potential newcomers, connecting with groups, and developing leadership skills.[26] Given the sometimes fractious nature of the Democratic coalition and the party's emphasis on different groups (as opposed to Republicans' emphasis on ideology),[27] and the distaste from some toward "establishment Democrats," crafting and coordinating coalitional activities is challenging but necessary.

Elections and Trust

Can we counter distrust in government simply with explicit defenses of government and the good it can do? There are some issues that enjoy broad support for government involvement: environmental regulation and spending, expanding health coverage and supporting education, and serving public health in the face of pandemics and other crises.[28]

The congressional elections of 2018 are a good case in point. The top issue of the 2018 midterms elections was health care. Democrats made major gains by emphasizing the need for government to maintain preexisting conditions protections, a policy that limits insurance companies from denying certain coverage, and to avoid cuts that would have resulted from repealing the Affordable Care Act. In this climate, even GOP members began to campaign by promising to expand and protect health care. These regulatory and policy appeals are rarely tied explicitly to a defense of *government itself* as a public bulwark against private power—but they could be.

Whether they recognize it or not, many Americans experience the good of government, sometimes even as they denigrate it in the abstract. Campaigning by naming and claiming the benefits of government can rebuild our trust in it. Good governance and the strong national polity it can nurture are essential ingredients for rebuilding trust. Electoral strategies aimed at increasing trust in government should take account of how policies affect citizens' understandings of themselves as civic actors. Strategies should above all aim to build trust between Americans, because lateral social trust influences support for policies that might affect others and for redistributive policies in general.[29]

Research on campaign messages shows that an emphasis on shared values increases the appeal of policies and candidates that support government improving people's lives. The Race-Class Narrative Project tested and used messages that talk about coming together across lines of race and class, point to times Americans unified and achieved their goals, and discuss racial scapegoating as a strategy to divide people that is carried out by "wealthy special interests." Proponents of this approach found some evidence that calling out racially divisive tactics and linking them "to economic concerns allows audiences, including whites, to see that their well-being is tied to rejecting racial resentment" and garnered higher support for increasing education funding, creating jobs that pay well, and increasing the affordability of health care. However, while 59 percent of the population can be moved by race-class narrative messages, they are also affected by voices from the right that emphasize security and the need "to take care of our own people first."[30] Other research on "moral reframing," such as work by sociologists Jan Voelkel and Robb Willer, found that talking about progressive policies and candidates using conservative ideas such as "patriotism, family and respect for tradition" could increase support for them among conservative voters, especially if these voters saw such candidates as having values similar to their own.[31]

Electoral activities aimed at promoting political trust should take into account the reality that many voters process information through personal experiences.[32] Marriage equality referendum campaigns from two states demonstrate how successful campaigns took account of this dynamic.[33] Maine and Washington state campaigns appealed to a range of voters who knew gay and lesbian people as friends, coworkers, and family members. Instead of emphasizing marriage as a right, they focused on the reason why straight people married—love and commitment—and framed gay and lesbian couples in the same way. Campaign ads told the stories of people who had changed their minds on same-sex marriage, like a grandfather in rural Maine and a male minister in Washington State. Canvassers used long "persuasion conversations" to shift people's positions rather than quick efforts to discern voters' views or try to convince them to vote. TV spots were warm, conversational, and noncombative.

In that campaign and elsewhere, tone matters. As a study by political scientists Joshua Kalla and David Brookman shows, when canvassers shared stories about immigrants and transgender people and used a nonjudgmental approach, this reduced the resistance people felt and decreased exclusionary attitudes.[34] In an assessment, Kalla and Brookman found that in efforts focused on people's views about the 2020 candidates and the stakes of the election, "deep canvassing," an approach that stresses "sharing narratives about personal experiences" and asking and listening nonjudgmentally, could shift voters while enabling them to feel respected.[35]

Campaigns could employ similar approaches in discussing policies that regulate business and support health care and social welfare. An intensive effort by Working America, a project of the AFL-CIO that canvassed voters year-round, connected to 450,000 voters in seventeen states. Matt Morrison, the executive director of the organization, found that one way to ease distrust toward politics and politicians is to first *listen* to voters. "Beginning the conversation by asking, 'What matters to you?' instead of telling voters what should matter to them gets a more receptive audience. Next, when we introduce new information by telling voters about something they don't know rather than telling them that what they think they know is wrong, you can see the light come on."[36]

What Working America learned is that when swing voters "can discuss and reason out loud, they can connect powerful stories from their own lives to pragmatic progressive policies—only if they hear about them." Changing electoral strategies is important, because, as Morrison writes, "Our current politics fail to engage working people in a conversation about what matters to them and to draw connections between their lived experience and the reason they should cast a ballot in the first place."[37]

But winning someone's vote only matters when those votes can matter. Part of any electoral strategy to promote trust in government must include securing more democratic voting laws and practices. At the same time, voting laws are not the only policies that affect the political system and people's stake in it. As policy feedback research has demonstrated, policies affect politics.[38] Citizens feel disempowered by policies that at first glance do not seem to respond to voting or elections. People who live in communities with a great deal of contact with the criminal justice system tend to feel disempowered and disrespected by the government.[39] Thus, while fighting to overcome laws and court decisions that suppress the vote, intensive mobilizing strategies aimed at populations who feel especially disenfranchised may have to be developed.

Policies can also empower citizens and spark civic action. When the GI Bill was instituted after World War II, more American adults went to college, and with that came a sense of empowerment and the resources that are usually associated with more political participation. The same goes for health care. Medicare created stakeholders and constituents who were and remain very sensitive to any threats and cutbacks to the program.[40] While the Affordable Care Act required all states to expand Medicaid, in 2012 the Supreme Court ruled expansion was an option. Research shows that turnout increased in places where Medicaid was expanded and suggests that further expansion could increase voting even more.[41] But stigmatizing approaches to Medicaid and adding extra burdens to getting coverage and services are disempowering.[42]

Again, the story of the ACA applies here. Its passage produced a backlash in 2010 and sparked a Tea Party movement in opposition, but under Trump, Republicans could still not muster the legislative support necessary to repeal or replace it. And in 2018 the Democrats won back the House in part by running on a pro-government and health-care reform platform. What policies are passed and how they were designed can encourage people to see themselves as having a stake in the system and better enable them to participate.

INSTITUTIONS AND TRUST IN GOVERNMENT

While the general conservative strategic impulse was to stoke distrust in government, the GOP often found itself controlling at least some levers of power in the post-Nixon era. And so the Republican weaponization of distrust was aimed strategically at institutions the GOP did not control as they sought to expand the powers of the institution that they did control. These arguments were often made to sound like consistent reads of ostensibly fixed constitutional principles, but they shifted with the political winds. Divided party control of government and alternating party control of Congress and the presidency complicated the strategic use of distrust in the United States.

Some efforts to shift institutional powers are expected in a system of checks and balances. As James Madison wrote in *Federalist* 51, to prevent any single institution from having too much power, the Constitution gave "to those who administer each department the necessary constitutional means and personal motives to resist encroachments of the others."[43] But abruptly reinterpreting constitutional meanings based on the results of the last election is not what he had in mind. Nor would he abide any individual or single institution standing as the sole arbiter of his or her or its own power. As he wrote in *Federalist* 10, "No man is allowed to be a judge in his own cause, because his interest would certainly bias his judgment, and, not improbably, corrupt his integrity."[44] When considered over time, the vacillations and the degree of partisan situational constitutionalism are stunning in their frequency and ultimately harm stable governance and fealty to the constitution over a party or officeholder.

But certain instances of situational constitutionalism are particularly dangerous and damaging. In *How Democracies Die*, Steven Levitsky and

Daniel Ziblatt describe four key indicators of authoritarian behavior: weak support for or a rejection of the democratic rules of the game, denying the legitimacy of political opponents, tolerating or encouraging violence, and a willingness to curtail civil liberties of the media and political opponents. Fundamental democratic norms can be weakened if actors put aside good faith presumptions and democratic forbearance, actions that can lead to the backsliding of democracy.[45]

The Trump administration and its expansion of presidential power brought with it an unprecedented threatening of political norms. Trump cast doubt on the legitimacy of elections (even an election he won) and exerted budgetary control over funds for a border wall after Congress made contrary decisions. The administration took a highly aggressive stance on the "unitary executive" theory of presidential leadership, and Trump singled out administrative actors—members of the "deep state"—whom he believed thwarted his will.

Conservative leaders have also undermined institutional norms. The GOP-controlled Wisconsin and Michigan legislatures stripped the governorship of various powers after Democrats won these positions. In recent years, nearly a dozen state legislatures (mostly controlled by Republicans) tried to expand or reduce the number of judges on their Supreme Courts; two states, both Republican-led, succeeded.[46] Senate majority leader Mitch McConnell blocked the Senate from its constitutional obligation to provide advice and consent to President Obama regarding a Supreme Court vacancy.

Increasing trust in institutions should include promoting a sort of civic education that acknowledges the potentially lasting effects of polarization on our constitutional understandings. As Americans are polarized and divided, they tie themselves too closely to one party and separate themselves too starkly from the other. This happens to the detriment of shared ties of social capital, economic fortunes, patriotism, and even constitutionalism. Perhaps what has been most striking about situational constitutionalism is that it revealed how little faith citizens and political elites alike have in the Constitution itself, raising the question of just how much the Constitution matters to conservatives willing to switch course at a moment's notice when political situations change.[47]

Civic educators—including not only college and university instructors but also K–12 teachers—could aim to teach the Constitution and equip students with the skills to think for themselves about what the Constitution means and what it prescribes. Expanding on and reinforcing these efforts, public relations campaigns and concerted efforts by organizations such as the National Endowment for the Humanities, the American Political Science Association, and the American Historical Association, as well as museums and other cultural institutions, should reinforce these civic aims, allowing individuals to hone their beliefs about the Constitution and the political system. With these supports, citizens would be more equipped to comfortably and consistently apply nonpartisan views of the appropriate functions of the system independent of who currently controls the levers of power and to stick to them—even when they are inconvenient. Such civic education should teach Americans to be more comfortable with ambiguity, conflict, and controversy and to accept that people with whom they disagree might yet be acting in good faith. Fellow citizens are "not enemies, but friends," as Abraham Lincoln put it, and this means some institutional tactics, however savvy, are unacceptable. Should the rebirth of this constitutional faith reach critical mass, it could even be a criterion by which we judge our elected leaders and restore the constitutional common ground on which trust might be rebuilt.

Restoring our faith in institutions through civic education may seem too long and too optimistic. Negative partisanship and long-standing electoral incentives from within the Republican Party make this a difficult task. And we cannot extinguish self-interest or the tendency for people to rationalize policies that disproportionately favor them. But as journalist Greg Sargent argues, Democrats should not engage in a wholesale tit-for-tat or "unilaterally disarm in the face of Republican hardball." Instead, they should "do all they can do to make the system more rewarding for fair play."[48] Institutions that promote minority rule should be scrutinized and, to the extent possible and reasonable, reformed. We can also shift incentives for elites to write rules that make voting systems fairer and more accessible, stimulate activism, and bring in new voters or at least strike out anti-democratic incentives.

When possible, oversight and institutional checks should be both fair and robust. Weakening transparency and accountability merely for partisan reasons shields elected officials from the consequences of their actions. Unchecked partisanship leads to groupthink and a discounting of expertise. A lack of expertise, in turn, makes the federal government less effective, as seen in Trump's mishandling of the COVID-19 epidemic, which led to preventable deaths and an economic decline. Whereas more successful and functioning governments across the globe mitigated the pandemic's impact, the U.S. response allowed the contagion to spread at extraordinary levels, resulting in human and economic losses unmatched in American history.[49]

Even before the pandemic, sidelining experts was par for the course in the Trump administration. Doing so served the desires of wealthy donors and corporate interests to undermine regulatory actions that protected health and labor rights. Indeed, while Trump employed populist rhetoric and adopted an in-your-face demeanor to appeal to his base, his policies served the wealthy. Although Trump emulated the prior conservative pattern of using government to support his favored constituencies (such as a massive bailout of farmers to cushion the blow of Trump's trade war), his rhetoric and a great deal of his policy agenda aimed to shrink government. At the same time, even as his message shifted in a new and more extreme direction, Trump was not the first to undermine the administrative state substantively or symbolically.[50] As political scientist Theda Skocpol notes, "Today's Trumpified GOP" has been built on "a dually radicalized synthesis years in the making—a marriage of convenience between anti-government free-market plutocrats and racially anxious ethno-nationalist activists and voters."[51] Rebuilding administrative capacity and preventing corruption would improve government operations and promote citizens' trust and support of public endeavors.[52]

The Trump years laid bare fault lines that can be exploited by those who do not respect institutional norms. As legal scholars Josh Chafetz and David Pozen suggest, the blatant flouting of constitutional norms may even attract more public attention and generate a greater backlash than slowly eroding norms.[53] So legislative steps should also be part of our strategies to restore and promote trust. Just as the corruption of the Gilded Age and the Watergate scandal led to new anti-graft laws and campaign finance regulation, new legislation can prevent corruption, shield nonpartisan civil service employees from political pressure, and protect government watchdogs and whistleblowers. Advocates for new laws should articulate a new public philosophy that telegraphs what would constitute appropriate and inappropriate uses of state power and institutional prerogatives without regard to specific policy questions or particular constitutional showdowns or crises.

POLICY AND TRUST

In the opening chapter of this book, we quoted sociologist William Gamson: trust, he said, is "the creator of collective power" and "the loss of trust is the loss of system power, the loss of a generalized capacity for authorities to commit resources to attain collective goals."[54]

This is true for many policies, especially redistributive ones. In this book, we have examined health-care reform as our through-line case, because it has been a perennial target for strategic uses of distrust.

At the dawn of the modern conservative movement, Ronald Reagan argued against Medicare, which he called an effort to impose statism and socialism on the American people.[55] From then on, the GOP efforts decried government interventions into health care as "socialistic," overbearing, even deadly. While strategic uses of distrust in government were employed against the unsuccessful Clinton health reform push, later in the 1990s and into the twenty-first century, more incremental efforts to attain greater coverage and to prevent retrenchment in gains made were aided by positive elite rhetoric in support of health care, mobilized publics, supportive public opinion, and effective policy designs.

During the Obama years, opponents of health reform again characterized the Affordable Care Act as socialism and claimed it would unleash unfeeling bureaucrats to become arbiters of life and death for the American people. But while the Tea Party mobilized citizens in opposition to the policy, pro-ACA citizen activism helped push reform through Congress. The law would not have existed without the mobilization of citizens to generate big legislative majorities and for further reforms afterward.

Fast-forward to the Trump administration. In 2017, activists pushed the federal government to keep its commitment to health coverage, and the GOP's efforts to "repeal and replace" Obamacare failed. By 2018, polls from the Pew Research Center showed a sharp increase in the percentage of voters, including key Republican demographics, who believe that ensuring health care is the federal government's responsibility.[56]

How much citizens trust government to provide health care hinges on how they see other players in the system. For instance, the average citizen trusts insurance companies even less than the federal government. This means regulating insurance companies and mandating coverage for preexisting conditions is quite popular. Americans have minimal trust in pharmaceutical companies, too, and so they support greater federal regulation and intervention there as well.[57]

But the Trump administration's handling of policy and the Republican war on the Affordable Care Act may have decreased the average American's trust that government can be counted on to consistently and competently administer and carry out health policies. In 2018, focus groups of former

Clinton voters found a common sentiment: "Before this particular administration, I had a lot more trust in the government, whether I agreed with what they had or not. I'm comfortable with a system that is run by the government, and I would have said that without equivocating. But right now, I'm a little bit iffy on it."[58]

How the policy is designed also determines whether citizens support it. For instance, in health-care policy, maintaining freedom of choice is consistent with the strong strain of individualism in American political culture. Early in the Clinton presidency, Americans supported expanding coverage in general but then opposed a key, poorly understood mechanism, the proposed health-care alliances. Recent data also show that while Americans want the government to do more, most also support maintaining other forms of health coverage.[59]

Universal coverage proposals and plans such as Medicare buy-in and early Medicare take account of this opinion landscape and would be less disruptive to the existing health-care system.[60] The political scientist Jacob Hacker argues that the path to universal coverage also requires attention to "policy sustainability," meaning that policies must be designed so they are entrenched and thus able to be built upon subsequently.[61]

To combat distrust, Democrats (and anyone else who might seek to build public confidence in government) should seek to reduce administrative burdens, aggressively pronounce government successes, name and claim popular government policies like Social Security and Medicare, and advertise the advantages of the political system and its necessity for enacting the public good. Taking lessons from the public relations campaigns of corporations, political scientist Amy Lerman argues that government can regain trust if it governs well, takes responsibility for failures, and emphasizes what government does that the private sector does not and cannot do.[62]

Because citizens often do not recognize that they have used a government program, regaining trust requires making the less visible more visible and sparking discussion about the connections between public action and opportunity.[63] More self-conscious policy design and positive elite rhetoric about government might increase trust.

Just as strategic efforts focused on organizations, elections, institutions, and policy have contributed to distrust in government, the efforts to counteract this war with government and rebuild trust must be equally planned and equally strategic. We must take account of what research shows about building coalitions and developing appropriate leaders for such a coalition; study public opinion and plan effective campaign structures and messages that promise deliverable government action; restore constitutional faith and institutional balance and counter democratic backsliding and other efforts to weaken norms; and build the trust and make the case for engineering effective public policies all the while pointing out that the public policies that the public approves of are, in fact, government.

Those who govern must earn the public's trust, and American history has demonstrated that trust is hard-won. Making policies work, touting policy successes, and recognizing and addressing policy failures could counteract strategic uses of distrust in government. Highlighting incompetent government and providing alternatives could increase appreciation for expertise and professionalism.

It has taken a long time and much effort to erode our trust in government. Rebuilding and fostering that trust will be neither easy nor quick. But the damage of distrust in the political system is too great to allow it to continue unchecked. These counterstrategies are critical first steps to take if we wish to make peace with government and ensure its responsiveness and accountability to popular control.

AFTERWORD

We completed this manuscript in the fraught weeks and months after the 2020 elections. Though the incumbent president Donald Trump was soundly defeated in November, initially the GOP seemed to show remarkable staying power in Congress. Republicans gained seats in the House and maintained control of the Senate (until losing two January 5, 2021 runoff elections in Georgia). What we saw during the COVID crisis, the 2020 campaign, and in the election's turbulent wake, which culminated in a violent insurrection of Trump supporters at the United States Capitol, demonstrates that the broad trend delineated in this book and its dangerous development under Donald Trump are likely to persist.

In the midst of 2020's COVID-19 pandemic, many looked to government, particularly the National Institutes of Health's infectious disease director Anthony Fauci, for expertise and direction. But Trump undermined public confidence in Fauci's expertise and his own administration's guidelines to curb the contagion. His distrustful response found receptive audiences among those who are primed to think that government always fails and who are skeptical or even disdainful toward science and experts.

Trump left key elements of pandemic response to the states, and his administration stoked distrust toward governors who promoted public health measures like wearing masks, social distancing, and lockdowns. On April 17, he tweeted "LIBERATE MICHIGAN," "LIBERATE MINNESOTA," and "LIBERATE VIRGINIA"—all states led by Democratic governors.[1] Many Republican governors followed Trump's lead and downplayed efforts to slow the contagion, which they framed as unnecessary limits on freedom.

With Trump's flawed COVID response as backdrop to the campaign, many voters worried that the virus would continue unabated and its economic and human devastation would go unaddressed. As Joe Biden held a persistent lead over Trump in national polling—even before the pandemic hit—Trump ran for reelection the way he won it the first time: not to win a majority of voters but instead by eking out another electoral college victory. He planned to do this by mobilizing his base and, predictably, building on their discontent.

Following the May 25 killing of George Floyd by a Minneapolis police officer, race became a national conversation. In large cities and small towns, Americans held Black Lives Matter protests in what was estimated to be "the largest movement in the country's history."[2] While Trump initially expressed sympathy to George Floyd's family, he went on to rail against Black Lives Matter and use racial appeals to rally his base and appeal to suburban women. Trump also criticized education on slavery and race in the United States and issued guidance to prohibit government agencies and contractors from teaching about racism. His campaign's law and order messaging was reminiscent of previous GOP efforts. It suggested that liberal elites were not on the side of "real Americans," which meant white Americans.

The Republican Party cleaved to Trump. Likewise, they promoted distrust in the media and in government. Rather than putting forth a national party platform for 2020, the national convention ratified a one-page resolution stating that no new positions would replace its 2016 document. They excoriated the media, endorsed Trump, and adopted his agenda.[3] This is yet another example of how distrust became the organizational glue of the GOP coalition.

All the while Trump was widening the Republican coalition in troubling ways. Besides marshaling traditional GOP constituencies, he winked at the hyper-distrustful fringe, like the QAnon conspiracy movement, which believes Democratic elites are Satan-worshipping pedophiles. Although the Department of Homeland Security identified violent right-wing white supremacist extremists as "the most persistent and lethal threat" to the United States,[4] in the September presidential debate, Trump encouraged the Proud Boys, a white-nationalist hate group, to "stand back and stand by."[5]

In October, when a militia group in Michigan was arrested for plotting the kidnapping of Democratic governor Gretchen Whitmer, Trump nevertheless continued his attacks on Whitmer. Echoing their 2016 anti–Hillary Clinton refrain, his supporters chanted "lock her up" at Trump's rallies.[6] Saying, "I have watched the president wedge a deeper divide in our country," Whitmer charged Trump with "sowing division and putting leaders, especially women leaders, at risk. And all because he thinks it will help his reelection."[7]

On September 18, Supreme Court associate justice Ruth Bader Ginsburg died, creating a vacancy on the court less than two months before the election. In another somersaulting instance of situational constitutionalism, Senate Republicans, led by Mitch McConnell, reversed their purported principles that had kept them from confirming Merrick Garland, whom Barack Obama had appointed to replace Antonin Scalia, who died in February 2016. Back then, they said they would not confirm such an appointment during an election year. In 2018, Senator Lindsey Graham said, "If an opening comes in the last year of President Trump's term, and the primary process has started, we'll wait to the next election," and added, looking at the television camera, "hold the tape."[8] But the Republican Senate, with Graham as Judiciary Committee chairman, filled Ginsburg's seat less than two weeks before the election. It confirmed Trump's appointee, Amy Coney Barrett, a young judge vetted and approved by the Federalist Society.

Throughout 2020, Trump returned to his playbook again and again, often undermining public confidence in a fair election system. Trump charged that the Democratic nominating process had been "rigged" against Bernie Sanders, questioned the security of mail-in ballots, and dubbed polls that had him behind as "suppression polls."[9]

On election night, with many states counting their early and mail-in ballots (methods that Democrats disproportionately preferred) after they counted the same-day ballots, the method that Trump voters were more likely to employ, Trump's early-reported swing state margins dwindled and then disappeared.

Trump outperformed the polls and was aided by a head start in the electoral college that made victory a possibility even with another popular vote loss. Trump may also have been aided by his campaign's decision to engage in large-scale rallies and door-to-door mobilization during the pandemic. Marshaling cultural arguments, like claims that Democrats wanted to defund the police and that they backed socialism, Trump increased support from Latino voters and improved turnout from white adults without a college degree. Meanwhile, Trump and his supporters spread disinformation about Biden and his family via right-wing media and social media in the hope of making the election a "choice election" rather than a referendum on Trump's first-term performance.[10]

Joe Biden nevertheless defeated Trump. Biden appealed to a wide spectrum of voters and was propelled by grassroots organizations and by increased Democratic support in the suburbs. Undoing Trump's 2016 surprise states, Biden rebuilt the "blue wall" states of Wisconsin, Michigan, and Pennsylvania, and his campaign remade the electoral college map by winning Georgia and Arizona, states a Democrat had not won since 1992 and 1996, respectively. Biden won a substantial majority of electoral votes—306—the same amount Trump had won in 2016 and had called a landslide.[11]

Yet in the weeks following the election, Trump continued to claim that he had actually won and that the election was rigged. He railed against the media especially, using messages of distrust for strategic purposes. As the votes were counted and Biden's victory became apparent, Trump questioned voting machines, leveled vague charges of "fraud" (especially against vote tallies in cities), spurred supporters to protest outside election boards, and launched scores of ultimately unsuccessful lawsuits to stop the counts or to throw out votes where his campaign thought this could help him win, all while refusing to concede the election and blocking the transition.

Trump's claims that the election was stolen from him are consistent with his party's decades-long unsupported contentions of election fraud and its efforts to strategically employ distrust in government. Many Republican leaders were slow to acknowledge Biden's win, as some chose to back Trump's unsubstantiated claims. Former Speaker of the House Newt Gingrich claimed that urban political machines in Atlanta, Detroit, and Philadelphia were corrupt and were trying to "steal the presidency." He suggested that the attorney general could have poll workers locked up.[12] Several days after the election, House Republican minority leader Kevin McCarthy proclaimed that Trump had won and advised, "Everyone who is listening: Do not be quiet. Do not be silent about this. We cannot allow this to happen before our very eyes."[13]

In a dynamic similar to the Tea Party mobilization that confronted President Obama, some postelection protests were "organized by prominent, well-funded pro-Trump groups such as Tea Party Patriots, Women for America First, Turning Point USA and Freedom Works USA." Steve Bannon and *Breitbart* were involved in creating a #StopTheSteal Facebook group that was removed from the platform.[14] Like the Tea Party, some adopted extremist rhetoric. In one instance, a "Facebook user posted an image with the text: 'I don't know why we are surprised about the vote, we all saw it coming and we know how it will end. Neither side is going to concede. Time to clean the guns, time to hit the streets.' "[15]

The distrustful rhetoric boiled over on January 6, 2021 when attendees of a "Stop the Steal" rally stormed the U.S. Capitol in a violent uprising against Congress's pro forma certification of the Presidential election results. True to form for a GOP that for decades had stoked distrust, the "Stop the Steal" event was promoted by several GOP members of Congress, and President Donald Trump addressed the crowd with remarks that included setting the crowd on foot toward the Capitol building. As the aftermath and investigations continued to unfold, there were calls for the resignation of multiple House members and Senators thought to be complicit in the insurrection, over 100 arrests, and the impeachment of Donald Trump for "incitement" of the insurrection. That impeachment, Trump's second in less than thirteen months, passed the House by a 232 to 197 vote that included ten House Republicans voting to impeach.

But, demonstrating Trump's continued hold on key GOP constituencies, the rest of the House Republicans voted against impeachment and some state Republican parties used extreme, conspiratorial rhetoric and censured elected officials who backed impeachment.[16] In all, the Republicans' denial of the democratic legitimacy of the 2020 election, with its air of distrust, grievance, and victimhood, suggests that neither Trump nor Trumpism will fade from American politics. Trump has indicated that he may run for president again. Whether he does or not, he will remain a force in Republican politics, leading many Republicans to continue to avoid confronting him, his agenda, and his followers.

While most voters rejected Trump, he remade the Republican Party. It became a party that valued, above all, loyalty to him. And it built on its long history of strategic uses of distrust in government. With few exceptions, Republicans tacitly agreed and sometimes even echoed Trump's disdain for democratic norms, checks, and balances. They engaged in a shift toward "illiberal values" such as "low commitment to political pluralism, demonization of political opponents, disrespect for fundamental minority rights and encouragement of political violence."[17] The fact that the electoral failure was visited more on Trump than on Republicans will likely further convince the GOP of the benefits of anger, illiberalism, and distrust.

This distrust, which Donald Trump peddled throughout 2020, has deep roots in the Republican Party and in American political culture more generally. As journalist Anne Applebaum wrote in the *Atlantic* after the elections, "Trump not only exploited this democratic deficit to win the White House, but he expanded it while in office."[18] The Trump presidency is over, but the Republican strategy that preceded it and was fed by it lives on.

This battle between trust and distrust, between unity and disunity, will rage on. Moving on from the politics of distrust involves building up trust in elections, political organizations, institutions, and policy—all areas where conservatives have benefited from extant distrust.

Still, there was a hint of rejection of the strategy of distrust in the election results. On the day media outlets declared he had won the presidency, President-elect Joe Biden called for Americans to come together, saying that it was "the time to heal in America," and pledging to "work with all my heart for the confidence of the whole people, to win the confidence of all people." Perhaps making government work well in a time of crisis may build trust. As political scientist Ryan LaRochelle pointed out, it was "conservatives' decades-long war on the safety net and the government's administrative capacity that made our society particularly vulnerable to the pandemic's impact."[19] It is possible, too, that the broader public reaction to the political violence in the U.S. Capitol, borne of stoked distrust and aimed at overturning the 2020 election, might lead most Americans to step back from the brink and to ask hard questions about how to heal our distrustful divides. Biden's pledge and the work of our leaders and citizens cannot guarantee that we will rebuild this lost social and political trust, but they are at least steps in the right direction: away from the war with government and the weaponization of distrust.

NOTES

1. WEAPONIZING DISTRUST

1. Deena Zaru, "Sasse Warns of 'Weaponizing Distrust' After Trump's Media Attacks," *CNN*, July 2, 2017, https://www.cnn.com/2017/07/02/politics/ben-sasse-donald-trump-media-attacks/index.html.

2. State of the Union, *CNN*, July 2, 2017, transcript available at http://transcripts.cnn.com/TRANSCRIPTS/1707/02/sotu.01.html.

3. Sasse supported Trump on 97 percent of floor votes in 2017 and 94 percent in 2019. "CQ Vote Studies: Presidential Support—Trump Divided, Conquered," *CQ Magazine*, February 12, 2018; "CQ Vote Studies: Presidential Support—Trump's Last Hurrah," *CQ Magazine*, February 25, 2019.

4. Jack Citrin and Laura Stoker, "Political Trust in a Cynical Age," *Annual Reviews in Political Science* 21, no. 1 (2018): 49–70, 51.

5. Citrin and Stoker, "Political Trust in a Cynical Age," 52–53.

6. Marc Hetherington, "Why Polarized Trust Matters," *The Forum* 13, no. 3 (2015): 445–58, 445.

7. Hetherington, "Why Polarized Trust Matters," 446; see also Marc J. Hetherington and Thomas J. Rudolph, *Why Washington Won't Work: Polarization, Political Trust, and the Governing Crisis* (Chicago: University of Chicago Press, 2015).

8. Luke Keele, "Social Capital and the Dynamics of Trust in Government," *American Journal of Political Science* 51, no. 2 (2007): 241–54; Andrew Wroe, "Economic Insecurity and Political Trust in the United States," *American Politics Research* 44, no. 1 (2016): 131–63; see also Hetherington and Rudolph, *Why Washington Won't Work*.

9. John R. Hibbing and Elizabeth Theiss-Morse, *Congress as Public Enemy: Public Attitudes Toward American Political Institutions* (New York: Cambridge University Press, 1995); John R. Hibbing and Elizabeth Theiss-Morse, *Stealth Democracy: Americans' Beliefs About How Government Should Work* (New York: Cambridge University Press, 2002).

10. Matt Levendusky, *How Partisan Media Polarize America* (Chicago: University of Chicago Press, 2013); Jeffrey M. Berry and Sarah Sobieraj, *The Outrage Industry: Political Opinion Media and the New Incivility* (New York: Oxford University Press, 2016).

11. Hetherington and Rudolph, *Why Washington Won't Work*, chaps. 2, 4.

12. This legitimating role of the out-party was best explored by Robert Dahl in "The American Opposition: Affirmation and Denial," in *Political Opposition in Western Democracies*, ed. Robert A. Dahl (New Haven: Yale University Press, 1966), 34–69.

13. See, e.g., Joseph S. Nye Jr., Philip D. Zelikow, and David C. King, eds., *Why People Don't Trust Government* (Cambridge, Mass.: Harvard University Press, 1997); Joseph Cooper, ed., *Congress and the Decline of Public Trust* (Boulder, Colo.: Westview Press, 1999); John R. Hibbing and Elizabeth Theiss-Morse, eds., *What Is It About Government That Americans Dislike?* (Cambridge: Cambridge University Press, 2001); Hetherington and Rudolph, *Why Washington Won't Work*; Marc J. Hetherington and Jonathan Weiler, *Authoritarianism and Polarization in American Politics* (New York: Cambridge University Press, 2009).

14. William Gamson, *Power and Discontent* (Homewood, Ill.: Dorsey Press, 1968), 42–43. As sociologist Dietrich Rueschemeyer contends, ideas and beliefs "can have lasting consequences for divided or unified responses to the same broad set of problems." Broad political and historical change involves both shifting ideas and transformations in politics, including the fluctuating nature and strength of political coalitions, institutions, and public policies. Political scientist Rogers Smith, for instance, posits a "spiral of politics," recognizing that, as contexts vary over time, the construction of ideas and interests, coalition formation and competition, the capture and use of governing institutions, and the consequent modifications of contexts and new ideas propel the spiral further. Dietrich Rueschemeyer, "Why and How Ideas Matter," in *The Oxford Handbook of Contextual Political Analysis*, ed. Robert E. Goodin and Charles Tilly (Oxford: Oxford University Press, 2006), 244. See, especially, Brian J. Glenn, "The Two Schools of American Political Development," *Political Studies Review* 2 (2004): 153–65; Robert C. Lieberman, "Ideas, Institutions, and Political Order," *American Political Science Review* 96 (2002): 697–712; Rogers M. Smith, "Ideas and the Spiral of Politics: The Place of American Political Thought in American Political Development," *American Political Thought* 3 (2014): 126–36; George Thomas, "Political Thought and Political Development," *American Political Thought* 3 (2014): 114–25.

15. Benedict Anderson, *Imagined Communities* (New York: Verso, 1991), 6.

16. Rogers Smith, *Political Peoplehood: The Roles of Values, Interests, and Identities* (Chicago: University of Chicago Press, 2015), 42

17. Garry Wills, *Cincinnatus: George Washington and the Enlightenment* (Garden City, N.Y.: Doubleday, 1984); Barry Schwartz, *George Washington: The Making of an American Symbol* (Ithaca, N.Y.: Cornell University Press, 1990); Edward G. Lengel, *Inventing George Washington: America's Founder, in Myth and Memory* (New York: Harper, 2011).

18. Chris Capozzola, *Uncle Sam Wants You: World War I and the Making of the Modern American Citizen* (New York: Oxford University Press, 2008); Wendy Wall, *Inventing the "American Way": The Politics of Consensus from the New Deal to the Civil Rights Movement* (New York: Oxford University Press, 2008).

19. Political parties have performed—to varying degrees of success—this "integrative" function throughout American political history. Walter Dean Burnham contended "the major task of American politics" was "building a nation out of a congeries of regions and peoples." Moreover, "if the social context in which a two-party system operates is extensively fragmented along regional, ethnic, and other lines, its major components will tend to be overwhelmingly concerned with coalition building and internal conflict management." Walter Dean Burnham, "Party Systems and the Political Process," in *Current Crisis in American Politics* (New York: Norton, 1982), 100.

20. See Rogers Smith, "Beyond Tocqueville, Myrdal, and Hartz: The Multiple Traditions in America," *American Political Science Review* 87 (1993): 549–66; James Morone "Political Culture: Consensus, Conflict and Culture War," in *The Oxford Handbook of American Political Development*, ed. Richard M. Vallely, Suzanne Mettler, and Robert C. Lieberman (Oxford: Oxford University Press, 2016), 132–47.

21. Smith, *Political Peoplehood*, 42.

22. Elizabeth Theiss-Morse, *Who Counts as an American? The Boundaries of National Identity* (New York: Cambridge University Press, 2009).

23. John E. Transue, "Identity Salience, Identity Acceptance, and Racial Policy Attitudes: American National Identity as a Uniting Force," *American Journal of Political Science*, 51 (2007): 78–91, 80. Research suggests this dynamic is at work in other countries as well. A study by Matthew Wright and Tim Reeskens of individuals from the United States and fifteen other industrialized countries discovered that greater immigrant diversity was associated with a sense of cultural threat and perceived economic threats, and a national identity that was relatively restrictive and ascriptive, rather than something immigrants could achieve; Matthew Wright and Tim Reeskens, "Of What Cloth Are the Ties that Bind? National Identity and Support for the Welfare State across 29 European Countries," *Journal of European Public Policy* 20, no. 10 (2013): 1443–63. Similarly, after analyzing multiple studies of national identity and immigration in many developed countries, David Miller and Sundas Ali conclude that "support for social justice, in societies where ethnically distinct immigrant groups are prominent, may increase if the civic components of national identity—feeling committed to the society and its values, respecting its institutions, etc.—become relatively more important in people's eyes, while the ethnic components—being born in the country, belonging to the dominant ethnic group, etc.—become less so." As the authors point out, it also matters if immigrants are defined as within the community and consistent with its civic identity. David Miller and Sundas Ali, "Testing the National Identity Argument," *European Political Science Review* 6, no. 2 (2014): 237–59, 255. Moreover, social solidarity is part of why different subnations adopt more or less generous social welfare policies; see, e.g., Prerna Singh, *How Solidarity Works for Welfare: Subnationalism and Social Development in India* (Cambridge: Cambridge University Press, 2016). Singh compares several states in India and finds that lack of collective identity undermines the sense of the popular good and is associated with weak support for social welfare programs.

24. Jack Citrin, "Comment: The Political Relevance of Trust in Government," *American Political Science Review* 68, no. 3 (September 1974): 973–88, 982.

25. Vivien Hart, *Distrust and Democracy: Political Distrust in Britain and America* (New York: Cambridge University Press, 1978), 53. Pollock found that "politically

competent, cynical individuals favor high initiative modes of influence—campaigning and contacting, as well as protest behavior"; Philip H. Pollock, "The Participatory Consequences of Internal and External Political Efficacy: A Research Note," *Western Political Quarterly* 36, no. 3 (September 1983): 400–9. On this point, see also Stephen C. Craig, "The Mobilization of Political Discontent," *Political Behavior* 2, no. 2 (1980): 189–209, 204–5.

26. Gamson, *Power and Discontent*, 48.

27. Christopher S. Parker and Matthew A. Barreto, *Change They Can't Believe In: The Tea Party and Reactionary Politics in America* (Princeton, N.J.: Princeton University Press, 2013), 223–34, 240.

28. Bert Useem and Michael Useem, "Government Legitimacy and Political Stability," *Social Forces* 57, no. 3 (March 1980): 840–52, 841. Notably, this hinges, too, on the "trust differential" in terms of public assessments of those in charge and those who would lead the opposition; Nilson and Burzotta Nilson found, for example, that "a pro-protest orientation develops out of *both* low trust in established elites and high trust in challenging elites"; Douglas C. Nilson and Linda Burzotta Nilson, "Trust in Elites and Protest Orientation: An Integrative Approach," *Political Behavior* 2, no. 4 (1980): 385–404, 387.

29. Theda Skocpol and Vanessa Williamson, *The Tea Party and the Remaking of Republican Conservatism* (New York: Oxford University Press, 2013), 162; Parker and Barreto, *Change They Can't Believe In*, 229.

30. Nancy MacLean, *Democracy in Chains: The Deep History of the Radical Right's Stealth Plan for America* (New York: Viking, 2017); Jane Mayer, *Dark Money: The Hidden History of the Billionaires Behind the Rise of the Radical Right* (New York: Anchor Books, 2017); Theda Skocpol and Alexander Hertel-Fernandez, "The Koch Network and Republican Party Extremism," *Perspectives on Politics* 14, no. 3 (September 2016): 681–99; Steven Teles, *The Rise of the Conservative Legal Movement: The Battle for Control of the Law* (Princeton, N.J.: Princeton University Press, 2008).

31. Lawrence R. Jacobs and Robert Y. Shapiro, *Politicians Don't Pander: Political Manipulation and the Loss of Democratic Responsiveness* (Chicago: University of Chicago Press, 2000), xv.

32. Gamson, *Power and Discontent*, 45.

33. Pew Research Center, "Public Trust in Government: 1958–2017," interactive report accompanying "Public Trust in Government Remains Near Historic Lows as Partisan Attitudes Shift," May 3, 2017, http://www.people-press.org/2017/05/03/public-trust-in-government-1958-2017/; http://assets.pewresearch.org/wp-content/uploads/sites/5/2017/05/03145544/05-03-17-Trust-release.pdf. Despite this general difference, with Donald Trump in the White House, this report did note a sharp decline in Democratic trust in 2017.

34. Hetherington, "Why Polarized Trust Matters"; Hetherington and Rudolph, *Why Washington Won't Work*; Pew Research Center, "Public Trust in Government, 1958–2017."

35. Davide Morisi, John T. Jost, and Vishal Singh, "An Asymmetrical 'President-in-Power' Effect," *American Political Science Review* 113, no. 2 (2019): 614–20.

36. William L. Lunch and Peter W. Sperlich, "American Public Opinion and the War in Vietnam," *Western Political Quarterly* 32, no. 1 (March 1979): 21–44, 43.

37. Hart, *Distrust and Democracy*, 182. Notably, the distrust from the left seemed to compel southern conservatives, for at least a time, to champion the state; they "switched for a while . . . wanting duties imposed on the rebellious by authoritative efficiency and confidential expertise (i.e., FBI spying)"; Garry Wills, *A Necessary Evil: A History of Distrust in Government* (New York: Simon & Schuster, 1999), 19–20.

38. Wills, *A Necessary Evil*, 288.

39. Citrin, "Comment: The Political Relevance of Trust in Government," 976; Wills, *A Necessary Evil*, 17.

40. On asymmetric polarization, see Thomas E. Mann and Norman J. Ornstein, *It's Even Worse Than It Looks: How the American Constitutional System Collided with the New Politics of Extremism* (New York: Basic Books, 2016). There is a great deal of literature on partisan polarization focused on whether it is more an elite or mass phenomenon. See, especially, Alan Abramowitz, *The Polarized Public: Why American Government Is so Dysfunctional* (Boston: Pearson, 2013); Alan Abramowitz, *The Disappearing Center: Engaged Citizens, Polarization, and American Democracy* (New Haven, Conn.: Yale University Press, 2011); Morris P. Fiorina, Samuel J. Abrams, and Jeremy C. Pope, *Culture War? The Myth of a Polarized America*, 3rd ed. (New York: Longman, 2010); Daniel J. Hopkins and John Sides, *Political Polarization in American Politics* (New York: Bloomsbury, 2015).

41. Matt Grossman and David A. Hopkins, *Asymmetric Politics: Ideological Republicans and Group Interest Democrats.* (New York: Oxford University Press, 2016).

42. Jacob S. Hacker and Paul Pierson, *American Amnesia: How the War on Government Led Us to Forget What Made America Prosper* (New York: Simon & Schuster, 2016), 259.

43. Although race has been a—perhaps *the*—perennial issue of American national politics, partisan racialized politics have not always been the way they are now. There are huge literatures on race and politics in the United States demonstrating its persistent impact as well as shifts. For two recent works of note showing continuity and change, see Avidit Achharya, Matthew Blackwell, and Maya Sen, *Deep Roots: How Slavery Still Shapes Southern Politics* (Princeton, N.J.: Princeton University Press, 2018); Michael Tesler, *Post-Racial or Most-Racial? Race and Politics in the Obama Era* (Chicago: University of Chicago Press, 2016).

44. Thomas E. Nelson and Donald R. Kinder, "Issue Frames and Group-Centrism in American Public Opinion," *Journal of Politics* 58, no. 4 (1996): 1055–78; Marc J. Hetherington, *Why Trust Matters: Declining Political Trust and the Demise of American Liberalism* (Princeton, N.J.: Princeton University Press, 2005).

45. Hacker and Pierson, *American Amnesia*, 250–51.

46. See Christopher Baylor, *First to the Party: The Group Origins of Political Transformations* (Philadelphia: University of Pennsylvania Press, 2018); Paul S. Herrnson, "The Roles of Party Organizations, Party-Connected Committees, and Party Allies in Elections," *Journal of Politics* 71, no. 4 (October 2009): 1207–24; Gregory Koger, Seth Masket, and Hans Noel, "Partisan Webs, Information Exchange and Party Networks," *British Journal of Political Science* 39 (2009): 633–53; Daniel Schlozman, *When Movements Anchor Parties: Electoral Alignments in American History* (Princeton, N.J.: Princeton University Press, 2015); Richard M. Skinner, Seth E.

Masket, and David A. Dulio, "527 Committees and the Political Party Network," *American Politics Research* 40 (2011): 60–84.

47. Both Eisenhower and Nixon were "preemptive" presidents whose presidencies were defined within the context of Franklin Delano Roosevelt's New Deal reconstruction; see Stephen Skowronek, *The Politics That Presidents Make* (Cambridge, Mass: Harvard University Press, 1993); Douglas B. Harris, "Dwight Eisenhower and the New Deal: The Politics of Preemption," *Presidential Studies Quarterly* 27, no. 2 (Spring 1997): 333–42.

48. See, e.g., Mitt Romney's statement on this in 2007: "Press Release—The Romney Agenda: The Three-Legged Republican Stool," October 15, 2007. Online by Gerhard Peters and John T. Woolley, The American Presidency Project, https://www.presidency.ucsb.edu/documents/press-release-the-romney-agenda-the-three-legged-republican-stool.

49. Sam Rosenfeld, *The Polarizers: Postwar Architects of Our Partisan Era* (Chicago: University of Chicago Press, 2017), 80.

50. Once constructed, this ideological movement served to "link" anti-communism groups, "meld" the ideas espoused with these groups with religious conservatives, and eventually facilitate the onboarding of southerners disaffected by the Democrats' embrace of the state to secure civil rights and promote the Great Society; the anti-state coalition expanded further still with anti-tax revolts and a Christian Right; Rosenfeld, *The Polarizers*, 81, 176.

51. Rosenfeld, *The Polarizers*, 260–1.

52. Berkeley Center for Right-Wing Studies, CCSRWM-People for the American Way Collection of Political Ephemera (1980–2004), https://crws.berkeley.edu/archives.

53. Anthony Downs, *An Economic Theory of Democracy* (New York: Harper, 1957).

54. If centrism reigns in some electoral strategies, as was the case for Dwight Eisenhower's "modern Republicanism," for example, or Bill Clinton's "New Democratic" movement, parties sometimes nominate more extreme candidates. The need to appeal to the base in the recent presidential nominating contests has produced atypically strong candidacies of candidates running to the left (Howard Dean, Barack Obama, and Bernie Sanders to name but a few) and the right (Pat Robertson, Ron Paul, Ted Cruz, and Donald Trump). The tendency to placate the extremes is in evidence for statewide, congressional, and local candidates as well.

55. Anthony King, *Running Scared: Why America's Politicians Campaign Too Much and Govern Too Little* (New York: Basic Books, 1997).

56. Anonymous interview with House Republican leadership staffer, June 5, 2008.

57. Hacker and Pierson describe the process of largely unchanged, steady conservatives *seeming* increasingly moderate due to the changing context around them. *American Amnesia*, 240–42.

58. Richard F. Fenno Jr., *Home Style: House Members in Their Districts* (New York: HarperCollins, 1978), 167–68.

59. Benjamin Ginsberg and Martin Shefter, *Politics by Other Means: Politicians, Prosecutors, and the Press from Watergate to Whitewater* (New York: Norton, 1990).

60. See J. Richard Piper, *Ideologies and Institutions: American Conservative and Liberal Governance Prescriptions Since 1933* (Lanham, Md.: Rowman & Littlefield, 1997); see also "Presidential-Congressional Power Prescriptions in Conservative Political Thought Since 1933," *Presidential Studies Quarterly* 21 (1991): 35–54; " 'Situational

Constitutionalism' and Presidential Power: The Rise and Fall of the Liberal Model of Presidential Government," *Presidential Studies Quarterly* 24 (1994): 577–94.

61. This was most elaborated by Reagan's Justice Department, where Attorney General Ed Meese articulated a robust "unitary executive" theory of governance that called, atypically for twentieth-century conservatives, for stronger presidential leadership.

62. Liberals also participate in "situational constitutionalist" politics, vacillating in their celebrations of presidential and congressional power depending on which institutions they control.

63. John W. Kingdon, *Agendas, Alternatives and Public Policies*, 2nd ed. (Boston: Pearson, 1993); Richard F. Fenno Jr., *Congressmen in Committees* (Boston: Little Brown, 1973).

64. On policy feedback, see Andrea Campbell, "Policy Makes Mass Politics," *Annual Review of Political Science* 15 (2012): 333–51; Paul Pierson, "When Effect Becomes Cause: Policy Feedback and Political Change," *World Politics* 45 (1993): 595–628; Suzanne Mettler, *The Submerged State: How Invisible Government Policies Undermine American Democracy* (Chicago: University of Chicago Press, 2011); Suzanne Mettler and Joe Soss, "The Consequences of Public Policy for Democratic Citizenship: Bridging Policy Studies and Mass Politics," *Perspectives on Politics* 2 (2004): 55–72; Andrea Campbell, *How Policies Make Citizens: Senior Political Activism and the American Welfare State* (Princeton, N.J.: Princeton University Press, 2003).

65. Christopher Howard argues that the hiddenness of some policy programs produces "a state that helps resolve the conflicting feelings that Americans have about government. In the abstract, most Americans want limited government. When asked about specific social programs or needy groups, Americans are much more supportive." Christopher Howard. "The Welfare State," in *The Oxford Handbook of American Political Development*, ed. Richard M. Vallely, Suzanne Mettler, and Robert C. Lieberman (Oxford: Oxford University Press, 2016), 625–42.

66. Hacker and Pierson, *American Amnesia*, 310.

67. Hacker and Pierson, *American Amnesia*.

68. Douglas B. Harris, "Dwight Eisenhower and the New Deal: The Politics of Preemption," *Presidential Studies Quarterly* 27 (1997): 333–42.

69. Kingdon, *Agendas, Alternatives and Public Policies*; Hacker and Pierson, *American Amnesia*, 146, 242.

70. Mann and Ornstein, *It's Even Worse than it Looks*, 98–100; Hacker and Pierson, *American Amnesia*, 310.

71. Anne Schneider and Helen Ingram, "Social Construction of Target Populations: Implications for Politics and Policy," *American Political Science Review* 87, no. 2 (June 1993): 334–47. This concept has been applied to a wide array of policies; see, Jonathan J. Pierce, Saba Siddiki, Michael D. Jones, Kristin Schumacher, Andrew Pattison and Holly Peterson "Social Construction and Policy Design," *Policy Studies Journal* 42, no. 1 (2014): 1–29.

72. Schneider and Ingram, "Social Construction of Target Populations," 342.

73. Virginia A. Chanley, "Trust in Government in the Aftermath of 9/11: Determinants and Consequences," *Political Psychology* 23 (2002): 469–83; Amy Fried, "Terrorism as a Context of Coverage Before the Iraq War," *International Journal of Press/ Politics* 10 (2005): 125–32; Brian J. Gaines, "Where's the Rally? Approval and Trust of the President, Cabinet, Congress, and Government Since September 11," *PS— Political Science and Politics* 35 (2002): 531–36; Mark J. Hetherington and Michael

Nelson, "Anatomy of a Rally Effect: George W. Bush and the War on Terrorism," *PS—Political Science and Politics* 36 (2003): 37–42; Theda Skocpol, "Will 9/11 and the War on Terror Revitalize American Democracy?," *PS—Political Science and Politics* 35 (2002): 537–40; Joshua Woods, "The 9/11 Effect: Toward A Social Science of the Terrorist Threat," *Social Science Journal* 48 (2011): 213–33.

74. On race and the American state in the twentieth century, see Robert C. Lieberman, *Shifting the Color Line: Race and the American Welfare State* (Cambridge, Mass.: Harvard University Press, 2008); Ira Katznelson. *When Affirmative Action Was White: An Untold History of Racial Inequality in Twentieth-Century America* (New York: Norton, 2005); Desmond S. King and Rogers M Smith, "Racial Orders in American Political Development," *American Political Science Review* 99, no. 1 (2005): 75–92.

75. Charles Murray, *Losing Ground: American Social Policy, 1950–1980* (New York: Basic Books, 1984).

76. Nicholas J. G. Winter. "Beyond Welfare: Framing and the Racialization of White Opinion on Social Security," *American Journal of Political Science* 50, no. 2 (2006): 400–20.

77. Of an exceptionally large literature, see, especially, Jill Quadagno, *The Color of Welfare: How Racism Undermined the War on Poverty* (New York: Oxford University Press, 1994); Martin Gilens, *Why Americans Hate Welfare: Race, Media and the Politics of Antipoverty Policy* (Chicago: University of Chicago Press, 1999); Ange-Marie Hancock, *The Politics of Disgust: The Public Identity of the Welfare Queen* (New York: NYU Press, 2004).

78. Hetherington, *Why Trust Matters*, 4.

79. See, e.g., Citrin, "Comment: The Political Relevance of Trust in Government"; the quote is from John Samples, *The Fallacy of Campaign Finance Reform* (Chicago: University of Chicago Press, 2006), 108.

80. Hart, *Distrust and Democracy*, xii.

81. Amy Fried, *Muffled Echoes: Oliver North and the Politics of Public Opinion* (New York: Columbia University Press, 1997).

82. Fried, *Muffled Echoes*, 9.

2. TRUST AND DISTRUST IN AMERICAN POLITICAL DEVELOPMENT

1. Garry Wills, *A Necessary Evil: A History of American Distrust of Government* (New York: Basic Books, 1999), 19.

2. Edmund Burke, "Speech on Conciliation with the Colonies," March 22, 1775, *The Founders' Constitution*, accessed March 16, 2018, http://press-pubs.uchicago.edu /founders/documents/v1ch1s2.html.

3. Bernard Bailyn, *The Ideological Origins of the American Revolution* (Cambridge, Mass.: Harvard University Press, 1967), 119.

4. It was likely a prevalent view in Europe too, just made more effective in America; see Max Edling, *A Revolution in Favor of Government: Origins of the U.S. Constitution and the Making of the American State* (New York: Oxford University Press, 2008), 222.

5. David Brian Robertson, *The Constitution and America's Destiny* (New York: Cambridge University Press, 2005), 83–99, 88.

6. Edling, *A Revolution in Favor of Government*, 29.

7. Note, for example, the scope of government authority (and relative unity of purpose) envisioned in the Virginia Plan; on the centralizing aims of these original intentions, see Gordon Wood, *The Creation of the American Republic* (New York: Norton, 1969); Robertson, *The Constitution and America's Destiny*.

8. Kenneth R. Bowling "A Tub to the Whale": The Founding Fathers and Adoption of the Federal Bill of Rights. *Journal of the Early Republic* 8, no. 3 (1988): 223–51.

9. Edling, *A Revolution in Favor of Government*, 224, 228.

10. Saul Cornell, *The Other Founders: Anti-Federalism and the Dissenting Tradition in America, 1788–1828* (Chapel Hill: University of North Carolina Press, 1999).

11. *The Federalist Papers*: No. 14, The Avalon Project: Documents in Law, History, https://avalon.law.yale.edu/18th_century/fed14.asp. Subsequent references will appear in the text.

12. Edling, *A Revolution in Favor of Government*, 9.

13. James Sterling Young, *The Washington Community, 1800–1828* (New York: Columbia University Press, 1966), 59.

14. Dorothy Ross, "Lincoln and the Ethics of Emancipation: Universalism, Nationalism, Exceptionalism." *Journal of American History* 96, no. 2 (2011): 379–399, 385.

15. Abraham Lincoln, "Inaugural Address," March 4, 1861, online by Gerhard Peters and John T. Woolley, *American Presidency Project*, https://www.presidency.ucsb.edu/node/202167.

16. Abraham Lincoln, "House Divided Speech," June 16, 1858, accessed April 7, 2018, http://www.abrahamlincolnonline.org/lincoln/speeches/house.htm.

17. Cecilia Elizabeth O'Leary, " 'Blood Brotherhood': The Racialization of Patriotism, 1865–1918," in *Bonds of Affection: Americans Define Their Patriotism*, ed. John Bodnar (Princeton, N.J.: Princeton University Press, 1996), 53–81, 55.

18. Vivien Hart, *Distrust and Democracy: Political Distrust in Britain and America* (New York: Cambridge University Press, 1978), 83.

19. Hart, *Distrust and Democracy*, 86.

20. William Graham Sumner, *What Social Classes Owe to Each Other* (New York: Harper & Brothers, 1883), 145. The phrase "forgotten man" was, oddly enough, used by both Franklin D. Roosevelt and Donald Trump. See Franklin D. Roosevelt, "Radio Address from Albany, New York: 'The "Forgotten Man" Speech,' " April 7, 1932, online by Gerhard Peters and John T. Woolley, *American Presidency Project*, https://www.presidency.ucsb.edu/node/288092; Donald J. Trump, "Inaugural Address," January 20, 2017, online by Gerhard Peters and John T. Woolley, *American Presidency Project*, https://www.presidency.ucsb.edu/node/320188.

21. See David W. Blight, *Race and Reunion: The Civil War in American Memory* (Cambridge, Mass.: Harvard University Press, 2002); Stuart McConnell, "Reading the Flag: A Reconsideration of the Patriotic Cults of the 1890s," in *Bonds of Affection: Americans Define Their Patriotism*, ed. John Bodnar (Princeton, N.J.: Princeton University Press, 1996), 102–119; John Pettegrew, " 'The Soldier's Faith': Turn-ofthe-Century Memory of the Civil War and the Emergence of Modern American Nationalism," *Journal of Contemporary History* 31, no. 1 (January 1996): 49–73.

22. Russell Alexander Alger, *The Spanish-American War* (New York: Harper & Brothers, 1901); Joseph Smith, *The Spanish-American War, 1895–1902: Conflict in the Caribbean and the Pacific* (New York: Routledge, 2013), 101–102.

23. O'Leary, "Blood Brotherhood," 77–78.
24. Alger, *The Spanish-American War*, 7.
25. On the populist casting of politics as the people versus the interests, see John Gerring, *Party Ideologies in America, 1828–1996* (New York: Cambridge University Press, 1998), chap. 6.
26. Rogers Smith, *Political Peoplehood: The Roles of Values, Interests, and Identities* (Chicago: University of Chicago Press, 2015), 168.
27. Sidney M. Milkis, *Political Parties and Constitutional Government* (Baltimore: Johns Hopkins University Press, 1999), 5.
28. Chris Capozzola, *Uncle Sam Wants You: World War I and the Making of the Modern American Citizen* (New York: Oxford University Press, 2008), 12, 209.
29. David R. Mayhew, "Wars and American Politics," *Perspectives on Politics* 3, no. 3 (2005): 473–93, 477–78.
30. See Milkis, *Political Parties and Constitutional Government*.
31. Franklin D. Roosevelt, "Inaugural Address," online by Gerhard Peters and John T. Woolley, *American Presidency Project*, https://www.presidency.ucsb.edu/node /208712. Roosevelt's use of "sacred" followed other religious imagery in the speech. Speaking of monopolists, he said, "The money changers have fled from their high seats in the temple of our civilization. We may now restore that temple to the ancient truths. The measure of the restoration lies in the extent to which we apply social values more noble than mere monetary profit."
32. See, esp., Alan Brinkley, *The Age of Reform: New Deal Liberalism in Recession and War* (New York: Knopf, 1995).
33. Samuel H. Beer, "In Search of a New Public Philosophy," in *The New American Political System*, ed. Anthony King (Washington, D.C.: American Enterprise Institute, 1978), 5, 7.
34. Kevin Kruse, *One Nation Under God* (New York: Basic Books, 2015); Kim Phillips-Fein, *Invisible Hands: The Businessmen's Crusade Against the New Deal* (New York: Norton, 2010).
35. Eric Schickler and Devin Caughey, "Public Opinion, Organized Labor, and the Limits of New Deal Liberalism, 1936–1945," *Studies in American Political Development* 25 (October 2011): 162–89.
36. Harry S. Truman, "Special Message to the Congress Presenting a 21-Point Program for the Reconversion Period," September 6, 1945. Harry S. Truman Presidential Library (HSTPL). https://www.trumanlibrary.gov/library/public-papers/128 /special-message-congress-presenting-21-point-program-reconversion-period.
37. Harry S. Truman, "Special Message to the Congress Recommending a Comprehensive Health Program," November 19, 1945. HSTPL, https://www.trumanlibrary.gov/library /public-papers/192/special-message-congress-recommending-comprehensive -health-program.
38. Jonathan Oberlander and Theodore R. Marmor, "The Road Not Taken: What Happened to Medicare for All?," in *Medicare and Medicaid at 50: America's Entitlement Programs in the Age of Affordable Care*, ed. Alan B. Cohen, David C. Colby, Keith Walloo, and Julian E. Zelizer (New York: Oxford University Press, 2015), 57.
39. Ira Katznelson, *Fear Itself: The New Deal and the Origins of Our Time* (New York: Norton, 2013), 24.

40. Anthony Champagne, Douglas B. Harris, James W. Riddlesperger Jr., and Garrison Nelson, *The Austin-Boston Connection: Five Decades of House Democratic Leadership, 1937–1989* (College Station, Tex.: Texas A&M University Press, 2009).

41. Milkis, *Political Parties and Constitutional Government*; James T. Patterson, *Congressional Conservatism and the New Deal* (Lexington, Ky.: University of Kentucky Press, 1967).

42. Champagne et al., *The Austin-Boston Connection*, 252–58.

43. Indeed, the generations who grew up during World War II were highly civically engaged, and scholarly public opinion surveys found high levels of trust in government in the immediate postwar era. This generation maintained trust and engagement for decades. See Suzanne Mettler, *Soldiers to Citizens: The G.I. Bill and the Making of the Greatest Generation* (Oxford: Oxford University Press, 2005); Robert D. Putnam, *Bowling Alone: The Collapse and Revival of American Community* (New York: Simon & Schuster, 2000).

44. Amy Fried, *Pathways to Polling: Crisis, Cooperation and the Making of Public Opinion Professions* (New York: Routledge, 2011). This 1942 survey is discussed on p. 57.

45. Daniel Kryder, *Divided Arsenal: Race and the American State During World War II* (Cambridge: Cambridge University Press, 2001); Fried, *Pathways to Polling*; Jean M. Converse, *Survey Research in the United States: Roots and Emergence 1890–1960* (Berkeley: University of California Press, 1987).

46. "Assails Elmer Davis: Rankin Says His OWI Is Wrecking Democratic Party in South," *New York Times*, March 9, 1943.

47. Office of War Information, "Negroes and the War," 1942, available via the Smithsonian, National Museum of African American History and Culture, https://transcription.si.edu/view/10156/NMAAHC-1EBE4167A4DB2_2001. See Chester Williams to Tom Elliot, memo, June 25, 1943, folder for Office of War Information II, papers of John Winant, Franklin D. Roosevelt Library, Hyde Park, N.Y. Other criticisms involved duplication with other agencies, internal inefficiencies, suspicion regarding centralizing such work and the potential involvement of OWI in the 1944 election, and questions about the American public being "propagandized." See also Harold F. Gosnell, "Obstacles to Domestic Pamphleteering by OWI in World War II," *Journalism Quarterly* 23, no. 4 (1946): 360–69; Sydney Weinberg, "What to Tell America: The Writers' Quarrel in the Office of War Information," *Journal of American History* 55, no. 1 (June 1, 1968): 73–89.

48. See Lauren Rebecca Sklaroff, "Constructing G.I. Joe Louis: Cultural Solutions to the 'Negro Problem' During World War II," *Journal of American History* 89, no. 3 (2002): 958–83; Kenneth B. Clark, "Morale of the Negro on the Home Front: World Wars I and II," *Journal of Negro Education* 3 (1943): 417–28.

49. Ira Katznelson, *When Affirmative Action Was White: An Untold Story of Racial Inequality in Twentieth Century America* (New York: Norton, 2005); Mettler, *Soldiers to Citizens*.

50. See Christopher Baylor, "First to the Party: The Group Origins of the Partisan Transformation on Civil Rights, 1940–1960," *Studies in American Political Development* 27 (October 2013): 111–41; Christopher Baylor, *First to the Party: The Group Origins of Political Transformation* (Philadelphia: University of Pennsylvania Press, 2018); Paul Frymer, *Black and Blue: African-Americans, the Labor Movement, and*

the Decline of the Democratic Party (Princeton, N.J.: Princeton University Press, 2007); Eric Schickler, *Racial Realignment: The Transformation of American Liberalism, 1932–1965* (Princeton, N.J.: Princeton University Press, 2016).

51. Steven White, "Civil Rights, World War II and US Public Opinion," *Studies in American Political Development* 30, no. 1 (April 2016): 38–61.

52. For an extended treatment of this change, see Gerring, *Party Ideologies in America*, 15.

53. This quotation is Gerring's from *Party Ideologies in America*, 15.

54. Kruse, *One Nation Under God*; Mark A. Smith, *The Right Talk: How Conservatives Transformed the Great Society Into the Economic Society* (Princeton, N.J.: Princeton University Press, 2009).

55. Clark Clifford to Harry S. Truman, November 19, 1947, confidential memo to the president [Clifford-Rowe memorandum], political file, 12–13, Clifford Papers, HSTPL. https://www.trumanlibrary.gov/library/research-files/memo-clark-clifford-harry-s-truman?documentid=NA&pagenumber=1

56. "Analysis of the Southern Democratic Revolt," ca. September 1948, memo, president's secretary's files, voting statistics, 3, Truman Papers, HSTPL. https://www.trumanlibrary.org/whistlestop/study_collections/1948campaign/large/docs/documents/index.php?documentid=7-1&pagenumber=3.

57. Schickler, *Racial Realignment*, 270.

58. On this, see Douglas B. Harris, "Dwight Eisenhower and the New Deal: The Politics of Preemption," *Presidential Studies Quarterly* 27 (Spring 1997): 333–42.

59. Eisenhower to Nixon, in Louis Galambos, ed., *The Papers of Dwight Eisenhower* 13: 1366 (Baltimore, MD: Johns Hopkins University Press, 1989); for more on this, see Harris, "Dwight Eisenhower and the New Deal."

60. David Blumenthal and James A. Morone, *The Heart of Power: Health and Politics in the Oval Office* (Berkeley: University of California Press, 2009), 109.

61. The Kerr-Mills Act created the Medical Assistance for the Aged Program in 1960. Part of the Social Security Act, it required a means test but gave states latitude in setting coverage and specific benefits. By 1963, only 28 states and the District of Columbia signed up to participate in the program, and it was widely judged to be a failure. Theodore R. Marmor, *The Politics of Medicare*, 2nd ed. (New York: A. de Gruyter, 2000); Jonathan Engel, *Poor People's Medicine: Medicaid and American Charity Care Since 1965* (Durham, NC: Duke University Press, 2006); David G. Smith and Judith D. Moore, *Medicaid Politics and Policy, 1965–2007* (New Brunswick, N.J.: Transaction Publishers, 2008).

62. Quoted in Marmor, *The Politics of Medicare*, 31.

63. Oberlander and Marmor, "The Road Not Taken: What Happened to Medicare for All?," 12.

64. Ronald Reagan, "Ronald Reagan Speaks Out Against Socialized Medicine," 1981, recording available at https://www.youtube.com/watch?v=kDnxxsjVr2o, transcript by authors.

65. Blumenthal and Morone, *The Heart of Power*; Marmor, *The Politics of Medicare*; Julian E. Zelizer, "The Contentious Origins of Medicare and Medicaid," in Cohen et al., *Medicare and Medicaid at 50*, 3–20.

66. Julian E. Zelizer, "The Contentious Origins of Medicare and Medicaid," 15. On race in passing and implementing Medicare, also see David Barton Smith, "Civil Rights

and Medicare: Historical Convergence and Continuing Legacy," in Cohen et al., *Medicare and Medicaid at 50*, 21–38; Blumenthal and Morone, *The Heart of Power*.

67. Beer, "In Search of a New Public Philosophy," 15.

68. The fact that these arguments dovetailed with those against communism, the other chief threat to American liberty, helped to reinforce the Republican Party's anti-state rhetoric and solidify party support around these key themes.

69. Phyllis Schlafly, *A Choice Not an Echo* (Alton, Ill.: Pere Marquette Press, 1964), 6, 7.

70. Leah Wright Riguer, *The Loneliness of the Black Republican: Pragmatic Politics and the Pursuit of Power* (Princeton, N.J.: Princeton University Press, 2015), 52.

71. Richard M. Nixon, "Address Accepting the Presidential Nomination at the Republican National Convention in Miami Beach, Florida," August 8, 1968, online by Gerhard Peters and John T. Woolley, *American Presidency Project*, https://www.presidency.ucsb.edu/node/251302.

72. Richard M. Scammon and Ben J. Wattenberg, *The Real Majority* (New York: Coward, McCann & Geoghegan, 1970), 57.

73. This quotation is taken from a memo obviously authored by Pat Buchanan (based on its similarities to other documents that specify Buchanan as the author), "The Elections of '70 and '72," box 48, folder 30, Contested Materials Collection, Richard M. Nixon Library, https://www.nixonlibrary.gov/sites/default/files/virtuallibrary/documents/contested/contested_box_48/Contested-48-30.pdf.

74. Advising Nixon, Buchanan quoted Scammon and Wattenberg's observation: "*In no Southern State are there enough Presidential Democrats to put together a statewide majority* . . . Although the divorce [between Democrats and the South] may not be final the question now is which of the two suitors the South will accept: Wallaceite or Republican." Patrick J. Buchanan, memorandum for the president, "The Elections of '70 and '72," box 48, folder 30, Contested Materials Collection, Richard M. Nixon Library, https://www.nixonlibrary.gov/sites/default/files/virtuallibrary/documents/contested/contested_box_48/Contested-48-30.pdf.

75. Patrick J. Buchanan, memorandum for the president, "The Veep and the Campaign of 1970," August 24, 1970, box 48, folder 30, Contested Materials Collection, Richard M. Nixon Library, https://www.nixonlibrary.gov/sites/default/files/virtuallibrary/documents/contested/contested_box_48/Contested-48-30.pdf.

76. On the Mehlman apology, see Mike Allen, "RNC Chief to Say It Was Wrong to 'Exploit' Racial Conflict for Votes," *Washington Post*, July 14, 2005, http://www.washingtonpost.com/wp-dyn/content/article/2005/07/13/AR2005071302342.html; Nixon 1968 Acceptance Speech, Miama Beach, Florida, August 8, 1968; online by Gerhard Peters and John T. Woolley, *The American Presidency Project*, https://www.presidency.ucsb.edu/node/256650. There were three other mentions of African Americans in the speech, but this is the only one with reference to policy.

77. Joseph E. Lowndes, *From the New Deal to the New Right: Race and the Southern Origins of Modern Conservatism* (New Haven, Conn.: Yale University Press, 2008), 7. See also Robert P. Jones, *White Too Long: The Legacy of White Supremacy on American Christianity* (New York: Simon & Schuster, 2020).

78. Angie Maxwell and Todd Shields, *The Long Southern Strategy: How Chasing White Voters in the South Changed American Politics* (New York: Oxford University Press, 2019).

79. Nancy MacLean, *Democracy in Chains: The Deep History of the Radical Right's Stealth Plan for America* (New York: Viking, 2017); Jane Mayer, *Dark Money:*

The Hidden History of the Billionaires Behind the Rise of the Radical Right (New York: Anchor Books, 2017); Theda Skocpol and Alexander Hertel-Fernandez, "The Koch Network and Republican Party Extremism," *Perspectives on Politics* 14, no. 3 (September 2016): 681–99; Steven Teles, *The Rise of the Conservative Legal Movement: The Battle for Control of the Law* (Princeton, N.J.: Princeton University Press, 2008).

80. 1968 Republican Platform. The GOP was also beginning to argue for stronger presidential leadership in areas of concern to conservatives. Two claims to enhance presidential power are notable: the first promised "presidential leadership" to "buttress state and local government," and the second proposed to create a "Presidential Office of Executive Management" aimed at eliminating bureaucratic overlap and inefficiencies. "Republican Party Platforms: Republican Party Platform of 1968," August 5, 1968, online by Gerhard Peters and John T. Woolley, *American Presidency Project*, https://www.presidency.ucsb.edu/documents/republican-party -platform-1968.

81. "Republican Party Platforms: Republican Party Platform of 1972," August 21, 1972, online by Gerhard Peters and John T. Woolley, *American Presidency Project*, https://www.presidency.ucsb.edu/documents/republican-party-platform-1972.

82. Barton Gellman. *Angler: The Cheney Vice Presidency* (New York: Penguin, 2008), 101.

83. Recommended changes include "elimination of proxy voting," "full public disclosure of financial interests by Members and divestiture of those interests which present conflicts of interest," and "changes in Democratic Caucus rules on binding of members. "Republican Party Platforms: Republican Party Platform of 1976," August 18, 1976, online by Gerhard Peters and John T. Woolley, *American Presidency Project*, https://www.presidency.ucsb.edu/documents/republican-party -platform-1976.

84. William F. Buckley Jr., "Our Mission Statement," *National Review*, November 19, 1955, https://www.nationalreview.com/1955/11/our-mission-statement-william-f -buckley-jr.

85. Dubbing this "American amnesia," political scientists Jacob S. Hacker and Paul Pierson show that at least the intraparty effort begun at the *National Review* had, by the late twentieth century, succeeded, as anti-government "Randians" (devotees of Ayn Rand) had taken over the GOP with the aim of undermining government altogether: "Trust but verify," they say, became "distrust and defeat." Jacob S. Hacker and Paul Pierson, *America Amnesia: How the War on Government Led Us to Forget What Made America Prosper* (New York: Simon & Schuster, 2017), 198.

86. Geoffrey Kabaservice, *Rule and Ruin: The Downfall of Moderation and the Destruction of the Republican Party, From Eisenhower to the Tea Party* (New York: Oxford University Press, 2012), 25.

87. Theda Skocpol and Vanessa Williamson, *The Tea Party and the Remaking of Republican Conservatism* (New York: Oxford University Press, 2016), 35.

88. Lloyd A. Free and Hadley Cantril, *The Political Beliefs of Americans* (New Brunswick, N.J.: Rutgers University Press, 1967).

89. Albert H. Cantril and Susan Davis Cantril, *Reading Mixed Signals: Ambivalence in American Public Opinion About Government* (Washington, D.C.: Woodrow Wilson Center Press, 1999), 25.

90. See J. Richard Piper, "'Situational Constitutionalism' and Presidential Power: The Rise and Fall of the Liberal Model of Presidential Government," *Presidential*

Studies Quarterly 24, no. 3 (Summer 1994): 577–94; J. Richard Piper, *Ideologies and Institutions: American Conservative and Liberal Governance Prescriptions Since 1933* (Lanham, Md.: Rowman & Littlefield, 1997).

3. HERE TO HELP? MOVEMENT CONSERVATISM AND THE STATE IN THE REAGAN ERA

1. Ronald Reagan, "The President's News Conference," August 12, 1986, online by Gerhard Peters and John T. Woolley, *American Presidency Project*, https://www.presidency.ucsb.edu/documents/the-presidents-news-conference-957.

2. Chicago's white population dropped from 49.6 percent in 1980 to 45.4 percent in 1990. The black population declined just slightly, decreasing from 39.8 percent to 39.1 percent, while the Hispanic population surged from 14 percent to 19.6 percent. See table 14 in Campbell Gibson and Kay Jung, "Historical Census Statistics on Population Totals by Race, 1790 to 1990, and by Hispanic Origin, 1970 to 1990, for Large Cities and Other Urban Places in the United States" (Working Paper No. 76, U.S. Census Bureau, Population Division, Washington, D.C., February 2005), https://www.census.gov/content/dam/Census/library/working-papers/2005/demo/POP-twps0076.pdf.

3. Reagan, "The President's News Conference," August 12, 1986.

4. Theodore J. Lowi, *The End of the Republican Era* (Norman: University of Oklahoma Press, 1995), 159.

5. With a 36-seat gain, House Republicans won 192 seats, tying the amount that they had after Nixon's 1968 and 1972 victories, effectively wiping out the effects of the 48-seat loss after Watergate in 1974.

6. See William Leuchtenberg, *In the Shadow of FDR* (Ithaca, N.Y.: Cornell University Press, 1983).

7. Douglas B. Harris, "Dwight Eisenhower and the New Deal: The Politics of Preemption," *Presidential Studies Quarterly* 27 (Spring 1997): 333–42.

8. Pew Research Center, "Public Trust in Government: 1958–2014," accessed August 7, 2016, http://www.people-press.org/2014/11/13/public-trust-in-government.

9. Thomas W. Evans, *The Education of Ronald Reagan: The General Election Years and the Untold Story of His Conversion to Conservatism* (New York: Columbia University Press, 2006), 4.

10. Robert Mann, *Becoming Ronald Reagan: The Rise of a Conservative Icon* (Lincoln: University of Nebraska Press, 2019), 109–110, 113.

11. Evans, *The Education of Ronald Reagan*, 4.

12. Ronald W. Reagan, *An American Life* (New York: Simon & Shuster, 1990), 134; see also Mann, *Becoming Ronald Reagan*, 111–12.

13. Leuchtenberg, *In the Shadow of FDR*.

14. Students for a Democratic Society, "Port Huron Statement," June 15, 1962, *Sixties Project*, http://www2.iath.virginia.edu/sixties/HTML_docs/Resources/Primary/Manifestos/SDS_Port_Huron.html.

15. Barry Goldwater, "Address Accepting the Presidential Nomination at the Republican National Convention in San Francisco," July 16, 1964, online by Gerhard Peters and John T. Woolley, *American Presidency Project*, https://www.presidency.ucsb.edu/node/216657.

16. Opposition to fluoridation, a conservative reaction to purported paternalism and government overreach, shared by the John Birch Society, took on dire proportions and conspiratorial tones as conservative opponents leveled charges ranging from the claim that fluoridation led to cancer to the idea that it was a communist plot; see Donald R. McNeil, "America's Longest War: The Fight Over Fluoridation, 1950–," *Wilson Quarterly* 9, no. 3 (Summer 1985): 140–53, 149.

17. Pew Research Center, "Public Trust in Government: 1958–2014," accessed August 7, 2016, http://www.people-press.org/2014/11/13/public-trust-in-government.

18. Quoted in Rick Perlstein, *Nixonland: The Rise of a President and the Fracturing of America* (New York: Scribner, 2008), 71.

19. Ronald Reagan, "Inaugural Address," January 5, 1967, Ronald Reagan Presidential Library, Simi Valley, Calif. (hereafter RRPL), https://www.reaganlibrary.gov/research/speeches/01051967a.

20. Jackson K. Putnam, "Governor Reagan: A Reappraisal," *California History* 83, no. 4 (2006): 24–45, 24.

21. Putnam, "Governor Reagan," 32–34, 45.

22. Andrew E. Busch, *Reagan's Victory: The Presidential Election of 1980 and the Rise of the Right* (Lawrence: University Press of Kansas, 2005), 50.

23. As governor of California, Reagan could be more pragmatic than his rhetoric. Despite his later links to the religious right, in 1967, Governor Reagan signed a bill liberalizing abortion laws. See, esp., Lou Cannon, *Governor Reagan: His Rise To Power* (New York: PublicAffairs, 2003).

24. Craig Shirley, *Reagan's Revolution: The Untold Story of the Campaign That Started It All* (Nashville, TN: Thomas Nelson, 2010), 80–83; Richard P. Nathan and Fred C. Doolittle, *Reagan and the States* (Princeton, N.J.: Princeton University Press, 2014), 47–48. Perlstein notes this made Reagan vulnerable to charges that his policies would lead states to raise taxes. Rick Perlstein, *The Invisible Bridge: The Fall of Nixon and the Rise of Reagan* (New York: Simon & Schuster, 2014), 595–96.

25. Samuel Beer, "In Search of a New Public Philosophy," in *The New American Political System*, ed. Anthony King (Washington, D.C.: AEI Press, 1977), 38; Martin Schram, *Running for President, 1976: The Carter Campaign* (New York: Stein and Day, 1977), 227.

26. David E. Rosenbaum, "Social Security a Major Issue in Florida as Primary Day Nears," *New York Times*, March 5, 1976.

27. Tip O'Neill with William Novak, *Man of the House: The Life and Political Memoir of Speaker Tip O'Neill* (New York: Random House, 1987), 337.

28. Ronnie Dugger, *On Reagan: The Man & His Presidency* (New York: McGraw Hill, 1983), 200–201.

29. Perlstein, *The Invisible Bridge*, 603. See also p. 338 for a selection from a 1975 radio address in which Reagan refers to "a strapping young fella with a big basket of groceries who pays for them in food stamps."

30. "'Welfare Queen' Becomes Issue in Reagan Campaign," *New York Times*, February 15, 1976. Regarding Reagan-era social welfare policy, see Paul Pierson, *Dismantling the Welfare State? Reagan, Thatcher and the Politics of Retrenchment* (Cambridge: Cambridge University Press, 1995); John O'Connor, "US Social Welfare Policy: The Reagan Record and Legacy," *Journal of Social Policy* 27, no. 1 (January 1998): 37–61; W. Elliot Brownlee and Hugh Davis Graham, eds., *The Reagan Presidency: Pragmatic Conservatism and Its Legacies* (Lawrence: University Press of Kansas, 2003).

31. Dugger, *On Reagan*, 200–201.

32. Kandy Stroud, *How Jimmy Won: The Victory Campaign from Plains to the White House* (New York: William Morrow, 1977), 245.

33. Jules Witcover, *The Marathon: The Pursuit of the Presidency, 1972–1976* (New York: Viking, 1977), 476.

34. Gerald M. Pomper, Ross K. Baker, Charles E. Jacob, Wilson Carey McWilliams, and Henry A. Plotkin, *The Election of 1976: Reports and Interpretations* (New York: David McKay, 1977), 25.

35. Busch, *Reagan's Victory*, 47–48.

36. The electoral benefits of conservative distrust were likely reinforced for Reagan and his strategists when an atypical foray into compromise cost him support. Reagan's announcement that Pennsylvanian moderate Richard Schweiker would be his running mate should he get the nomination "enrag[ed] a number of conservative delegates"; Pomper et al., *The Election of 1976*, 25. Indeed, conservative Clifton White wrote that the Schweiker choice "was a pragmatist's masterpiece. The only problem was that it ignored the ideological realities not only with the Republican Party, but increasingly in the country at large." White believed that this "horrified" conservatives and "cut the heart out of some of Ronald Reagan's most loyal supporters"; he believed, too, that it cost Reagan delegate support from within Schweiker's own state. F. Clifton White and William J. Gill, *Why Reagan Won: A Narrative History of the Conservative Movement, 1964–1981* (Regnery, 1981), 179.

37. Rick Perlstein. *Reaganland: America's Right Turn, 1976–1980* (New York: Simon and Schuster, 2020), 33.

38. "Republican Party Platforms: Republican Party Platform of 1980," July 15, 1980, online by Gerhard Peters and John T. Woolley, *American Presidency Project*, http://www.presidency.ucsb.edu/ws/?pid=25844. The GOP sought to limit congressional spending authority by advocating a constitutional amendment to require a balanced budget except in "national emergency" instances where a two-thirds vote could approve a deficit budget. Ironically, the platform then advocated more congressional action, including "use of the Congressional veto, sunset laws, and strict budgetary control of the bureaucracies." They also argued for greater congressional oversight of the bureaucracy in 1980 but advocated none of this in 1984.

39. Ronald Reagan, "Address Accepting the Presidential Nomination at the Republican National Convention in Detroit," July 17, 1980, online by Gerhard Peters and John T. Woolley, *American Presidency Project*, http://www.presidency.ucsb.edu/ws/?pid=25970.

40. Barton Gellman, *Angler: The Cheney Busch, Vice Presidency* (New York, Penguin, 2008), 101.

41. *Reagan's Victory*, 23.

42. Busch *Reagan's Victory*, 21.

43. Lowi, *The End of the Republican Era*, 195.

44. V. O. Key Jr., "A Theory of Critical Elections," *Journal of Politics* 17, no. 1 (February 1955): 3–18; Walter Dean Burnham, "Party Systems and the Political Process," in *Current Crisis in American Politics* (New York: Norton, 1982); Walter Dean Burnham, *Critical Elections and the Mainsprings of American Politics* (New York: Norton, 1970).

45. Eric Schickler, *Racial Realignment: The Transformation of American Liberalism, 1932–1965* (Princeton, N.J.: Princeton University Press, 2016).

46. Walter Dean Burnham, "The 1980 Earthquake: Realignment, Reaction, or What?," in The *Hidden Election: Politics and Economics in the 1980 Presidential Campaign*, ed. Thomas Ferguson and Joel Rogers (New York: Pantheon, 1981), 98–140, 109.

47. Everett Carl Ladd, "The Reagan Phenomenon and Public Attitudes Toward Government," in *The Reagan Presidency and the Governing of America*, ed. Lester M. Salamon and Michael S. Lunds (Washington, D.C.: Urban Institute, 1984), 221–49, 222, 248.

48. Lowi, *The End of the Republican Era*, 141,160, 114.

49. Eisenhower and Nixon should be understood as "preemptive" presidents in the context of FDR's New Deal; see Stephen Skowronek, *The Politics That Presidents Make* (Cambridge, Mass.: Harvard University Press, 1993); Douglas B. Harris, "Dwight Eisenhower and the New Deal: The Politics of Preemption," *Presidential Studies Quarterly* 27, no. 2 (Spring 1997): 333–42.

50. Lowi, *The End of the Republican Era*, 180.

51. Ladd, "The Reagan Phenomenon and Public Attitudes Toward Government," 222.

52. Ladd, "The Reagan Phenomenon and Public Attitudes Toward Government," 226.

53. Benjamin Ginsberg and Martin Shefter, "The Presidency and the Organization of Interests," *The Presidency and the Political System*, 2nd ed., ed. Michael Nelson, (Washington, D.C.: CQ Press, 1988), 311–330.

54. Augustus B. Cochran III, *Democracy Heading South: National Politics in the Shadow of Dixie* (Lawrence: University Press of Kansas, 2001), 9–10.

55. Thomas Byrne Edsall with Mary D. Edsall, *Chain Reaction: The Impact of Race, Rights, and Taxes on American Politics* (New York: Norton, 1992), 149.

56. Thomas E. Cavanagh and James L. Sundquist, "The New Two-Party System," in *The New Direction in American Politics*, ed. John E. Chubb and Paul E. Peterson (Washington, D.C.: Brookings, 1985), 33–67, 49, 53.

57. Angie Maxwell and Todd Shields, *The Long Southern Strategy: How Chasing White Voters in the South Changed American Politics* (New York: Oxford University Press, 2019); Daniel K. Williams, "Jerry Falwell's Sunbelt Politics: The Regional Origins of the Moral Majority," *Journal of Policy History* 22 (2010), 125–47.

58. Cavanagh and Sundquist, "The New Two-Party System," 64–65.

59. Ronald Reagan, "Inaugural Address," January 20, 1981, RRPL, https://www.reaganlibrary.archives.gov/archives/speeches/1981/12081a.htm.

60. Joseph White and Aaron Wildavsky, *The Deficit and the Public Interest: The Search for Responsible Budgeting in the 1980s* (Berkeley: University of California Press, 1990), 137.

61. Reagan, "Inaugural Address," January 20, 1981.

62. White and Wildavsky, *The Deficit and the Public Interest*, 106.

63. White and Wildavsky, *The Deficit and the Public Interest*, 106–107.

64. Ronald Reagan, "Address Before a Joint Session of the Congress on the Program for Economic Recovery," February 18, 1981. American Presidency Project. https://www.presidency.ucsb.edu/documents/address-before-joint-session-the-congress-the-program-for-economic-recovery-0.

65. Adam Clymer, "Governors Oppose Reagan on Medicaid," *New York Times*, February 24, 1981, A1.

66. Richard S. Williamson, "The 1982 New Federalism Negotiations," *Publius* 12, no. 2 (1983): 11–32; Shanna Rose, *Financing Medicaid: Federalism and the Growth of America's Health Care Safety Net*, 1st ed. (Ann Arbor: University of Michigan Press, 2013); Gareth Davies, "The Welfare State," in *The Reagan Presidency: Pragmatic Conservatism and Its Legacies*, ed. W. Elliot Brownless and Hugh Davis Graham (Lawrence: University of Kansas Press, 2003), 209–32.

67. Spencer Rich, "Reagan Budget Means Drastic Cuts in Medicare and Medicaid Programs," *Washington Post*, August 21, 1981.

68. David L. Ginsberg. "Health Care Policy in the Reagan Administration: Rhetoric and Reality," *Public Administration Quarterly* 11, no. 1 (1987): 59–70.

69. Vic Fingerhut to Congress leaders, "Subject: What Democrats Should Do Tonight, Tomorrow, the Day After, and Next Week in Response to the President's Speech and the GOP PR Follow-Up," September 24, 1981, press relations box 18, folder "Democratic Response to the State of the Union Address, December 1983–January 1984," Tip O'Neill Congressional Papers, John J. Burns Library, Boston College, Chestnut Hill, Mass., [TPO].

70. Hugh Heclo and Rudolph G. Penner, "Fiscal and Political Strategy in the Reagan Administration," in *The Reagan Presidency: An Early Assessment*, ed. Fred I. Greenstein (Baltimore: Johns Hopkins University Press, 1983), 21–47, 36.

71. Heclo and Penner, "Fiscal and Political Strategy in the Reagan Administration," 36

72. Geoffrey Kabaservice, *Rule and Ruin: The Downfall of Moderation and the Destruction of the Republican Party, From Eisenhower to the Tea Party* (New York: Oxford University Press, 2012), 363–68, 119; Frank J. Thompson, "Medicaid Rising: The Perils and Potential of Federalism," in *Medicare and Medicaid at 50: America's Entitlement Programs in the Age of Affordable Care*, ed. Alan B. Cohen, David C. Colby, Keith A. Wailoo, and Julian E. Zelizer (New York: Oxford University Press, 2015), 191–212. Reagan was met with serious and effective opposition in Congress. For example, Representative Henry Waxman (D-CA), the chair of the Commerce Committee Subcommittee on Health, opposed the Medicaid cap and was key in establishing Medicaid's Disproportionate Share Hospital Program, which created a higher share of federal funds in the federal–state match and expanded Medicaid eligibility.

73. Quoted in Robert Ajemian, "Tip O'Neill on the Ropes," *Time*, May 18, 1981, 17.

74. Speaker's daily press conference, June 17, 1981, folder 11-1, "Press Conference Transcripts January–June 1981," press relations box 11, TPO.

75. White and Wildavsky, *The Deficit and the Public Interest*, 135–36.

76. Reagan's letter to Congressional leaders about the Social Security System, July 18, 1981. https://www.ssa.gov/history/reaganstmts.html.

77. Richard P. Nathan, "The Reagan Presidency in Domestic Affairs," in *The Reagan Presidency: An Early Assessment*, ed. Fred I. Greenstein (Baltimore: Johns Hopkins University Press, 1983), 48–81, 50.

78. Nathan, "The Reagan Presidency in Domestic Affairs," 62.

79. White and Wildavsky, *The Deficit and the Public Interest*, 173–74.

80. James Fallows, "The Spend-Up," *Atlantic*, July 1986.

81. Joseph Cooper and William F. West, "Presidential Power and Republican Government: The Theory and Practice of OMB Review of Agency Rules," *Journal of Politics* 50, no. 4 (1988): 864–95, 873, 876.

82. Theodore J. Lowi, *The Personal President: Power Invested, Promise Unfulfilled* (Ithaca, N.Y.: Cornell University Press, 1985), 159.

83. Gillis Long and Geraldine Ferraro talking points, October 1982; Jim Wright speaking at the Speaker's daily press conference, July 1982, folder "Budget Constitutional Amendment on Balanced Budget, April-July 1982," press assistant files, box 16, TPO.

84. Long and Ferraro talking points, October 1982.

85. Scott Spitzer, "Reagan's Silent Majority: Conservative Welfare Politics After Nixon," paper presented at the annual meeting of the Western Political Science Association, Hollywood, Calif., 2013, 35–36.

86. Themes and Issues of the 1982 Campaign, July 21, 1982, folder "Polling Information— 1982" (6 of 6), box 65, Michael Deaver collection, RRPL, https://www.reaganlibrary .gov/sites/default/files/digitallibrary/smof/dcos/deaver/box-065/40-137-7065200 -065-006-2016.pdf.

87. J. Brooks Flippen, *Jimmy Carter, the Politics of Family, and the Rise of the Religious Right* (Athens: University of Georgia Press, 2011), 329–31.

88. See Justin Fox, "The Mostly Forgotten Tax Increases of 1982–1993," *Bloomberg*, December 15, 2017.

89. Francis X. Clines, " 'Historic Realignment' Seen by Reagan on Election Day," *New York Times*, October 31, 1984.

90. Clines, " 'Historic Realignment' Seen By Reagan On Election Day."

91. "National Exit Polls Table," *New York Times*, November 5, 2008, https://www.nytimes .com/elections/2008/results/president/national-exit-polls.html.

92. Louis Harris remarks to the House Democratic Caucus, October 3, 1984, TPO.

93. Louis Harris remarks to the House Democratic Caucus, October 3, 1984.

94. "Republican Party Platforms: Republican Party Platform of 1984," August 20, 1984, online by Gerhard Peters and John T. Woolley, *American Presidency Project*, http:// www.presidency.ucsb.edu/ws/?pid=25845.

95. Ronald Reagan, "Remarks Accepting the Presidential Nomination at the Republican National Convention in Dallas, Texas," August 23, 1984, online by Gerhard Peters and John T. Woolley, *American Presidency Project*, http://www.presidency.ucsb.edu /ws/?pid=40290.

96. Ronald Reagan, "Address Before a Joint Session of the Congress on the State of the Union," February 6, 1985, online by Gerhard Peters and John T. Woolley, *American Presidency Project*, http://www.presidency.ucsb.edu/ws/?pid=38069.

97. Ronald Reagan, "Inaugural Address," January 21, 1985, online by Gerhard Peters and John T. Woolley, *American Presidency Project*, http://www.presidency.ucsb.edu /ws/?pid=38688.

98. Reagan, "Inaugural Address," January 21, 1985.

99. Richard S. Englund, "The Catastrophic Health Care Blunder," *American Spectator*, November 1988, 25–30, 28.

100. "A National Brushfire Survey of Public Attitudes," prepared for the Republican National Committee, December 14–15, 1985, "Decision-Making Information Polls" series, box 9, David Chew Papers, RRPL.

101. Otis Bowen, interview, Miller Center, University of Virginia, Ronald Reagan Presidential Oral History Project, November 8 and 9, 2001. Bowen is often credited as the primary driving force for the legislation; see Carolyn Thompson. "The

Cabinet Member as Policy Entrepreneur," *Administration & Society* 25, no. 4 (1994): 395–409.

102. Ronald Reagan, "Address Before a Joint Session of Congress on the State of the Union," February 4, 1986, online by Gerhard Peters and John T. Woolley, *American Presidency Project*, http://www.presidency.ucsb.edu/ws/?pid=36646.

103. See Richard J. Ellis, *The Development of the American Presidency*, 2nd ed. (New York: Routledge, 2012), 451.

104. Charlie Savage, *Takeover: The Return of the Imperial Presidency and the Subversion of American Democracy* (Boston: Little, Brown, 2007), 47.

105. It is worth pointing out that this view that a president should step in to provide coordination and centralization to an otherwise fractionalized political system is Wilsonian too; for the quotation, see "Separation of Powers: Legislative–Executive Relations" and Stephen J. Markman, memorandum to Edwin Meese III, "Subject: Separation of Powers," April 30, 1986, RG 60 folder OLP, April–May 1986, part 1, box 86, Department of Justice Files, National Archives & Records Administration, Washington, DC [NARA], 25–26. See also the descriptions under "Miscellaneous" on 9–11, 16.

106. There is not a little irony in the fact that these purportedly "strict construction-ists" sounded quite a bit like Woodrow Wilson in terms of admitting frustrations with separation of powers, complaining that Congress was too divided to provide national leadership (with a strong Speaker or president), and asserting a stron-ger democratic role for the president; again, the quotation is from "Separation of Powers: Legislative-Executive Relations" and Markman memorandum to Edwin Meese III, "Subject: Separation of Powers," April 30, 1986. See also the descriptions under "Miscellaneous" on 16.

107. Jeffrey K. Tulis, *The Rhetorical Presidency* (Princeton, N.J.: Princeton University Press, 1987).

108. "Separation of Powers: Legislative-Executive Relations" and Markman memoran-dum to Edwin Meese III, "Subject: Separation of Powers," April 30, 1986. See also the descriptions under "Miscellaneous" on 28.

109. "Separation of Powers: Legislative–Executive Relations" and Stephen J. Markman, memorandum to Edwin Meese III, "Subject: Separation of Powers," April 30, 1986, RG 60 folder OLP, April–May 1986, part 1, box 86, Department of Justice Files, NARA, 8, 17.

110. In one notable example, there seemed to be some concern (that proved correct when Democrats recaptured the Senate only months later) that Democratic gains in the Senate would produce more conflict over judicial appointments. The report read: "In the next two years President Reagan can expect to see renewed attempts by Senate Democrats to inject philosophical criteria into the examination of judi-cial nominees. In preparation for future Supreme Court confirmation battles, the President's opponents in the Senate will seek to block individual conservative candidates for the lower courts and make philosophical disagreement a legitimate ground of opposition"; "Separation of Powers: Legislative Executive Relations," 31.

111. "Separation of Powers: Legislative–Executive Relations" and Stephen J. Markman, memorandum to Edwin Meese III, "Subject: Separation of Powers," April 30, 1986, RG 60 folder OLP, April–May 1986, part 1, box 86, Department of Justice Files, NARA, 33.

112. Samuel A. Alito Jr. to the Litigation Strategy Working Group, February 5, 1986, "Using Presidential Signing Statement to Make Fuller Use of the President's Constitutionally Assigned Role in the Process of Enacting Law," accession 060-89-269, box 6, folder "SG/Litigation Strategy Working Group," Department of Justice Files of Stephen Galebach, 1985–1987, NARA, https://www.archives.gov/files/news/samuel-alito/accession-060-89-269/Acco60-89-269-box6-SG-LSWG-AlitotoLSWG-Feb1986.pdf.

113. Walter Dellinger, "The Legal Significance of Presidential Signing Statements," memorandum opinion for the Counsel to the President, November 3, 1993, https://www.justice.gov/file/20446/download.

114. Matthew Crenson and Benjamin Ginsberg, *Presidential Power: Unchecked & Unbalanced* (New York: Norton, 2007), 198.

115. "Separation of Powers: Legislative–Executive Relations" and Stephen J. Markman, memorandum to Edwin Meese III, "Subject: Separation of Powers," April 30, 1986, RG 60 folder OLP, April–May 1986, part 1, box 86, Department of Justice Files, NARA, 16.

116. Crenson and Ginsberg, *Presidential Power*, 245.

117. David Stockman, *The Triumph of Politics: How the Reagan Revolution Failed* (New York: Harper & Row, 1986), 159, 200, as quoted in Skowronek, *The Politics Presidents Make*, 418.

118. Health and Human Services secretary Otis Bowen told his staff that, in the first cabinet meeting after the elections, President Reagan said that making health care available at affordable prices and addressing catastrophic care costs in particular remained administration goals. "Report of the Highlights of the Senior Staff Meeting, November 12, 1986," Health and Human Services Staff Meetings, 1986 November–December 1986, box 14, folder 20, series 7, "Catastrophic Health Reform, 1985–1991," Otis T. Bowen Papers (hereafter OTBP), Ball State University Archives and Special Collections, Alexander M. Bracken Library, Muncie, Indiana.

119. See Theodore Draper, *A Very Thin Line: The Iran Contra Affairs* (New York: Simon & Schuster, 1991); Amy Fried, *Muffled Echoes: Oliver North and the Politics of Public Opinion* (New York: Columbia University Press, 1997); Malcolm Byrne, *Iran-Contra: Reagan's Scandal and the Unchecked Abuse of Presidential Power* (Lawrence, Kansas: University Press of Kansas, 2014).

120. Otis Bowen, interview.

121. Joseph Antos, interviewed by David Smith and Judy Moore, CMS Oral History Project. Centers on Medicare and Medicaid Services, August 13, 2003.

122. Reagan's Gallup job approval, which had been as high as 68 percent in May of 1986, had dropped below 50 percent by year's end, where it would stay with few exceptions throughout 1987. Gallup Presidential Approval Center, Ronald Reagan, https://news.gallup.com/interactives/185273/presidential-job-approval-center.aspx.

123. Brock may have had a greater "understanding of the problems," Bowen later said, "because he and I were the only two in the entire cabinet who had ever run for election." Otis Bowen, interview by Philip V. Scarpino, Tobias Leadership Center, Indiana University, January 23, 2007, https://tobiascenter.iu.edu/research/oral-history/audio-transcripts/bowen-otis.html

124. "Minutes. Domestic Policy Council. December 12, 1986," Domestic Policy Council, December 1986, box 14, folder 11, OTBP.

125. Otis Bowen, interview. In the oral history, Bowen read from his notes from the final cabinet meeting before Reagan signed off on the Bowen approach in February 1987. Moreover, Bowen made nearly the same statements in other meetings. See "Minutes, Domestic Policy Council, December 12, 1986"; "Minutes, Domestic Policy Council," December 23, 1986, box 139, folder DPC Meeting no. 73 (with President), Ralph C. Bledsoe Papers, RRPL.

126. Miller advised Reagan against supporting the bill, telling the president, "When you send it up to Capitol Hill and it comes back, it'll be far worse. And you'll have to sign it because it has your name on it." James Miller, interview, Miller Center, University of Virginia, Ronald Reagan Presidential Oral History Project, November 4, 2001. Earlier, Bowen and Miller had clashed about various budgetary matters, including funding for AIDS programs, with Miller prioritizing limiting spending to pursue deficit reduction.

127. Charles D. Hobbs and Peter Germanis, "Memorandum for Domestic Policy Council, Subject: Catastrophic Health Insurance," December 22, 1986, box 14, folder 11, OTBP. Bowen's response memo (n.d., in the same folder) elided these ideological concerns but rather focused on administrative and cost issues as well as the unlikelihood Congress would support a program based on vouchers. Miller's statement was from a December 3, 1986, meeting of the Domestic Policy Council, where Sprinkle also "felt we should restrain public spending." "Minutes, Domestic Policy Council," December 3, 1986, Domestic Policy Council, 1986 Dec.; box 14, folder 11, OTBP.

128. According to a memorandum from Eugene Hickock of the Justice Department, proposals should support a "minimalist role for government" and reflect the "belief that the role of government, as a rule, should be limited to providing an environment conducive to the efficient operation of the private market and the exercise of judgment and responsibility by families, and communities." Eugene Hickock (DOJ/OLC), memo to Joe Antos, "Memorandum, Recommendations for the Health Policy Group to the Domestic Policy Council," December 9, 1986, box 14, folder "Catastrophic Illness Insurance (Originals) (3)," Ralph C. Bledsoe Papers, RRPL. See also Robert Pear, "Reagan Advisors Oppose Key Point of Health Plan," New York Times, December 16, 1986, A1.

129. Phil N. Truluck, letter to Don Regan, December 11, 1986, box 14, folder "Catastrophic Illness Insurance (Originals) (2)," Ralph C. Bledsoe Papers, RRPL.

130. Spencer Rich, "Catastrophic Illness Insurance Backed," Washington Post, November 21, 1986.

131. Interestingly, about six months later, the Heritage Foundation privately expressed their own political fears relating to health care, floating a mandate for basic and catastrophic coverage as a way of heading off broader Democratic proposals leading toward universal coverage. According to a report prepared by the Heritage Foundation and White House staff for President Reagan, "While this would be opposed by some libertarians and many of the self employed, it is difficult to see any other way of defusing what appears to be irresistible pressure for steps to deal with the problem of underinsurance. Failure to put the onus on individuals will only feed the momentum towards mandatory "free" health care paid largely by employers—and taxpayers." T. Kenneth Cribb Jr., "Strategic Plan for Domestic Affairs," with cover letter to Howard H. Baker dated June 4, 1987, folder "Ed Feulner

(1)," box 2, Howard H. Baker Jr. files, RRPL, https://www.reaganlibrary.gov/public
/digitallibrary/smof/cos/bakerhoward/box-002/40-27-6912132-002-009-2017.pdf.

132. U.S. House and U.S. Senate, eds., *Iran-Contra Investigation: Joint Hearings before
the House Select Committee to Investigate Covert Arms Transactions with Iran and
the Senate Select Committee on Secret Military Assistance to Iran and the Nicaraguan Opposition: One Hundredth Congress, First Session* (Washington: U.S. G.P.O,
1988); William S. Cohen and George J. Mitchell, *Men of Zeal: A Candid Inside Story
of the Iran-Contra Hearings* (New York: Viking, 1988).

133. See Gordon S. Jones and John A. Marini, eds., *The Imperial Congress: Crisis in
the Separation of Powers* (New York: Pharos Books. 1988); quoted passage from
Gordon S. Jones' introduction to part 2, p. 104. In "Overthrowing Oligarchy,"
Jones provided a rationale for the "situational constitutionalism" as a conservative
attempt to counter any dominant institution, awhile acknowledging that conservatives had been pro-Congress in the mid-twentieth century and might be again
under different circumstances: see, esp., 296–7.

134. Jones and Marini, *The Imperial Congress*, 1.

135. Michael E. Hammond and Peter M. Weyrich, "Legislative Lords: Gag Rules and
Permanent Staff," in Jones and Marini, *The Imperial Congress*, 237.

136. See the following chapters from *The Imperial Congress*: Gordon S. Jones, "Overthrowing Oligarchy," 301; Herman A. Mellor, "Congressional Micromanagement:
National Defense," 107–29; and John Hiram Caldwell, "Congressional Micromanagement: Domestic Policy," 130–50.

137. Thomas G. West, "Restoring the Separation of Powers," in Jones and Marini, *The
Imperial Congress*, 311.

138. Gordon Crovitz, "The Criminalization of Politics," in Jones and Marini, *The
Imperial Congress*, 239.

139. Hammond and Weyrich, "Legislative Lords," 224.

140. Hammond and Weyrich, "Legislative Lords," 223.

141. Hammond and Weyrich, "Legislative Lords," 223.

142. Gordon S. Jones and John A. Marini, "General Introduction," in Jones and Marini,
The Imperial Congress, 1.

143. Gabriel Prosser, "Comes the Revolution," in Jones and Marini, *The Imperial Congress*,
332–3.

144. Jones, "Overthrowing Oligarchy," 297.

145. Thomas G. West, "Restoring the Separation of Powers," in Jones and Marini, *The
Imperial Congress*, 317. Arguing that Republicans must become a "party of constitutional government," West contended, "Such a political party must be, at least at
first, the anti-Congress party. *Limited government means a limited Congress*" (324,
italics in original).

146. Cribb, "Strategic Plan for Domestic Affairs."

147. Many coalition partners were named in the "Strategic Plan for Domestic Affairs,"
(p. 47) which, depending on the initiative, included the Heritage Foundation,
Concerned Women for America, National Right to Life Committee, the American
Legislative Exchange Council (ALEC), the U.S. Chamber of Commerce, the
National Taxpayers Union, the Reason Foundation, Citizens for a Sound Economy,
the Cato Institute, Armey's Budget Commandoes, the Republican Research Committee (U.S. House), the Rockford Institute, and the Free Congress Foundation,
among others.

148. The most detailed research on MCCA remains Carolyn Thompson, "The Political Evolution of the Medicare Catastrophic Health Care Act of 1988" (PhD diss., Johns Hopkins University, 1990). Another fine source is Richard Himelfarb, *Catastrophic Politics: The Rise and Fall of the Medicare Catastrophic Coverage Act of 1988* (University Park: Pennsylvania State University Press, 1985).

149. Keith A. Wailoo, "The Era of Big Government: Why It Never Ended," in *Medicare and Medicaid at 50: America's Entitlement Programs in the Age of Affordable Care*, ed. Alan B. Cohen, David C. Colby, Keith A. Wailoo, and Julian E. Zelizer (New York: Oxford University Press, 2015), 238. While there was public controversy later, which led to the MCCA being repealed under President George H. W. Bush, disputes during its development and passage were largely constrained and were addressed within governmental circles.

150. Robert B. Porter, memorandum for John A. Sununu, "Subject: Statements on Catastrophic Care," April 19, 1989, 29142-006—1998-0004-F[1]—Catastrophic Illness (1989)—George H. W. Bush Presidential Records—Chief of Staff, White House Office of—Sununu, John, Files—Issues Files. George H. W. Bush Presidential Library, College Station, Tex. (hereafter GHWBPL).

151. Porter, memorandum for John A. Sununu, "Subject: Statements on Catastrophic Care," April 19, 1989.

152. Himelfarb, *Catastrophic Politics*.

153. John Rother, interview by Ed Berkowitz, August 27, 2002, CMS Oral History Project, Centers for Medicare and Medicaid Services, https://www.cms.gov/About -CMS/Agency-Information/History/Downloads/CMSOralHistory_Medicare-.pdf

154. Brian Biles, interview by Ed Berkowitz, October 9, 2002, CMS Oral History Project, Centers for Medicare and Medicaid Services, https://www.cms.gov/About -CMS/Agency-Information/History/Downloads/CMSOralHistory_Medicare-.pdf

155. Health economist Gail Wilensky, who headed Medicare and Medicaid soon after MCCA was repealed, held: "We took a piece of legislation that was passable and sustainable, and more was added to it than high-income seniors were willing to finance by redistribution of their money to low-income seniors . . . But it wasn't that there wasn't a problem initially being addressed; it's just that the passage of the bill was in fact too much, and we weren't honest with seniors about who would ultimately be paying the bill." Quoted in *Principle Over Politics? The Domestic Policy of the George H.W. Bush Presidency*, ed. Richard Himelfarb and Rosanna Perotti (Westport, Conn.: Prager, 2004), 290.

156. Martin Tolchin, "Retreat in Congress; The Catastrophic-Care Debacle—A Special Report—How the New Medicare Law Fell on Hard Times in a Hurry," *New York Times*, October 9, 1989, http://www.nytimes.com/1989/10/09/us/retreat-congress-catastrophic-care-debacle-special-report-new-medicare-law-fell.html.

157. Robert B. Porter, memorandum for John A. Sununu, "Subject: Recommended Discussion with Rep. Bill Archer," April 4, 1989, GHWBPL.

158. Letter to Dan Rostenkowski from President Bush. April 21, 1989. GHWBPL.

159. Nicholas E. Calio, memorandum for John A. Sununu, "Subject: Letter from Ways and Means Republicans About Administration Position on Catastrophic Care Coverage, May 1, 1989, GHWBPL. The memo introduces a April 27, 1989 letter from GOP members of the Ways and Means Committee, GHWBPL.

160. Senate Finance Committee staffer Marina Weiss reported she had heard that "Chief of Staff Sununu had told President Bush, to stay away from the debate over

the act, in fact from health care issues generally and this in particular." Marina Weiss, interviewed by Edward Berkowitz, July 17, 2002, CMS Oral History Project, Centers for Medicare and Medicaid Services, https://www.cms.gov/About-CMS /Agency-Information/History/Downloads/CMSOralHistory_Medicare-.pdf.

161. As Rostenkowski remembered, "People in my neighborhood in Chicago were angry at me. This legislation would never cost them a dime because the increases were not for people at this financial level. And they had pickets against me and they chased me down the avenue." Dan Rostenkowski, interview by Ed Berkowitz, December 4, 2002, CMS Oral History Project, Centers for Medicare and Medicaid Services, https://www.cms.gov/About-CMS/Agency-Information/History/Downloads /CMSOralHistory_Medicare-.pdf. For a contemporaneous account, see William Recktenwald, "Insurance Forum Turns Catastrophic for Rostenkowski," *Chicago Tribune*, August 18, 1989, http://articles.chicagotribune.com/1989-08-18/news /8901050673_1_senior-citizens-congressman-dan-rostenkowski-health-insurance For a discussion that places this incident into the context of how the elderly have been socially transformed by health policy, see Mark Schlesinger, "Medicare and the Social Transformation of American Elders," *Medicare and Medicaid at 50: America's Entitlement Programs in the Age of Affordable Care*, ed. Alan B. Cohen, David C. Colby, Keith A. Wailoo, and Julian E. Zelizer (New York: Oxford University Press, 2015).

162. Tolchin, "Retreat in Congress."

163. Rother, interview by Ed Berkowitz, August 27, 2002.

164. White House press conference transcript, September 12, 1989, GHWBPL.

165. See Mark A. Peterson, "Reversing Course on Obamacare: Why Not Another Medicare Catastrophic?," *Journal of Health Politics, Policy and Law*, 43, no. 4 (2018): 605–50.

166. Richard Darman, director of OMB, memo to President Bush, "Enrolled Bill H.R. 3607—Medicare Catastrophic Care Act of 1989," December 11, 1989, GHWBPL. Bush's and Reagan's Health and Human Services secretaries saw President Bush as doing little to defend the program. See Bowen, interview, November 8–9, 2001; Louis Sullivan, interview by Ed Berkowitz, September 16, 2002, CMS Oral History Project, Centers for Medicare and Medicaid Services, https://www.cms.gov /About-CMS/Agency-Information/History/Downloads/CMSOralHistory _Medicare-.pdf.

167. David Blumenthal and James A. Morone, *The Heart of Power: Health and Politics in the Oval Office* (Berkeley: University of California Press, 2009). See also Thomas Rice, Katherine Desmond, and Jon Gabel, "The Medicare Catastrophic Coverage Act: A Post-Mortem," *Health Affairs* 9, no. 3 (1990), https://www.healthaffairs.org /doi/full/10.1377/hlthaff.9.3.75

168. David E. Rosenbaum, "Bush Rejects Stopgap Bill After Budget Pact Defeat," *New York Times*, October 6, 1990; John J. Pitney and William Connelly Jr., *Congress's Permanent Minority? Republicans in the U.S. House* (Lanham, Md.: Rowman & Littlefield, 1994), 32–34.

169. See Heclo and Penner, "Fiscal and Political Strategy in the Reagan Administration," 27. This idea that the public was willing to give Reagan time before rendering judgment about the effectiveness of the economic program was in evidence in Carl Everett Ladd's analysis of first-term polling; Everett Carl Ladd, "The Reagan Phenomenon and Public Attitudes Toward Government," in *The Reagan*

Presidency and the Governing of America ed. Lester M. Salamon and Michael S. Lund (Washington, D.C.: Urban Institute, 1984), 221–49, 224.

170. These are from the 1983 and 1985 State of the Union addresses, respectively. Ronald Reagan, "Address Before a Joint Session of the Congress on the State of the Union," January 25, 1983, online by Gerhard Peters and John T. Woolley, *American Presidency Project*, http://www.presidency.ucsb.edu/ws/?pid=41698; Ronald Reagan, "Address Before a Joint Session of the Congress on the State of the Union," February 6, 1985, online by Gerhard Peters and John T. Woolley, *American Presidency Project*, https://www.presidency.ucsb.edu/node/258923.

171. Ronald Reagan, "Address Before a Joint Session of Congress on the State of the Union," January 25, 1988, online by Gerhard Peters and John T. Woolley, *American Presidency Project*, http://www.presidency.ucsb.edu/ws/?pid=36035.

172. Frances Fox Piven, "Institutions and Agents in the Politics of Welfare Cutbacks," in *Remaking America: Democracy and Public Policy in an Age of Inequality*, ed. Joe Soss, Jacob S. Hacker, and Suzanne Mettler (New York: Russell Sage Foundation, 2007), 151.

173. Rick Perlstein, "Exclusive: Lee Atwater's Infamous 1981 Interview on the Southern Strategy," *Nation*, November 13, 2012, https://www.thenation.com/article/exclusive -lee-atwaters-infamous-1981-interview-southern-strategy.

174. Indeed, free market liberalism always benefited from its untestability. It never existed as its more ardent proponents imagined it, particularly given the large degree of promotional policies that subsidized business in the nineteenth century. It was only after decades of the government cradling American industry in its hands through protectionism and subsidy that conservatives would discover "laissez faire" after the government's promotional role was accompanied by regulation. The ship had more than sailed with the growth of state management and regulation in the twentieth century.

175. Nathan, "The Reagan Presidency in Domestic Affairs," 63.

176. Skowronek, *The Politics That Presidents Make*, 429.

177. Nathan, "The Reagan Presidency in Domestic Affairs," 78.

178. See J. Richard Piper, *Ideologies and Institutions: American Conservative and Liberal Governance Prescriptions Since 1933* (Lanham, Md.: Rowman & Littlefield, 1997); see also "Presidential-Congressional Power Prescriptions in Conservative Political Thought Since 1933," *Presidential Studies Quarterly* 21 (1991): 35–54; and " 'Situational Constitutionalism' and Presidential Power: The Rise and Fall of the Liberal Model of Presidential Government," *Presidential Studies Quarterly* 24 (1994): 577–94.

179. Sidney M. Milkis and Jesse H. Rhodes, "George W. Bush, the Republican Party and the 'New' American Party System," *Perspectives on Politics* 5 (2007): 461–88, 467.

180. Bill Barr, memo, "Common Legislative Encroachments on Executive Branch Authority," July 27, 1989, https://www.justice.gov/file/24286/download.

181. Charlie Savage and Maggie Haberman, "Trump Weighs Bringing Back William Barr as Attorney General," *New York Times*, December 6, 2018, https://www.nytimes .com/2018/12/06/us/politics/william-barr-attorney-general-trump.html

182. Quote from Dick Cheney, Gellman, *Angler*, 97, 98. Dick Cheney, "Congressional Overreaching in Foreign Policy," in *Foreign Policy and the Constitution*, ed. Robert A. Goldwin and Robert A. Licht (Washington, D.C.: AEI Press, 1990), 101–22.

4. A REVOLUTION AGAINST GOVERNMENT? THE PROMOTION OF DISTRUST IN THE CLINTON ERA

1. Bill Clinton, "Oklahoma City Speech," April 23, 1995, http://www.presidentialrhetoric .com/historicspeeches/clinton/oklahomacity.html.

2. "William J. Clinton: Remarks to the American Association of Community Colleges in Minneapolis, Minnesota—April 24, 1995," accessed February 2, 2021, https://www .presidency.ucsb.edu/documents/remarks-the-american-association-community -colleges-minneapolis-minnesota.

3. Todd S. Purdum, "Clinton Assails the Preachings of the 'Militias,'" *New York Times*, May 6, 1995.

4. Just three months before the bombing, just 21 percent trusted government. "Public Trust in Government: 1958–2014" (Pew Research Center for the People and the Press, November 13, 2014), http://www.people-press.org/2014/11/13/public -trust-in-government.

5. On the importance of his aggressive tactics and antiestablishment views to Gingrich's rise, see Douglas B. Harris, "Legislative Parties and Leadership Choice: Confrontation or Accommodation in the 1989 Gingrich-Madigan Whip Race," *American Politics Research* 34, no. 2 (March 2006): 189–222; Matthew N. Green and Douglas B. Harris, *Choosing the Leader: Leadership Elections in the U.S. House of Representatives* (New Haven, Conn.: Yale University Press, 2019).

6. Julian E. Zelizer, *Burning Down the House: Newt Gingrich, the Fall of a Speaker and the Rise of the Republican Party* (New York: Penguin, 2020), 11; Douglas B. Harris, "Sack the Quarterback: The Strategies and Implications of Congressional Leadership Scandals," in *Scandal! An Interdisciplinary Approach to the Consequences, Outcomes, and Significance of Political Scandals*, ed. Alison Dagnes and Mark Sachleben (New York: Bloomsbury, 2014), 29–50.

7. Dan Balz and Ronald Brownstein, *Storming the Gates: Protest Politics and the Republican Revival* (Boston: Little, Brown, 1996), 15.

8. This is not to neglect the important international crises that did occupy the Clinton years but only to observe that electoral politics and policy disputes were domestically focused; for a good summary of foreign policy matters in the Clinton years, see Russell L. Riley, n.d., "Bill Clinton: Foreign Affairs," Miller Center, U.S. Presidents – Bill Clinton, University of Virginia, https://millercenter.org/president/clinton/foreign -affairs.

9. Newt Gingrich, "If House Republicans Are Ever to Become a Majority: The Requirements for a Break with 36 Years of Failure," box 44, folder 1, Mickey Edwards Collection, Carl Albert Center Congressional and Political Collections, University of Oklahoma, Norman, Oklahoma [MEC]. See, too, Gordon S. Jones and John A. Marini, eds., *The Imperial Congress: Crisis in the Separation of Powers* (New York: Pharos, 1988).

10. Anonymous interview with press staff member to Newt Gingrich, by Douglas B. Harris, September 7, 2000.

11. Jon Kyl, COS Chairman to COS Members, "Re: 24 February Planning Session," March 1, 1989, box 81, folder 19, MEC.

12. Gingrich, "If House Republicans Are Ever to Become a Majority."

13. Gingrich, "If House Republicans Are Ever to Become a Majority."

14. Gingrich, "If House Republicans Are Ever to Become a Majority."
15. Agenda 7/9, Leadership Files, box 15, folder "Dear Republican Colleague Notebook 1992 (3)," Robert H. Michel Papers, The Dirksen Congressional Center, Pekin, IL [RHM].
16. See Green and Harris, *Choosing the Leader*, 83–85.
17. The 1988 Republican Platform, August 16, 1988, online by Gerhard Peters and John T. Woolley, American Presidency Project, https://www.presidency.ucsb.edu /node/273433.
18. Republicans also claimed in 1988 that the House "Ethics Committee has become a shield for Democrats" where members "protect their cronies"; maintained that Democrats "stole a congressional seat," a reference to the seating of a Democrat after a contested Indiana election; charged that leaders "rig adoption of substantive legislation on mere procedural grounds"; and asserted that Democratic leaders "viciously penalize independent Democrats who vote their conscience." "Republican Party Platforms: Republican Party Platform of 1988," August 16, 1988, online by Gerhard Peters and John T. Woolley, *American Presidency Project*, https://www .presidency.ucsb.edu/documents/republican-party-platform-1988.
19. "Republican Party Platforms: Republican Party Platform of 1992," August 17, 1992, online by Gerhard Peters and John T. Woolley, *American Presidency Project*, https://www.presidency.ucsb.edu/documents/republican-party-platform-1992.
20. See, for example, James C. Cleveland, ed., *We Propose: A Modern Congress* (New York: McGraw-Hill, 1966); Melvin Laird, ed., *Republican Papers* (Garden City, N.Y.: Anchor Books); John J. Rhodes, *The Futile System: How to Unchain Congress and Make the System Work Again* (Garden City, N.Y.: EPM Publications, 1976). On how Robert Michel was advocating for this more conservative "restoration" well into the 1980s and 1990s, see Douglas B. Harris, "Anticipating the Revolution: Michel and Republican Congressional Reform Efforts," in *Robert H. Michel: Leading the Republican House Minority*, ed. Frank Mackaman and Sean Q Kelly (Lawrence, KS: University Press of Kansas, 2019), 186–215.
21. Garry Wills, *Reagan's America* (New York: Penguin, 2000), 1.
22. Jon F. Hale, "The Making of the New Democrats," *Political Science Quarterly* 110:2 (Summer 1995): 207–32.
23. They also sought to answer the charges that Democrats were too "soft on crime" and "weak on national defense."
24. Laura [Nichols], "Re: Message Grid Discussion Points for Tuesday Message Meeting," undated memorandum to TO, CH, MW, KB, box 841, folder 9 "Message Group Tallygrid, 1991–1993," Richard A. Gephardt Collection, Missouri History Museum, St. Louis, MO [RAG].
25. Douglas B. Harris, "The Democratic Leadership Council and New Democratic Issues," paper presented at the annual meeting of the Southern Political Science Association, Atlanta, Georgia, 1994; Douglas B. Harris, "Modern Republicanism and New Democrats: Issue Convergence and the Selective Emphasis Strategy of Party Competition" paper presented at the annual meeting of the Northeastern Political Science Association, Providence, Rhode Island, 1994.
26. William J. Clinton, "Address Accepting the Presidential Nomination at the Democratic National Convention in New York," July 16, 1992, online by Gerhard Peters and John T. Woolley, *American Presidency Project*, https://www.presidency.ucsb

.edu/node/220260. On the more general point, see Stephen Skowronek, *The Politics Presidents Make: Leadership from John Adams to Bill Clinton* (Cambridge, Mass.: Harvard University Press, 1997), 447–52; Stephen Skowronek, *Presidential Leadership in Political Time: Reprise and Reappraisal* (Lawrence: University Press of Kansas, 2008), 105–13.

27. See Pew Research Center, "Public Trust in Government 1968–2017," http://www.people-press.org/2017/05/03/public-trust-in-government-1958-2017.

28. Balz and Brownstein, *Storming the Gates*, 15, 162, 192.

29. Nigel Ashford, "The Republican Policy Agenda and the Conservative Movement," in *The Republican Takeover of Congress* ed. Dean McSweeney and John E. Owens (New York: St. Martin's, 1998), 96–117, 101.

30. Major Garrett, *The Enduring Revolution: How the Contract with America Continues to Shape the Nation* (New York: Crown Forum, 2005), 58–60.

31. Balz and Brownstein, *Storming the Gates*, 15.

32. Anthony Fabrizio and John McLaughlin to Robert H. Michel, "Staff-Van Der Meid," February 4, 1993, box 4, folder "Campaign 1992, Republican Poll," RHM.

33. See, for example, Michelle Alexander, *The New Jim Crow: Mass Incarceration in the Age of Colorblindness* (New York: New Press, 2010).

34. Paul Starr, "The Hillycare Mythology," *American Prospect*, September 13, 2007. http://prospect.org/article/hillarycare-mythology.

35. See, esp., Jacob Hacker, *The Road to Nowhere: The Genesis of President Clinton's Plan for Health Security* (Princeton, N.J.: Princeton University Press, 1997) According to staffer Chris Jennings, Clinton later concluded that health reform would have had a better chance if it had been pursued after welfare reform, as this would have "enhanced the public's confidence that he and the Democrats got it, that there are some things that government is overdoing." Said Jennings, "There was a sense that government was providing too much dependency as opposed to empowerment." Chris Jennings and Jeanne Lambrew, April 17 and 18, 2003, Oral history, Miller Center, Presidential Oral Histories. Bill Clinton Presidency, University of Virginia, https://millercenter.org/the-presidency/presidential-oral-histories/chris-jennings-and-jeanne-lambrew-oral-history.

36. Theda Skocpol, *Boomerang: Health Care Reform and the Turn Against Government* (New York: Norton, 1997), 115.

37. Rahm Emanuel, Memorandum for Mark Gearan, George Stephanopoulos, "Subject: Crime Initiatives," June 2, 1993, box 8. folder "Crime Poll [OA/ID 3828]," Emanuel Papers, William J. Clinton Presidential Library. Little Rock, Arkansas. [hereafter WJCPL].

38. House Republican Conference, Rep. Dick Armey, Chairman, "Worse Than the Disease? An Analysis of the Clinton Approach to Health Care," August 25, 1993, Health Care Task Force, segment 10, box 5, folder "HC [Health Care]—Republican Reports [OA/ID 3516]" Robert Boorstin collection, WJCPL.

39. Armey, "Worse Than the Disease?"

40. Armey, "Worse Than the Disease?," said that these public reactions would occur "if the Clinton plan leads to a rationing of health care, tight limits on choices of personal physicians, and exceedingly high taxes," claims they were to make about the plan as the debate unfolded.

41. Haynes Johnson and David S. Broder, *The System: The American Way of Politics at the Breaking Point* (Boston: Little, Brown, 1996), xii, 11–12

42. Gary L. Carpenter, "Coverdell, Fellow Republicans Push Alternative to Clinton Plan," Associated Press clipping, October 12, 1993, Health Care Task Force, segment 10, box 5. folder "HC [Health Care]—GOP Attacks," Boorstin collection, WJCPL.

43. Haley Barbour, memorandum to Republican leaders, "Focus on Health Care— The Clinton Plan," September 17, 1993, Health Care Task Force, segment 10, box 5, folder "HC [Health Care]—GOP Attacks," Boorstin collection, WJCPL.

44. The phrase was used 208 times during the 103rd Congress. "Government-run health care," "big government health care," "health care bureaucracy," and "social- ized medicine," and similar language were also quite common. Amy Fried and Douglas B. Harris, "On Red Capes and Charging Bulls: How and Why Conserva- tive Politicians and Interest Groups Promoted Public Anger," in *What Is It About Government That Americans Dislike?*, ed. John R. Hibbing and Elizabeth Theiss- Morse (New York: Cambridge University Press, 2001), 157–74, 170.

45. Barbour, memorandum to Republican leaders, "Focus on Health Care—The Clinton Plan."

46. February 18, 1993. Cited in Fried and Harris, "On Red Capes and Charging Bulls," 170.

47. Quotes compiled in a memo for the Clinton Health Care Task Force, n.d., Health Care Task Force, segment 7, box 5. folder 2 "Republicans—General [OA/ID 3664], Edelstein Collection, WJCPL.

48. William Kristol, memo to Republican leaders, Project for the Republican Future, "Defeating President Clinton's Health Care Proposal," December 2, 1993, Health Care Task Force, segment 10, box 5, folder "HC [Health Care]—Republican Reports [OA/ID 3516]," Robert Boorstin collection, WJCPL.

49. William Kristol, memo to Republican leaders, Project for the Republican Future, "Why Republicans Should Oppose 'Universal Coverage, '" April, 7, 1994, segment 10, box 5, folder "HC [Health Care]—Republican Reports [OA/ID 3516]," Robert Boorstin collection, WJCPL.

50. Eric Felten, *The Ruling Class: Inside the Imperial Congress* (Washington, D.C.: Regnery, 1993), 6.

51. Edwin J. Feulner Jr., foreword to Felten, *The Ruling Class*, ix–x.

52. Felten, *The Ruling Class*, 73, 97.

53. Felten, *The Ruling Class*, 25, 29.

54. Felten, *The Ruling Class*, 79.

55. Felten, *The Ruling Class*, 46.

56. Quotes from Rahm Emanuel and Bruce Reed, memorandum for the president, "Subject: Introduction to Crime Strategy," February 18, 1994, box 9, folder "Intro to Crime Strategy [1] [OA/ID 3828]," Emanuel papers, WJCPL. In the same folder, see also Rahm Emanuel, memorandum for the president, "Subject: Communica- tions. Strategy for Crime & Violence," February 18, 1994. Also see Rahm Emanuel and Bruce Reed, memorandum for Mack McLarty, "Subject: Crime Bill Strategy," January 7, 1994, box 7, folder "Crime Bill Communication [OA/ID 3828]," Emanuel papers, WJCPL. Hollan found Clinton successfully shifted the ownership of the crime issue toward Democrats and associated prevention with crime fighting.

David B. Hollan, "He's Stealing My Issues! Clinton's Crime Rhetoric and the Dynamics of Issue Ownership," *Political Behavior* 26 (2004): 95–124.

57. Paul Starr, *Remedy and Reaction: The Peculiar American Struggle Over Health Care Reform* (New Haven, Conn.: Yale University Press, 2011), 117.

58. Bill Kristol also opposed the Cooper plan, calling it "a gigantic leftward social policy gamble by the Democrats, one that should be impossible to win given everything the United States has learned over the past 25 years about the failures of big-government liberalism," William Kristol, memo to Republican leaders, Project for the Republican Future, "Defeating the Coming Clinton-Cooper Compromise," February 10, 1994, Health Care Task Force, segment 7, box 5, folder 2 "Republicans—General [OA/ID 3664]," Edelstein collection, WJCPL.

59. Starr, *Remedy and Reaction*, 116.

60. Skocpol, *Boomerang*, 139.

61. Health Care Task Force, segment 10, box 9, folder "HC [Health Care]: HIAA [Health Insurance Association of America] Ads [OA/ID 3514]," Robert Boorstin collection, WJCPL.

62. See Raymond L. Goldsteen, Karen Goldsteen, James H. Swan, and Wendy Clemeña, "Harry and Louise and Health Care Reform: Romancing Public Opinion," *Journal of Health Politics, Policy and Law* 26, no. 6 (2001): 1325–52; Darrell M. West, Diane Heith, and Chris Goodwin, "Harry and Louise Go to Washington: Political Advertising and Health Care Reform," *Journal of Health Politics, Policy and Law* 21, no. 1 (1996): 35–68.

63. Johnson and Broder, *The System*, 428.

64. Memo on February 15, 1994, event at the National Press Club, Health Care Task Force, segment 7, box 5, folder 2 "Republicans—General [OA/ID 3664], Edelstein collection, WJCPL.

65. Health Care Task Force, segment 10, box 6, folder "HC [Health Care]: Direct Mail Campaigns [OA/ID 3514]," Robert Boorstin collection, WJCPL.

66. An advertisement script by the Project for the Republican Future responding to the 1994 State of the Union address focused on government harming quality and coverage and predicted "rationing" and "waiting lines." Health Care Task Force, segment 10, box 14, folder "HC [Health Care]: Opposition TV Ads [OA/ID 3514]," Robert Boorstin collection, WJCPL.

67. Skeptics included prominent Senate Democrats. Appropriations Committee chair Robert Byrd blocked a White House effort to add health care to a budget reconciliation bill, which would have avoided a filibuster. Daniel Patrick Moynihan, chair of the Senate Finance Committee, through which any health reform bill had to pass, did not think the system needed fundamental reform and favored prioritizing welfare reform. Skocpol, *Boomerang*, 101; Starr, *Remedy and Reaction*, 108. See also Balz and Brownstein, *Storming the Gates*, 253.

68. Johnson and Broder, *The System*, 310–11.

69. Chris Jennings and Steve Edelstein, memo to Hillary Rodham Clinton, "Re: Meeting with Senator Wellstone," February 24, 1994," Health Care Task Force, segment 7, box 42, folder "Congressional Briefing Memos—First Lady 1994 [2] [OA/ID 3681]," Edelstein collection, WJCPL.

70. Edelstein and Martin, memo on health care congressional briefing, "Re: Paul Wellstone D-MN," July 5, 1994, Health Care Task Force, segment 7, box 4 of 62, folder

"Edelstein, Steve [Congress]. Congressional profiles written for the cabinet: Pena, Frederico (Transportation) [OA/ID3669] [Congress]. WJCPL.

71. Johnson and Broder, *The System*, 275–77.

72. For more on congressional statements linking Whitewater to health care and distrust, see Fried and Harris, "On Red Capes and Charging Bulls," 170–71.

73. These concerns had a long history. As sociologist Michael Javen Fortner notes, the post–World War II anti-drug and crime activism of a "black silent majority" in Harlem helped create the Rockefeller drug laws; these influenced decades of punitive crime policy. Michael Javen Fortner, *Black Silent Majority: The Rockefeller Drug Laws and the Politics of Punishment* (Cambridge, Mass.: Harvard University Press, 2015).

74. Katharine Q. Seelye, "Provision on Death Penalty Is Slowing Anti-Crime Bill," *New York Times*, June 26, 1994.

75. Pat Griffin and Ron Klain through Mack McLarty, memorandum for the president, "Subject: Crime Bill—Legislative Strategy," June 18, 1994, "Records Concerning Rahm Emanuel, Special Assistant to the President, 1993–1999," box 8, folder "Crime and Conference Strategy [OA/ID 3828]," FOIA number 2009-0140-F collection, WJCPL.

76. See Talking Points for CBC Calls. July 7, 1994; Recommended Telephone Call. July 22, 1994; and Memorandum for the President. July 22, 1994. From: Rahm Emanuel, Bruce Reed, Ron Klain. Subject: Q&A on Racial Justice Act. box 11, folder "Racial Justice [OA/ID 3828]," Emanuel papers, WJCPL.

77. Ronald Brownstein, "Crime Bill Likely to Omit 'Racial Justice' Measure," *Los Angeles Times*, July 15, 1994, http://articles.latimes.com/1994-07-15/news/mn-15839 _1_racial-justice.

78. Quoted in Helen Dewar, "Senate Gives Up on Health Care, Passes Crime Bill," *Washington Post*, August 26, 1994.

79. There is an extensive literature on how racial stereotypes, rhetoric, and symbols are used and to what effect. See, for instance, Jon Hurwitz and Mark Peffley, "Playing the Race Card in the Post–Willie Horton Era: The Impact of Racialized Code Words on Support for Punitive Crime Policy," *Public Opinion Quarterly* 69 (2005): 99–112; Tali Mendelberg, *The Race Card* (Princeton, N.J.: Princeton University Press, 2001).

80. Darren Wheelock and Douglas Hartmann, "Midnight Basketball and the 1994 Crime Bill Debates: The Operation of a Racial Code," *Sociological Quarterly* 38 (2001): 315–42, 328.

81. Jerry Lewis (R-CA) in 140, *Congressional Record*, August 17, 1994, H8510.

82. John Duncan (R-TN) in 140, *Congressional Record*, August 20, 1994, H23363.

83. Christopher Cox (R-CA) in 140, *Congressional Record*, August 18, 1994, H23140-1.

84. Gwen Ifill, "Spending in Crime Bill: Prevention or Just Pork?," *New York Times*, August 16, 1994, http://www.nytimes.com/1994/08/16/us/spending-in-crime-bill -prevention-or-just-pork.html.

85. Wheelock and Hartmann, "Midnight Basketball and the 1994 Crime Bill Debates."

86. Craig Shirley & Associates, "Clinton, Reno Presented First "Crimebusters Action Kits," August 4, 1994, box 8, folder "GOP [Grand Old Party] Notes [1] [OA/ID 3828]," Emanuel papers, WJCPL.

87. NRA ad w/ Charlton Heston, box 7, folder "Crime Bill Strategy [2] [OA/ID 3828]," Emanuel papers, WJCPL.

88. Michael Wilbon, "The GOP's Midnight Madness," *Washington Post*, August 19, 1994. https://www.washingtonpost.com/archive/sports/1994/08/19/the-gops-midnight -madness/c9dc11d4-b9c1-4939-93c4-2f1c717eca72/?utm_term=.cab1e51e18e2.
89. "A Retrospective on Health Reform, October 1994, Background," 9; Clinton presidential records, First Lady's Office, series/staff member—First Lady's Press Office, subseries—Lisa Caputo, OA/ID 10250, folder "Health Care Retrospective," WJCPL. https://clinton.presidentiallibraries.us/files/original/98c973424df54abc47599358d2 8ee4bf.pdf.
90. "A Retrospective on Health Reform, October 1994, Background," 2, 3, 14.
91. Madelyn Hochstein and Gene Wright, "The Story of Health Care Reform as Told by the American People," 3; First Lady's Office and Pam Cicetti, "Health—Polling [folder 2] [2]," Clinton digital library, accessed September 11, 2017, https://clinton .presidentiallibraries.us/items/show/42629.
92. The report by Hochstein and Wright referred to a "Rip Van Winkle effect," as if people slept through the year. Hochstein and Wright, "The Story of Health Care Reform as Told by the American People."
93. As Clinton staffer Mike Lux put it, the administration "needed to focus more on turning more of our efforts to educating, energizing and mobilizing those constituencies who we are counting on to be our base: labor, seniors, those with disabilities, African-American, Hispanic, nurses, social workers, pharmacists, the mental health community, single payer activists, and other liberal Democratic activists." While there was outreach, these groups lacked the necessary passion for policy success because of the bill's complexity, which made it hard to explain, and the "lack of trust that our allies place in us in terms of compromising on the things that matter the most to them (mostly because of bruises from past fights.)." Mike Lux, memorandum for distribution, "Subject: Mobilizing the Base," February 21, 1994, First Lady's Office and Pam Cicetti, "Health - Communications, Message [2]," Clinton Digital Library, accessed January 26, 2021, https://clinton .presidentiallibraries.us/items/show/42550.
94. Stanley Greenberg. October 11, 2007. Oral history. Miller Center, Presidential Oral Histories. Bill Clinton Presidency. University of Virginia. https://millercenter.org /the-presidency/presidential-oral-histories/stanley-greenberg-oral-history-2007.
95. Chris Jennings and Jeanne Lambrew, April 17 and 18, 2003, Oral history, Miller Center, Presidential Oral Histories, Bill Clinton Presidency, University of Virginia. https://millercenter.org/the-presidency/presidential-oral-histories/chris-jennings -and-jeanne-lambrew-oral-history.
96. Frank Luntz to Republican leaders, "Re: Public Reaction to 'The Contract,'" September 2, 1994, reprinted in Garrett, *The Enduring Revolution*, 303.
97. Balz and Brownstein, *Storming the Gates*, 253.
98. Ed Gillespie and Bob Schellhas, eds., *Contract with America* (New York: Times Books, 1994), 7, 21. According to the GOP's book on the Contract, "Passage of the *Contract* will dramatically change the way Washington does business, and change the business that Washington does," producing "a fundamental restructuring of government" (22–23).
99. Gillespie and Schellhas, *Contract with America*, 189.

100. See undated notes, box 2809, folder "House GOP Leadership Projects Through December 1993," Newt Gingrich Papers, University of West Georgia Special Collections, Carrollton, Georgia [NLG].

101. Garrett, *The Enduring Revolution*, 56.

102. Gillespie and Schellhas, *Contract with America*, 4.

103. See John B. Bader, *Taking the Initiative: Leadership Agendas in Congress and the "Contract with America"* (Washington, D.C.: Georgetown University Press, 1996); Douglas B. Harris, "House Majority Party Leaders' Uses of Public Opinion Information," *Congress & the Presidency* 32, no. 2 (2005): 133–55; Lawrence Jacobs, Eric Lawrence, Robert Y. Shapiro, and Steven S. Smith, "Congressional leadership of Public Opinion," *Political Science Quarterly* 113 (1998): 21–42; Amy Fried and Douglas B. Harris, "Governing with the Polls," *Historian* 72 (2010): 321–53.

104. Frank Luntz, "From Minority to Majority: A Strategy for the Republican House Leadership," January 27, 1994, box 2629, folder "Planning/Strategy Memos," NLG.

105. Gillespie and Schellhas, *Contract with America*, 8.

106. Gillespie and Schellhas, *Contract with America*, 5–8, 13.

107. Gingrich communications staffer, interviewed by Harris, September 7, 2000.

108. Gillespie and Schellhas, *Contract with America*, 79, 115, 125.

109. According to Gingrich, talk radio was oppositional and helped fortify the conservative movement; Newt Gingrich, *To Renew America* (New York: HarperCollins, 1995), 211. In a study of Rush Limbaugh's listeners, Jamieson and Cappella found they strongly distrusted Washington, particularly when Democrats are in charge. Kathleen Hall Jamieson and Joseph N. Cappella, *Echo Chamber: Rush Limbaugh and the Conservative Media Establishment* (New York: Oxford University Press, 2008), 127–28.

110. Anonymous interview with Gingrich press staffer by Douglas B. Harris, September 7, 2000.

111. Balz and Brownstein, *Storming the Gates*, 167.

112. William Gamson, *Power and Discontent* (Homewood, Ill.: Dorsey Press, 1968), 48.

113. James G. Gimpel, *Legislating the Revolution: The Contract with America in Its First 100 Days* (Boston: Allyn & Bacon, 1996), 17–19; Bader, *Taking the Initiative*, 183–188.

114. Garrett, *The Enduring Revolution*, 13.

115. Ed Goeas to Republican Conference, "Re: A Contract with the American Voters," August 10, 1994, reprinted in Garrett, *The Enduring Revolution*, 299–301, 301.

116. See Gimpel, *Legislating the Revolution*, esp. appendix A8, 152–53; Bader, *Taking the Initiative*; Garrett, *The Enduring Revolution*.

117. Ashford, "The Republican Policy Agenda and the Conservative Movement," 97, 104–105.

118. Dick Armey and John Boehner to Republican Members of Congress, "Re: Contract Coalitions and Outreach," December 26, 1994, reprinted in Garrett, *The Enduring Revolution*, 313–14, 313.

119. Tony Blankley as quoted in Elizabeth Drew, *Showdown: The Struggle Between the Gingrich Congress and the Clinton White House* (New York: Touchstone, 1997), 32.

120. Garrett, *The Enduring Revolution*, 80–83.

121. Garrett, *The Enduring Revolution*, 83.

122. House Republican Conference, "Background: The Contract with America," box 96-54 "Republican Contract with America," Barbara Vucanovich Records, Univeristy of Nevada, Reno Special Collections Department, [BFV].

123. Gillespie and Schellhas, *Contract with America*, 79.

124. Ashford, "The Republican Policy Agenda and the Conservative Movement," 101.

125. Armey and Boehner, to Republican Members of Congress, "Re: Contract Coalitions and Outreach."

126. Ashford, "The Republican Policy Agenda and the Conservative Movement," 99. Others who closely observed the 1994 election noted the role of public anger toward Clinton and government. See Gary C. Jacobson, "The 1994 House Elections in Perspective," *Political Science Quarterly* 111, no. 2 (Summer 1996): 203-23; Linda Killian, *The Freshmen: What Happened to the Republican Revolution?* (Boulder, Colo.: Westview Press, 1998); Balz and Brownstein, *Storming the Gates*.

127. Ashford, "The Republican Policy Agenda and the Conservative Movement," 100.

128. Gingrich, *To Renew America*, 115.

129. Luntz to Republican leaders, "Re: Public Reaction to 'The Contract,'" September 2, 1994, reprinted in Garrett, *The Enduring Revolution*, 304.

130. Quoted in Balz and Brownstein, *Storming the Gates*, 54.

131. Balz and Brownstein, *Storming the Gates*, 30; see also Douglas L. Koopman, *Hostile Takeover: The House Republican Party, 1980-1995* (Lanham, Md.: Rowman & Littlefield, 1996), 25. As Steve Gunderson told Nicol Rae, "The Contract with America focused on what united the party—economic issues—and not what divided us;" Nicol C. Rae, *Conservative Reformers: The Republican Freshmen and the Lessons of the 104th Congress* (New York: Routledge, 1998), 39, 39-40. GOPAC's Joe Gaylord, one of the contract's strategists, said, "There was a conscious effort to attract the Perot vote in the '94 campaign, and one of the ways that manifested itself was there were no social issues in the Contract"; Garrett, *The Enduring Revolution*, 86.

132. Rae, *Conservative Reformers*, 40.

133. Balz and Brownstein, *Storming the Gates*, 56.

134. Jacobson, "The 1994 House Elections in Perspective," 211.

135. Gillespie and Schellhas, *Contract with America*, 183.

136. Gillespie and Schellhas, *Contract with America*, 3.

137. Kerry [Knott] to Dick [Armey], "Re: Tomorrow Night and Beyond November 7, 1994," box 40, folder 32, Richard K. Armey Papers, Carl Albert Center Congressional and Political Collections, University of Oklahoma, Norman, Oklahoma [RKA].

138. Drew, *Showdown*, 30.

139. Drew, *Showdown*, 33.

140. Anonymous interview with press staff member to Newt Gingrich, by Douglas B. Harris, September 7, 2000.

141. Bill Paxon, "Dear Republican Colleague: NRCC April Recess Action Plan," April 5, 1995, box 40, folder 36, RKA.

142. Killian, *The Freshmen*, 64.

143. Ashford, "The Republican Policy Agenda and the Conservative Movement," 97.

144. Gingrich, *To Renew America*, 71.

145. Gingrich, *To Renew America*, 73.

146. Paxon, "Dear Republican Colleague: NRCC April Recess Action Plan."

147. Paxon, "Dear Republican Colleague: NRCC April Recess Action Plan."
148. Paxon, "Dear Republican Colleague: NRCC April Recess Action Plan."
149. Douglas B. Harris, "The Rise of the Public Speakership," *Political Science Quarterly* 113 (Summer 1998): 193–212.
150. Drew, *Showdown*, 114–15.
151. Drew, *Showdown*, 116.
152. On situational constitutionalism, see J. Richard Piper, "Presidential-Congressional Power Prescriptions in Conservative Political Thought Since 1933," *Presidential Studies Quarterly* 21 (1991): 35–54; J. Richard Piper, "'Situational Constitutionalism' and Presidential Power: The Rise and Fall of the Liberal Model of Presidential Government," *Presidential Studies Quarterly* 24 (1994): 577–94.
153. "Separation of Powers: Legislative-Executive Relations," and Stephen J. Markman, memorandum to Edwin Meese III, "Subject: Separation of Powers," April 30, 1986, RG 60 folder OLP, April–May 1986, part 1, box 86, Department of Justice Files, National Archives and Records Administration, Washington, DC [NARA], 17, 21.
154. Newt Gingrich, foreword to *The Imperial Congress: Crisis in the Separation of Powers*, ed. Gordon S. Jones and John A. Marini (Pharos Books, 1988), x–xi.
155. Gingrich, foreword, *The Imperial Congress*, x–xi.
156. Newt Gingrich's remarks in *Masters of the House: Congressional Leaders Over Two Centuries*, ed. Roger H. Davidson, Susan Webb Hammond, and Raymond W. Smock (Boulder, Colo.: Westview Press, 1998).
157. William J. Clinton, press conference, April 18, 1995, http://www.presidency.ucsb.edu/ws/index.php?pid=51237.
158. William F. Connelly Jr., "Newt Gingrich—Professor and Politician: The Anti-Federalist Roots of Newt Gingrich's Thought," *Southeastern Political Review* 27, no. 1 (March 1999): 103–27, 116.
159. Connelly, "Newt Gingrich—Professor and Politician," 115.
160. Republican Party Platform of 1992.
161. House Republican Conference, "Quarterly Report, January–March 1993," box 57, folder 21, RKA.
162. Internal House GOP document from the summer of 1994, reprinted in Garrett, *The Enduring Revolution*, 296; see also p. 17.
163. John Boehner, "Dear Republican Colleague," January 23, 1995, box 56, folder 10, RKA.
164. See Skowronek, *Presidential Leadership in Political Time*, 103–104.
165. Bob Franks, memorandum for Republican members and staff, "Subject: The Budget Message, Now Through May 1," box 56, folder 2, RKA.
166. On these efforts, see David Maraniss and Michael Weisskopf, *Tell Newt to Shut Up* (New York: Touchstone, 1996); Lawrence R. Jacobs and Robert Y. Shapiro, *Politicians Don't Pander: Political Manipulation and the Loss of Democratic Responsiveness* (Chicago: University of Chicago Press, 2000).
167. Randall Strahan and Daniel J. Palazzolo, "The Gingrich Effect," *Political Science Quarterly* 119, no. 1 (Spring 2004): 89–114, 104.
168. "Luntz Research: Words that Work," September 29, 1996, Debate Preparation, box 2514, folder "Luntz," NLG.
169. "House Republican National Strategic Plan for 1996," PowerPoint, box 2426, folder "Strategic Plan for 1996," NLG.

170. Jamieson and Cappella, *Echo Chamber*, 133–34.

171. Glen Bolger to senior congressional staff, "Re: Observations on the National Political Environment—What It Means for Our Message," May 31, 1996, box 2601, folder "Polling," NLG.

172. William J. Clinton, "Address Before a Joint Session of the Congress on the State of the Union," January 23, 1996, http://www.presidency.ucsb.edu/ws/?pid=53091. The language of "reconstruction" acknowledges Skowronek's *The Politics Presidents Make* and *Presidential Leadership in Political Time*.

173. Quoted in Will Marshall, "Controversy: Why Did Clinton Win?," *American Prospect*, March–April 1997, http://prospect.org/article/controversy-why-did-clinton-win.

174. See Russell L. Riley, "Bill Clinton: Campaigns and Elections," n.d., Miller Center, U.S. Presidents – Bill Clinton, University of Virginia, https://millercenter.org/president /clinton/campaigns-and-elections.

175. Ashford, "The Republican Policy Agenda and the Conservative Movement," 114.

176. Haley Barbour, chairman, to Republican leadership, "Subject: Post-Election Survey Summary," January 14, 1997, box 2514, folder "Other Polling," NLG.

177. Balz and Brownstein, *Storming the Gates*, 180.

178. "New Luntz Survey on Taxes for Dick Armey *As Tax Day Approaches, Tempers Flare*," April 11, 1997, box 13, folder 11, RKA.

179. Frank Luntz to interested parties, "Re: Talking About Taxes," June 24, 1997, box 2211, folder "Outreach," NLG.

180. GOPAC, "Communications Strategies for our Governing Majority," July 1997, box 2420, folder "Communication GOPAC," NLG.

181. John F. Harris and Helen Dewar, "President Vetoes Flood Relief Bill," *Washington Post*, June 10, 1997.

182. ELC Retreat Document, September 9, 1997, box 2426, folder "ELC Retreat," NLG.

183. Andy to Kerry, Brian, Michele, Tyler, "Subject: Freedom and Responsibility Speech," March 26, 1997, box 55, folder 14, RKA.

184. "Re: FDA Reform Strategy," September 23, 1997, box 55, folder 14 "Armey, Legislative—House Majority Leader Planning for the 105th Congress, March–December 1997," RKA.

185. "Re: Fall Property Rights Agenda," September 22, 1997, box 55, folder 14 "Armey, Legislative—House Majority Leader Planning for the 105th Congress, March–December 1997," RKA.

186. "Smaller, Smarter Government Project," 1998, box 55, folder 15, RKA.

187. "Goal of Chairman's Meeting," February 1–5, 1998, box 24, folder 15, RKA.

188. Oversight Department to Armey Office, "Re: Draft Waste Plan," May 5, 1999, box 55, folder 9, RKA.

189. Lee Walczak and Richard S. Dunham, "Newt Gingrich's 'Goals for a Generation,' " *Business Week*, April 6, 1998.

190. Poll results from RNC national polling, dated January 5–8, 1998, box 2149, folder "Newt Memos," NLG.

191. House Republican Communications Playbook, draft, July 20, 1998, box 2423, folder "Communications Playbook," NLG.

192. Kerry [Knott] to Dick [Armey], "Re: Tomorrow Night and Beyond November 7, 1994."

193. Jacob S. Hacker and Paul Pierson, *American Amnesia: How the War on Government Led Us to Forget What Made America Prosper* (New York: Simon & Schuster, 2017), 198.

194. Quotation from Balz and Brownstein, *Storming the Gates*, 95. See also internal polling regarding how to use the budget surplus of the late 1990s; undated memorandum, "To Newt, From: Copy," box 2420, folder "Health Care Campaign," NLG.

5. "WE'RE ALL MAD HERE": THE TEA PARTY AND THE OBAMA ERA

1. Barack Obama, "Remarks by the President at a Campaign Event in Roanoke, Virginia," July 13, 2012, https://obamawhitehouse.archives.gov/the-press-office/2012 /07/13/remarks-president-campaign-event-roanoke-virginia.
2. Steve Peoples and Jim Kuhnhenn, "Romney Accuses Obama of Casting Shame on Success," *Boston.com*, July 17, 2012, http://archive.boston.com/news/politics/articles /2012/07/17/romney_on_attack_in_pa_obama_collects_texas_cash.
3. Hendrik Hertzberg, "We Built It," *New Yorker*, August 29, 2012, https://www .newyorker.com/news/hendrik-hertzberg/we-built-it.
4. "Transcript: Rep. Paul Ryan's Convention Speech," *National Public Radio*, August 29, 2012, https://www.npr.org/2012/08/29/160282031/transcript-rep-paul-ryans -convention-speech.
5. Aaron Blake, "Obama's 'You Didn't Build That' Problem," *Washington Post*, July 18, 2012, https://www.washingtonpost.com/blogs/the-fix/post/obamas-you-didnt-build -that-problem/2012/07/18/gJQAJxyotW_blog.html?utm_term=.58444b40c534.
6. Indeed, all social movements must balance the tensions between feeding a movement's popular strength but guarding its messaging and articulating its views to people in power.
7. Marc Hetherington, "Why Polarized Trust Matters," *The Forum* 13, no. 3 (2015): 445–58.
8. Marvin Olasky, *Compassionate Conservatism: What It Is, What It Does, and How It Can Transform America* (New York: Free Press, 2000). Notably, George W. Bush wrote the foreword to this book.
9. U.S. House of Representatives. Select Committee on Ethics, In the Matter of Representative Newt Gingrich, H Report 105-1, January 17, 1997, 10, https://www .congress.gov/congressional-report/105th-congress/house-report/1/1?s=1&r=13.
10. On this point (and the dubiousness of the public opinion claim), see Fay Lomax Cook, Jason Barabas, and Benjamin I. Page, "Policy Elites Invoke Public Opinion: Polls, Policy Debates, and the Future of Social Security," in *Navigating Public Opinion: Polls, Policy, and the Future of American Democracy*, ed. Jeff Manza, Fay Lomax Cook, and Benjamin I. Page (Oxford University Press, 2002), 141–70, 158.
11. Sidney M. Milkis and Jesse H. Rhodes, "George W. Bush, the Republican Party, and the 'New' American Party System," *Perspectives on Politics* 5, no. 3 (September 2007): 461–88, 472.
12. Richard B. Cheney, Oral History, March 16 and 17, 2000, Presidential Oral Histories, George H. W. Bush Presidency, Miller Center, University of Virginia, https:// millercenter.org/the-presidency/presidential-oral-histories/richard-b-cheney-oral -history-secretary-defense.
13. Barton Gellman, *Angler: The Cheney Vice-Presidency* (New York: Penguin, 2008), 105.

14. Chris Cillizza, "Why George W. Bush Was Right," *Washington Post*, January 31, 2013, https://www.washingtonpost.com/news/the-fix/wp/2013/01/31/why-george-w-bush-was-right-on-immigration/?utm_term=.6704e830e2e4.

15. On the importance of trust and legitimacy in the aftermath of the financial crisis, see Philip A. Wallach, *To the Edge: Legality, Legitimacy, and the Responses to the 2008 Financial Crisis* (Washington, D.C.: Brookings Institution, 2015).

16. President Barack Obama, "Inaugural Address," January 21, 2009, http://obamawhitehouse .archives.gov/blog/2009/01/21/president-barack-obamas-inaugural-address.

17. Robert Draper, *When the Tea Party Came to Town* (New York: Simon & Schuster, 2012), xii.

18. As Skocpol and Jacobs point out, the timing and conditions of the economic crash politically disadvantaged Obama compared to Franklin Roosevelt. Roosevelt came to power years after an economic crash, not as it was occurring, and the recovery Obama presided over did little to counter the skewed distribution of wealth and income. See Theda Skocpol and Lawrence R. Jacobs, "Reaching for a New Deal: Ambitious Governance, Economic Meltdown, and Polarized Politics," in *Reaching for a New Deal: Ambitious Governance, Economic Meltdown, and Polarized Politics in Obama's First Two Years*, ed. Theda Skocpol and Lawrence R. Jacobs (New York: Russell Sage Foundation, 2011), 1–50.

19. Texas Republican House member Jeb Hensarling claimed that the Bush administration had forced Republicans to "choose between financial meltdown on the one hand and taxpayer bankruptcy and the road to socialism on the other." In Carl Hulse, "Conservatives Viewed Bailout Plan as Last Straw," *New York Times*, September 26, 2008.

20. See, for example, Faiz Shakir, "Limbaugh: 'I Hope Obama Fails,'" *Think Progress*, January 20, 2009, https://thinkprogress.org/limbaugh-i-hope-obama-fails -83bde6a9780f.

21. Barack Obama, *A Promised Land* (New York: Crown, 2020), 263. See also Michael Grunwald, *The New New Deal: The Hidden Story of Change in the Obama Era* (New York: Simon & Schuster, 2012).

22. Theda Skocpol and Vanessa Williamson, *The Tea Party and the Remaking of Republican Conservatism* (New York: Oxford University Press 2012), 105.

23. On the Koch network, see Theda Skocpol and Alexander Hertel-Fernandez, "The Koch Network and Republican Party Extremism," *Perspectives on Politics* 14, no. 3 (2016): 681–99.

24. Christopher W. Schmidt, "Popular Constitutionalism on the Right: Lessons from the Tea Party," *Denver University Law Review* 88, no. 3 (2011): 523–57.

25. See Sean Wilenz, "Confounding Fathers: The Tea Party's Cold War Roots," *New Yorker*, October 11, 2010, https://www.newyorker.com/magazine/2010/10/18 /confounding-fathers; Jared A. Goldstein, "The Tea Party Movement and the Perils of Popular Originalism," *Arizona Law Review*, 53 (2011): 827–66, https://papers .ssrn.com/sol3/papers.cfm?abstract_id=1777466.

26. Kevin Arceneaux and Stephen P. Nicholson, "Who Wants to Have a Tea Party? The Who, What, and Why of the Tea Party Movement," *P.S. Political Science and Politics* 45 (October 2012): 700–10; Andrew J. Perrin, Steven J. Tepper, Neal Caren, and Sally Morris, "Political and Cultural Dimensions of Tea Party Support, 2009–2012," *Sociological Quarterly* 55 (2014): 625–52.; Daniel Tope, Justin T. Pickett, and Ted

Chiricos, "Anti-Minority Attitudes and Tea Party Movement Membership," *Social Science Research* 51 (2015): 322–37.

27. Christopher Parker, "Race and Politics in the Age of Obama," *Annual Review of Sociology* 42 (2016): 217–30, 225.

28. Rogers Smith, "Beyond Tocqueville, Myrdal, and Hartz: The Multiple Traditions in America," *American Political Science Review* 83 (1993): 549–66.

29. Arceneaux and Nicholson, "Who Wants to Have a Tea Party?," 704.

30. Bryan Gervais and Irwin L. Morris, *Reactionary Republicanism: How the Tea Party in the House Paved the Way for Trump's Victory* (New York: Oxford University Press, 2018), 25. See also Vanessa Williamson, Theda Skocpol, and John Coggin, "The Tea Party and the Remaking of Republican Conservatism," *Perspectives on Politics* 9 (March 2011): 25–43, 33.

31. Skocpol and Williamson, *The Tea Party and the Remaking of Republican Conservatism*, 56.

32. Sam Stein, "Newt Gingrich Slammed for Saying Obama May Hold 'Kenyan, Anti-Colonial' Worldview," *HuffingtonPost*, September 12, 2010.

33. Amy Gardner, "Gauging the Scope of the Tea Party Movement in America," *Washington Post*, October 24, 2010, https://www.washingtonpost.com/wp-dyn/content /article/2010/10/23/AR2010102304000.html; Jill LePore, *The Whites of Their Eyes: The Tea Party's Revolution and the Battle Over American History* (Princeton, N.J.: Princeton University Press, 2010); James P. Melcher and Amy Fried, "Tea Talk: The Rhetoric of Tea Party Governors" (paper presented at the New England Political Science Association Annual Meeting, Portsmouth, NH, 2012); and Skocpol and Williamson, *The Tea Party and the Remaking of Republican Conservatism*.

34. Francis B. Prior, "Quality Controlled: An Ethnographic Account of Tea Party Messaging and Action," *Sociological Forum* 29, no. 2 (June 2014): 301–17, 307.

35. Prior, "Quality Controlled," 309.

36. Christopher F. Karpowitz, J. Quin Monson, Kelly D. Patterson, and Jeremy C. Pope, "Tea Time in America? The Impact of the Tea Party Movement on the 2010 Midterm Elections," *P.S. Political Science and Politics* 44 (April 2011): 303–309, 303; Williamson, Skocpol, and Coggin, "The Tea Party and the Remaking of Republican Conservatism"; Perrin et al., "Political and Cultural Dimensions of Tea Party Support," 627.

37. Williamson, Skocpol, and Coggin "The Tea Party and the Remaking of Republican Conservatism;"; Perrin et al., "Political and Cultural Dimensions of Tea Party Support"; Jeff Nesbit, *Poison Tea: How Big Oil and Big Tobacco Invented the Tea Party and Captured the GOP* (New York: St. Martin's, 2016).

38. Williamson, Skocpol, and Coggin, "The Tea Party and the Remaking of Republican Conservatism"; Perrin et al., "Political and Cultural Dimensions of Tea Party Support"; Charles S. Bullock III and M. V. Hood, "The Tea Party, Sarah Palin, and the 2010 Congressional Elections: The Aftermath of the Election of Barack Obama," *Social Science Quarterly* 93 (2012): 1424–35; Karpowitz et al., "Tea Time in America? The Impact of the Tea Party Movement on the 2010 Midterm Elections."

39. Pew Research Center, "Trust in Government Nears Record Low, but Most Federal Agencies Are Viewed Favorably," October 18, 2013, https://www.people-press .org/2013/10/18/trust-in-government-nears-record-low-but-most-federal-agencies -are-viewed-favorably.

40. This is a point that we noted many years ago when we first noted these patterns in 1990s politics; Amy Fried and Douglas B. Harris, "On Red Capes and Charging Bulls: How and Why Conservative Politicians and Interest Groups Promoted Public Anger," in *What Is It About Government That Americans Dislike?*, ed. John R. Hibbing and Elizabeth Theiss-Morse (Cambridge: Cambridge University Press, 2001), 157–74.

41. Williamson, Skocpol, and Coggin, "The Tea Party and the Remaking of Republican Conservatism," 29.

42. Rachel M. Blum, *How the Tea Party Captured the GOP: Insurgent Factions in American Politics* (Chicago: University of Chicago Press, 2020), 31.

43. Jacob S. Hacker, "The Road to Somewhere: Why Health Reform Happened, or Why Political Scientists Who Write About Public Policy Shouldn't Assume They Know How to Shape It," *Perspectives on Politics* 8 (2010): 861–76; Jonathan Oberlander, "Long Time Coming: Why Health Reform Finally Passed," *Health Affairs* 29 (2010): 1112–16; Paul Starr, *Remedy and Reaction: The Peculiar American Struggle Over Health Care Reform* (New Haven: Yale University Press, 2011).

44. Richard Kirsch, *Fighting for Our Health: The Epic Battle to Make Health Care a Right in the United States* (Albany, N.Y.: Rockefeller Institute Press, 2012); Marc Stier, *Grassroots Advocacy and Health Care Reform* (New York: Palgrave Macmillan, 2013). Health Care for America Now (HCAN) served as a coalition for passing the Affordable Care Act. They framed the choice as between profit-seeking insurance companies and patients and, according to them, "ran an unprecedented field program of 1,000 groups in 50 states representing 30 million people" and "complemented the work on the ground with paid advertising and an aggressive earned media program." See "Health Care for America Now," accessed August 8, 2018, http://healthcareforamericanow.org/about/history.

45. Oberlander, "Long Time Coming: Why Health Reform Finally Passed," 1113.

46. Mollyann Brodie, Drew Altman, Claudia Deane, Sasha Buscho, and Elizabeth Hamel, "Liking the Pieces, Not the Package: Contradictions in Public Opinion During Health Reform," *Health Affairs* 29 (2010): 1125–30, 1126.

47. Frank Luntz, "The Language of Healthcare 2009," http://www.politico.com/pdf /PPM116_luntz.pdf). Subsequent quotes from Luntz are to this source unless otherwise noted. Mike Allen noted that Luntz was "involved in creating much of the language Republican lawmakers used from 1994 through 2004, but was tossed out by the House leadership in 2005. One of his successes was popularizing the phrase 'death tax' for "inheritance tax"; Mike Allen "Frank Luntz Warns GOP: Health Reform Is Popular," *Politico*, May 5, 2009, http://www.politico.com/news /stories/0509/22155.html.

48. U.S. House of Representatives, 111th Congress. First Session. *Congressional Record*, Vol. 155, No. 100. July 7, 2009, H7727-7728.

49. U.S. House of Representatives, 111th Congress. First Session. *Congressional Record*, Vol. 155, No. 107. July 16, 2009, H8274.

50. U.S. House of Representatives, 111th Congress, Second Session. *Congressional Record*, Vol. 156, No. 30. March 4, 2010, H1107.

51. The evolution of this misinformation is elaborated in Brendan Nyhan's "Why the 'Death Panel' Myth Wouldn't Die," *Forum* 8, no. 1 (2010): 6–10.

52. Sarah Palin, "Statement on the Current Health Care Debate," Facebook, August 7, 2009, https://www.facebook.com/note.php?note_id=113851103434.

53. Quoted by Starr, *Remedy and Reaction*, 212.
54. Brian Montopoli, "Grassley Warns of Government Pulling Plug 'On Grandma,'" *CBS News*, August 12, 2009, http://www.cbsnews.com/news/grassley-warns-of-government -pulling-plug-on-grandma.
55. Quoted by Starr, *Remedy and Reaction*, 212–13.
56. Brodie et al., "Liking the Pieces, Not the Package: Contradictions in Public Opinion During Health Reform," 1126.
57. Daniel J. Hopkins, "The Exaggerated Life of Death Panels: The Limits of Framing Effects in the 2009–2012 Health Care Debate," 2013, https://papers.ssrn.com/sol3 /papers.cfm?abstract_id=2163769.
58. James N. Druckman, Jordan Fein, and Thomas J. Leeper, "A Source of Bias in Public Opinion Stability," *American Political Science Review* 106 (2012): 430–54.
59. Nyhan, "Why the 'Death Panel' Myth Wouldn't Die," 16.
60. Nyhan, "Why the 'Death Panel' Myth Wouldn't Die."
61. Glenn Kessler, "Sarah Palin, 'Death Panels' and 'Obamacare,'" *Washington Post*, June 27, 2012; Jason Millman, "It's Time to Bury the 'Death Panel' Myth for Good. Is This the Way to Do It?," *Wonkblog* (blog),*Washington Post*, September 17, 2014, http://www.washingtonpost.com/blogs/wonkblog/wp/2014/09/17/its-time-to -bury-the-death-panel-myth-for-good-is-this-the-way-to-do-it.
62. David M. Frankford, "The Remarkable Staying Power of 'Death Panels,'" *Journal Of Health Politics, Policy & Law* 40 (2015): 1083–95, 1085–86.
63. Obama, *A Promised Land*, chapter 17.
64. Amy E. Lerman, Meredith L. Sadin, and Samuel Trachtman, "Policy Uptake as Political Behavior: Evidence from the Affordable Care Act," *American Political Science Review* 111, no. 4 (2017): 755–70.
65. Andrea Louise Campbell, "Policy Feedbacks and the Impact of Policy Designs on Public Opinion," *Journal of Health Politics, Policy & Law* 36 (2011): 961–73, 966.
66. Skocpol and Williamson, *The Tea Party and the Remaking of Republican Conservatism*, 60.
67. Gareth Davies and Martha Derthick, "Race and Social Welfare Policy: The Social Security Act of 1935," *Political Science Quarterly* 112 (1997): 217–35; Lisa Disch, "The Tea Party: A 'White Citizenship Movement?,'" in *Steep: The Precipitous Rise of the Tea Party*, ed. Lawrence Rosenthal and Christine Trost (Berkeley: University of California Press, 2012), 133–51; Michael Henderson and D. Sunshine Hillygus, "The Dynamics of Health Care Opinion, 2008—2010: Partisanship, Self-Interest, and Racial Resentment," *Journal of Health Politics, Policy & Law* 36 (2011): 945–60; Ira Katznelson, *Fear Itself: The New Deal and the Origins of Our Time* (New York: Norton & Company, 2013); Douglas L. Kriner and Andrew Reeves, "Responsive Partisanship: Public Support for the Clinton and Obama Health Care Plans," *Journal of Health Politics, Policy and Law* 39 (2014): 717–49; Michael Tesler, *Post-Racial or Most Racial: Race and Politics in the Obama Era* (Chicago: University of Chicago Press, 2016); Nicholas J. G. Winter, "Beyond Welfare: Framing and the Racialization of White Opinion on Social Security," *American Journal of Political Science* 50 (2006): 400–20.
68. Martha Shanahan, "5 Memorable Moments When Town Hall Meetings Turned to Rage," *National Public Radio: It's All Politics*, August 7, 2013, http://www.npr.org/sections/its allpolitics/2013/08/07/209919206/5-memorable-moments-when-town-hall-meetings -turned-to-rage.

69. Patricia Antsett and Kathleen Gray, "Tempers Flare Over Health Care Plan," *Detroit Free Press*, August 7, 2009.
70. Kirsch, *Fighting for Our Health*, 199.
71. Ian Urbina, "Beyond Beltway, Health Debate Turns Hostile," *New York Times*, August 7, 2009, A1. The pro-ACA group Health Care for America Now, in coalition with other groups, organized supporters of the health reform law to attend town meetings as well; see Kirsch, *Fighting for Our Health*.
72. Daniel P. Gitterman and John C. Scott, " 'Obama Lies, Grandma Dies': The Uncertain Politics of Medicare and the Patient Protection and Affordable Care Act," *Journal of Health Politics Policy and Law*, 36 (2011): 555–63, 555.
73. Kirsch, *Fighting for Our Health*, 201.
74. Caitlin Duffy, *Vilifying Obamacare: Conservative Tropes of Victimage in the 2009 Health Care Debates* (M.A. thesis, Wake Forest University, 2013).
75. Lawrence Rosenthal and Christine Trost, *Steep: The Precipitous Rise of the Tea Party* (Berkeley: University of California Press, 2012), 11–12.
76. Thomas E. Mann, "American Politics on the Eve of the Mid-term Elections: Fall from Grace," *World Today* 66, no. 11 (November 2010): 20–22, 21.
77. Gary C. Jacobson, for one, attributes the rise of conservative opposition to Obama to the McCain–Palin campaign's efforts to capitalize on Obama's name, background, and associations, which, Jacobson claims, were "bound to vibrate the racist, xenophobic, anti-intellectual, and anti-elitist as well as antiliberal strands woven into the fabric of right win populist thinking"; Gary C. Jacobson, "Legislative Success and Political Failure: The Public's Reaction to Barack Obama's Early Presidency" *Presidential Studies Quarterly* 41, no. 2 (June 2011): 220–43 223.
78. Skocpol and Jacobs, "Reaching for a New Deal," 21.
79. Ken Blackwell and Ken Klukowski, *The Blueprint: Obama's Plan to Subvert the Constitution and Build an Imperial Presidency* (Guilford, CT: Lyons Press, 2010), 26–27.
80. Anita Dunn, "The Truth About 'Czars,' " September 16, 2009, https://www.whitehouse.gov/blog/2009/09/16/truth-about-czars.
81. Jake Sherman, "Bachmann Forms Tea Party Caucus," *Politico*, July 16, 2010, https://www.politico.com/story/2010/07/bachmann-forms-tea-party-caucus-039848; Mara Liasson, "Tea Party: It's Not Just Taxes, It's the Constitution," *National Public Radio*, July 14, 2010, https://www.npr.org/templates/story/story.php?storyId=128517427.
82. Gervais and Morris, *Reactionary Republicanism*, 180.
83. Jacobson, "Legislative Success and Political Failure," 230.
84. Gervais and Morris, *Reactionary Republicanism*, 56–57.
85. But, as E. J. Dionne wrote, "The book contained no second thoughts about policies and actions that had plainly hurt the Republicans in 2006 and 2008: the Iraq War, the Schiavo case, the handling of Hurricane Katrina, the tax cuts and the other economic policies that ended in the Great Recession"; E. J. Dionne *How the Right Went Wrong* (New York: Simon & Shuster, 2016), 234.
86. Eric Cantor in Eric Cantor, Paul Ryan, and Kevin McCarthy, *Young Guns: A New Generation of Conservative Leaders* (New York: Threshold Editions, 2010), 20.
87. Kevin McCarthy, in Cantor, Ryan, and McCarthy, *Young Guns*, 172.
88. Thomas E. Mann and Norman J. Ornstein, *It's Even Worse Than It Looks: How the American Constitutional System Collided with the New Politics of Extremism* (New York: Basic Books, 2012), 10.

89. Paul Ryan's comments in the roundtable, in Cantor, Ryan, and McCarthy, *Young Guns*, 6.

90. Paul Ryan, in Cantor, Ryan, and McCarthy, *Young Guns*, 122.

91. Kevin McCarthy in the roundtable, in Cantor, Ryan, and McCarthy, *Young Guns*, 11.

92. Chris Good's interview with Hecker was printed in "How the Contract from America Got Started," *Atlantic*, April 16, 2010, https://www.theatlantic.com/politics /archive/2010/04/how-the-contract-from-america-got-started/39028.

93. The document was reprinted in Chris Good, "Tea Partiers Release Document of Principles," *Atlantic* April 14, 2010, https://www.theatlantic.com/politics/archive /2010/04/tea-partiers-release-document-of-principles/38922.

94. "A Pledge to America," https://www.washingtonpost.com/wp-srv/politics/documents /GOP_pledge_09222010.pdf.

95. Angie Maxwell and T. Wayne Parent, "The Obama Trigger: Presidential Approval and Tea Party Membership," *Social Science Quarterly* 93, no. 5 (December 2014): 1384–1401, 1398. With conservative antigovernment rhetoric a perennial force in American political thought that various movements have tapped into, to the extent that the Tea Party was motivated and unified merely by anti-Obama sentiment, its cohesiveness and force was likely to "wane after President Obama leaves office" (1398).

96. The Tea Party breakdown seemed quite important to the voting, even in the Rubio–Crist race. "Rubio got 86 percent support from those who said they sup-ported the Tea Party (40 percent of voters) and 44 percent from voters who were neutral to the Tea Party (24 percent). Crist gained 55 percent of the voters who opposed the Tea Party while Meek got support from 39 percent of those voters (32 percent of the total). While those who supported the Tea Party overwhelmingly voted for Rubio, 61 percent of exit poll respondents said that the Tea Party was not a factor in their overall vote decision"; Sean D. Foreman, "Florida Senate Race (Crist v. Meek v. Rubio): The Rise of Rubio and Fall of Crist," in *The Roads to Congress 2010*, ed. Sean D. Foreman and Robert Dewhirst (Lanham, Md.: Lexington Books, 2011), 222–23.

97. Robert G. Boatright, *Getting Primaried: The Changing Politics of Congressional Primary Challenges* (Ann Arbor: University of Michigan Press, 2013), 180, 183, 203.

98. Boatright, *Getting Primaried*, 6; John Sides, Michael Tesler, and Lynn Vavreck, *Identity Crisis: The 2016 Presidential Campaign and the Battle for the Meaning of America* (Princeton, N.J.: Princeton University Press, 2018), 38; Boatright, "The 2014 Congressional Primaries in Context" (paper presented at the Campaign Finance Institute and the Brookings Institution, September 30, 2014), 10–11.

99. Maxwell and Parent, "The Obama Trigger," 1390.

100. Jacobson, "Legislative Success and Political Failure," 240; Gary C. Jacobson, "The Republican Resurgence in 2010," *Political Science Quarterly* 126, no. 1 (Spring 2011): 27–52, 34–35.

101. For a brief description of these races, see Congressional Quarterly, *Congress and the Nation 2009–2012: Politics and Policy in the 111th and 112th Congresses*, ed. Dave Tarr (Washington, D.C.: Sage/CQ Press, 2014), 24–25.

102. Congressional Quarterly, *Congress and the Nation*, 22.

103. Jacobson, "Legislative Success and Political Failure," 239, 234.

104. Congressional Quarterly, *Congress and the Nation*, 23.
105. Alan I. Abramowitz, "Expect Confrontation, Not Compromise: The 112th House of Representatives Is Likely to Be the Most Conservative and Polarized House in the Modern Era," *P.S. Political Science and Politics* 44, no. 2 (April 2011): 293–295, 293.
106. All three are quoted in Andy Barr, "The GOP's No-Compromise Pledge," *Politico*, October 28, 2010.
107. Jacobson, "The Republican Resurgence in 2010," 38.
108. Thomas E. Mann and Norman J. Ornstein, *It's Even Worse Than It Looks*, xxii.
109. Dick Armey, "Stay True to Principle, Constitution," *Politico*, January 18, 2011, https://www.politico.com/story/2011/01/stay-true-to-principle-constitution-047697.
110. Schmidt, "Popular Constitutionalism on the Right: Lessons from the Tea Party," 542–44.
111. "House's 63rd Attempt to Dismantle Obamacare Fails Also," *Newsweek*, February 2, 2016, https://www.newsweek.com/houses-63rd-attempt-dismantle-obamacare-fails-also-422418.
112. Mann and Ornstein, *It's Even Worse Than It Looks*, 82, 187, 213.
113. Robert Draper, "How Kevin McCarthy Wrangles the Tea Party in Washington," *New York Times*, July 13, 2011, https://www.nytimes.com/2011/07/17/magazine/how-kevin-mccarthy-wrangles-the-tea-party.html.
114. These quotations are from Senator Chuck Hagel and Republican congressional staff member Mike Lofgren; both are quoted in Mann and Ornstein, *It's Even Worse Than It Looks*, 54.
115. Gervais and Morris, *Reactionary Republicanism*, 185.
116. Mann and Ornstein, *It's Even Worse Than It Looks*, 218.
117. Sides, Tesler, and Vavreck, *Identity Crisis*, 38–39.
118. Leigh A. Bradberry and Gary C. Jacobson, "The Tea Party and the 2012 Presidential Election," *Electoral Studies* 40 (2014): 1–9, 3.
119. Bradberry and Jacobson, "The Tea Party and the 2012 Presidential Election," 8.
120. "The 2012 Republican Platform, August 27, 2012," online by Gerhard Peters and John T. Woolley, *American Presidency Project*, accessed September 15, 2015, https://www.presidency.ucsb.edu/documents/2012-republican-party-platform.
121. Dick Morris and Eileen McGann, *Power Grab: Obama's Dangerous Plan for a One-Party Nation* (West Palm Beach, FL: Humanix, 2014).
122. "The 1992 Republican Party Platform," August 17, 1992, online by Gerhard Peters and John T. Woolley, *American Presidency Project*, https://www.presidency.ucsb.edu/node/273439.
123. "The 2012 Republican Party Platform."
124. Juraj Medzihorsky, Levente Littvay, and Erin K. Jenne, "Has the Tea Party Era Radicalized the Republican Party? Evidence from Text Analysis of the 2008 and 2012 Republican Primary Debates," *P.S. Political Science and Politics* (October 2014): 806–12, 807.
125. Gary C. Jacobson, "How the Economy and Partisanship Shaped the 2012 Presidential and Congressional Elections," *Political Science Quarterly* 128, no. 1 (Spring 2013): 1–28, 10.
126. Bradberry and Jacobson, "The Tea Party and the 2012 Presidential Election," 4.
127. Jacobson, "How the Economy and Partisanship Shaped the 2012 Presidential and Congressional Elections," 31.

128. Republican National Committee, *Growth and Opportunity Project*, 2013, https://assets.documentcloud.org/documents/623664/republican-national-committees-growth-and.pdf.

129. See Grace Wyler, "The GOP's Plan To Save Itself Involves Destroying Grassroots Conservatives," *Business Insider*, March 18, 2013, https://www.businessinsider.com/rnc-paul-tea-party-grassroots-gop-autopsy-2013-3; Thomas B. Edsall, "The Republican Autopsy Report," *New York Times*, March 20, 2013, https://opinionator.blogs.nytimes.com/2013/03/20/the-republican-autopsy-report.

130. Tim Alberta, *American Carnage: On the Front Lines of the Republican Civil War and the Rise of President Trump* (New York: Harper, 2019), 161, 162–63; Seung Min Kim, "Senate Passes Immigration Bill," *Politico*, June 27, 2013, https://www.politico.com/story/2013/06/immigration-bill-2013-senate-passes-093530.

131. Lauren Cohen Bell, David Elliot Meyer, and Ronald Keith Gaddie, *Slingshot: The Defeat of Eric Cantor* (Washington, D.C.: CQ Press, 2015), 85–86, 101.

132. Matthew N. Green, *Legislative Hardball: The House Freedom Caucus and the Power of Threat-Making in Congress* (New York: Cambridge University Press, 2019), 10.

133. Green, *Legislative Hardball*, 9.

134. "Speaker Boehner Resigns from Congress, Victory for Tea Party," *Chicago Tribune*, September 25, 2015; see also Jay Newton-Small, "House Speaker John Boehner Calls It Quits," *Time*, September 25, 2015.

135. Green, *Legislative Hardball*, 43–45.

136. Todd S. Purdum, "The Cannibal Party: Being a GOP House Speaker Might Be the Worst Job in Washington," *Politico Magazine*, September 2015, https://www.politico.com/magazine/story/2015/09/boehner-resignation-house-speaker-history-213193.

137. Mike DeBonis, Robert Costa, and Rosalind S. Helderman, "House Majority Leader Kevin McCarthy Drops Out of Race for House Speaker," *Washington Post*, October 8, 2015; the letter, reprinted by the *Post*, is from Walter B. Jones to conference chair Cathy McMorris Rodgers, dated October 6, 2015. On some of the speculation here, see Matthew Yglesias, "The Affair Allegations That Derailed Kevin McCarthy's Quest for the Speakership, Explained," *Vox*, October 9, 2015, https://www.vox.com/2015/10/9/9488323/mccarthy-ellmers-affair.

138. For more on this race and on speakership challenges, see Matthew N. Green and Douglas B. Harris, *Choosing the Leader: Leadership Elections in the U.S. House of Representatives* (New Haven: Yale University Press, 2019).

139. Green, *Legislative Hardball*, 46; Green and Harris, *Choosing the Leader*, 26–27.

140. Jennifer Steinhauer, "Paul Ryan Faces Tea Party Forces That He Helped Unleash," *New York Times*, March 2, 2016.

141. Tony Badger, "The Lessons of the New Deal: Did Obama Learn the Right Ones?," *History* 97, no. 1 (January 2012): 99–114, 113.

142. Jacobson, "The Republican Resurgence in 2010," 33–34.

143. Geoffrey M. Kabaservice, *Rule and Ruin: The Downfall of Moderation and the Destruction of the Republican Party, from Eisenhower to the Tea Party* (New York: Oxford University Press, 2012).

144. John Gerring, *Party Ideologies in America, 1828–1996* (New York: Cambridge University Press, 1998), 143, 145.

145. Mann and Ornstein, *It's Even Worse Than It Looks*.

146. Colleen M. Grogan and Sunggeun (Ethan) Park, "The Racial Divide in State Medicaid Expansions," *Journal of Health Politics Policy and Law* 42 (2017): 539–72.
147. Indeed, given the advanced average age of the Tea Party members and their consistent conservatism, it is to be expected that most of them, individually, have switched commitments on whether the Congress or the President should be dominant as partisan realities in Washington have changed over the last decades.

6. "PUNCH GOVERNMENT IN THE FACE": ANGER IN THE TRUMP ERA

1. United States of America v. Internet Research Agency LLC, et al., Case 1:18-cr -OOO32 DLC, 12.
2. United States of America v. Internet Research Agency, 6.
3. Special Counsel Robert S. Mueller III, *Report on the Investigation Into Russian Interference in the 2016 Presidential Election* (Washington, D.C.: U.S. Department of Justice, March 2019), 4 (hereafter, Mueller Report).
4. United States of America v. Internet Research Agency, 14.
5. *(U) Report of the Select Committee on Intelligence United States Senate on Russian Active Measures Campaigns and Interference in the 2016 U.S. Election*, Volume 5, *Counterintelligence Threats and Vulnerabilities*, vii. United States Senate, 116th Congress, 2020. See also Renee DiRest, Kris Shaffer, Becky Ruppel, David Sullivan, Robert Matney, Ryan Fox, Jonathan Albright, and Ben Johnson, "The Tactics & Tropes of the Internet Research Agency," *New Knowledge*, 2018.
6. United States of America v. Internet Research Agency, 17; this is also in the Mueller Report, 23.
7. Kathleen Hall Jamieson, *Cyberwar: How Russian Hackers and Trolls Helped Elect a President: What We Don't, Can't, and Do Know* (New York: Oxford University Press, 2018).
8. Theda Skocpol and Vanessa Williamson, *The Tea Party and the Remaking of Republican Conservatism* (New York: Oxford University Press, 2012).
9. The press release, entitled "Donald J. Trump Statement on Preventing Muslim Immigration," was covered widely, including in Rebecca Shabad, "Donald Trump Calls for 'Total and Complete Shutdown' of Muslims Entering U.S.," *CBS News*, December 7, 2015, https://www.cbsnews.com/news/donald-trump-calls-for-total-and -complete-shutdown-of-muslims-entering-u-s/.
10. Aaron Blake, "Trump Tries to Re-write His Own History on Charlottesville and 'Both Sides,' " *Washington Post*, April 26, 2019, https://www.washingtonpost.com /politics/2019/04/25/meet-trump-charlottesville-truthers.
11. We explore Trump's use of this strategy in 2016 and examine early signs of its use in 2020 in "In Suspense: Donald Trump's Efforts to Undermine Public Trust in Democracy," *Society* 57 (October 2020): 527–33.
12. Michael D. Shear, "Trump Reacts to Cohen Raid, Syria and More: An Annotated Transcript," *New York Times*, April 9, 2018, https://www.nytimes.com/2018/04/09 /us/politics/trump-cohen-mueller-full-transcript.html.
13. Shear, "Trump Reacts to Cohen Raid."

14. See Philip Rucker and Robert Costa, "Bannon Vows a Daily Fight for 'Decon-struction of the Administrative State,'" *Washington Post*, February 23, 2017, https://www.washingtonpost.com/politics/top-wh-strategist-vows-a-daily-fight-for-deconstruction-of-the-administrative-state/2017/02/23/03f6b8da-f9ea-11e6-bf01-d47f8cf9b643_story.html.

15. Donald P. Moynihan, "Populism and the Deep State: The Attack on Public Service Under Trump," May 21, 2020, 9, https://ssrn.com/abstract=3607309 or http://dx.doi.org/10.2139/ssrn.3607309.

16. Joseph Fishkin and David E. Pozen, "Asymmetric Constitutional Hardball," *Columbia Law Review* 118 (2018): 915–82, 923.

17. President Donald J. Trump (@realdonaldtrump), "An 'extremely credible source' has called my office and told me that @BarackObama's birth certificate is a fraud." Twitter, August 6, 2012, 4:23:00 p.m. Using scare quotes in deeming the source "extremely credible," Trump seemed to have tipped his hand about the question-able veracity of the discredited and illogical birther claim.

18. The question posed was: "Do you think people who actively and publicly question whether Barack Obama was truly born in the United States are just nutty con-spiracy theorists, or do you think there is cause to wonder where he was born and its important enough to justify their actions" ($N = 914$ registered voters ±3 percent), Fox News Poll, Anderson Robbins Research/Shaw & Company Research, April 3–5, 2011, https://www.foxnews.com/projects/pdf/FoxNews_Poll_ObamaBirth.pdf.

19. Philip Klinkner, "The Causes and Consequences of 'Birtherism,'" (paper presented at the 2014 Annual Meeting of the Western Political Science Association), 4, http://www.wpsanet.org/papers/docs/Birthers.pdf.

20. Joshua Green, *Devil's Bargain: Steve Bannon, Donald Trump, and the Storming of the Presidency* (New York: Penguin, 2017), 106.

21. Rachel M. Blum. *How the Tea Party Captured the GOP: Insurgent Factions in American Politics* (Chicago: University of Chicago Press, 2020), 105

22. "Here's Donald Trump's Presidential Announcement Speech," *Time*, June 16, 2015, https://time.com/3923128/donald-trump-announcement-speech.

23. "Here's Donald Trump's Presidential Announcement Speech."

24. Benjy Sarlin, "GOP Rivals Accuse Donald Trump of Encouraging Violence at Rallies," *Time*, March 12, 2016. https://www.nbcnews.com/politics/2016-election/gop-rivals-accuse-donald-trump-encouraging-violence-rallies-n537101.

25. See Garrett Epps, "Ted Cruz is a Natural-Born Citizen," *Atlantic*, January 14, 2016, https://www.theatlantic.com/politics/archive/2016/01/donald-trump-ted-cruz-birther-argument/424104. On Rubio, see Janell Ross, "Marco Rubio Now Faces Donald Trump's All-Too-Predictable Birther Blueprint," *Washington Post*, February 22, 2016, https://www.washingtonpost.com/news/the-fix/wp/2016/02/22/marco-rubio-now-faces-donald-trumps-all-too-predictable-birther-blueprint.

26. Marc Hetherington, "Trust in Trump Comes from Lack of Trust in Government," *Brookings FixGov* (blog), September 16, 2015, https://www.brookings.edu/blog/fixgov/2015/09/16/trust-in-trump-comes-from-lack-of-trust-in-government.

27. Trent Franks, as quoted in Tim Alberta, *American Carnage: On the Front Lines of the Republican Civil War and the Rise of President Trump* (New York: HarperCollins, 2019), 345.

28. Trump's ability to win the nomination (and the surprising success of Bernie Sanders' insurgency) revealed how porous American national parties have become. Reforms dating back as far back as the Progressive Era that weakened political parties' control over the nomination of candidates coupled with reforms of the 1960s and 1970s at the presidential level that weakened conventions and democratized party nominations made it possible for insurgent candidates to express rank-and-file voter dissatisfactions and to drive deeply into the nominating process. If John McCain was sometimes a maverick and Mitt Romney was an "electable" if moderate alternative, Trump was open in articulating an antiestablishment message that included the Republican Party apparatus.

29. President Donald J. Trump (@realdonaldtrump), "Jeb Bush had a tough night at the debate. Now he'll probably take some of his special interest money, he is their puppet, and buy ad's," Twitter, December 16, 2015, 10:20:57 a.m. Here and throughout, we relied on the searchable database of the Trump Twitter Archive: https://www.thetrumparchive.com/.

30. President Donald J. Turmp (@realdonaldtrump), "Everybody is laughing at Jeb Bush-spent $100 million and is at bottom of pack. A pathetic figure!" Twitter, February 8, 2016, 11:38:00 a.m.; "Poor @JebBush spent $50 million on his campaign, I spent almost nothing. He's bottom (and gone), I'm top (by a lot). That's what U.S. needs!" Twitter, December 24, 2015, 3:10:14 p.m.; "So, I have spent almost nothing on my run for president and am in 1st place. Jeb Bush has spent $59 million & done. Run country my way!" Twitter, December 29, 2015, 9:39:30 a.m.; "I would feel sorry for @JebBush and how badly he is doing with his campaign other than for the fact he took millions of $'s of hit ads on me," Twitter, December 31, 2015, 10:07:18 a.m.; "@JebBush is a low energy 'stiff' who should focus his special interest money on the many people ahead of him in the polls. Has no chance!" Twitter, January 2, 2016, 7:17:12 a.m.; "Low energy candidate @JebBush has wasted $80 million on his failed presidential campaign. Millions spent on me. He should go home and relax!" Twitter, January 21, 2016, 9:32:57 a.m.; and "After spending $89 million, @JebBush is at the bottom of the barrel in polls. He is ashamed to use the name 'Bush' in ads. Low energy guy!" Twitter, January 22, 2016, 10:42:18 a.m.

31. President Donald J. Trump (@realdonaldtrump), Twitter, February 3, 2016, 08:47:33 a.m.

32. President Donald J. Trump (@realdonaldtrump), Twitter, February 3, 2016, 09:10:53 a.m.; President Donald J. Trump (@realdonaldtrump), "Based on the fraud committed by Senator Ted Cruz during the Iowa Caucus, either a new election should take place or Cruz results nullified," Twitter, February 3, 2016, 09:28:59 a.m.; President Donald J. Trump (@realdonaldtrump), "The State of Iowa should disqualify Ted Cruz from the most recent election on the baiss that he cheated- a total fraud!" Twitter, February 3, 2016, 02:25:08 p.m.

33. Joshua J. Dyck, Shanna Pearson-Merkowitz, and Michael Coates, "Primary Distrust: Political Distrust and Support for the Insurgent Candidacies of Donald Trump and Bernie Sanders in the 2016 Primary," PS: Political Science and Politics 51, no. 2 (April 2018): 351–357, 353. "Feeling" thermometer evaluations of Trump also revealed a substantial difference between "trusters," who were more likely to rate Rubio and Cruz (an average of the two) 8 points higher than Trump, while "distrusters" rated Trump 15 points higher than Rubio/Cruz (355).

34. Donald J. Trump(@realdonaldtrump), "Just watched @marcorubio on television. Just another all talk, no action politician. Truly doesn't have a clue! Worst voting record in Sen." Twitter, September 24, 2015, 10:23:41 p.m. "Lightweight Marco Rubio was working hard last night. The problem is, he is a choker, and once a choker, always a choker! Mr. Meltdown.," Twitter, February 26, 2016, 11:38:36 a.m.; Little Marco Rubio, the lightweight no show Senator from Florida is just another Washington politican," Twitter, " February 26, 2016, 12:50:23 p.m.; "Fraud lightweight Marco made a TV ad on TrumpU featuring 2 people who signed these letters: https://t.co/sSpFBn6Rux https://t.co/KFmotmqfnN," Twitter, March 6, 2016, 12:32:42 p.m.
35. President Donald J. Trump (@realdonaldtrump), Twitter, March 12, 2016, 01:06:24 p.m.
36. Even in the 2016 platform's preamble, the GOP expressed the party's belief "in the Constitution as our founding document" and stated that "the Constitution was not written as a flexible document, but as our enduring covenant." See Republican Party Platforms, 2016 Republican Party Platform Online by Gerhard Peters and John T. Woolley, The American Presidency Project, https://www.presidency.ucsb.edu/node/318311.
37. Republican objections to the unilateral use of presidential power were not limited to domestic policy. The GOP also raised objections to executive agreements replacing Senate-approved treaties as the modus operandi of the executive branch, proclaiming that "a new Republican executive will work with the Congress to reestablish constitutional order in America's foreign relations. All international executive agreements and political arrangements entered into by the current Administration must be deemed null and void as mere expressions of the current president's preferences"; 2016 Republican Party Platform.
38. Similarly, they claimed that Obama's National Labor Relations Board had become "patronizing and controlling," leaving "workers in a form of peonage to the NLRB"; 2016 Republican Party Platform.
39. Republicans also devoted considerable attention to well-worn conservative objections to an "activist judiciary." Using dire language, the GOP claimed: "an activist judiciary that usurps power properly reserved to the people through other branches of government" was a "critical threat" and a "national crisis" that could only be addressed by having a Republican president "to fill [existing and anticipated] vacancies on the [Supreme] Court" as well as congressional action "to use the check of impeachment for judges who unconstitutionally usurp Article I powers"; 2016 Republican Party Platform.
40. Republican Party Platforms, 2016 Republican Party Platform Online by Gerhard Peters and John T. Woolley, The American Presidency Project, https://www.presidency.ucsb.edu/node/318311.
41. Ed O'Keefe, "Dozens of GOP Delegates Launch New Push to Halt Donald Trump," *Washington Post*, June 17, 2016, https://www.washingtonpost.com/politics/dozens-of-gop-delegates-launch-new-push-to-halt-donald-trump/2016/06/17/e8dcf74e-3491-11e6-8758-d58e76e11b12_story.html; Patrick Healy and Jonathan Martin, "Ted Cruz Stirs Convention Fury in Pointed Snub of Donald Trump," *New York Times*, July 20, 2016, https://www.nytimes.com/2016/07/21/us/politics/ted-cruz-donald-trump-mike-pence-rnc.html.
42. Stephen Collinson, Tal Kopan, and Tom LoBianco, "Convention Drama: Trump Campaign Stops Rules Rebellion," CNN, July18, 2020, https://www.cnn.com/2016/07/18/politics/rnc-procedural-votes-rules-committee/index.html.

43. Craig Allen Smith, " 'I Alone' vs. 'Stronger Together': Contrasting Visions in the 2016 Nomination Acceptance Address," *American Behavioral Scientist* 61 (2017): 966–85, 973.
44. Smith, " 'I Alone' vs. 'Stronger Together,' " 973.
45. Dan Roberts, "Dump Trump? Paul Ryan Leaves Door Open to Republican Convention Revolt," *Guardian*, June 19, 2016, https://www.theguardian.com/us-news/2016 /jun/19/paul-ryan-donald-trump-republican-convention.
46. Ezra Klein, "Donald Trump's Success Reveals a Frightening Weakness in American Democracy," *Vox*, November 7, 2016, http://www.vox.com/policy-and-politics/2016 /11/7/13532178/donald-trump-american-democracy-weakness.
47. Klein, "Donald Trump's Success Reveals a Frightening Weakness in American Democracy."
48. Ella Nilsen, "The Mueller Indictments Reveal the Timing of the DNC Leak Was Intentional," *Vox*, July 13, 2018, https://www.vox.com/2018/7/13/17569030/mueller -indictments-russia-hackers-bernie-sanders-hillary-clinton-democratic-national -convention.
49. "Trump Addresses Media in Florida; Trump: I Hope Russia Can Find Clinton's E-Mails," press conference transcript, *CNN*, July 27, 2016, http://transcripts.cnn .com/TRANSCRIPTS/1607/27/ath.02.html
50. Mueller Report, 49.
51. Mueller Report, 54.
52. United States of America v. Internet Research Agency, 17.
53. Mueller Report, 22.
54. Mueller Report, 14.
55. Mueller Report, 33.
56. Mueller Report, 33–34.
57. Mueller Report, 48.
58. Mueller Report, 136, 7.
59. Mueller Report, 141.
60. Michael Zoorob and Theda Skocpol, "The Overlooked Organizational Basis of Trump's 2016 Victory," in *Upending American Politics: Polarizing Parties, Ideological Elites, and Citizen Activists from the Tea Party to the Anti-Trump Resistance*, ed. Theda Skocpol and Caroline Tervo (New York: Oxford University Press, 2020), 96, 97.
61. He had done this earlier in his candidacy as well. In fall 2015 (several months before the first 2016 primary), Trump asserted that finding a replacement for the ACA could be done easily and inexpensively. He told an interviewer there were "many different ways to fix it . . . Everybody's got to be covered. This is an un-Republican thing for me to say." Trump asserted, "I am going to take care of everybody . . . Everybody's going to be taken care of much better than they're taken care of now." When asked how people would receive coverage, he replied, "I would make a deal with existing hospitals to take care of people." When queried who would pay health-care costs, Trump replied, "the government's gonna pay for it. But we're going to save so much money on the other side. But for the most it's going to be a private plan and people are going to be able to go out and negotiate great plans with lots of different competition with lots of competitors with great companies and they can have their doctors, they can have plans, they can have

everything." Donald Trump, interview by Scott Pelley, *60 Minutes*, September 27, 2015, https://www.cbsnews.com/news/donald-trump-60-minutes-scott-pelley.

62. "Trump: Repealing And Replacing Obamacare Is Going To Be 'So Easy,'" video clip posted on October 25, 2016, *RealClear Politics*, https://www.realclearpolitics.com/video/2016/10/25/trump_repealing_obamacare_is_going_to_be_so_easy.html.

63. Evan Saltzman and Christine Eibner, "Donald Trump's Health Care Reform Proposals: Anticipated Effects on Insurance Coverage, Out-of-Pocket Costs, and the Federal Deficit" (Commonwealth Fund, September 23, 2016), https://www.commonwealthfund.org/publications/issue-briefs/2016/sep/donald-trumps-health-care-reform-proposals-anticipated-effects.

64. Ryan Teague Beckwith, "President Trump Is Back to Complaining, Without Evidence, About Rigged Elections. This Time, It's 2018," *Time*, July 24, 2018, https://time.com/5347269/donald-trup-russia-interfere-2018-election-democrats.

65. "Full Transcript: Third 2016 Presidential Debate," *Politico*, October 20, 2016, https://www.politico.com/story/2016/10/full-transcript-third-2016-presidential-debate-230063.

66. "Full Transcript: Third 2016 Presidential Debate."

67. Duncan J. Watts and David M. Rothschild, "Don't Blame the Election on Fake News. Blame It on the Media," *Columbia Journalism Review*, December 5, 2017 [italics in original], https://www.cjr.org/analysis/fake-news-media-election-trump.php.

68. Dan Schill and Rita Kirk, "Angry, Passionate, and Divided: Undecided Voters and the 2016 Presidential Election," *American Behavioral Scientist* 61 (2017): 1056–76, 1060.

69. Schill and Kirk, "Angry, Passionate, and Divided," 1070.

70. Schill and Kirk, "Angry, Passionate, and Divided," 1060.

71. Pamela S. Shockley, Sherwyn P. Morreale, and Carmen Stavrositu, "Voters' Perceptions of Trust in 2016 Presidential Candidates, Clinton and Trump: Exploring the Election's Outcome," *American Behavioral Scientist* 63, no. 7 (2019): 856–87. Contrasting evaluations of both candidates on a range of issues were related to patterns of support in statistically significant ways, including that Clinton's overall advantages on trust might explain her popular vote victory, while Trump's trust advantages on terrorism and national security, particularly in swing states, might have helped him to eke out margins in enough states to win the electoral college.

72. "Trust and the U.S. Presidential Election," 2017 Edelman Trust Barometer, slide 6 of 30, https://www.edelman.com/trust2017/trust-and-us-presidential-election.

73. "Trust and the U.S. Presidential Election," 2017 Edelman Trust Barometer.

74. Uri Friedman, "Why Trump Is Thriving in an Age of Distrust," *Atlantic*, January 20, 2017.

75. Lee Drutman, "Political Divisions in 2016 and Beyond: Tensions Between and Within the Two Parties" (Democracy Fund Voter Study Group, June 2016), https://www.voterstudygroup.org/publications/2016-elections/political-divisions-in-2016-and-beyond.

76. Drutman, "Political Divisions in 2016 and Beyond."

77. Joshua Green, *Devil's Bargain: Steve Bannon, Donald Trump, and the Nationalist Uprising* (New York: Penguin, 2017), 205, 208.

78. Josh Marshall, "Trump Rolls Out Anti-Semitic Closing Ad," *Talking Points Memo*, November 5, 2016, https://talkingpointsmemo.com/edblog/trump-rolls-out-anti -semitic-closing-ad.

79. Daniel Polti, "Is Donald Trump's Closing Campaign Ad Anti-Semitic?," *Slate*, November 6, 2016, https://slate.com/news-and-politics/2016/11/is-donald-trumps -closing-campaign-ad-anti-semitic.html; Niraj Chokshi, "Trump Accuses Clinton of Guiding Global Elite Against U.S. Working Class," *New York Times*, October 13, 2016, https://www.nytimes.com/2016/10/14/us/politics/trump-comments-linked -to-antisemitism.html.

80. Emily Ekins, "The Five Types of Trump Voters: Who They Are and What They Believe" (Democracy Fund Voter Study Group, June, 2017), https://www .voterstudygroup.org/publications/2016-elections/the-five-types-trump-voters.

81. Ekins, "The Five Types of Trump Voters: Who They Are and What They Believe."

82. Philip Klinkner, "The Easiest Way to Guess If Someone Supports Trump? Ask If Obama Is a Muslim," *Vox*, June 2, 2016, https://www.vox.com/2016/6/2/11833548 /donald-trump-support-race-religion-economy.

83. Alan Abramowitz, *The Great Alignment: Race, Party Transformation, and the Rise of Donald Trump* (New Haven: Yale University Press, 2018), 129.

84. Regarding this shift over time, contrast the analysis of Tali Mendelberg in *The Race Card: Campaign Strategy, Implicit Messages, and the Norm of Equality* (Princeton, N.J.: Princeton University Press, 2001) with that of Nicholas A. Valentino, Fabian G. Neuner, and L. Matthew Vandenbroek, "The Changing Norms of Racial Political Rhetoric and the End of Racial Priming," *Journal of Politics* 80, no. 3 (July 2018): 757–71.

85. John Sides, Michael Tesler, and Lynn Vavreck, *Identity Crisis: The 2016 Presidential Campaign and the Battle for the Meaning of America* (Princeton, N.J.: Princeton University Press, 2018) 176, 71. The tie between deservingness and race is key. As Nicholas Winter found, "This linkage has led to Social Security being viewed implicitly as a 'white' program, in much the same way as welfare has been branded as 'black.' " Nicholas J. G. Winter, *Dangerous Frames: How Ideas about Race and Gender Shape Public Opinion* (Chicago: University of Chicago Press, 2008), 9. See also Ashley Jardina, *White Identity Politics* (Cambridge: Cambridge University Press, 2019).

86. Trump won states worth 306 electoral votes but only officially recorded 304 due to the actions of two "faithless electors" who voted for Rand Paul and John Kasich rather than for Trump.

87. Uri Friedman, "Why Trump Is Thriving in an Age of Distrust," *Atlantic*, January 20, 2017.

88. President Donald J. Trump (@realdonaldtrump), Twitter, November 27, 2016, 7:31:54 p.m.

89. Donald Trump, interview by Lesley Stahl, *60 Minutes*, November 13, 2016, https:// www.cbsnews.com/news/60-minutes-donald-trump-family-melania-ivanka -lesley-stahl.

90. Heather Caygle, "Ryan: Trump's Comments 'Textbook Definition' of Racism," *Politico*, June 7, 2016, https://www.politico.com/story/2016/06/paul-ryan-trump -judge-223991; Tim Alberta, " 'Mother Is Not Going to Like This': The 48 Hours That Almost Brought Down Trump," *Politico Magazine*, July 10, 2019, https://www

.politico.com/magazine/story/2019/07/10/american-carnage-excerpt-access
-hollywood-tape-227269.

91. Mary Louise Kelly, "How the Relationship Between Trump and His Spy Chiefs Soured," *NPR*, October 29, 2019, https://www.npr.org/2019/10/29/773127809/how -the-relationship-between-trump-and-his-spy-chiefs-soured. This was but one of many instances; as Kelly, an NPR correspondent, put it, "This story of mistrust could have started [in] a dozen different places."

92. President Donald J. Trump (@realdonaldtrump), "Intelligence agencies should never have allowed this fake news to 'leak' into the public. One last shot at me. Are we living in Nazi Germany?" Twitter, January 11, 2017, 7:48:52 a.m.

93. "CQ Vote Studies: Presidential Support—Trump Divided, Conquered," *CQ Magazine*, February 12, 2018.

94. Donald J. Trump, "The Inaugural Address" January 20, 2017, https://www.whitehouse .gov/briefings-statements/the-inaugural-address.

95. Erica Chenoweth and Jeremy Pressman, "This Is What We Learned by Counting the Women's Marches," *Washington Post*, February 7, 2017, https://www.washingtonpost .com/news/monkey-cage/wp/2017/02/07/this-is-what-we-learned-by-counting -the-womens-marches; Marie Berry and Erica Chenoweth, "Who Made the Women's March?," in *The Resistance: The Dawn of the Anti-Trump Opposition Movement*, ed. David S. Meyer and Sidney Tarrow (New York: Oxford University Press, 2018).

96. Michael C. Dorf and Michel S. Chu, "Lawyers as Activists: From the Airport to the Courtroom," in *The Resistance: The Dawn of the Anti-Trump Opposition Movement*, ed. David S. Meyer and Sidney Tarrow (New York: Oxford University Press, 2018).

97. Michael S. Schmidt, Mark Mazzetti, and Matt Apuzzo, "Trump Campaign Aides Had Repeated Contacts with Russian Intelligence," *New York Times*, February 14, 2017, https://www.nytimes.com/2017/02/14/us/politics/russia-intelligence-communications -trump.html.

98. President Donald J. Trump (@realdonaldtrump), Twitter, February 15, 2017, 7:19:18 a.m. and 08:13:10 a.m.

99. Philip Rocco, "The Anti-Analytic Presidency Revisited," *The Forum* 15, no. 2 (2017): 363–78, 365.

100. Jathan Sadowski, "The Much-Needed and Sane Congressional Office That Gingrich Killed Off and We Need Back," *Atlantic*, October 26, 2012, https://www.theatlantic .com/technology/archive/2012/10/the-much-needed-and-sane-congressional-office -that-gingrich-killed-off-and-we-need-back/264160; Tim Hanrahan, "On Twitter, Trump Has Long and Colorful History of Climate Skepticism," *Wall Street Journal*, June 1, 2017; Jacob Carter, Gretchen Goldman, Genna Reed, Peter Hansel, Michael Halpern, and Andrew Rosenberg, Union of Concerned Scientists, "Sidelining Science Since Day One: How the Trump Administration Has Harmed Public Health and Safety in Its First Six Months," July 13, 2017, https://www.ucsusa.org/resources /sidelining-science-day-one; Brad Plumer and Coral Davenport, "Science Under Attack: How Trump is Sidelining Researchers and Their Work," *New York Times*, December 28, 2019.

101. Charles Stewart III, "Trump's Controversial Election Integrity Commission Is Gone. Here's What Comes Next," Monkey Cage, *Washington Post*, January 4, 2018, https://www.washingtonpost.com/news/monkey-cage/wp/2018/01/04/trumps -controversial-election-integrity-commission-is-gone-heres-what-comes-next.

102. Matthew Dunlap, letter to Mike Pence and Kris Kobach, August 3, 2018, http:// paceidocs.sosonline.org/PDF/Dunlap%20PACEI%20Docs%20Findings%20 letter%20-%20FINAL.080318.pdf.

103. Amy E. Lerman, Meredity L. Sadin, and Samuel Trachtman, "Policy Uptake as Political Behavior: Evidence from the Affordable Care Act," *American Political Science Review* 111, no. 4 (2017): 755–70.

104. James Morone, "Health Policy and White Nationalism: Historical Lessons, Disruptive Populism, and Two Parties at a Crossroads," *Journal of Health Politics, Policy and Law* 43, no. 4 (2018): 683–706, 684.

105. Jacob S. Hacker and Paul Pierson, "The Dog That Almost Barked: What the ACA Repeal Fight Says About the Resilience of the American Welfare State," *Journal of Health Politics, Policy and Law* 43, no. 4 (2018): 551–77. Moreover, as Hacker and Pierson noted, "The Republicans' repeal drive was not a stand-alone goals. It was part of an integrated strategy that centered on freeing up fiscal space for large tax cuts," 566.

106. See Congressional Budget Office, *Cost Estimation, Better Care Reconciliation Act of 2017*, June 26, 2017. Regarding the earlier House version, see Congressional Budget Office, July 19, 2017, *Cost Estimation, Obamacare Repeal Reconciliation Act of 2017*; Henry C. Jackson, "Six Promises Trump Has Made About Health Care," *Politico*, March 13, 2017, https://www.politico.com/story/2017/03/trump -obamacare-promises-236021.

107. Kaiser Health News, "Summary of the American Health Care Act," May 2017, http://files.kff.org/attachment/Proposals-to-Replace-the-Affordable-Care-Act -Summary-of-the-American-Health-Care-Act.

108. Colleen M. Grogan and Sunggeun (Ethan) Park, "The Politics of Medicaid: Most Americans Are Connected to the Program, Support Its Expansion, and Do Not View It as Stigmatizing," *Milbank Quarterly* 95 (2017): 749–82.

109. Lunna Lopes, Liz Hammel, Ashley Kirzinger, Audrey Kearney, and Mollyann Brodie, "KFF Health Tracking Poll—November 2019: Health Care in the 2020 Election, Medicare-for-All, and the State of the ACA," November 20, 2019, https:// www.kff.org/health-reform/poll-finding/kff-health-tracking-poll-november-2019.

110. Amy Fried, "How Maine People Moved Sen. Collins and Stopped Trumpcare," *Bangor Daily News*, August 8, 2017, http://pollways.bangordailynews.com/2017/08 /08/national/collins-deserves-praise-but-lets-not-forget-the-maine-people-who -influenced-her.

111. Lara Putnam and Theda Skocpol, "Middle America Reboots Democracy," *Democracy: A Journal of Ideas*, February 20, 2018, https://democracyjournal.org /arguments/middle-america-reboots-democracy.

112. Jessica Schubel, "House ACA Repeal Bill Puts Children with Disabilities and Special Health Care Needs at Severe Risk" (Center on Budget and Policy Priorities, June 14, 2017), https://www.cbpp.org/research/health/house-aca-repeal-bill-puts -children-with-disabilities-and-special-health-care-needs.

113. Charlotte Alter and Haley Sweetland Edward, "The United Patients of America," *Time*, July 13, 2017, https://time.com/4856231/the-united-patients-of-america.

114. Fried, "How Maine People Moved Sen. Collins and Stopped Trumpcare"; John Cassidy, "How Susan Collins Helped Save Obamacare," *New Yorker*, September 26, 2017; Jaclyn Rice, "Susan Collins on Spontaneous Applause at Maine Airport: 'It Was Just Amazing,'" *Boston Globe*, July 31, 2017.

115. Sara Rosenbaum, "The (Almost) Great Unraveling," *Journal of Health Politics, Policy and Law* 43, no. 4 (2018): 579–603, 579.

116. Jonathan Oberlander, "Repeal, Replace, Repair, Retreat—Republicans' Health Care Quagmire," *New England Journal of Medicine* 377, no. 11 (2017): 1001–1003.

117. Selena Simmons-Duffin, "Trump Is Trying Hard to Thwart Obamacare. How's That Going?," *NPR Online*, October 14, 2019, https://www.npr.org/sections/health -shots/2019/10/14/768731628/trump-is-trying-hard-to-thwart-obamacare-hows-that -going.

118. Jan Hoffman and Abby Goodnough, "Trump Administration Files Formal Request to Strike Down All of Obamacare," *New York Times*, May 1, 2019, https://www .nytimes.com/2019/05/01/health/unconstitutional-trump-aca.html.

119. "Remarks by President Trump and American Taxpayers on Tax Reform," December 13, 2017, https://www.whitehouse.gov/briefings-statements/remarks -president-trump-american-taxpayers-tax-reform.

120. "Remarks by President Trump and American Taxpayers on Tax Reform," December 13, 2017.

121. See Suzy Khimm, "Trump Cuts Red Tape at White House Event Touting Deregula- tion," December 14, 2017, https://www.nbcnews.com/politics/white-house/trump -cuts-red-tape-white-house-event-touting-deregulation-n829851.

122. Glen Bolger, to Interested Parties, "Re: Surviving the 2018 Election," November 9, 2017, https://pos.org/surviving-the-2018-election.

123. A search of the word "Mueller" on the Trump Twitter Archive produced 69 such tweets from January 1, 2018, to December 31, 2018, http://www.trumptwitterarchive .com/archive.

124. Charlie Savage, "Barr Bridges the Reagan Revolution and Trump on Executive Power," *New York Times*, November 18, 2019, https://www.nytimes.com/2019/11/18/us /politics/barr-executive-power-trump.html.

125. Bill Barr, memo to Deputy Attorney General Rod Rosenstein and Assistant Attor- ney General Steve Engel, "Re: Mueller's 'Obstruction' Theory," June 8, 2018, https:// www.documentcloud.org/documents/5638848-June-2018-Barr-Memo-to-DOJ -Muellers-Obstruction.html.

126. Indeed, when Barr delivered a speech to the Federalist Society in Washington, D.C., in which he defended Trump's broad use of presidential power (and ridi- culed his unnamed "friends on the other side" who complained that Trump was " 'shredding' constitutional norms," he complained about Obama's use of power: "Measures taken by this [Trump] Administration seem a bit tame when compared to some of the unprecedented steps taken by the Obama Administration's aggres- sive exercises of Executive power—such as, under its DACA program, refusing to enforce broad swathes of immigration law." Attorney General William Barr, "Remarks before the Federalist Society's 2019 National Lawyers Convention," November 15, 2019, https://www.justice.gov/opa/speech/attorney-general-william- p-barr-delivers-19th-annual-barbara-k-olson-memorial-lecture.

127. White House, "Remarks by President Trump and President Putin of the Russian Federation in Joint Press Conference," July 16, 2018, https://www.whitehouse.gov /briefings-statements/remarks-president-trump-president-putin-russian-federation -joint-press-conference.

128. White House, "Remarks by President Trump and President Putin of the Russian Federation in Joint Press Conference," July 16, 2018.

129. White House, "Remarks by President Trump and President Putin of the Russian Federation in Joint Press Conference," July 16, 2018.

130. Editorial Board, "Trump's Tariffs Spawn Exemptions, Then His Own Big Government," *USA Today*, August 29, 2018, https://www.usatoday.com/story/opinion /2018/08/29/trump-steel-aluminum-tariffs-spawn-exemptions-big-government -editorials-debates/1055050002.

131. Laura Reiley, "Trump's $16 Billion Farm Bailout Will Make Rich Farmers Richer, Report Says," *Washington Post*, July 31, 2019, https://www.washingtonpost.com /business/2019/07/31/trumps-billion-farm-bailout-will-make-rich-farmers-richer -hasten-small-farm-failure-study-says.

132. Dan Charles, "Farmers Got Billions from Taypayers in 2019, and Hardly Anyone Objected," *NPR* December 31, 2019, https://www.npr.org/sections/thesalt/2019/12 /31/790261705/farmers-got-billions-from-taxpayers-in-2019-and-hardly-anyone -objected.

133. Jim Tankersley, "U.S. Budget Deficit to Top $1 Trillion for Next Decade," *New York Times*, January 28, 2020, https://www.nytimes.com/2020/01/28/business/trillion -budget-deficit-cbo.html.

134. Jane Coaston, "Eminent Domain, the Big-Government Tactic Trump Needs to Use to Build the Wall, Explained," *Vox*, January 18, 2019, https://www.vox.com /policy-and-politics/2019/1/18/18176893/eminent-domain-trump-border-wall-gop.

135. David Frum, "The Mystery of the Disappearing Security Clearance," *Atlantic*, January 13, 2019, https://www.theatlantic.com/politics/archive/2019/01/does-john -brennan-have-security-clearance/579772.

136. "Statement from 60 Former CIA Officials Regarding the Removal of Security Clearances," August 17, 2018. Statement available from CNN's Jim Sciutto tweet, @ jimsciutto, "Breaking: In new letter, 60 Fmr CIA officers protest Trump on clear-nacnes: 'We believe equally strongly that former govt officials have the right to express their unclassified views on what they see as critical national security issues without fear of being punished for doing so," Twitter, August 17, 2018, 5:35 p.m., https://twitter.com/jimsciutto/status/1030568706705948678.

137. See President Donald J. Trump (@realdonaldtrump), "Study the late Joseph McCarthy, because we are now in period with Mueller and his gang that make Joseph McCarthy look like a baby! Rigged Witch Hunt," Twitter, August 19, 2018, 8:24:38 a.m.; President Donald J. Trump (@realdonaldtrump), "Alan Dershowitz: 'These are not crimes. He (Mueller) has no authority to be a roving Commissioner. I don't see any evidence of crimes.' This is an illegal Hoax that should be ended immediately. Mueller refuses to look at the real crimes on the other side. Where is the IG REPORT?," Twitter, November 29, 2018, 10:04:34 p.m.

138. Of Trump, David A. Graham said, "No other mainstream GOP figure has been so willing to make the brazen claims Trump has about the integrity of American elections generally, or about the democratic process itself"; David A. Graham "Democracy, Interrupted," *Atlantic*, January 13, 2019, https://www.theatlantic.com /politics/archive/2019/01/trump-continues-to-attack-rigged-elections/580030.

139. Beckwith, "President Trump Is Back to Complaining, Without Evidence, About Rigged Elections. This Time, It's 2018."

140. Christopher Cadelago and Brent D. Griffiths, "Trump, at Rally, Hints at Conspiracy Theories for Migrant Caravan," *Politico*, October 18, 2018, https://www.politico .com/story/2018/10/18/trump-migrant-caravan-montana-rally-915044.

141. Christopher Cadelgo and Ted Hesson, "Why Trump Is Talking Nonstop About the Migrant Caravan," *Politico*, October 23, 2018, https://www.politico.com/story/2018/10/23/trump-caravan-midterm-elections-875888.

142. John Fritze and Christopher Schnaars, "President Trump Latches Onto Migrant Caravan as Top Issue in Midterms," *USA Today*, October 25, 2018, https://www.usatoday.com/story/news/politics/elections/2018/10/25/donald-trump-migrant-caravan-could-help-gop-midterms/1742669002.

143. David Jackson, Susan Page, and John Fritze, "Exclusive: President Trump Vows to Send as Many Troops to the Border 'As Necessary' To Stop Caravan," *USA Today*, October 23, 2018.

144. President Donald J. Trump (@realdonaldtrump), Twitter, October 22, 2018, https://twitter.com/realDonaldTrump/status/1054354059535269888.

145. Will Somer, Lachlan Markay, Asawin Suebsaeng, and Sam Stein, "Trump's Own Team Knows His Caravan Claims Are Bullshit," *Daily Beast*, October 24, 2018, https://www.thedailybeast.com/trumps-own-teams-know-his-caravan-claims-arent-true-dont-particularly-care?source=twitter&via=desktop; see also Adam Serwer, "Trump's Caravan Hysteria Led to This," *Atlantic*, October 28, 2018, https://www.theatlantic.com/ideas/archive/2018/10/caravan-lie-sparked-massacre-american-jews/574213.

146. Alexander Burns and Astead W. Herndon, "Trump and GOP Candidates Escalate Race and Fear as Election Ploys," *New York Times*, October 22, 2018, https://www.nytimes.com/2018/10/22/us/politics/republicans-race-divisions-elections-caravan.html.

147. William K. Rashbaum, Alan Feuer, and Adam Goldman, "Pipe Bombs Investigation Turns Toward Florida as More Trump Critics Are Targeted," *New York Times*, October 25, 2018, https://www.nytimes.com/2018/10/25/nyregion/bomb-explosive-device.html.

148. Jack Healy, Julie Turkewitz, and Richard A. Oppel Jr., "Cesar Sayoc, Mail Bombing Suspect, Found an Identity in Political Rage and Resentment," *New York Times*, October 27, 2018, https://www.nytimes.com/2018/10/27/us/cesar-altieri-sayoc-bomber.html?action=click&module=RelatedLinks&pgtype=Article.

149. Paul P. Murphy, "Bowers Blamed Jews for Helping 'Invaders' in the Migrant Caravans," *CNN*, October 27, 2018, https://www.cnn.com/us/live-news/pittsburgh-synagogue-shooting/h_0c180f52c8d032fd47eef570cc5065c2.

150. Maggie Haberman and Mark Landler, "A Week After the Midterms, Trump Seems to Forget the Caravan," *New York Times*, November 13, 2018, https://www.nytimes.com/2018/11/13/us/politics/trump-caravan-midterms.html; Eugene Scott, "Before the Midterms, Trump Harped on the Migrant Caravan. Since Then, He Hasn't Brought It Up," *Washington Post*, November 8, 2018, https://www.washingtonpost.com/politics/2018/11/08/before-midterms-trump-harped-migrant-caravan-since-then-he-has-barely-mentioned-it; Aaron Rupar, "Fox News Barely Mentions Caravan First Morning After Midterms," *Vox*, November 7, 2018, https://www.vox.com/2018/11/7/18071658/fox-news-caravan-midterm-elections.

151. Gary C. Jacobson, "Extreme Referendum: Donald Trump and the 2018 Midterm Elections," *Political Science Quarterly* 134, no.1 (2019): 9–38, 13.

152. Jacobson, "Extreme Referendum," 13.

153. Ashlyn Still, Chris Kahn, and Grant Smith, "American Anger," *Reuters*, October 24, 2018, https://graphics.reuters.com/USA-ELECTION-POLL-ANGER/010080XQ1RD/index.html.

154. Quoted in Chris Kahn and Grant Smith, "Americans' Anger May Help Democrats in Nov. 6 Vote: Reuters/Ipsos Poll," *Reuters*, October 24, 2018, https://www.reuters.com/article/us-usa-election-poll-anger/americans-anger-may-help-democrats-in-nov-6-vote-reuters-ipsos-poll-idUSKCN1MY18T.
155. Kahn, and Smith, "American Anger"; Jacobson, "Extreme Referendum," 14, 31.
156. Senator Marsha Blackburn, "Blackburn Votes to Acquit President Trump," February 5, 2020, https://www.blackburn.senate.gov/2020/2/blackburn-votes-acquit-president-trump.

7. MAKING PEACE WITH GOVERNMENT

1. Rick Perlstein, *Before the Storm: Barry Goldwater and the Unmaking of the American Consensus* (New York: Hill and Wang, 2001), 110.
2. Geoffrey Kabaservice, *Rule and Ruin: The Downfall of Moderation and the Destruction of the Republican Party, from Eisenhower to the Tea Party* (Oxford University Press, 2012), 112, 113.
3. Barry Goldwater's Nomination Acceptance Speech, July 16, 1964. In *The Republican Party: Documents Decoded*, ed. Douglas B. Harris and Lonce H. Bailey (Santa Barbara, CA: ABC-CLIO, 2014), 114.
4. Pew Research Center, "Public Trust in Government: 1958–2019," April 11, 2019. https://www.pewresearch.org/politics/2019/04/11/public-trust-in-government-1958-2019.
5. William E. Leuchtenberg, *In the Shadow of FDR: From Harry Truman to George W. Bush*, rev., updated ed. (Ithaca, N.Y.: Cornell University Press, 2001).
6. Franklin D. Roosevelt, "1944 State of the Union Address," January 11, 1944; online by Gerhard Peters and John T. Woolley, The American Presidency Project, https://www.presidency.ucsb.edu/node/210825.
7. Douglas B. Harris, "Partisan Framing in Legislative Debates," in *Winning with Words: The Origins and Impact of Framing*, ed. Brian F. Schaffner and Patrick J. Sellers (New York: Routledge, 2010), 41–59.
8. Shanto Iyengar, Yphtach Lelkes, Matthew Levendusky, Neil Malhotra, and Sean J. Westwood, "The Origins and Consequences of Affective Polarization in the United States," *Annual Review of Political Science* 22 (2019): 129–46.
9. Lilliana Mason, *Uncivil Agreement: How Politics Became Our Identity* (Chicago: University of Chicago Press, 2018); Daniel J. Hopkins, *The Increasingly United States: How and Why American Political Behavior Nationalized* (Chicago: University of Chicago Press, 2018); Michael Tesler, *Post-Racial or Most-Racial? Race and Politics in the Obama Era* (Chicago: University of Chicago Press, 2016).
10. Jay D. Hmielowski, Myiah J. Hutchens, and Michael A. Beam, "Asymmetry of Partisan Media Effects? Examining the Reinforcing Process of Conservative and Liberal Media with Political Beliefs, Political Communication," *Political Communication* 37, no. 6 (2020): 852–68.
11. Alexander Hertel-Fernandez, "Policy Feedback as Political Weapon: Conservative Advocacy and the Demobilization of the Public Sector Labor Movement," *Perspectives on Politics* 16 (2018): 364–79.
12. Davide Morisi, John T. Jost, and Vishal Singh, "An Asymmetrical "President-in-Power" Effect," *American Political Science Review* 113, no. 2 (2019): 614–20.

13. James Fishkin and David E. Pozen, "Asymmetric Constitutional Hardball," *Columbia Law Review* 118 (2018): 915–82.

14. Matt Grossman and David A. Hopkins, *Asymmetric Politics: Ideological Republicans and Group Interest Democrats* (New York: Oxford University Press, 2016), 329.

15. Indeed, the Constitution of 1787 was designed to take account of enslaved persons of African descent, and constitutional changes were made after the Civil War. The New Deal Democratic coalition was upended after Democrats embraced civil rights; the coalition came under strain after President Harry Truman's late-1940s executive actions. The white South left the coalition after the rise of the civil rights movement, and President Lyndon Johnson's passage of civil rights, voting rights, and Great Society legislation in the 1960s.

16. See, esp., Marisa Abrajano and Zoltan L. Hajnal, *White Backlash: Immigration, Race, and American Politics* (Princeton, N.J.: Princeton University Press, 2015).

17. Alan I. Abramowitz, *The Great Alignment: Race, Party Transformation, and the Rise of Donald Trump* (New Haven, Conn.: Yale University Press, 2018), 46, 50.

18. Ismail K. White and Chryl N. Laird, *Steadfast Democrats: How Social Forces Shape Black Political Behavior* (Princeton, N.J.: Princeton University Press, 2020).

19. Maureen A. Craig, Julian M. Rucker, and Jennifer A. Richeson, "Racial and Political Dynamics of an Approaching 'Majority-Minority' United States," *Annals of the American Academy of Political and Social Science* 677, no. 1 (May 2018): 204–14; John Sides, Michael Tesler, and Lynn Vavreck, *Identity Crisis: The 2016 Presidential Campaign and the Battle for the Meaning of America* (Princeton, NJ: Princeton University Press, 2019).

20. Ryan D. Enos, "Causal Effect of Intergroup Contact on Exclusionary Attitudes," *Proceedings of the National Academy of Sciences USA* 111, no. 10 (2014): 3699–3704. See also Ryan D. Enos, *The Space Between Us: Social Geography and Politics* (New York: Cambridge University Press, 2017).

21. Jacob Hacker and Paul Pierson, *American Amnesia: How the War on Government Led Us to Forget What Made America Prosper* (New York: Simon & Schuster, 2016).

22. Nicholas Carnes, *The Cash Ceiling: Why Only the Rich Run for Office—and What We Can Do About It* (Princeton, N.J.: Princeton University Press, 2018), 200.

23. Gavin Jenkins, "The Sessions Where Working-Class Democrats Learn to Take Down the GOP," *Vice*, February 19, 2019, https://www.vice.com/en_us/article/evebw7/the-sessions-where-working-class-democrats-learn-to-take-down-the-gopt.

24. Eitan Hersh, *Politics Is for Power: How to Move Beyond Political Hobbyism, Take Action and Make Real Change* (New York: Scribner, 2020), 157.

25. Leah E. Gose, Theda Skocpol, and Vanessa Williamson, "Saving America Once Again, from the Tea Party to the Anti-Trump Resistance," in *Upending American Politics: Polarizing Parties, Ideological Elites, and Citizen Activists from the Tea Party to the Anti-Trump Resistance*, ed. Theda Skocpol and Caroline Tervo (New York: Oxford University Press, 2020), 191–211.

26. Scholars Strategy Network, "How to Revitalize America's Local Political Parties," January 30, 2019, https://scholars.org/contribution/how-revitalize-americas-local-political-parties.

27. Grossman and Hopkins, *Asymmetric Politics*.

28. To be sure, candidates across the political spectrum have long argued they would protect popular government programs. While their policies in office contradicted

their rhetoric, Republicans have claimed during campaigns that they were going to protect popular government programs. For instance, in 2012, the GOP claimed the Affordable Care Act undermined Medicare. In 2016, while stoking distrust against elites, candidate Trump also recognized the power of pro-government language. During the campaign, Trump promised to "take care of everybody" with some unspecified but purportedly superior health-care program and to protect Social Security, Medicare, and Medicaid. Trump also pledged to raise taxes on the wealthy, in part by closing the carried interest loophole.

29. Marc J. Hetherington, *Why Trust Matters* (Princeton, N.J.: Princeton University Press, 2005).

30. Demos, *Race-Class Narrative, National Dial Survey Report*, May 2018, https://www .demos.org/sites/default/files/publications/LRP%20Report.Race-Class%20Narrative .National%20C3.Final_.2018.05.08_4.pdf.

31. Jan Gerrit Voelkel and Robb Willer, "Resolving the Progressive Paradox: Conservative Value Framing of Progressive Economic Policies Increases Candidate Support," May 8, 2019, https://ssrn.com/abstract=3385818 or http://dx.doi.org/10.2139/ssrn .3385818.

32. Katherine J. Cramer and Benjamin Toff, "The Fact of Experience: Rethinking Political Knowledge and Civic Competence," *Perspectives on Politics* 15 (2017): 754–70.

33. Amy Fried, Robert Glover, and Emily Shaw, "Organizing Voters for Marriage Equality: Electoral Strategies and Democratic Engagement in the U.S. Same-Sex Marriage Movement" (working paper, n.d.). https://www.academia.edu/12799360 /Organizing_Voters_for_Marriage_Equality_Electoral_Strategies_and_Democratic _Engagement_in_the_U_S_Same_Sex_Marriage_Movement.

34. Joshua L. Kalla and David E. Brookman, "Reducing Exclusionary Attitudes Through Interpersonal Conversation: Evidence from Three Field Experiments," *American Political Science Review* 114 (2020): 410–25.

35. People's Action, "How to Defeat Trump and Heal America: Deep Canvassing and Political Persuasion in the 2020 Presidential Election," 2020, https://peoplesaction .org/wp-content/uploads/2020/09/PA-ReportDeepCanvassingResults09.14- FINAL.pdf. See also Micah L. Shifry, "To Change Voters' Sympathies, It's Time to Go Deep," *American Prospect*, February 24, 2020, https://prospect.org/politics /change-voters-sympathies-deep-canvassing. The organization Changing the Conversation Together uses deep canvassing as its technique, arguing on its website that "By listening to voters' stories and sharing their own, deep canvassers invite voters to use their vote to combat the politics of hate and cruelty in the national arena"; https://www.ctctogether.org/about-us.

36. Matt Morrison, "The Best Way for Democrats to Win Working-Class Voters," *New York Times*, September 24, 2018. https://www.nytimes.com/2018/09/24/opinion /democrats-unions-working-class-voters-.html?action=click&module=Opinion& pgtype=Homepag.

37. Morrison, "The Best Way for Democrats to Win Working-Class Voters."

38. On policy design and policy feedback, see Pamela Herd and Donald P. Moynihan, *Administrative Burden: Policymaking by Other Means* (New York: Russell Sage, 2018); Daniel Béland, Philip Rocco, and Alex Waddan, "Policy Feedback and the Politics of the Affordable Care Act," *Policy Studies Journal* 47, no. 2 (May 2019): 395–422.

39. On overcoming negative political impacts of the carceral and custodial state, see, esp., Michael Leo Owens and Hannah L. Walker, "The Civic Voluntarism of

'Custodial Citizens': Involuntary Criminal Justice Contact, Associational Life, and Political Participation," *Perspectives on Politics* 16, no. 4 (December 2018): 990–1013; Amy E. Lerman and Vesla M. Weaver, *Arresting Citizenship: The Democratic Citizenship of American Crime Control* (Chicago: University of Chicago Press, 2014).

40. Andrea Campbell, *How Policies Make Citizens: Senior Political Activism and the American Welfare State* (Princeton, N.J.: Princeton University Press, 2003).

41. On past Medicaid expansions, see Jake Haselswerdt, "Expanding Medicaid, Expanding the Electorate: The Affordable Care Act's Short-Term Impact on Political Participation," *Journal of Health Politics, Policy and Law* 42, no. 4 (2017):667–95; Joshua D. Clinton and Michael W. Sances, "The Politics of Policy: The Initial Mass Political Effects of Medicaid Expansion in the States," *American Political Science Review* 112, no. 1 (2018): 167–85; Katherine Baicker and Amy Finkelstein, "The Impact of Medicaid Expansion on Voter Participation: Evidence from the Oregon Health Insurance Experiment," *Quarterly Journal of Political Science* 14, no. 4 (2019): 383–400. On the potential for future expansions to increase voting see Jake Haselswerdt, Michael Sances, and Sean McElwee, *The Missing Medicaid Millions* (Data for Progress, 2019), http://filesforprogress.org/memos/missing_medicaid_millions.pdf.

42. Jamila Michener, *Fragmented Democracy: Medicaid, Federalism, and Unequal Politics* (New York: Cambridge University Press, 2018).

43. *Federalist Papers* No. 51, The Avalon Project: Documents in Law, History, and Diplomacy. https://avalon.law.yale.edu/18th_century/fed51.asp.

44. *Federalist Papers* No. 10, https://avalon.law.yale.edu/18th_century/fed10.asp.

45. Steven Levitsky and Daniel Ziblatt, *How Democracies Die* (New York: Broadway Books, 2018); see, too, Nancy Bermeo, "On Democratic Backsliding," *Journal of Democracy* 27 (2016): 5–19; surveys by Bright Line Watch at http://brightlinewatch.org/surveys.

46. Marin K. Levy, "Packing and Unpacking State Courts," *William & Mary Law Review* 61 (2020): 1121–58.

47. On the long-standing importance of such faith, see Sanford Levinson, *Constitutional Faith* (Princeton, N.J.: Princeton University Press, 2012).

48. Greg Sargent, *An Uncivil War* (New York: HarperCollins, 2018), 165.

49. Though we recognize that the virus resurged even in countries that initially handled its impacts well, the overall point about successful governance is borne out in cross-national studies that link better governance to mitigation of spread; see Lung-Chang Chien and Ro-Ting Lin, "COVID-19 Outbreak, Mitigation, and Governance in High Prevalent Countries," *Annals of Global Health* 86 (1): 119; https://www.annalsofglobalhealth.org/articles/10.5334/aogh.3011/.

50. David E. Lewis, "Deconstructing the Administrative State," *Journal of Politics* 81 (2019): 767–89.

51. Theda Skocpol, "The Elite and Popular Roots of Contemporary Republican Extremism," in *Upending American Politics: Polarizing Parties, Ideological Elites, and Citizen Activists from the Tea Party to the Anti-Trump Resistance*, ed. Theda Skocpol and Caroline Tervo (New York: Oxford University Press, 2020), 22.

52. Ryan Rafaty, "Perceptions of Corruption, Political Distrust, and the Weakening of Climate Policy," *Global Environmental Politics* 18 (2018): 106–29; Thomas J. Bollyky, Sawyer Crosby, and Samantha Kiernan, "Fighting a Pandemic Requires Trust," *Foreign Affairs*, October 23, 2020, https://www.foreignaffairs.com/articles/united-states/2020-10-23/coronavirus-fighting-requires-trust?utm_campaign=tw_daily_soc&utm_source=twitter_posts&utm_medium=social.

53. Josh Chafetz and David E. Pozen, "How Constitutional Norms Break Down," *UCLA Law Review* 65 (2018): 1430–1959.

54. William Gamson, *Power and Discontent* (Homewood, Ill.: Dorsey, 1968), 42–43. As sociologist Dietrich Rueschemeyer contends, ideas and beliefs "can have lasting consequences for divided or unified responses to the same broad set of problems." Broad political and historical change involves both shifting ideas and transformations in politics, including the fluctuating nature and strength of political coalitions, institutions, and public policies. Political scientist Rogers Smith, for instance, posits a "spiral of politics," recognizing that, as contexts vary over time, the construction of ideas and interests, coalition formation and competition, the capture and use of governing institutions, and the consequent modifications of contexts and new ideas propel the spiral further. Dietrich Rueschemeyer, "Why and How Ideas Matter," in *The Oxford Handbook of Contextual Political Analysis*, ed. Robert E. Goodin and Charles Tilly (March 2006), 244. See, esp., Brian J. Glenn, "The Two Schools of American Political Development," *Political Studies Review* 2 (2004): 153–65; Robert C. Lieberman, "Ideas, Institutions, and Political Order," *American Political Science Review* 96 (2002): 697–712; Rogers M. Smith, "Ideas and the Spiral of Politics: The Place of American Political Thought in American Political Development," *American Political Thought* 3 (2014): 126–36; George Thomas, "Political Thought and Political Development," *American Political Thought* 3 (2014): 114–25.

55. Ronald Reagan, "Ronald Reagan Speaks Out Against Socialized Medicine," ca. 1981, YouTube, October 13, 2009, https://www.youtube.com/watch?v=kDnxxsjVr20 (transcriptby authors).

56. While there were partisan differences, in 2017, 52 percent of Republicans with incomes over $30,000 saw providing health care as a governmental responsibility. This surge of support persisted in 2018, when 60 percent saw health care as a responsibility of the federal government, while 37 percent did not. Kristin Bialik, "More Americans Say Government Should Ensure Health Care Coverage," Pew Research Center, January 13, 2017, http://www.pewresearch.org/fact-tank/2017/01/13/more-americans -say-government-should-ensure-health-care-coverage; Jocelyn Kiley, "Most Continue to Say Ensuring Health Care Coverage Is Government's Responsibility," Pew Research Center, October 3, 2018, http://www.pewresearch.org/fact-tank/2018/10/03 /most-continue-to-say-ensuring-health-care-coverage-is-governments-responsibility.

57. For instance, in a February 2019 Kaiser poll, only 25 percent said they trusted drug companies to price their products fairly; 25 percent is a combination of those who chose "a lot" or "somewhat." Large majorities across political parties, and 86 percent overall, favor enabling the federal government to negotiate for lower drug prices. But this support reverses to 66 percent opposition if people are told arguments from opponents, such as negotiations would mean limiting research and development on new drugs or limiting Medicare recipients' prescription coverage. Ashley Kirzinger, Lunna Lopes, Bryan Wu, and Mollyann Brodie, "KFF Health Tracking Poll—February 2019: Prescription Drugs," Kaiser Family Foundation, 2019, https://www.kff.org/health-reform/poll-finding/kff-health -tracking-poll-february-2019-prescription-drugs.

58. Dylan Scott, "Why Donald Trump Makes Democratic Voters Uneasy About Medicare-for-All," *Vox*, February 8, 2018, https://www.vox.com/policy-and-politics/2018/2/8 /16655796/democrats-medicare-for-all-clinton-voters-trump.

59. For instance, in the 2017 Pew poll, 28 percent favored a single national program, with 29 percent supporting a mix of public and private programs. A March 2018 Kaiser Family Foundation poll found that 59 percent supported Medicare for all with a much larger majority, 75 percent backing Medicare for all if people wanted it, while "people who currently have other coverage can keep what they have." Ashley Kirzinger, Bryan Wu, and Mollyann Brodie, "Kaiser Health Tracking Poll— March 2018: Views on Prescription Drug Pricing and Medicare-for-All Proposals," Kaiser Family Foundation, March 23, 2018, https://www.kff.org/health-costs /poll-finding/kaiser-health-tracking-poll-march-2018-prescription-drug-pricing -medicare-for-all-proposals.

60. Jonathan Cohn, "2 Liberal Democrats Are Promoting a Twist on 'Medicare for All,'" *HuffPost*, February 17, 2019, https://www.huffpost.com/entry/deluaro-schakowsky -medicare-for-america-all_n_5c672cc6e4b05c889d1f4bc9.

61. Jacob S. Hacker, "Medicare Expansion as a Path as Well as a Destination: Achieving Universal Insurance Through a New Politics of Medicare," *Annals of the American Academy of Political and Social Science* 685, no. 1 (2019): 135–53. See also Jamila Michener, "Medicaid and the Policy Feedback Foundations for Universal Healthcare," *Annals of the American Academy of Political and Social Science* 685, no. 1 (2019): 116–34.

62. Amy L. Lerman, *Good Enough for Government Work: The Public Reputation Crisis in America (And What We Can Do to Fix It)* (Chicago: University of Chicago Press, 2019).

63. The public supports an array of government actions, even when people say they think government is too big and does too much. Individuals dislike "regulation" as a general proposition but support regulations to help consumers and workers and produce a safer, cleaner environment. Moreover, as Suzanne Mettler has shown, people consistently underestimate the extent to which they have used government programs; these misunderstandings are often an artifact of how policies have been designed in the United States. See Suzanne Mettler, *The Submerged State: How Invisible Government Policies Undermine American Democracy* (Chicago: University of Chicago Press, 2011).

AFTERWORD

1. President Donald J. Trump (@realdonaldtrump), "LIBERATE VIRGINIA, and save your great 2nd Amendment. It is under siege!," Twitter, April 17, 2020, 11:25:45 a.m.; "LIBERATE MICHIGAN!" Twitter, April 17, 2020, 11:22:41 a.m.; and "LIBERATE MINNESOTA!," Twitter, April 17, 2020, 11:21:48 a.m.

2. Larry Buchanan, Quoctrung Bui, and Jugal K. Patel, "Black Lives Matter May Be the Largest Movement in U.S. History," *New York Times*, July 3, 2020, https://www .nytimes.com/interactive/2020/07/03/us/george-floyd-protests-crowd-size.html.

3. Republican National Committee, "Resolution Regarding the Republican Party Platform," 2020, https://prod-cdn-static.gop.com/docs/Resolution_Platform_2020.pdf.

4. Department of Homeland Security, "Homeland Threat Assessment," October 2020, 18. https://www.dhs.gov/sites/default/files/publications/2020_10_06_homeland -threat-assessment.pdf.

5. The Commission on Presidential Debates, September 29, 2020 Debate Transcript, https://www.debates.org/voter-education/debate-transcripts/september-29-2020-debate-transcript/.

6. Meagan Vazquez, "Trump Appears to Give a Pass to the Domestic Kidnapping Plot Against Whitmer," CNN, October 27, 2020, https://www.cnn.com/2020/10/27/politics/trump-gretchen-whitmer-kidnapping-michigan/index.html.

7. Gretchen Whitmer, "The Plot to Kidnap Me," Atlantic, October 27, 2020, https://www.theatlantic.com/ideas/archive/2020/10/plot-kidnap-me/616866.

8. Matthew Daly, "GOP Senators Confront Past Comments on Supreme Court Vote," AP, September 19, 2020, https://apnews.com/article/election-2020-ruth-bader-ginsburg-elections-us-supreme-court-courts-1c42ab69fe886d1b2133129006918e7f.

9. Amy Fried and Douglas B. Harris, "In Suspense: Donald Trump's Efforts to Undermine Public Trust in Democracy," Society 57 (2020): 527–33, https://doi.org/10.1007/s12115-020-00526-y.

10. Emily Dreyfuss, "Trump's Tweeting Isn't Crazy. It's Strategic, Typos and All," New York Times, November 5, 2020, https://www.nytimes.com/2020/11/05/opinion/sunday/trump-twitter-biden-misinformation.html.

11. Trump seemed to have won 306 Electoral Votes in 2016 but officially recorded only 304 due to two faithless electors from Texas, one voting for Rand Paul and the other voting for John Kasich: "2016 Electoral College Results, National Archives and Records Administration, https://www.archives.gov/electoral-college/2016.

12. Justin Baragona, "Newt Gingrich: Bill Barr Should Arrest Poll Workers," Daily Beast, November 6, 2020, https://www.thedailybeast.com/newt-gingrich-calls-on-attorney-general-bill-barr-to-arrest-poll-workers?ref=scroll.

13. Tim Alberta, "The Election That Broke the Republican Party," Politico, November 6, 2020, https://www.politico.com/news/magazine/2020/11/06/the-election-that-broke-the-republican-party-434797.

14. Tina Nguyen and Mark Scott, "Trump-linked Figures Have Boosted #StopTheSteal Movement," Politico, November 6, 2020, https://www.politico.com/news/2020/11/06/trump-linked-figures-boosted-stopthesteal-movement-434733.

15. Nguyen and Scott, "Trump-linked Figures Have Boosted #StopTheSteal Movement."

16. Aaron Blake, "As Trump Departs, His Extremes Live on in State GOPs," Washington Post, January 25, 2021, https://www.washingtonpost.com/politics/2021/01/25/trump-departs-his-extremes-live-state-gops/.

17. Anna Lührmann, Juraj Medzihorsky, Garry Hindle, and Staffan I. Lindberg, "New Global Data on Political Parties," V-Dem Institute, October 2020, https://www.v-dem.net/media/filer_public/b6/55/b6553f85-5c5d-45ec-be63-a48a2abe3f62/briefing_paper_9.pdf.

18. Anne Applebaum, "Trump Won't Accept Defeat. Ever," Atlantic, November 6, 2020, https://www.theatlantic.com/ideas/archive/2020/11/trumps-forever-campaign-is-just-getting-started/617021.

19. Ryan LaRochelle, "Decades of Conservative Governance Has Worsened the Coronavirus Crisis," Washington Post, April 7, 2020, https://www.washingtonpost.com/outlook/2020/04/07/decades-conservative-governance-has-worsened-coronavirus-crisis.

INDEX

Page numbers in *italics* indicate figures or tables.

188; national unity threatened by, 19–20; party polarization and, 8–9; as politically useful, 20; political system easing of, 209–10; in postwar U.S., 33–42; race and, 9–11; in right-wing politics, 19; roots of, 21–24; southern conservatives and, 229n37; strategy of, 42–45; Tea Party and, 7, 123–24, 135, 140, 160, 269n95; D. Trump creating, 194–96, 219–20, 222, 274n33; violence from, 193–94, 219; weaponizing, 1–2, 4, 224

disunity, 24–27

Dole, Bob, 54, 93, 102, 116

domestic terrorism, 86

Douglass, Frederick, 27

Douglas, Helen Gahagan, 49

Downs, Anthony, 13

drug companies, 80, 138, 215, 288n57

Drutman, Lee, 178

Duffy, Caitlin, 143

Dukakis, Michael, 78, 81, 92

Duncan, John, 103

Dunlap, Matthew, 183

Dyck, Joshua, 169

Economic Recovery Tax Act, 60

economics, 25, 264nn18–19; Contract with America and, 260n131; Democrats criticizing Reagan policy of, 65; distress in, 131; federal government power in, 205; insecurity in, 4; issues in, 135; voodoo, 78, 92

Edelman Trust Barometer, 177

Edling, Max, 24

Edsall, Thomas, 59

Eisenhower, Dwight D., 10, 17, 36, 38, 49, 197, 230n47

Ekins, Emily, 178

electioneering strategies, 90

elections, 195, 208–9, 222

electoral benefits, 11, 13–15, 241n36

electoral college, 22, 93, 180, 278n86

electoral realignment, 10, 56–59, 66–67, 75, 89–90, 117, 121

elites, 3, 7–8, 124, 198, 201

email scandal, 177

Emanuel, Rahm, 96

eminent domain, 191

end-of-life counseling, 140–41

Energy Task Force, 128

equality, of race, 203–4

Equal Rights Amendment, 55

evangelicals, 40, 55, 59, 65, 67, 170, 175, 199

executive branch, 71, 128

executive leadership, 15–16, 85, 125

executive power, 69–70, 151

experts, sidelining of, 182–83, 213–14

extreme candidates, 230n54

Fabrizio, Anthony, 94

Fallows, James, 64

Farmers' Alliance chapter, 26

farming, 46, 190

far-right groups, 13, 134–35

Fauci, Anthony, 219

federal government, 17, 288n57; authority of, 22; Congressional expenditures of, 41; conservatives fight against, 34; economic insecurity and, 4; economic power and, 205; institutions of, 16; police powers of, 65; public opinion of, 3–4, 118; Republicans blamed for shutdown of, 120; trust in, 139–40

federalism, 22, 83

Federalist Papers, 23, 72, 112–13, 211

Federalist Society, 164, 221, 281n126

federal spending, 39, 44 46–47, 52–53, 60–61, 64, 82–83, 106, 126, 129, 131, 200

Feinstein, Dianne, 192

Felten, Eric, 98–99

Fenno, Richard, 14

Feulner, Edwin, 99

Fierce, Don, 88

financial crisis (2008), 123, 129–30, 199–200

fiscal policy, 29–30

Fiske, Robert, 101

Fitzwater, Marlin, 80

Flake, Jeff, 180

Floyd, George, 220

fluoridation, 240n16

Ford, Gerald, 48, 52–54

foreign policy, 60, 66, 72–73, 154